D1389677

RH

Hamilton Harty
Musical Polymath

Music in Britain, 1600–2000

ISSN 2053-3217

Series Editors:
BYRON ADAMS, RACHEL COWGILL, AND PETER HOLMAN

This series provides a forum for the best new work in the field of British music studies, placing music from the early seventeenth to the late twentieth centuries in its social, cultural, and historical contexts. Its approach is deliberately inclusive, covering immigrants and emigrants as well as native musicians, and explores Britain's musical links both within and beyond Europe. The series celebrates the vitality and diversity of music-making across Britain in whatever form it took and wherever it was found, exploring its aesthetic dimensions alongside its meaning for contemporaries, its place in the global market, and its use in the promotion of political and social agendas.

Proposal or queries should be sent in the first instance to Professors Byron Adams, Rachel Cowgill, Peter Holman, or Boydell & Brewer at the addresses shown below. All submissions will receive prompt and informed consideration.

Professor Byron Adams,
Department of Music – 061, University of California, Riverside, CA 92521-0325
email: byronadams@earthlink.net

Professor Rachel Cowgill,
School of Music, Cardiff University, 31 Corbett Road, Cardiff CF10 3EB
email: cowgillre@cardiff.ac.uk

Professor Peter Holman,
School of Music, University of Leeds, Leeds, LS2 9JT
email: p.k.holman@leeds.ac.uk

Boydell & Brewer, PO Box 9, Woodbridge, Suffolk, IP12 3DF
email: editorial@boydell.co.uk

Previously published volumes in this series are listed at the back of this volume.

Hamilton Harty
Musical Polymath

Jeremy Dibble

THE BOYDELL PRESS

First published 2013
The Boydell Press, Woodbridge
ISBN 978 1 84383 858 6

The Boydell Press is an imprint of Boydell & Brewer Ltd
PO Box 9, Woodbridge, Suffolk IP12 3DF, UK
and of Boydell & Brewer Inc.
668 Mt Hope Avenue, Rochester, NY 14620-2731, USA
website: www.boydellandbrewer.com

The publisher has no responsibility for the continued existence
or accuracy of URLs for external or third-party internet websites
referred to in this book, and does not guarantee that any content
on such websites is, or will remain, accurate or appropriate.

A CIP catalogue record for this book is available from the British Library

Papers used by Boydell & Brewer Ltd are natural, recyclable
products made from wood grown in sustainable forests

Designed and typeset in Adobe Minion Pro by
David Roberts, Pershore, Worcestershire

Printed and bound in Great Britain by
CPI Group (UK) Ltd, Croydon, CR0 4YY

For my twin sister Priscilla,
her husband Simon,
my nephews Timothy and Nicholas,
and my niece Alice.

Hamilton Harty, *c.* 1920

❧ Contents

Illustrations

❧ *Frontispiece*

Hamilton Harty (*c.* 1920)

❧ *Plates*
(between pp. 112 and 113)

1 Harty at the piano, aged 16 (1896)
2 Willam Harty (with his wife Annie seated centre) with the St Cecilia Society, Lisburn
3 Harty and Agnes Nicholls (Royal College of Music, Special Collections)
4 Agnes Nicholls Harty as Isolde (Royal College of Music, Special Collections)
5 Michele Esposito
6 Lieutenant Harty, Royal Navy, *c.* 1917
7 Harty with the Hallé Orchestra in the Manchester Free Trade Hall, 1923–4
8 Complimentary dinner given by Harty for the Hallé Orchestra, December 1923
9 Harty with his Honorary DMus, Manchester University, 1925
10 Harty with Esposito and members of the Hallé Orchestra, Dublin, 1926
11 Harty on the S.S. *President Roosevelt*, 1936
12 Harty at the Hollywood Bowl
13 Harty conducting Mendelssohn's *Elijah*, Sydney Town Hall, 20 June 1934
14 Harty on the carillon at Sydney University, June 1934
15 Harty, late 1930s
16 The interior of Harty's flat at Hove, *c.* 1940
17 Harty, a last photo (1940)

❧ *Text Figures*

1 Facsimile of the first movement of Harty's transcription of Handel's *Water Music* 142
2 Facsimile of the first movement of Harty's transcription of Handel's *Music for the Royal Fireworks* (Royal College of Music, Special Collections) 187
3 Facsimile of the opening of *With the Wild Geese* (Royal College of Music) 298

Unless otherwise shown, all the illustrations listed above are reproduced by permission of Queen's University, Belfast (Harty Collection MS 14).

Music Examples

Preface

I N the late nineteenth century the province of Ulster provided the world with its fair share of musical talent in the contrasting personalities of Charles Wood, Hamilton Harty, Herbert Hughes and Norman Hay. Arguably the most gifted of these was Harty, who, in my view, together with the Dublin-born Stanford, shared that remarkable 'spark' of natural talent, technically and inspirationally. Both pursued success in England and left their mark on the history of British music, but drew much of their character from the land of their birth. Having also completed studies of Charles Villiers Stanford, perhaps the greatest and most accomplished of all Irish composers, and Michele Esposito, the Neapolitan pianist and composer who made his home in Dublin for forty-six years, I thought it fitting to assess Harty in both his British and Irish contexts, and, regarding the latter, to appraise his identity within the sphere of Irish cultural nationalism. Born in Hillsborough, largely self-taught, he came under the wing of Esposito in Dublin before migrating to London. A great admirer of Stanford, Harty ploughed his own Irish furrow as a composer, but showed an extraordinary versatility as a brilliant accompanist – to some the finest these islands have ever produced – and as one of that dazzling catalogue of British conductors in the 1920s and 30s who achieved international standing. In this sense Harty's combination of abilities has probably never been equalled.

It would be impossible to undertake a study of Harty without paying tribute to the pioneering work of David Greer, which has proven to be invaluable in appraising Harty's achievements. It includes Greer's book *Hamilton Harty: His Life and Music* (1978), his edition of Harty's unfinished but nonetheless fascinating autobiography, *Hamilton Harty: Early Memories* (1979), numerous articles, and a biography of Elsie Swinton, *A Numerous and Fashionable Audience: The Story of Elsie Swinton* (1997). His meticulous work on the manuscripts has also been of considerable assistance.

In this study of Harty's life and work, and with the benefit of a larger number of primary sources, I have attempted to broaden the account of his remarkable career. In the first instance I have endeavoured to elucidate his early years as comprehensively as is possible from surviving sources at Hillsborough, Belfast and Dublin, and then his meteoric rise to prominence in London soon after 1901, when, without university or conservatoire qualifications, his astonishing talent as an accompanist – as yet a musical discipline unrecognised professionally – was soon in demand from the capital's most distinguished performers. This thread, in fact, continues throughout the book, for, though Harty later devoted his career to conducting, he never abandoned the art of accompanying or of participating in chamber music. Indeed, during his years with the Hallé a spot at each of the Thursday concerts was reserved for chamber music with the international soloists, and he made professional appearances as a pianist until two years before his death in 1941. What is astonishing about this dimension of his life is not only the amount of music he performed, both vocal and instrumental (including an appreciable number of world premieres or second performances), but the sheer number of musical personalities with whom he came into contact.

Harty intuitively linked accompanying with conducting, based on his observations of his idol Artur Nikisch, another brilliant accompanist and conductor. This is evident from his writings – some of them outspoken and controversial – which I have also attempted to integrate into the 'rationale' of his outlook and tastes as a practical musician and composer. His autodidacticism, for example, can be fairly linked with his intuitive and highly individual (even eccentric) approach to the composition of Berlioz, a composer he revered and placed above Wagner. I have also tried to rationalise Harty's distaste for twentieth-century musical intellectualism with the programmes he conducted, the works he studiously avoided, and also his general dislike of opera as a theatrical phenomenon (as strictly opposed to one in the concert hall or as a commercial recording).

I have attempted to reassess Harty's inimitable career as a conductor in several ways. His special, personal approach to conducting, an art in which he was, again, entirely self-taught, engendered immense loyalty at the Hallé from his players and his audience as well as the critic Samuel Langford. The charges of conservatism, made essentially by Neville Cardus of the *Manchester Guardian*, require a more balanced and comprehensive reappraisal. It is true that Harty avoided most of 'modernist' Stravinsky (including *The Rite of Spring*), most of Bartók, Hindemith, the works of the Second Viennese School and much of the later music of Holst and Vaughan Williams, and remained vehemently antipathetical to their contemporary 'cerebral' aesthetics. His belief that one's response to music was essentially emotional led him to be deeply conscious of his audience. Their endorsement and appreciation, he firmly maintained, ensured the survival of the Hallé Society through the difficult economic times which he inherited in 1920. This was particularly acute in the years immediately after the First World War, when Harty succeeded in turning the Hallé's deficit into a surplus; when times improved later in the 1920s it is noticeable that his programmes became more adventurous (though this again brought the threat of financial deficits, exacerbated by the onset of the Great Depression).

As a proselyte for the music of Berlioz, Harty's mission outstripped that of Beecham, especially with his landmark performances of the *Grande Messe des morts* and the *Symphonie funèbre et triomphale*, and it has now been forgotten that his interpretations of Brahms's symphonic music, then also considered conservative, even backward, helped to restore the reputation of the great Romantic Classicist to the towering position he enjoys today. Indeed, Harty's love of the Romantic giants – Berlioz, Wagner, Brahms, Tchaikovsky, Mahler and Sibelius – tells us much about the bent of his own musical language, which, for all its potent Irish inflections and assimilations, confesses an indebtedness to the Continental late nineteenth and early twentieth centuries. Through this particular 'refraction' it beceoms easier to understand Harty's natural affinity for the late British Romantics Stanford, Elgar and Delius, and for the younger generation of Bantock, Holbrooke and Bax, and how, in 'modernist' terms, this found an acceptable home in the music of Walton, Lambert and contemporary Italians such as Respighi, Casella and Pizzetti. Finally, I have also reassessed Harty's genius as a conductor of the Romantic orchestra in terms of both his *savoir faire* as an orchestrator, and the age of transcriptions and arrangements in which he lived. His transcriptions of Handel had a national following years before the early-music movement gained a foothold, and even now their sensitivity and luminosity are models of a once proud artform whose mission was to reach out and popularise.

In this volume I have tried to plot Harty's career in parallel with a personal life of some complexity. It has not been easy. Minute books from the Hallé and LSO, and the assiduous journalism of the *Manchester Guardian* have been invaluable in giving clues, as have the autobiographies of his contemporaries Neville Cardus, Landon Ronald, Gerald Jackson, Archie Camden and Isobel Baillie. Very little correspondence exists before 1914, and much of what does survive (mostly in the Harty archive at Queen's University, Belfast) is largely, though not exclusively, of a professional nature between him and other musicians. Save for a couple of letters, nothing has survived of his marriage with Agnes Nicholls. This, and their future estrangement, was a matter that Harty deliberately kept intensely private. However, I am extremely grateful to Christopher Bolland for making available to me thirty-one letters from Harty to his mother, Lorie Bolland, a serendipitous find made during the writing of this book. His permission to allow me to use these in the last two chapters has lent a quite new perspective to Harty's solitary existence during the 1920s and 1930s, as well as to the establishment of facts about his life hitherto unknown.

❧ *Acknowledgements*

There are many people and institutions I must thank for their assistance in the completion of this book.

First of all the Arts and Humanities Research Council, whose funding of a wider research study of Irish music between 1890 and 1990 (in collaboration with my colleague Dr Patrick Zuk) enabled me to complete research for this project. Without this funding the book would have taken considerably longer. In this regard, too, I should like to pay tribute to the sterling assistance of my colleague Dr Alasdair Jamieson, whose expert and enthusiastic help with unearthing primary and secondary sources on Harty, made possible by the AHRC funding, was both rewarding and invaluable. I must also thank Durham University and its Arts Faculty for extending financial assistance for travel, accommodation and research materials. Without this, the task of completing my study would have been more arduous.

To Diarmuid Kennedy and Brenda Robinson I owe much for helping me to navigate my way through the Harty Archive at Queen's University, Belfast, and to the Music Department at the university for granting permission to use manuscript and photographic materials. In a similar way I should like to acknowledge permission from the Royal College of Music. I am grateful to Simon

Walker at Hillsborough for showing me documents and manuscript material at St Malachi's Church in Hillsborough and for guiding me round the church and grounds. I extend my thanks to the archives of the Hallé and London Symphony Orchestra for use of minute books and letters, to the Hereford and Worcester County Records Office, to Bruce Chandler of Christ Church, Bray, for providing information about Harty's time at the church, and to Dr Peter Horton of the Royal College of Music. I should also like to express my appreciation to the New York Public Library and the Estate of Padraic Colum for use of correspondence between Colum and Harty. Special thanks also go to Kate and Ian Russell and Laura Ponsonby for use of passages from Hubert Parry's diaries, to Christopher Bolland who generously allowed me to use the correspondence between Harty and his mother, to Ruth Fleischmann for the inclusion of correspondence between Harty and her father, Aloys Fleischmann, and Diana Sparkes for providing me with correspondence between Harty and her father, Hubert Foss.

To the following I should also like to express my thanks for their support and interest in this project: David Greer, Lewis Foreman, Stephen Lloyd, Lionel Carley, Philip Hammond, Lucia Gri, Timothy Storey, Piers Lane, the Goldner Quartet, Barry Smith, Jonathan Clinch, Declan Farmer, Jan Smaczny, Philip Shields and Declan McGovern.

In bringing this project to successful conclusion I must also gratefully acknowledge the support of my friends and colleagues Patrick Zuk and Séamus de Barra, who provided the initial impetus to research both Harty and Esposito. To my mother, Pamela Dibble, and my cousin, Maureen Dibble, I should like to offer my thanks for offering me accommodation, and my wife Alison, who has always been there to support my obsession with British and Irish music.

JEREMY DIBBLE
Durham 2012

Abbreviations

ABC	Australian Broadcasting Commission
BBCSO	BBC Symphony Orchestra
BNL	*Belfast News Letter*
BNOC	British National Opera Company
C.	Columbia Records (Britain)
CB	Christopher Bolland
CBSO	City of Birmingham Symphony Orchestra
COL	Columbia Records (USA)
DOS	Dublin Orchestral Society
HPM	*Hillsborough Parish Magazine*
IAO	Incorporated Association of Organists
IT	*Irish Times*
LPO	London Philharmonic Orchestra
LSO	London Symphony Orchestra
MG	*The Manchester Guardian*
MT	*Musical Times*
PRMA	*Proceedings of the Royal Musical Association*
RIAM	Royal Irish Academy of Music
RAM	Royal Academy of Music
RCM	Royal College of Music
RDS	Royal Dublin Society
RF	Ruth Fleischmann
RMA	Royal Musical Association
RMCM	Royal Manchester College of Music
RNCM	Royal Northern College of Music
RNVR	Royal Navy Volunteer Reserve
SW	Simon Walker
WIT	*Weekly Irish Times*
GB-Belqb	Queen's University, Belfast, Harty Collection
GB-HWRO	Hereford and Worcester Records Office
GB-Lam	Royal Academy of Music (RAM)
GB-Lbl	British Library
GB-Lbbc	BBC Archives, Caversham
GB-Lcm	Royal College of Music (RCM)
GB-Mha	Hallé Archives, Manchester
GB-Mcm	Royal Northern College of Music (RNCM)
GB-ShP	Shulbrede Priory, Lynchmere, Sussex
US-NYp	New York, Public Library at Lincoln Center

'He was the child of that spirit-land of which Yeats sang,
whence he came for a while to make music for our heart's delight.'

Norman Hay, 1943

Hey diddle diddle, the flute and the fiddle,
They frolic for Hamilton Harty,
The trumpet and 'cello, they babble and bellow,
He's such a remarkable party.

The fiddle-bows flatten with fear at his baton,
The clarinets haste to their duty;
With energy tireless, he witches the wireless,
Enchanting the ether with beauty.

Smith's Weekly [Sydney, Australia], 19 May 1934

Hillsborough, Belfast and Dublin: A Musical Apprenticeship

A<small>T</small> the end of the nineteenth century the patronage of churches within the Anglican Communion was a common phenomenon. Many enjoyed the benefaction of wealthy Oxford and Cambridge colleges to pay the salaries of their incumbents and for the upkeep of church fabric – links that are still in many cases maintained today. Many village churches with a strong connection to adjacent landed families were generously supported; indeed, the provision of the church itself might well have come from the family coffers, the church obliging by acting as an appropriate burial place for their ancestors. One such edifice was the church of St Malachy, Hillsborough, in the Lisburn district of Co. Down. One of the finest examples of Gothic Revival architecture, it was built by the 1st Marquis of Downshire between 1760 and 1774 in anticipation, wrongly as it transpired, that it would be the diocesan cathedral of Co. Down. Though the Marquis, by the name of Wills Hill, may have been disappointed that his grand church was not honoured in the way he had hoped (the honour went to Down Cathedral, whose restoration the Marquis also helped to finance from 1790), his zeal for Hillsborough's reconstruction was in no way dampened. He went about modernising his house in the finest Georgian style, enthused by the sense of dynasty exhibited by his affluent forbears – beneficiaries of the Ulster Plantation who had developed and enlarged the estate over two centuries, and whose name, 'Hillsborough', had supplanted the original 'Cromghlinn' (as former land of the Irish Chieftain, Bryan McCrory Magennes). Hill's desire for fine surroundings was accentuated by his appetite for culture and beautification, not least in his determination to furnish his handsome church with a stipendiary parish choir (the first of its kind in Ireland) and a substantial three-manual organ in the west gallery, built by John Snetzler between 1772 and 1773, for which he paid the sum of £400.[1] To these notable resources he added the service of a professional organist, Michael Thompson, DMus, from London, who was in place to accompany the first service on 22 August 1773.[2]

Appointment of the organist (who enjoyed accommodation and security of tenure in a tied house close to the estate) and a special interest in the church's

---

[1] The employment of Snetzler was a major coup for Hills, since the Swiss organ builder had also provided instruments for Norwich Cathedral, Buckingham Palace, Peterhouse, Cambridge, the New Room, Bristol and Beverley Minster. See also A. Barnes and M. Renshaw, *The Life and Work of John Snetzler* (Aldershot: Ashgate, 1994).

[2] From time to time Thompson visited St Anne's, Belfast, where he occasionally assisted. At this time one may assume that Hillsborough not only outshone the church choirs of Belfast but also rivalled the one cathedral establishment with its own choir school at Armagh.

choral wellbeing continued to be a matter of family patronage for the Hills for the next century or so. In the late 1870s this responsibility fell to Lord Arthur Hill, the brother of the 5th Marquis of Downshire who had died in 1874.[3] An energetic Conservative MP for Down and a prominent Orangeman (as encapsulated by the *Spy* cartoon in *Vanity Fair*),[4] Hill took a benevolent approach to the estate and to his estate workers which earned him a popular reputation. His interest in the provision of good church music was undoubtedly fuelled by marriage to his second wife Annie Fortescue Harrison in 1877. Lady Arthur Hill, as she became known, was a competent composer; she is best remembered now for the music to Meta Orred's touching ballad of 1877 *In the Gloaming* ('In the gloaming, oh, my darling / When the lights are soft and low'), but her musical prowess extended as far as productions of an operetta, *The Ferry Girl*, produced at London's Savoy Theatre in May 1890, and later at the Gaiety Theatre, Dublin, in December 1894.[5] She and her husband were also in the habit of patronising musical events, including a concert in the Ulster Hall, Belfast, on 25 January 1896 which featured various vocal items by her.[6]

In 1878 the post of organist at Hillsborough fell vacant. The new appointee was William Michael Harty, a twenty-six-year-old Irishman with roots in the southwest of the country. William Harty's parents had moved from their native Limerick to Dublin sometime during the late 1850s or early 1860s.[7] William became a choirboy in Christ Church Cathedral as well as at Christ Church, Bray, and took lessons from Robert Prescott Stewart, a recent appointment to the Professorship of Music at Trinity College, Dublin, and organist at both Christ Church and St Patrick's Cathedrals. Stewart was reputed to have remarked: 'Harty looks like a perfect little angel – but he is a devil!'.[8] While in post as organist at St Nicholas's Church, Dundalk, he met his wife Annie Elizabeth (née Richards) during a visit to Greystones, Co. Wicklow, to christen a new organ (his recital was heard by no less than a young Charles Villiers Stanford).[9] This scant information was imparted by one of Hamilton Harty's sisters, Alice; we know nothing more of William before his appointment at Hillsborough, other than that he was clearly a highly capable musician and organist and that he brought

---

[3] Hill maintained the estate at Hillsborough until the coming of age of the 6th Marquis in 1892.

[4] See *Vanity Fair*, 21 August 1886.

[5] See *MT* 31 (1890), 346, and *MT* 36 (1895), 40. Lady Hill's operetta was in fact given its initial airing in a concert performance at St George's Hall on 3 December 1883: *MT* 25 (1884), 22.

[6] See *MT* 37 (1896), 176. Lady Hill's chamber organ, built by George Pike England in 1795, originally located in Hillsborough Castle, was transferred to the parish church where it remains a rare and treasured feature. See also R. I. Stoupe, *Hillsborough Parish Church: The Organs* (Belfast, 1972).

[7] John Barry, *Hillsborough: A Parish in the Ulster Plantation* (Belfast: William Mullan, 1962), 65.

[8] Barry, *Hillsborough*, 65.

[9] Barry, *Hillsborough*, 65.

to the appointment at Hillsborough a new and broad vitality that extended well beyond the organ loft and the choir stalls.[10] As Hamilton Harty later recalled:

> he [William] led an exceedingly busy musical life and travelled extensively all over the northern countryside, giving organ recitals, training choirs and teaching various instruments, including the organ, piano, violin and cello. Besides this he had a wonderful reputation as a teacher of singing and most of the most famous solo singers of his time in Ireland were his pupils.[11]

William Harty's position as organist and peripatetic music teacher allowed him and his growing family a modest, middle-class existence. 'The salary of a country organist in those days, added to the fees which could be made by private teaching, represented an income which might support a large family in a modestly comfortable fashion but which left nothing over for extras.'[12] This was a fact pugnaciously corroborated by Edith Harty, after Stephen Williams had conspicuously strayed from the truth in an obituary talk for the BBC on 20 February 1941:

> Your remarks anent the death of my brother, Sir Hamilton Harty, over the air last night while doubtless given in all good faith erred lamentably in one respect and in that respect caused considerable pain to myself and another member of my family. You said 'he was the son of a "poor" Organist ...' My father was one of the best-known musical figures in the north of Ireland in his day; ran two choral societies and taught music in Belfast and all over the north. So much for his musical attainments. But your remarks can also be construed to suggest he was poverty stricken and here you were equally wide of the mark. My father brought up a large family (10 children) in comfortable surroundings, gave them first-class educations and several have made their mark in places all over the world in their respective spheres. No one would have resented your unfortunate remark more than would the subject of your talk.[13]

Surviving photographs of a well-dressed gentleman confirm that William Harty enjoyed a secure and happy existence at Hillsborough and had no reason to move on to another appointment. (He died in post in 1918.) Yet, interviewed in America in the early 1930s, Harty maintained that the family existence was in fact meagre:

> My parents were very poor. All Ireland is poor. We were a big family and we had such hard times to take care of everybody. My father brooded a great deal over our slavery which was the result of our poverty, but my mother – she was the only one

---

[10] See John Barry, 'Hillsborough Years', in *Hamilton Harty: His Life and Music*, ed. David Greer (Belfast: Blackstaff Press, 1978), 1–22, at 3n.

[11] H. H. Harty, 'Autobiography' (handwritten, *c.* 1941), *GB-Belqb*, MS 14. Harty was very ill when he began his memoirs, and he only completed twenty-seven pages. They have been reproduced and edited by David Greer as *Hamilton Harty: Early Memories* (Belfast: The Queen's University, 1979).

[12] Harty, 'Autobiography'.

[13] Greer, *Hamilton Harty: Early Memories*, 17n. The obituary also appeared in *The Listener*.

for whom life seemed perfect and complete. She had brought her children into the world and that was what she was on earth to do. She was like a queen and moved regally about in our house wholly because she had been successful in her own life. But my father always craved liberty and he felt that no one ever could arrive at his goal until he was unhampered by the responsibilities and the cares that kill the spirit. He often talked to me of how cruelly our existence, ground out in want, crushed the finest in every man. And I believe that myself.[14]

On arriving from his previous post at Dundalk, William and his wife already had three children: William (age unknown), John (born in 1876) and Edith (born 1878). Herbert Hamilton (known as 'Bertie' by his close family)[15] was the first to be born at Hillsborough, on 4 December 1879, and another six followed:[16] Alice in 1882, Harold in 1883, George Frederick in 1885, Annie May in 1886 (though she lived for little more than a year), Irene in 1889 and Archibald in 1891. Herbert Hamilton had in fact been born in quite modest accommodation at No. 14 Main Street in Hillsborough, just up the hill from the church. But not long afterwards William was given leave to occupy the much more substantial 'organist's house' at 25 Ballynahinch Road, where he remained until his death in 1918. This was a fine, spacious property, and it accommodated a contented household, full of music. If William Harty was not teaching, playing the organ or taking choir practices, he was teaching his own children to play. 'How he found time in the midst of all this work to teach his own children … I shall never understand,' Hamilton Harty recollected, 'and I fear it must often have been a very weary man who listened, after a hard day, to our performances, and who so gently corrected us and set us fresh tasks.'[17]

On 11 November 1880, not long after William Harty and his family arrived at Hillsborough, a St Cecilia Musical Society was founded at a meeting at Hillsborough Castle under the aegis of Lady Arthur Hill.[18] William Harty was to be its conductor. Weekly choir practices took place at Hillsborough and two other nearby towns of Lisburn and Dromore. The first concert took place in the Orange Hall at Lisburn on 24 March 1881, and the first one at Hillsborough was held in the Castle on 9 November 1881. These were the two most common venues, though sometimes the ballroom or schoolhouse at Hillsborough were also used. In November 1883 each town became financially autonomous with its own president and vice-president, though William Harty remained, by unanimous consent, the conductor of all three constituent societies.[19] Many of the concerts

---

[14] L. W. Armsby, 'The Irish Composer-Conductor: Sir Hamilton Harty', in L. W. Armsby, *Musicians Talk: Impressions of Musicians, with Plates* (New York: Dial Press, 1935), 144–8, at 145–6.

[15] BBC Northern Ireland and North of England Home Service talk, 3 Oct. 1951.

[16] Herbert Hamilton was baptised on 4 Sept. 1880 at St Malachi's. Such was William Harty's status as organist that the baptism was undertaken by John Gibbs, Archdeacon of Downshire (rather than the local rector).

[17] Harty, 'Autobiography'.

[18] Greer, *Hamilton Harty: Early Memories*, 18n. See also *BNL*, 11 Nov. 1896.

[19] 'St Cecilia Musical Society', *BNL*, 28 Nov. 1883.

were recorded in the *Hillsborough Parish Magazine* and from time to time there was mention in the *Belfast News Letter*. The repertoire performed was, on the whole, modest and chosen to suit a choral demography of all ages, from children to the elderly. The choral works of Alfred Gaul often featured (works such as *The Holy City*, all eminently suited to amateur choral societies), along with Haydn's *The Creation*, Gade's *The Erl King's Daughter*, Mendelssohn's psalms, and Macfarren's *May Day*.[20] There were also songs, duets and instrumental pieces, some of them played by Lord and Lady Hill, Canon Frank McClintock (the future Dean of Armagh Cathedral)[21] and members of the Harty family. In 1896 an article in the *Belfast News Letter* noted that, of late, some thought that the Society was in a state of 'decadence', but that after fees for membership had been reduced, many new members had joined, injecting the Society with a new lease of life. The choir, freshly energised, went on to win prizes in the newly inaugurated Feis Ceoil, the Irish competitive festival founded in 1897.[22]

Herbert Hamilton Harty grew up amid this fertile hive of musical activity at Hillsborough, in an environment he would always hold dear:

> Built for the most part on the side of a hill and surrounded by trees, it [Hillsborough] looks, to those who see it for the first time, much more English than Irish. There are good reasons for that which any history of the 'North' will explain more fully and more accurately than I can or need to do here. It is necessary, however, to mention its distinguished and beautifully situated church, with its long avenues of magnificent trees, for my father was organist and choirmaster of this church (for 40 years, as a tablet by the altar testifies) and all my early musical training was connected with its musical service.[23]

Years later, as an acclaimed professional musician, he would recall his boyhood in Hillsborough with a fondness that extended beyond pure nostalgia. In spite of the village's 'English' impression and his Anglican upbringing, Harty retained a strong sense of his Irish, indeed of his Ulster, identity, and, judging by the fondness with which he embraced the whole of Ireland and its culture, he remained conscious of his deeper roots through both his parents even after

---

[20] Annie Patterson, 'Herbert Harty', *WIT*, 7 July 1900.

[21] Canon Frank McClintock was a highly competent pianist and a close friend of Charles Villiers Stanford at Cambridge University where they were both members of the Cambridge University Musical Society (CUMS). Stanford and McClintock often played duets for the CUMS chamber concerts and McClintock appeared as the solo pianist in Stanford's early Piano Concerto in B flat on 3 June 1873, and in Beethoven's Piano Concerto No. 3 on 21 May 1875. With Stanford he visited Berlin and the Schumann Festival at Bonn in 1873: Jeremy Dibble, *Charles Villiers Stanford: Man and Musician* (Oxford: Oxford University Press, 2002), 50 *passim*.

[22] The first Feis Ceoil took place in Dublin 1897 and the second in Belfast in 1898. This pattern was repeated in 1899 and 1900 but afterwards Dublin became the permanent venue. William Harty entered the St Cecilia Society in the Belfast competition of 1898 and won third prize. The following year, in Dublin, the choir won second prize, and in Belfast in 1900 they took first prize.

[23] Harty, 'Autobiography'.

partition in 1921. In 1920 he was strangely quick to deny that Irish folk-music had been a significant part of his childhood:

> I am sorry I can't bring folk-music into the story. Such little folk-music as there used to be in my native County Down was not Irish, but Scottish. Music in my early impressions did not mean fiddlers at fairs or immemorial drinking-songs in taverns, or indeed anything more Bohemian or picturesque than my father's organ-playing.[24]

Yet there were 'fair days' at Hillsborough twice a month, and the folk-music, whether Scottish or Irish, was very much part of the animated scene of farm animals, market traders and visitors from all over the county.[25] Such music was most likely to have been provided by the so-called 'Mountainy Men', impoverished farmers who, eking a living from the poor upland soil, frequented the lowland fairs with their fiddles, tin whistles and pipes to earn a meagre supplement to their scant incomes.

Harty's general education was 'a very chancy and irregular affair' in which compulsory attendance every morning of the National School was at best sporadic, and what instruction he received at home was invariably 'interrupted for musical reasons.'[26] Much of his schooling took place at home with his mother and, according to his sister Alice, he ceased to attend formal lessons at the National School after he was twelve.[27] But apart from assisting his father with duties in the adjoining stable, and enjoying the fresh air of the adjacent countryside, he increasingly devoted his time to music and to instrumental practice, essentially on the piano and organ. 'I do not remember ever having commenced to learn music,' he recalled as a twenty-year-old; 'I fancy I must always have played a little.'[28] 'I am often asked who were my principal masters in music,' Harty recounted in 1920. 'Beyond my father (and mother) I never had any, although I learned so much later through the kindness and goodness of more famous colleagues.'[29] Many years later he related to an Australian reporter that he began learning the piano at four and was playing chamber music by the age of eight, though it has to be said that Harty was in the habit of elaborating the memories of his youth.[30] Harty's sense of autodidacticism – he neither received formal lessons outside Hillsborough nor went to a conservatoire or university – was to a large extent inculcated by the musical training and opinions he received from his mother, who was a violinist, and from his organist father: '[My father] was a born musician – self-taught, and an unbeliever in academic

---

[24] 'C.' [H. C. Colles], 'Hamilton Harty', *MT* 61 (1920), 227–30, at 227.

[25] See Barry, 'Hillsborough Years', 19.

[26] Ibid. See also Greer, *Hamilton Harty: Early Memories*, 16n.

[27] BBC talk, 3 Oct. 1951. The schoolrooms at Hillsborough still exist and can be found towards the front, to right and left, of the picturesque approach to Hillsborough Church.

[28] Patterson, 'Herbert Harty'.

[29] Harty, 'Autobiography'.

[30] *Bendigo Advertiser*, 8 May 1934.

teaching. Anyone, according to him, could learn to play a musical instrument if he had the will and just a hand-book to point to the rudiments.'[31] Although Harty conceded that such an education was inappropriate for an aspiring pianist to become a virtuoso, he nevertheless maintained that his father's methods, for him at least, were sound: 'The use of a modicum of technique for him was as a key wherewith to enter the delightful pastures and still waters of the classics. He set me on that way, and as a small boy I could play all "The Forty-Eight" of Bach by heart.'[32] This astonishing feat of memory, as part of his training, Harty retained throughout his career. The Hillsborough community also preserves an attractive anecdote connected with William Harty's Sunday school classes, held in the organ loft, where he apparently taught Bible stories through the medium of Handel's dramatic arias and choruses from the oratorios. True or not, this would certainly account for his son's lifelong enthusiasm for Handel's music.[33] In addition, much of the canonical repertoire was available in the form of piano duet.[34] As accompanist for the St Cecilia Society young Harty developed a brilliant technique of 'reading at sight [which] was of inestimable value to him.'[35] His skill in transposition – a phenomenon to those that witnessed it – he no doubt acquired in the organ loft; and his brilliance as a score-reader (which must have rivalled that of Arnold Bax), he refined through practical experience of the viola, and a more passing acquaintance with the cello, horn and cornet 'simply that I might get a good knowledge of the different clefs and transposing instruments'. This brought 'a certain ease and facility in transferring orchestral scores to the piano.'[36] Harty also undoubtedly possessed an extraordinary memory and could retain extensive passages of music after only a single hearing. This ability was relayed by the Dublin organist George Harrison, of St George's Church:

> Esposito … brought Harrison 13 pages of music, absolutely new, in manuscript, and asked him to play it over from him. He did so, and after he handed the manuscript back, young Harty who had been listening quietly in a darkened corner came forward and said he would like to test his memory. So he sat down at the piano and played the whole 13 pages of music right through correctly, after hearing it only once![37]

---

[31] [Colles], 'Hamilton Harty', 227. Although Harty continually reiterated that he only received instruction from his father, this is not entirely true: from Patterson, 'Herbert Harty', it is evident that he received tuition on the viola from T. J. Lindsay and some training in harmony and counterpoint from Joseph Smith.

[32] Patterson, 'Herbert Harty'.

[33] I am grateful to Simon Walker of Hillsborough Church for this appealing tale.

[34] Patterson, 'Herbert Harty'.

[35] Patterson, 'Herbert Harty'.

[36] Hamilton Harty, 'The Art of Pianoforte Accompaniment' (typescript, c. 1930), GB-Belqb MS 14/29/xiii.

[37] Extract from letter of Rev. W. Martin, Scrapbook A, 22, GB-Belqb.

William Harty also bequeathed to his son a robust technique in harmony and counterpoint, and a broad knowledge of the musical literature:[38]

> He had unerringly good taste in music and had managed to acquire a large and very complete library, not only of church music and organ music but of oratorios, symphonies, operas, chamber music, and of music for piano. His habit was to say – 'There is most of the greatest music that has been written: play through it, all of it – everything – and at the end you will have gained a good musical education.' For my part I took him at his word and consider the experience thus gained as the basis of any musical powers I may possess.[39]

The idea of a musical career – in emulation of his father – appears to have occurred to Harty early on.[40] In 1920 he said 'I can recall hearing as a small child the sonatas of Mozart and Beethoven being played every night downstairs as I lay falling to sleep.'[41] 'He practised the piano for hours even when he was very small,' Alice Harty recollected. 'Early in the morning before the rest of us were up, we'd hear scales being played for an hour. And when he came home from school for dinner, he used to rush to the piano again.'[42] On Sundays he sang in the Hillsborough church choir, sitting close to his father, and from about seven or eight he began to learn the organ, even though he was not tall enough to reach the pedals.[43] 'I had also to leave the upper 'swell' manual religiously alone and confine myself to the 'choir' and 'great',' he remembered.[44] The earliest reference to him in the *Hillsborough Parish Magazine* (which proudly chronicled his early career) was of a solo part in John Henry Hopkins's famous carol *We Three Kings* on 27 December 1891.[45] When old enough to manage the organ, he regularly deputised for his father, and, as he entered his teens, he increasingly took part as accompanist in concerts for the St Cecilia Society with his father and siblings.[46] When his technique had outstripped theirs, he appeared either as a soloist or with Lady Arthur Hill or Canon McClintock.[47] At home, meanwhile, there was a 'domestic' string quartet led by his mother. His sister Edith also played the violin, he the viola, and his father the cello. By all accounts the performances left much to be desired:

---

[38] Though not an active composer, William Harty published an Evening Service in G which was published by Novello in 1885 and dedicated to the Marchioness of Downshire. He was also the author of a *Masonic March* for organ: see Greer, *Hamilton Harty: Early Memories*, 13n.

[39] Harty, 'Autobiography'.

[40] BBC North of Ireland and North of England Home Service talk, 3 Oct. 1951.

[41] [Colles], 'Hamilton Harty', 227.

[42] BBC talk, 3 Oct. 1951.

[43] BBC talk, 3 Oct. 1951. See also Patterson, 'Herbert Harty'.

[44] Patterson, 'Herbert Harty'.

[45] Greer, *Hamilton Harty: Early Memories*, 13n.

[46] Patterson, 'Herbert Harty'.

[47] Greer, *Hamilton Harty: Early Memories*, 20n.

I don't recollect that we ever got through a quartet without many stops and a good deal of somewhat acrid discussion and insulting accusation – 'You hurried!' 'I didn't!' 'You made the wrong repeat!' 'Well, you did the same yesterday!' 'Why don't you tune correctly?' 'It's four in a bar, not three' etc., etc. And always my father's wise good-humoured 'Well it's all right, we'll start again. Come on – one, two, three, four![48]

But like all these experiences, it formed a larger part of Harty's gradual assimilation of the wider musical world.

At fourteen Harty was appointed organist and choirmaster of Magheragall (also known as Brookmount) Parish Church in Co. Antrim, with a yearly stipend of £12.[49] The job entailed playing twice on a Sunday, which meant taking the horse and carriage four miles there and back. The Vestry, mindful of Harty's youth, employed his father to train the choir until the son felt ready. The services at Magheragall were undemanding, and the organ, installed in the west gallery, was small. This location enabled the adolescent Harty to abscond during the sermons:

> I was chiefly interested in the belfry-tower because of the birds' eggs which could be taken there. Many a time during the sermon I slipped off the organ stool and with the aid of Ellen [Larmour] the sextoness climbed the crazy ladders to the nests, filling my hat with eggs, mostly starlings' eggs, and coming back just in time to finish the service.[50]

Harty recounted in his *Autobiography* that he was at Magheragall for 'some years', but after his 'official' appointment in February 1894 he was only in post there for about eighteen months, for on 21 November 1895 he was appointed organist at the much larger city church of St Barnabas, Duncairn Gardens, in Belfast.[51] This was, according to Harty himself, 'a church of a more important character.'[52] Completed in 1892, it was a new Victorian edifice that had been built to accommodate the burgeoning number of worshippers who had migrated

[48] Harty, 'Autobiography'.

[49] Harty stated in his autobiography that he was 'barely 12' when he began at Brookmount, and in the *MT* article of 1920 he stated his age as nine: [Colles], 'Hamilton Harty', 227. Alice Harty also recollected that he was twelve (BBC talk, 3 Oct. 1951), though the minutes of the Select Vestry at Magheragall record his appointment on 12 Feb. 1894, when Harty would have been fourteen (the *HPM* noted his appointment in March 1894). Greer notes that he may have been more informally in post before this time since the vacancy was longstanding: Greer, *Hamilton Harty: Early Memories*, 20–22n.

[50] Harty, 'Autobiography'. A variation of this boyhood hobby occurs in Patterson, 'Herbert Harty', where Harty admitted he was prone to raid the nests of birds in the thickets and hedges on his journeys along the wild roads to Brookmount, often nearly making him late: 'I played through the church service with my pockets full of eggs'.

[51] Select Vestry Minutes, St Barnabas' Church, Belfast. See also Greer, *Hamilton Harty: Early Memories*, 22n.

[52] Harty, 'Autobiography'.

from the country to seek work in Belfast's ever-expanding industrial landscape of mills, foundries and factories.[53] Harty's appointment was by no means unanimous. As one of a shortlist of three organists, he was selected only after a second ballot.[54] We know little of Harty's work at St Barnabas's except that he was only organist there for a year and that his resignation on 12 November 1896 was very probably provoked by mutual dissatisfaction. Minutes from the Select Vestry show that in April 1896 'it [was] to be conveyed to Mr Harty that the music of the services should be suitable for the congregation' and that, in the following August, he had to obtain permission to be absent.[55] Harty was not yet seventeen, but already, it seems, he was becoming restive.

In Belfast, Harty related, 'I met with many opportunities of increasing my experience in many branches of music besides purely church music. An excellent local violinist, T. J. Lindsay, was particularly kind and helpful.'[56] Lindsay, a Professor of Music at the Belfast Conservatoire, was a player of some ability; he led the orchestra of the Belfast Philharmonic Society and was active as a chamber music specialist at most of the significant music societies in the north of Ireland. Besides giving some tuition to Harty on the viola, Lindsay provided him with an entrée into Belfast's steadily growing musical life. He appeared with Lindsay in one of the Saturday Night Concerts at the Ulster Hall on 28 March 1896 as an accompanist, and as a rather average viola player he joined the Belfast Philharmonic Society run by Francis Koeller.[57] 'I don't think I can have been very helpful in this orchestra from a really musical point of view,' Harty recounted, 'for, to be frank, I lacked both tone and technique, but I learned a great deal in an orchestral sense which was to prove most useful to me in later days.'[58] It was perhaps advantageous to Harty's stage of development in 1896 that the Belfast Philharmonic (essentially a society of chorus and orchestra like its Dublin counterpart, the Dublin Music Society) was enjoying a period of expansion, in terms both of members and artistic horizons. Ticket prices were a little too high for some, which provoked complaints to the press, but the Society had to meet the costs of bringing professional players from the Hallé Orchestra in Manchester.[59] Harty therefore would have had the opportunity to play side by side with these professionals as well as semi-professionals and amateurs, though he is only mentioned as violist in the orchestra on one occasion, for a concert on 23 October 1896, featuring Mendelssohn's anthem 'Hear my prayer' and Beethoven's cantata *Calm Sea and Prosperous Voyage*. It appears, somewhat ironically, that he was not in the orchestra when the Society performed a concert

---

[53] St Barnabas was bombed at Easter 1941 during the 'blitz' of Belfast. A new church was built and opened in 1957. After amalgamation with St Paul's Church in 1992, the building was demolished in 1995.

[54] Greer, *Hamilton Harty: Early Memories*, 22n.

[55] Greer, *Hamilton Harty: Early Memories*, 22n.

[56] Harty, 'Autobiography'.

[57] For the concert, see 'Saturday Night Concerts', *BNL*, 30 Mar. 1896.

[58] Harty, 'Autobiography'.

[59] For the complaints, see *BNL*, 3 Mar. 1896.

version of Berlioz's *The Damnation of Faust* at the Ulster Hall (in March 1896, with the American baritone David Bispham as Mephistopheles), but it is more than likely that he was in the audience. This was by far the most ambitious musical venture the Society had undertaken and such was its impression on the Belfast audience that *Faust* was given a repeat performance on 27 November. By then Harty had departed for Dublin, but it is likely that he took part in rehearsals for the work in the months leading up to the concert. Indeed, it may well have been a crucial early formative experience in his particular and personal devotion to the music of the French composer.

Harty's work in Belfast and in the local area around Hillsborough now entailed performing chamber music, organ recitals (which were occasionally given with his father), orchestral concerts, and his church work. [60] This meant that he had to commute regularly back and forth from Hillsborough to Belfast; if he returned home late of an evening he was forced to walk the distance from Lisburn when there was no train to his home village. At this time he was preoccupied daily with improving his piano technique; with the assistance of an instrument which he now enjoyed in his own room at home, he was able to practise for hours each day with the aspiration of becoming a piano virtuoso.[61] At this juncture Harty's performing abilities as a pianist had really outstripped what Belfast could offer. There was employment, but it was increasingly unchallenging. Nor, beyond what his father could provide, was there sufficient counsel for the musical career that was becoming more and more inevitable day by day.[62] In fact, according to Harty's sister Alice, William Harty and his wife tried 'to put every difficulty in his way' along the path to becoming a professional musician.[63] This only fuelled his determination to succeed. Having observed an advertisement for an organist and choirmaster at Christ Church, Bray, Co. Wicklow,[64] he applied and was appointed on 6 November 1896, when he was just shy of seventeen.

Herbert Harty (as he was known at this time) hoped that Dublin could offer

---

[60] In 1898 Harty assisted his father with a recital at Hillsborough: 'Mr Herbert Harty contributed two pieces, "Pilgrim's Chorus, Tannhäuser", Wagner and Mendelssohn's "Sonata in F minor", displaying remarkable power of expression in each, and the solemn music rolled along the aisles with great effect. After the second item in the recital, the Rev. F. W. Hogan sang the solo, "O, God have mercy", from Mendelssohn's "St Paul", Mr Harty accompanying him on the organ': *BNL*, 15 July 1898.

[61] BBC talk, 3 Oct. 1951.

[62] It is a further indication of Harty's rapidly developing ability that he did not seek formal advice or tuition from either the newly founded Belfast City School of Music (founded 1891) or the Belfast Conservatoire (founded 1894), though it is apparent that he became acquainted with some of the teachers at the latter. Neither institution survived for long: see W. J. McCormack and P. Gillan, *The Blackwell Companion to Irish Culture* (Oxford: Blackwell, 1999), 401.

[63] BBC talk, 3 Oct. 1951.

[64] See Vestry Minutes, Christ Church, Bray; see also Greer, *Hamilton Harty: Early Memories*, 23n.

him more lucrative employment and greater musical satisfaction.[65] At the same time, home was not too far away. With a good rail service between Dublin and Belfast, he was still able to use his parental home at Hillsborough as an important and readily accessible haven:

> Though he had actually left his native Hillsborough ..., he always returned to his old home and the cherished scenes of his childhood at least once a year ... and often enough he would remain there for the major part of the summer, engaged the while upon writing one or other of his compositions.[66]

Christ Church, Bray, distinctive for its fine spire and unique peal of bells, was 'a large and important church with a good organ and a fine service of music'.[67] It had been built to accommodate Bray's expanding population, which had been growing since the coming of the railway in 1854, with funds principally furnished by the 11th Earl of Meath; he was still a major patron of the church when Harty arrived. The town, close to the Irish capital, enjoyed a sizeable middle-class professional population with a growing appetite for music and culture, one that ensured a healthy choral participation at the church. Moreover, Christ Church benefited from the presence of two highly cultivated clergymen, father and son, Archdeacon James G. Scott and curate George Digby Scott. (the latter of great help to Harty during his time there).

Having tendered his resignation from St Barnabas somewhat precipitately on 12 November, Harty moved into digs in Bray at Clara Villa, Herbert Road, and began work at Christ Church on 15 November. His principal duties were two Sunday services and a Friday evening practice. The parish had high hopes for him:

> Among the competitors for the post which Dr Figgis obtained was a young player of much promise, who was brought under our notice. He was not quite a stranger to Bray, for his father, William Harty, organist of Hillsborough, had begun his musical life as a boy in Bray choir. Mr Herbert Harty, who has been organist at St Barnabas' Church, in Belfast, took up Dr Figgis' work on the 15th November. He has shown that he knows well how to accompany a choir, and has played instrumental music with taste and facility. He gives us every reason to expect that he will make rapid improvement as our young organists before have done, and that, like Mr Martin, Mr Marchant, and Dr Figgis, he will win his spurs at Bray, and give us much pleasure in his playing when he has become familiar with our organ.[68]

---

[65] Harty is first listed in the *Bray Parish Report* for 1897.

[66] Quoted in Greer, *Hamilton Harty: Early Memories*, 23n. Harty also continued to appear from time to time as an accompanist for guest artists in Belfast Philharmonic concerts: see, for example, *Belfast Evening Telegraph*, 15 Feb. 1901; *MT* 41 (1901), 189. He returned to play for other occasions as organist in the Ulster Hall with his father: see *BNL*, 8 Dec. 1899.

[67] Harty, 'Autobiography'.

[68] *Bray Parish Quarterly Calendar* (Winter 1896–7), 2.

The organ, considered by some to be old-fashioned, was in fact a subject of some contention at the church and there was some suggestion that Figgis's move had been prompted by more modern organs available in Dublin. The news of Harty's appointment was therefore made with an exhortation that 'a wealthy private resident or friend may come forward …, as zealous men have done elsewhere, to provide the means of supplying a more modern and more complete instrument.[69] This was one task Harty did not see to fruition, but in compensation the young Ulsterman, with the help of local musicians, tried to expand the horizons at Bray with a broader range of concerts. In this he was encouraged by Digby Scott, who was especially knowledgeable about music and possessed 'an instinctive sympathy with the work and aspirations of a young man still uncertain of his path.'[70]

Harty's church work at Bray was not too onerous, but he was required to train the choir for full choral services, and larger works, such as Stainer's *Crucifixion*, were a regular fixture in Lent.[71] His one and only surviving anthem, *I Heard a Voice from Heaven*, was written on the death of Queen Victoria in January 1901 and sung specially at a packed service at Christ Church to commemorate her long reign.[72] In the same way as his predecessor, Harty gave numerous organ recitals at Christ Church, to which he devoted hours of practice.[73] Audiences at these recitals were already accustomed to choral and solo vocal items, but to these was now added the novel sound of a solo violin.[74] Very soon the church realised that they had gained a brilliant pianist as well as a fine organist. Harty was often invited to perform at meetings of the Christ Church branch of the

[69] *Bray Parish Quarterly Calendar* (Winter 1896–7), 2. A later review of Figgis's farewell organ recital at Christ Church on 3 Dec. 1896 continued the insinuation, commenting that 'Dr Figgis showed the capacities of the old organ to the best advantage; but still we could not but think how magnificent the effect would be if we had such an instrument as his new organ at St Matthias' placed where our organ is. For we should like to say for the benefit of anyone who is ambitious of purchasing a first-class organ, that it is but little use to spend money on a fine instrument if you do not then choose a building of good acoustic properties in which to place it; but we can confidently assert that if anyone would put a first-class organ in Christ Church they would find that all its beauties could be heard to the utmost advantage there': *Bray Parish Quarterly Calendar* (Spring 1897), 4.

[70] *Bray Parish Quarterly Calendar* (Winter 1896–7), 2. The ministry of the Scotts at Bray lasted from 1862 until 1943.

[71] On the *Crucifixion*, see *Bray Parish Quarterly Calendar* (Spring 1901), 2; (Summer 1901), 2.

[72] The manuscript of Harty's anthem is dated 'January 1901'. Its performance is recorded in the *Bray Parish Quarterly Calendar* (Spring 1901), 1: 'The music, arranged by the Rev. G. D. Scott and Mr. Herbert Harty, was most solemn and impressive, the opening sentences being borrowed from an unpublished setting of the Burial Service by Dykes: and the sentence from the Revelation admirably written for the occasion by our accomplished young organist.' The anthem was later sung at the funeral of Archdeacon Scott in January 1912: *IT*, 17 Jan. 1912.

[73] Harty, 'Autobiography'.

[74] *Bray Parish Quarterly Calendar* (Autumn 1898), 5.

Church of Ireland Temperance Society, and the recently formed Bray Musical Society wasted no time in recruiting him as an accompanist.[75] By 1899 Harty decided to institute a series of chamber concerts of his own in the Parochial Hall, but these foundered with small and sometimes non-existent audiences. In his autobiography Harty recorded a most disastrous launch to his concert series, for which his sister Edith invested a great deal of time in the preparation of refreshments aimed at those who might be regular subscribers. No-one came. Edith was deeply upset at the insult to her brother, but Harty himself expressed a certain relief mixed with a degree of cynicism and indignation:

> I've often wondered why we were let down so 'flat' on that occasion, but later experience of life has taught me that people, generally speaking, only come to entertainments when they are quite sure that nothing will be expected from them in return, and in this case there was the frightful possibility that they might be expected to subscribe to a series of concerts of classical music – how terrifying! I have never forgotten or forgiven that experience, more for the sake of my sister than for myself, for she was bitterly disappointed, whereas to be quite truthful I was relieved and delighted, for I am afraid I have never been what is called a 'good and easy mixer'.[76]

The *Bray Quarterly Calendar* also remarked after the second of Harty's concerts, where he was assisted by T. J. Lindsay, that the audience was diminutive, and feared (rightly) that this would convince its promoter to bring his venture to an end:

> A great musical treat was afforded to those who attended the Recital of Classical and Modern Music given by Mr H. H. Harty in the Parochial Hall, on Saturday afternoon, April 15th. With Mr Harty's own powers as a pianist everyone in Bray who takes any interest in musical matters is already well acquainted, and let it suffice to say that on this occasion he did himself full justice by a very artistic rendering of a most interesting and very varied selection of works for the piano. ... The only disappointing thing was the smallness of the audience, which we fear must have meant a real loss to Mr Harty, and this we regret on selfish grounds no less than on others, for it will be a great loss to us all if Mr Harty finds himself unable to continue giving these excellent recitals.[77]

Harty may have felt let down by his experiences at Bray, but with Dublin only ten miles to the north, new opportunities beckoned of which he took full advantage. In the Irish capital a new cultural momentum was in the air and there was a sense that a new and more serious attitude to music was emerging to rival that of the nation's obvious and much admired literary prowess. As Harty commented, 'she [Dublin] was still occupied in the making of that tradition, and though in the past many great musical names had been associated with her musical activities, she was still important and influential enough to attract

---

[75] See *Bray Parish Quarterly Calendar* (Spring 1898), 5–6; (Spring 1899), 6.

[76] Harty, 'Autobiography'.

[77] *Bray Parish Quarterly Calendar* (Summer 1899), 6.

to herself some of the best of contemporary musicians.'[78] Since 1886 the Royal
Dublin Society (RDS) had relied heavily on the advice and artistic leadership of
Michele Esposito, the senior professor of pianoforte at the Royal Irish Academy
of Music (RIAM), to oversee and participate in a seasonal series of chamber
concerts in the Society's lecture theatre in Leinster House, Kildare Street.
The concerts also drew upon other local professors from the RIAM, thereby
providing a regular and valuable platform for them to perform more challenging
repertoire and an opportunity for them to become better known.[79] Although
Harty did not take formal lessons at the RIAM, he evidently made himself
known there at an early stage and admired the work that was taking place:

> Good honest teaching and general integrity on the part of the principal teachers
> had begun to discourage that light-hearted facility and self-confidence which
> has always been the curse of native Irish musical talent. You were not really
> welcome at the RIAM, for instance, unless you were prepared to work hard and
> conscientiously at your chosen instrument, and to put self-respect and modesty
> before conceit and self-sufficiency.[80]

Harty befriended several of the Academy's most eminent teachers and former
pupils, and worked with them in the concert life of Bray and Dublin. It was
in this way that he rapidly developed an affinity for accompanying vocal and
instrumental soloists in chamber music and the repertoire of solo art song.
Mrs Scott Ffennell, a well-known singer of songs and ballads, promoted an
annual series of concerts in Dublin, and Harty was co-opted to accompany a
performance of Liza Lehmann's recently published cycle for solo quartet and
piano, *In a Persian Garden*.[81] Scott-Ffennell's son-in-law Gordon Cleather, a
professor of singing at the RIAM, appeared with Harty on several occasions, as
did the cellist Alexandrina Elsner, the violist Octave Grisard, and the violinists
P. J. Griffith, Patrick Delaney, Arthur Darley, and Adolph Wilhelmj (son of the
great German violinist August Wilhelmj, one-time Konzertmeister at Bayeuth),
the last of whom Harty had known from the Belfast Conservatoire. Harty also
accompanied the violinist Henri Verbrugghen (who frequently visited Dublin to
play at the RDS), and the sopranos Adelaide Mullen and Ella Russell, the latter in
the presence of Queen Victoria at the Viceregal Lodge during her visit to Ireland
in April 1900. Harty, who was later introduced to the queen, was presented with
an elaborate scarf pin.[82] At another of Scott Ffennell's concerts Harty became
acquainted with William Henry Squire, principal cellist in the Queen's Hall
Orchestra and a well-known player on the London circuit. Squire described his
first meeting with Harty with fond clarity:

[78] Harty, 'Autobiography'.

[79] See Jeremy Dibble, *Michele Esposito* (Dublin: Field Day Publications, 2010), 51–3.

[80] Harty, 'Autobiography'.

[81] See *IT*, 16 Jan. 1899.

[82] See *HPM* and the *Bray Parish Quarterly Calendar* (Summer 1900), 1–2. Harty later
presented his royal gift to his sister Alice: BBC talk, 18 June 1951.

> I became acquainted with my revered friend, Hamilton Harty, exactly fifty years
> ago, the occasion being a concert at the Rotunda, Dublin, in February 1901, for
> which I had been engaged. The first item on that programme was Grieg's now well-
> known Sonata for Cello and Piano. Arriving at the hall for morning rehearsal, I
> was confronted with a young man who, somewhat demurely, began apologising
> for having had so little time to prepare the work we were about to play, and which
> was new to him. His words perturbed me somewhat, but after playing a page or
> two together, I realised that my partner was not only a brilliant pianist, but a very
> gifted musician indeed; and his handling of some quite difficult accompaniments,
> which he was reading at sight, impressed me tremendously.[83]

Harty also became well known for accompanist skills at concerts given by
the larger choral bodies in Dublin, such as the University Choral Society, the
Orpheus Choral Society (directed by James Culwick), the Dublin Glee and
Madrigal Union, and the newly instituted Leinster Section of the Incorporated
Society of Musicians. But, without question, most influential on Harty at this
time was Esposito. Though he had almost certainly witnessed Esposito's playing
at concerts in the Irish capital, Harty appears to have first encountered the fiery
Italian – he described him aptly as a 'martinet'[84] – getting onto a train at Bray
station. Harty asked if he would take him as a pupil, whereupon, '"Show me
your hands", he [Esposito] said abruptly – "no, they are not good for piano – the
thumbs are too short!".' Harty was somewhat discouraged by this response, but
he then resolved to audition for Esposito's new orchestra, the Dublin Orchestral
Society (DOS), a brand new and ambitious enterprise that was launched on 1
March 1899. Harty's account of that meeting is as follows:

> He [Esposito] made an appointment at his house and I presented myself with viola,
> for the necessary audition. While waiting for him I noticed a MS full score lying
> open on a table, and glanced at it. It was a symphony and lay open at the Scherzo.
> Presently he came in and I proceeded to play something for him – an ordeal for
> us both. In a few minutes he stopped me and said seriously and with kindliness –
> 'you know, it is 'orrible! You cannot play that piece of music!' Feeling both nervous
> and disappointed I said 'Oh – do you think so? Well perhaps you like this piece
> better', and played from memory some of the bars of the principal theme of the
> Scherzo I had glanced at while waiting for him. His face changed – 'But – but
> *nobody* knows that. How you get it?' I explained and from that day I became, not
> indeed a regular pupil of the 'Maestro' but, a close friend who could look with
> complete confidence to him for help and advice. Indeed with the exception of my
> own father his was the ruling influence in my musical life.[85]

---

[83] See BBC talk, 3 Oct. 1951.

[84] Harty, 'Autobiography'.

[85] Harty, 'Autobiography'. A slightly different version of this event was detailed by
Harty in his obituary article 'Michele Esposito' for *The Irish Statesman*, 7 Dec.
1929, 276: see Dibble, *Michele Esposito*, 146–7. Harty suggests no exact date for
his story, but it raises some interesting questions. If Harty's audition took place
for the orchestra 'he had just founded', then it would suggest that the event took
place in 1899. However, the piece which Harty commited to memory suggests
that it was Esposito's 'Irish' Symphony – Esposito's only symphonic work – which

Though Harty always maintained that he was never 'officially' a pupil of Esposito, he nevertheless admitted to sending him everything he wrote for criticism, even as a mature and professional musician.[86] It is clear from at least two photographs of him and Esposito together – where Harty's hand can be seen affectionately grasping his mentor's arm – that his respect and admiration for the Italian remained undimmed.

With no surviving programmes for the DOS concerts, we cannot be sure of the date when Harty began to play with the orchestra, though we know that he was admitted as a violist.[87] If it was in or around 1899, when the orchestra was formed, then he would have enjoyed up to three years of orchestral experience under Esposito's baton. The DOS would have also have provided Harty with a modest but useful income, as well as the opportunity to assimilate a good deal of core repertoire.[88] There was also much to learn 'actively' in terms of orchestration and rehearsal technique. From this point of view, therefore, Harty, like the young Elgar before him, drew a vast amount of his orchestral *savoir faire* from immediate practical experience. Yet, as Harty admitted, 'the orchestra itself was not superlative', and the variable standard of playing, intonation and ensemble must have jarred by comparison with the professionalism of the Hallé Orchestra.[89] This famous orchestra gave two concerts in Dublin the year before the DOS was formed – on 7 and 8 March 1898, at the newly opened Lyric Hall, under the baton of Frederic Cowen. They were so well received that the orchestra returned to give two further concerts on 15 and 16 November in the same year, and again in 1900 and 1901, this time under Richter, to similar public approbation (much to the dissatisfaction of Esposito and the DOS who, with small audiences, were struggling to survive financially). Although Harty does not mention these visits in his autobiography, it seems inconceivable that he was not there, providentially, to hear Britain's finest orchestra.

As Harty acknowledged later, 'the years I spent in Dublin were important ones to me, for there I was brought into contact with music of all kinds and had many opportunities of improving my knowledge and understanding.'[90] This 'knowledge and understanding' extended well beyond his musical experience. At the very time Harty had arrived in Dublin Ireland's political consciousness was gathering momentum, particularly with thoughts of Home Rule, and the country as a whole was preoccupied with the revival of its culture, spearheaded by its wealth of literary genius and by antiquarians fascinated in the rich narrative of the nation's neglected history. During the 1890s alone Ireland had witnessed the birth of two Irish Literary Societies (one in London, the other in

the Italian entered for the Feis Ceoil in 1902. Given that Harty could not have auditioned in 1902, after he had left Dublin for London, it suggests that Esposito must have already composed either all or some of the 'Irish' Symphony some years before the Feis of 1902.

[86] [Colles], 'Hamilton Harty', 228.

[87] [Colles], 'Hamilton Harty', 227.

[88] See Dibble, *Michele Esposito*, 75 *passim*.

[89] Dibble, *Michele Esposito*, 75 *passim*.

[90] Harty, 'Autobiography'.

Dublin),[91] the Abbey Theatre, and the Gaelic League, as well as the emergence of major cultural luminaries such as George Moore, Augusta Gregory, W. B. Yeats and Douglas Hyde. Much of the focus was on poetry, fiction, and the revival of Irish myth and legend, and to this was added the potent agency of Irish folk music, one that had much power in the melodies of Thomas Moore, and which had also been harnessed with much enthusiasm by Stanford in *Songs of Old Ireland* in 1882 and in his later edition of *The Petrie Collection*, commissioned by the Irish Literary Society and published between 1902 and 1905. Indeed, Stanford, as the most prominent of Irish composers, enjoyed a degree of iconic status among Irish musicians, not least with the enormous success of his 'Irish' Symphony (1887) and his comic opera *Shamus O'Brien* (1896). Both these works enjoyed huge success in London, on tour throughout Britain and Ireland, and on New York's Broadway, and were accepted as expressions of authentic 'Irishness'. Yet the source of Stanford's cultural references was from London, which left Ireland's resident community of musicians to consider the major and compelling question of a school of Irish composers for themselves.

Of course, folksong was an obvious wellspring from which Irish musical creativity might find genuine and distinctive utterance; such was the *topos* of many European nations in their bid for national, and in many cases political, distinctiveness, and one that Annie Patterson urged at the Pan-Celtic Congress of 1901.[92] But there were inherent dangers, too, for the question arose whether an Irish identity could be expressed sincerely without the quotation or assimilation of the folk repertoire. In some quarters a narrow idea prevailed that arrangements of Irish airs were *sine qua non* towards such a goal, and some held the even narrower precept that Irish folk song *was* Irish music *de facto* (to the exclusion of Continental music, which was judged to be an alien phenomenon). This was a debate that raged in the preludial debates before 'An Feis Ceoil', an annual Irish national music festival, was launched in 1897.[93] A strong nationalist faction on the board of the Feis – who consisted of members of the National Literary Society and the Gaelic League – advocated that only traditional music should be promulgated. Thanks largely to the agitations of Esposito, Patterson, and members of the RIAM, who protested at the first public meeting of the Feis at the Mansion House on 15 June 1896, the festival's syllabus was broadened considerably. Moreover, Esposito also got his way in establishing a composers' competition that was open to all persons 'of Irish birth and parentage, whether resident in Ireland or elsewhere, as well as those of British or foreign parentage who have been resident in Ireland for three years' in order to encourage

---

[91] The Irish Literary Society was founded in London in 1892; the National Literary Society was founded by Yeats in Dublin the following year.

[92] *WIT*, 7 Sept. 1901. As a proselyte for the unique nature of Irish music, Patterson also delivered an important paper to the Musical Association on 13 April 1897, entitled 'The Characteristic Traits of Irish Music'. It was published in *PRMA*, 23rd sess. (1896–7), 91–111.

[93] For further discussion on this debate, see P. Zuk, 'Music and Nationalism', *Journal of Music in Ireland* 2(2) (2002), 5–10; 2(3) (2002), 25–30.

indigenous composition.[94] This initiative, above all others, acted as a vital spur to Harty's first musings as a composer.

A string quartet in A minor was completed on 28 March 1898, and Harty may have harboured designs of entering it for the Feis in 1899. The work, however, had numerous flaws, most of them revealing inexperience in handling large-scale form and tonal organisation (the under-length first movement is one such instance). For the 1899 Feis in Dublin he entered a violin sonata; this received no prize but was pronounced 'proximo' by the adjudicators.[95] For the 1900 Feis his String Quartet in F, Op. 1, was awarded first prize in the string quartet category, and a further award was given for his 'violin and piano duet'. The first movement of the quartet and of the duet (now lost) were subsequently performed at one of the evening concerts in the Wellington Hall in Belfast during the festival, and were considered auspicious indications of Harty's emerging talent:

> The first movement of the prize string quartet by Mr H. Harty was played by a quartet consisting of Miss Swan, Miss Munster, Miss L. Brett, and Miss M. Brett. This is an unquestionably clever composition, with a recurring melody of a very bright and pleasing character. This latter forms the chief subject of [the] movement, and is subjected to some very scholarly and ingenious developments. The piece was excellently played by the quartet of ladies. ... An excellent piano and violin duet, composed by Mr H. Harty and played by the composer and Mr T. J. Lindsay, next formed a very pleasing feature of the concert. The more Mr Harty's compositions are heard the more is the assurance conveyed of his exceedingly high gifts as a composer. He certainly occupies a high place among the younger generation of composers.[96]

This quartet was certainly an advance on the earlier Quartet in A minor, demonstrating a more assured handling of harmony and the polyphonic idiom of the string quartet. In general there is a much clearer comprehension of form, proportion, and textural balance than in the earlier work, and the scoring shows greater imagination, not least in the viola – Harty's 'part' – which features prominently. Moreover, the interesting cyclic connection between the Scherzo, its recurrence in the slow movement, and the quirky nature of the Finale must have caught the eye of the judges. However, what the critic of the *Irish Times* took for ingenuity in the first movement is in fact over-amplication, typical of a young, excessively ambitious imagination. Not only is the developmental phase of the movement long-winded, but so is the markedly over-elaborate exposition (of 111 bars) and recapitulation, both of which would have benefited from judicious surgery. The pastoral slow movement, though inventive in places, tends to monotony engendered essentially by excessive repetition of the initial

[94] See *MT* 36 (1896), 663–4.

[95] *HPM* (Mar. 1899); see Greer, *Hamilton Harty: Early Memories*, 23n. The manuscript of this work is now lost.

[96] 'Feis Ceoil: Competitions and Evening Concert', *IT*, 16 May 1900. An 'Introduction and Allegro' for violin and piano, almost certainly the 'duet', was later performed by Harty and Lindsay at a 'Grand Concert' in the Downshire National School on 12 October 1900.

thematic material, though, admittedly, this is prudently broken up by the cyclic recurrence of the Scherzo material. The vivacious and technically demanding Finale, which possesses musical ideas of lyrical interest and contrapuntal ingenuity, is an engaging if eccentric structure. Harty's developmental phase begins in a remarkably chromatic manner (curiously suggestive of Bruckner), which leads with some surprise to a false yet extended recapitulation of the opening thematic material in E flat major. Even more unexpected is the introduction of an entirely new episode before F major is restored for the final reprise which has by now taken on the rhetorical mantle of a 'rondo' theme. The Scherzo, which incorporated in a revised form the corresponding movement of the discarded Quartet in A minor, is the most successful conception. The 'will-o-the-wisp' style of the Scherzo material, redolent of the many instances in Mendelssohn, is controlled with impressive skill, as is the more cheerful demeanour of the Trio, where the cello features most prominently as soloist. But most striking in terms of technical adeptness is Harty's ability to rework the Scherzo. At first this process appears to take a contrapuntal departure, but a sudden curtailment on the dominant of C, and a pregnant pause, leads to a thoroughly Beethovenian shift to A flat replete with a recapitulation of material from the Trio. The tonal recovery is then effected by a clever combination of this material and the rapid semiquaver motion of the Scherzo, first in E flat and subsequently, through another Beethovenian upward shift to the dominant of A, smoothing the way to a final restatement of the Scherzo's principal idea.[97]

One of the consequences of being a prize-winner at the Feis was a higher profile in the Irish press. As part of her series of biographical articles for *Weekly Irish Times*, Annie Patterson produced a feature on 'Herbert Harty' in July 1900 in which she also drew particular attention to his aptitude as an accompanist.[98] This was, after all, how Harty was principally known in Dublin. After settling in the Irish capital in 1896 he had initially still considered the possibility of becoming a soloist, and set about a demanding programme to improve his technique:

> Generally speaking I devoted the mornings to hard and rather despairing technical pianoforte practice, for I thought in my innocence that determination and concentration could solve all problems, even the most difficult ones. That this did not prove to be so was not because of lack of trying on my part, and at least I gained from all this study a fairly good all-round technique which was to be most useful to me in later developments.[99]

By 1900, however, he recognised that his first aspiration was no longer realistic. Moreover, as is clear from his autobiography, he realised that he knew

---

[97] In his autobiography Harty maintained that he was 'not proud' of his early quartets 'for they [were] naturally enough immature in style and unfinished in craftsmanship'. Yet he still acknowledged, with some justification, they exuded a 'certain lyrical freedom'.

[98] Patterson, 'Herbert Harty'.

[99] Harty, 'Autobiography'.

little of the higher branches of piano technique, and that he could not acquire it purely through his own resources. A different type of career therefore beckoned:

> As time went on I began to realize that, work as hard as I might, I was never likely to develop into a famous solo pianist, in spite of a certain facility and understanding of the pianoforte. So I gave up this dream and turned to another possibility, the possibility that is to say of becoming something a little outstanding as an accompanist. I had already become fairly well known in that capacity, and was assured by various artists visiting Ireland that I should find plenty of work and success in London.[100]

In fact, during 1900 Harty's horizons as an accompanist had started to extend beyond the confines of Dublin and Belfast. In April 1900 Adolph Wilhelmj asked Harty to join him on a tour of the Continent with an initial concert in Berlin.[101] Later that year he was recruited by several English concert promoters, including the well-known Birmingham-based impresario Sidney Harrison (manager of Adelina Patti), to act as accompanist in tours of various British cities.[102] Apparently '[Harrison] was a perfect skin-flint while negotiations were proceeding, but once the contract was signed nothing could exceed his generosity and kindness.'[103] It was this kind of work and the possibility of working with more regular and prestigious artists that persuaded Harty to consider moving to London. This sentiment was confirmed in the *Bray Parish Quarterly Calendar*, which stated that he had an 'opening for a wider career in London',[104] and that 'he [hoped] to find a better sphere for the development and employment of his talents than in Ireland.'[105] After his afternoon concert at the Rotunda with Squire in Dublin on 19 February 1901 Harty announced to his colleague that 'he was leaving for London the day following to take up an organ appointment at All Saints', Norfolk Square, Paddington.'[106] The people at Bray were extremely sorry to see him leave, not only because he had maintained a

---

[100] Harty, 'Autobiography'.

[101] *IT*, 29 Mar. 1900. See also *Bray Parish Quarterly Calendar* (Summer 1900), 2.

[102] That Harty participated in a Scottish tour organised by Methuen & Simpson in November 1900, with the singers Madame Belle Cole, Helen Trust, Jack Robertson, and Fred Williams, and the violinist Hilda Gee, is evident from concerts at the Kinnaird Hall on 19 November (see *Courier and Argus*, 13 and 15 Nov. 1900), and the Greenock Town Hall on 24 November (see *Glasgow Herald*, 26 Nov. 1900).

[103] Harty, 'Autobiography'.

[104] *Bray Parish Quarterly Calendar* (Spring 1901), 2.

[105] *Bray Parish Quarterly Calendar* (Summer 1901), 2.

[106] See BBC talk, 3 Oct. 1951. As Greer has pointed out, Harty's account in his autobiography maintained that it was Squire who 'advised me seriously to consider pursuing my career in London'. But the Vestry Minutes of Norfolk Square confirm that he had already been offered the post before the concert in Dublin took place. Moreover, Harty announced his departure to the Vestry of Christ Church, Bray, in a letter of 11 Jan. 1901. The *Bray Parish Quarterly Calendar* (Summer 1901), 2, confirms that he left London 'in [sic] the end of February'.

high standard of church music at Christ Church, but also because he had been a major force for good in bringing music to the local community. His next step would launch him into a more demanding environment, where, in a relatively short time, he would enjoy a pre-eminent position as one of Britain's finest and most sought-after accompanists.

London (1):
A Pre-eminent 'Collaborator'
and Aspiring Composer

IN moving to England, Harty counted himself among a steady trickle of artists who left Ulster to join the ever-expanding Irish diaspora overseas. Belfast had outstripped Dublin as the industrial capital of Ireland, and, with its predominant Protestant work ethic and expanding middle classes, it valued the rewards of growing individual wealth engendered by the burgeoning professions of finance, medicine and engineering (particularly maritime). However, that wealth did not translate into a propensity for the visual arts, the written word or music-making. Consequently, without the necessary infrastructure or patronage, musicians like Harty followed in the footsteps of Arthur O'Leary, Charles Villiers Stanford and Charles Wood in search of more fertile pastures. The Belfast-born Herbert Hughes, Harty's junior by three years, would continue this diaspora a few years later.

As he had always done, Harty consulted his father about leaving Ireland. William Harty was against the idea, largely because he was anxious about his son's ability to make ends meet, but, recognising that Herbert was old enough to fend for himself, he relented: 'I suppose you are best judge of what you should do.'[1] Moving to London was full of uncertainty for the twenty-one-year-old Irishman. He held no qualifications, had no means of 'entering' society, and he was far from well off; yet, at the same time, he knew there was no realistic alternative, there being little prospect of gaining wider experience in Dublin. More importantly, he was also aware of negative attributes among his compatriot musicians, ones he later elucidated to Colles of the *Musical Times*: 'Well, the Irish musical student is greatly facile, and still more greatly indolent. He reaches a certain point and then drifts. Ireland offers him no scope; yet, as a rule, he is reluctant to leave home. That did not hold good with me.'[2] But, with the exception of Squire, he had virtually no contacts in London and he had no professional credentials – a university degree or qualification from a musical conservatoire – to reinforce his professional standing. In fact, the only employment he could rely on was his organist post. On his arrival he took rented rooms at 34 Southwick Street, Hyde Park West (parallel with Praed Street in Paddington), so as to be close to All Saints', but after beginning his contract at the church, things went badly. The incumbent disapproved of Harty's florid style of playing, so Harty resigned after just a week. 'I was young and 'touchy' in those days', he admitted later, 'and when the vicar – kind and considerate in many ways – took it on himself to criticise my style of playing I immediately

---

[1] BBC talk, 18 June 1951.

[2] *MT* 61 (1920), 228.

resigned. I can appreciate now that he meant well.'³ The priest at All Saints', the Rev. William Boyd, was in fact a musical man who appreciated the organist's craft. As a musician himself, he had authored the tune *Pentecost*, which was often sung to John Monsell's *Fight the Good Fight*. During the 1890s he took on a young Edward Bairstow as organist for four years before Bairstow moved on to Wigan Parish Church. 'Then came Mr Hamilton Harty, from Ireland,' Boyd recounted, cryptically, but evidently proud of the association. 'But, as we both of us soon discovered that his métier lay in a direction other than of organ playing, he left to ascend the ladder of accompanists, and I am told he has no superior in London.'⁴

The potential of making a living solely from accompanying others suggested itself only days after Harty arrived. On 22 March, while lunching with Squire, a brougham arrived with a message from a wealthy society patroness, Lady Violet Brassey, who wanted some musical entertainment that evening at her premises at 24 Park Lane. Squire, who was accustomed to this type of employment, took Harty with him, 'and many a time later,' Squire recalled, 'he would remind me that I had provided him with his first paid engagement as an accompanist in London.'⁵

In his first few years in London Harty was short of money. He took most of his meals out because he lived in lodgings, but sometimes he forewent food altogether. When he did eat, it could be a frugal affair – an 'inadequate diet of buns and tea'.⁶ Yet Edwardian London, lively and prosperous, offered much to excite a young, impressionable musician. A great deal of new Continental music had reached the capital's concert halls. It was possible to hear the works of Richard Strauss (a regular visitor in the early years of the twentieth century), Reger, Humperdinck, Bruckner, Dvořák, Debussy, Ravel, Charpentier, Chabrier, Dukas and Puccini, and later in the decade, the music of Mahler, Schoenberg, Skryabin. Through the offices of Beecham and Diaghilev, the late nineteenth-century Russians (Borodin, Balakirev, Rimsky-Korsakov and Mussorgsky) and Stravinsky would be readily available for British audiences to savour. Elgar's music was at its zenith, and while the works of Parry and Stanford had, to some extent, been eclipsed, their pupils – such as Vaughan Williams, Gustav Holst, Roger Quilter, Frank Bridge, John Ireland, Samuel Coleridge-Taylor and William Hurlstone – were emerging names, as were the former RAM students Granville Bantock, Josef Holbrooke, Arnold Bax and York Bowen. More providentially for Harty, who in Dublin had only properly witnessed the proficiency of Esposito, the cult of the international conductor was gathering considerable momentum with the likes of Hans Richter, Artur Nikisch, Henry Wood, Landon Ronald and Thomas Beecham, and with Continental figures such as Richard Strauss, Fritz

³ Harty, 'Autobiography'.

⁴ *MT* 48 (1907), 170. One of Harty's distinguished successors at All Saints' was the blind organist William Wolstenholme.

⁵ BBC talk, 3 Oct. 1951, *GB-Lbbc*. See also quoted extracts in Squire's diary, Scrapbook A, 45, *GB-Belqb*.

⁶ Agnes Nicholls, speaking in a BBC documentary broadcast 3 Oct. 1951 by the North of Ireland and North of England Home Service.

Steinbach, Willem Mengelberg and Vasily Safonov (not to mention such figures as Elgar, who was a major attraction). As part and parcel of their towering personalities and *savoir faire*, professional orchestral playing in London was rapidly expanding and entering a new era in which the late-nineteenth-century Teutonic dominance of symphonic music, and the Italian supremacy in opera, were being challenged by a broader, more cosmopolitan taste for things French, Spanish, Czech, Russian and Scandinavian.

Although Harty secured few engagements at first, which often meant sending home reassuring but untrue accounts to his parents informing them that all was well,[7] by 1902 his reputation had begun to develop at a pace which would soon be unstoppable. As he told Colles: 'I worked at accompanying, and enthrallingly interesting I found it, with such a variety of music does one thus become acquainted, and with such a variety of artists – little and big – but all human.'[8] In her article for the *Weekly Irish Times* in July 1900 Annie Patterson highlighted Harty's unique talent as accompanist, intimating, even then, that this was the young man's chosen path of career. 'It is work,' he explained to Patterson, 'that suits me admirably and I like it better than anything else.'[9] It was particularly Harty's role as an accompanist of singers and as a pianist in chamber music that cemented his reputation in Dublin. He had the uncanny knack of understanding, even anticipating, the intention of a solo artist. In addition to his more-than-adequate technique, he possessed a beautiful, singing touch and the ability to shape melodic phrases that remained legendary to all those who played with him.[10] Yet he was also aware of his special ability to sight-read and transpose. 'These', Harty asserted, 'are the two things the average accompanist is usually quite unable to do.'[11] That Harty had discovered this ability, and indeed his potential for employment, had been revealed during a concert he remembered at Bray:

> A short time ago … when the Bray Musical Society gave a performance of Barnett's 'Ancient Mariner', the piano was very much 'up,' in fact to such an extent that the sopranos were totally unable to sing the numerous As and B flats with which the work abounds. So, when the time approached for the concert, we decided there was only one thing to be done, and that was to transpose the whole work down – part of it a semitone and part a whole tone. Well, I did this at the performance, and I believe it went all right, but it was necessary to keep very much on the alert, as it was not easy to remember always whether one was playing a tone or a semitone down. We thought first of all of putting on the posters, 'The whole played and sung at the *normal pitch*,' in imitation of the announcement of the Moody-Manners

[7] Harty, 'Autobiography'.

[8] *MT* 61 (1920), 228.

[9] Patterson, 'Herbert Harty'.

[10] Leonard Hirsch recounted after his audition for the Hallé orchestra in 1922 that he could remember nothing of how he played, only 'how wonderfully Harty accompanied me on the piano': Leonard Hirsch, 'Memories of Sir Hamilton', in *Hamilton Harty: His Life and Music*, ed. David Greer (Belfast: Blackstaff Press, 1978), 67–74, at 67.

[11] Patterson, 'Herbert Harty'.

Opera Company, but this was finally negative, one very good reason for doing so being that most of the work was being done a good deal *below* normal pitch.[12]

Edward Bairstow recalled Harty's phenomenal ability during a concert in the Drill Hall, Wigan, in which Harry Plunket Greene appeared as soloist:

> H. P. G. … sang Stanford's 'Songs of the Sea'. This time he brought with him as accompanist Hamilton Harty, then just rising to fame in London. He had been organist to Boyd at All Saints for a short time till he found his feet. There was only one concert grand in Wigan and that was tuned to the old pitch, impossible for H. P. G. I therefore got a small grand as well at low pitch. When we came to rehearse, H. P. G. found that the smaller grand was ineffectual in the long, thin Drill Hall. 'Transpose everything a semitone down, Ham,' said he, 'and play on the big piano.' Harty never turned a hair or made a mistake so far as I know. I turned over for him so that I was quite able to detect any slips. The first song on the programme was Schubert's *Litanei*.[13]

Harty's capacity to read scores was also a talent he felt was valuable, not simply to be able to hear a work on the piano, but also because it could be an invaluable tool for elaborating inadequate piano arrangements:

> The power to read orchestral music easily and to transfer it to the piano is useful in another way. Many works for solo instruments or for voice were not written originally with piano accompaniment. Indeed the arrangement for piano is seldom very full, and is often thin and bald in the extreme. The reason is that these arrangements are meant to be within the grasp of the average person, and because of this much detail has been omitted. There is nothing to prevent one, however, getting the original orchestral score and making one's own arrangement, or at least adding details to enrich what is already provided in the piano arrangement. Quite apart from the interest of this proceeding, it is extraordinary how such things for instance as Violin Concertos can be improved, when played with a piano accompaniment to which the method has been applied.[14]

That Harty put this into practice is evident from a concert of the Hallé Orchestra in 1921. Bantock's large-scale song-cycle *Omar Khayyám* was programmed, but the orchestral parts failed to arrive in time for the performance. To the amazement of the audience, and especially the orchestral players who remained on the platform throughout the performance, Harty simply read the entire work onto the piano and saved the day.[15]

Such was Harty's awareness of this 'art' that he attempted some years later to articulate it in an article called 'The Art of Pianoforte Accompaniment'. In this short, concise essay he was eager to stress those skills of sight-reading

[12] Patterson, 'Herbert Harty'.

[13] F. Jackson, *Blessed City: The Life and Works of Edward C. Bairstow* (York: William Sessions, 1996), 35. That Harty was frequently called upon to transpose his piano parts is evident from the manuscript and printed copies of his own songs where different keys are boldly ringed as a form of personal *aide-memoire*.

[14] Harty, 'The Art of Pianoforte Accompaniment'.

[15] See Hirsch, 'Memories of Sir Hamilton', 69.

and transposition which gained him a reputation for versatility, and a special loyalty and kudos among professionals. But he was also unwavering in his desire to see more young pianists adopt the skill, in part because it was a more than rewarding line of work for the plethora of qualified pianists emerging from music colleges, and also because, with commensurate fees, it was a viable means of making a living. More important, however, was the fact that Harty utterly disliked the term 'accompanist', deeming it a subordinate expression rather than one which described a notion of *equality* in performance. In this sense he was keen to proselytise a new status for the role:

> The chief cause for the neglect of the art of accompaniment is to be found in the absurd and unfortunate title 'accompanist', with all that it implies. Whatever may have been the justification for this name in the darkest early Victorian ages, it is now nothing but a stupid and misleading misnomer for a musician who is called upon to exhibit very rare and special qualities. 'Collaborator' would be more explanatory and a much more desirable description of a musician who spends his life interpreting such works as those for voice and piano of Schubert, Schumann, Brahms, Wolf, and Strauss – to say nothing of the rest of the great mass of music, both vocal and instrumental, with which he is always being brought into contact. I am sure the composers I have mentioned realised this to the full. Most of the songs of Hugo Wolf for instance are described by him as having been written for voice and pianoforte, not as songs with accompaniment for piano, and at Recitals of his songs, in order to emphasise the importance of the piano part, he always insisted upon the piano being fully opened, as it is when a Solo Pianist performs.[16]

Harty's plea for the art of accompaniment to be taken seriously was, even before his death, recognised by musical conservatoires. In 1943 the celebrated accompanist Ivor Newton sagaciously attributed the amelioration of standards to Harty:

> Hamilton Harty, who did more than anyone else to raise the standard of accompanying in England, told me that he devoted as much thought to preparing his share in a programme as if he were the soloist. The qualities an accompanist most needed, he thought, were technique and temperament, and the rare gift of tact.[17]

Yet, writing in the same year, Gerald Moore admitted that old prejudices died hard:

> I do not feel ashamed to call myself an accompanist, and yet to many the title is a brand signifying that the owner is of a slightly inferior caste. My loving aunt is not the only one who asks me why I do not become a solo pianist – even musicians have asked me the same question. Yet somebody must play accompaniments and that is the work I love. If men of recent times like Nikisch, Bruno Walter,

[16] Harty, 'The Art of Pianoforte Accompaniment'. Harty reiterated this plea in his autobiography, even suggesting that 'pianist' might be the most satisfactory term.

[17] Ivor Newton, 'At the Piano', *Music and Letters* 24(2) (1943), 107–10, at 109.

Hamilton Harty and Landon Ronald could do it, then it is good enough for me –
and you.[18]

Even more significantly, Harty ultimately attributed his facility as an
orchestral conductor to his years as, to use his term, a 'collaborator': 'When
Nikisch, that poetical Conductor, was asked to what he attributed a rather
special part of his skill – the faculty he possessed of making each player in the
Orchestra give a little more than his ordinary best – he replied "I think it is the
experience I have had of accompanying. That teaches one to feel with others".'[19]
   Besides the presence of Nikisch in London, there were other accompanists
with whom Harty had to compete. One of London's most seasoned and
experienced accompanists was Henry Bird, who had been signed up in 1891 by
Arthur Chappell as his official pianist for the Monday and Saturday Popular
Concerts at St James's Hall, very much in vogue during the second half of the
nineteenth century.[20] Bird, who was still in demand, worked with most of
the prominent solo instrumentalists and singers of his day, including Joseph
Joachim and Harry Plunket Greene, who also performed with Bird's one-time
pupil, Leonard Borwick. It was Greene and Borwick who pioneered the first
lieder (and piano) recitals in London in December 1893, recitals which broke
with the old form of miscellaneous concerts of instrumentalists, piano and
(usually) multifarious voices. Greene and Borwick worked together for ten years
in this way before their own international careers forced them to part company.[21]
Another pianist, Samuel Liddle, often accompanied them on tour to give
Borwick some respite, and after Borwick forged his solo career, Liddle's position
as an accompanist became well established. In addition, there were also Percy
Pitt, Frederick Kiddle (both of whom played for the Promenade Concerts), Frank
Lambert, York Bowen, C. A. Lidgey and Landon Ronald, who was the preferred
accompanist of figures such as Nellie Melba and Paolo Tosti and, through Tosti's
status as singing teacher to the royal family, was often pianist for state occasions
at Buckingham Palace, Balmoral and Windsor.[22]
   At first, with relatively few public engagements, Harty depended on the kind
of employment that aristocrats could provide in fashionable areas of London:

[18] Gerald Moore, *The Unashamed Accompanist* (London: Ascherberg, Hopwood &
   Crew, 1943), 6.
[19] Harty, 'The Art of Pianoforte Accompaniment', 6. Harty admired Nikisch's
   conducting but, like Gerald Moore after him, observed a rare quality in his
   ability as accompanist, one that he must have witnessed from the pioneering
   recordings of lieder he made in 1903 with the German soprano Elena Gerhardt
   and from the concerts that Gerhardt gave with Nikisch at the Bechstein Hall in
   London from 1906 until the war. Landon Ronald, who also forged his career as a
   conductor through early experiences as an accompanist, admired Nikisch above
   all conductors: Landon Ronald, *Myself and Others: Written Lest I Forget* (London:
   Sampson Low, Martson & Co., 1931), 70–71.
[20] See obituary, *MT* 57 (1916), 25–6; also 'Henry Richard Bird', *MT* 51 (1910), 289–90.
[21] H. Plunket Greene, 'Leonard Borwick: Some Personal Recollections', *Music &
   Letters* 7(1) (1926), 17–24, at 18.
[22] 'Landon Ronald', *MT* 51(1910), 217.

... there were many musical parties or 'At Homes' given at the houses of the richer classes, especially during 'the season'. Here a couple of operatic singers and a focus instrumentalist would provide a sufficiently attractive programme for a polite and appreciative audience. They took place generally at night, beginning at about 10.30 or 11 p.m. After about 2 hours' music there was supper and – for me at any rate – a walk home in the early dawn.[23]

However, he quickly fell in with Plunket Greene, at precisely the time when the Irish baritone's collaboration with Borwick was beginning to fragment. He was also able to rely on his connections with the Feis Ceoil which, by now, was a permanent fixture of Dublin's cultural life. In May 1901, while he was at the Feis to perform his prize-winning *Fantasiestücke*, he also accompanied Coleridge-Taylor's *Hiawatha* (a new work at that time) for the Dublin University Choral Society, gaining adulation from one of the soloists for his ability to transpose.[24] In fact, by 1902 Harty was employed as the festival's resident accompanist; this allowed him to witness the appearance of a young tenor from Athlone, John McCormack, who, not quite nineteen, won the festival's gold medal in 1903 by a comfortable margin. McCormack himself gave an account of that auspicious and fateful scene:

The hall was packed that first Feis afternoon ... several thousand people, many of whom had come miles to Dublin for that occasion. And every tenor and baritone and soprano and contralto had 'rooters'; but silent rooters, for applause was forbidden. I made my way to a spot in a corner of the hall, not far from the stage. In half an hour the judges called the first of the fourteen tenors who were competing, and the contest was on.

Eight of these tenors sang, and none of them disturbed materially my peace of mind. Three of the remaining five, however, did, one especially. This chap was William Rathbone, a matured singer and very evidently, by the actions of the audience, the favourite. ... Rathbone finished and stepped down from the platform. As he passed down the aisle toward the dressing-room, which brought him near me, I saw him take his left hand in his right and press it with congratulatory fervour. It may appear to have been a presumptuous act; I thought it such, and was inclined to smile. Also, that act of Rathbone's of shaking hands with himself on his assumed victory struck me as a trifle previous. It made something inside me rebel, and straightway there was born a resolve to teach him a lesson if I could.

... At any rate, all the undesirable part of my long-continued nervousness promptly vanished. And I walked, as my name was called, to the platform and over to the piano where Hamilton Harty sat waiting. Harty, now a distinguished composer, was the official accompanist for the Feis. But when my turn came he was tired.

... Well, we finally began. But Harty, as I intimated, was physically worn out. He wanted to get through and quickly; and he played the introductory measures of 'Tell Fair Irene' as though he had a train to make. It was a tempo twice as fast as [Vincent] O'Brien had taught me was the correct one; a tempo, likewise, too rapid

[23] Harty, 'Autobiography'.

[24] See Greer (ed.), *Hamilton Harty: His Life and Music*, 36.

to permit of good singing, to say nothing of interpreting Händel's music as he intended.

There was only one thing to do and I did it. I turned around and informed Harty I had learned the aria in a way different from the way he was playing it. 'Please take it just half as fast,' I requested. Instead of objecting he only smiled. He probably thought: 'The poor boy, well, let him have his way.' But I hadn't gone far before Harty settled down and played for me one of the finest accompaniments I have ever sung to. He was a sportsman to the tips of his talented fingers, and he gave me all there was musically in him.

With my last note there came from the audience a volley of applause. ... The gold medal I was awarded as winner of the tenor contest at the Feis decided my future.[25]

This serendipitous encounter cemented a lifelong friendship.[26]

Another tenor, Gregory Hast, whom Harty had befriended in Belfast, was one of the first artists, along with the great Charles Santley, that Harty accompanied at the newly opened Bechstein Hall.[27] This superb venue, located at 36 Wigmore Street, boasted one of the best acoustics in Europe and helped to establish the phenomenon of piano, vocal and instrumental recitals as a normal fixture of London life. Harty's appearances at the hall were so regular that, according to Gerald Moore, he was believed to have had his bed there.[28] Other venues, such as the Steinway Hall, Aeolian Hall, St James's Hall and Queen's Hall were also regular haunts. The pattern of Harty's life at this point was normally participation in miscellaneous programmes featuring an array of solo singers and instrumentalists, many of which were promoted either privately by individual artists or by corporate impresarios such as Chappell or Boosey for their weekly Ballad Concerts at St James's Hall. The quality of the artists must have been distinctly variable: the tenor Hirwen Jones, 'hardly

[25] John McCormack, *His Own Life Story* (New York: Small, Maynard & Co., 1918; repr. edn New York: Vienna House, 1973), 65–7, 69. A further account is imparted by Lily McCormack in *I Hear You Calling Me* (London: Allen, 1950), 99: 'In later years when he [Harty] had become a close friend, "Hale" said he got quite a shock when he saw a mere lad walk onto the platform to tackle such an intricate work. He gave him a nod and started the opening bars when the "mere lad" turned to him and said, "Oh, that's much too fast. I don't sing it as fast as that". Vastly amused at the naiveté of the boy, "Hale" said, "All right. Just show me how you like it". John hummed the beginning and they were off.'

[26] Harty also accompanied another aspiring tenor, James Joyce, during the 1904 Feis Ceoil in Dublin. McCormack, who was good friends with Joyce, persuaded him to enter. Unfortunately for Joyce, his refusal to undertake the compulsory sight-reading test disqualified him from the gold medal, and he had to make do with bronze: see Gordon T. Ledbetter, *The Great Irish Tenor* (London: Duckworth, 1977), 37.

[27] The Bechstein Hall, now the Wigmore Hall, was opened on 31 May 1901 with a concert given by Busoni and Ysaÿe.

[28] Gerald Moore, *Am I Too Loud?* (London: Hamish Hamilton, 1962), 92.

sang two consecutive bars in the same time',[29] and an inexperienced Violet Sydney smacked a little too much 'of the schoolroom',[30] but other concerts promised much for the young Irishman. The soprano Grainger Kerr included numerous unusual Russian songs by Glinka, Rimsky-Korsakov, Dargomizhky, Tchaikovsky and Balakirev;[31] Frederick Keel, soon to be well known for his *Four Salt-Water Ballads*, sang *Linden Lea* and *Blackmwore by the Stour* by an as yet unknown Vaughan Williams,[32] along with Liza Lehmann's song cycle *In a Persian Garden*.[33] But perhaps the most auspicious breakthrough for Harty was his collaboration with the Austrian violinist Fritz Kreisler, whose international career had only recently begun with a tour of the United States in 1900 and 1901. Kreisler is recorded as having made his London debut with Richter at St James's Hall on 12 May 1902, when he performed Beethoven's Violin Concerto, but according to Robin Legge of *The Saturday Review*, Kreisler was 'too "unknown" to risk "testing" in an important concert':

> But the unknown quantity tried his fortune in the provinces. For an engagement at a South Coast Resort an agent tendered him – Fritz Kreisler forsooth! – the elee-mosynary fee of five guineas for a recital for which Kreisler must provide his own accompanist. To him came a then unknown pianist-accompanist of quite outstanding ability. His name was Hamilton Harty and his fee was six guineas.[34]

Kreisler's career in Britain took off instantly and throughout 1902 he made a successful tour of the provinces. In London his first solo recital on 13 June was so popular that there was demand for a second, which took place on 12 December that year with Harty at the piano. The commotion that Kreisler's presence in London created among the capital's concert-goers was immense, for, as the critic of *The Times* commented after a recital in May 1903, he joined the ranks of Lady Hallé and Joachim in an undying tradition of classic violinists:

> In view of the much-discussed advance in recent years of the science of violin-playing and of the wide general interest in it, it is interesting to note the appearance in London concert-rooms within the last few days of three of the greatest exponents – Lady Hallé, Dr. Joachim, and Herr Kreisler. As the name of modern experts is legion, as they crowd upon each other almost in dozens, as the latest comer seems to go one better than his immediate predecessor, as the visits of the older generation are, so to say, 'angelic' in their comparative fewness, so one is a little apt to forget there have been giants in the earth before, brave men before these Agamemnons. Yet how quickly one is brought back, on hearing these giants, to realize that there has been no real advance either in the technique or

[29] *The Times*, 25 June 1902.
[30] *The Times*, 14 May 1903.
[31] *The Times*, 14 May 1903.
[32] *The Times*, 29 Nov. 1902. The concert took place at St James's Hall, 2 December 1902.
[33] *The Times*, 26 Feb. 1904.
[34] Robin Legge, in *The Saturday Review*, 7 Feb. 1931; also quoted in L. P. Lochner, *Fritz Kreisler* (New York: The Macmillan Co., 1950), 69.

in the artistic quality; and that all the *reclamé*, all the talking in the world, will not add a sufficiency of cubits to the stature of the newcomers to enable them to rise above their immediate predecessors. In a sense Herr Kreisler, who began a new series of recitals in St. James's Hall on Saturday afternoon, is an anachronism in that undoubtedly he, more than any other of his exact contemporaries, belongs to the race of giants of old, while himself still a young man. That he is in the royal line and will one day succeed to the possession of the giants, his still living predecessors, he makes quite evident at each appearance. He, more than the rest, seems imbued with the classic tradition, while fully alive to all that is called modern. His Paganini playing is as alert and vivacious as that of any other violinist, yet for him Paganini seems to mean more than mere brilliant technical display. His Bach, his playing of such pieces as a Corelli sarabande or a D'Angelis gigue, or an Ernst concerto, is not only well balanced and full of temperament, and shows not only the player's versatility and catholicity of taste, but a command of style and a sense of 'atmosphere' that only one in the royal line could show. Tried even in the keen fire of the recollection referred to above, Herr Kreisler, who was admirably accompanied by Mr. Hamilton Harty, comes out unscathed.[35]

Though he worked with other pianists in Britain, including Ernő Dohnányi, Kreisler remained strongly loyal to Harty and they often appeared together, not only in London (where he continued to attract large crowds in 1904 and 1905), but also in Harty's old stamping ground of Dublin (13 March 1903), Liverpool (October 1904), Belfast (October 1904, which included an arrangement Harty made for Kreisler of Chaminade's *Serenade*)[36] and Birmingham (September 1905). There were also royal engagements such as the private audience they received at Frogmore on 9 July 1903 (one of many that Kreisler received from the royal household during the next twelve years), and Harty was nearly always present when Kreisler appeared as soloist at the Chappell Ballad Concerts.[37]

By the end of 1902 Harty's reputation as an accompanist was spreading by word of mouth as much as by advertisement. At that time he encountered the soprano Agnes Nicholls, whose career as one of Britain's greatest sopranos of the twentieth century was already under way. Born on 14 July 1876, Agnes Helen Nicholls grew up in Cheltenham, a Regency spa town in the Cotswolds. Her father Albert Chapman Nicholls, a draper, and her mother Fanny Elizabeth (née Vent) were both music lovers. Indeed, Albert Nicholls duly recognised the musical talent of his daughter and allowed her to study the violin and piano at the RCM in 1893, but was against the notion of her becoming a singer. In 1894 Albert Nicholls suddenly died, at which juncture Agnes Nicholls resolved to apply for a scholarship in singing under the guidance of Alberto Visetti, which she won for a period of five years. As a student at the RCM she soon began to confirm her standing as a major talent; she sang for Queen Victoria at Windsor

---

[35] *The Times*, 11 May 1903.

[36] *Belfast Evening Telegraph*, 18 Oct. 1904. A study of the music Kreisler played at these concerts also reveals that Harty was one of the first to be party to Kreisler's 'pastiches' (the authorship of which was not revealed until 1935).

[37] See, for example, *The Times*, 21 Jan. 1907; 21 Feb. 1907.

and appeared in the RCM's opera productions under the direction of Stanford.[38] Such was the power and depth of her voice that Stanford was also able to perform the 'Liebestod' from *Tristan und Isolde* with her and the RCM Orchestra, a work with which she would be closely associated in later years.[39] After leaving the RCM in 1899 she soon began to receive important engagements as a soloist in oratorios, notably at the major choral festivals of the Three Choirs and Leeds, and she secured her first important role as the Dew Fairy in Humperdinck's *Hänsel und Gretel* at Covent Garden in 1901.[40]

Nicholls and Harty had in fact participated in the same concert in the 1902 Feis Ceoil, but it is unlikely that they actually met socially, for Nicholls did not recall the occasion: 'It was in the autumn of 1902 that I first met Hamilton Harty. A cellist friend of mine was to give a recital and asked if I would sing two groups. I consented, and she wrote recommending a young man named Harty as accompanist, as she had been unable to book Samuel Liddle. A few days later at my friend's house on a very crooked staircase, I met him.'[41] Two years older than Harty, Nicholls recalled her first impressions of the young Ulsterman who was not quite twenty-three:

> He was the best-looking man I ever saw – a 'soft' face, if one may so describe it, at times almost like a girl's; a great shock of hair – chestnut brown; brilliant blue eyes that seemed to look through you; and a lovely skin; very witty, very humorous, and with the softest voice and a literal gurgle of laughter when amused.[42]

After their first acquaintance Harty became a regular visitor at the Nicholls's house at 153 Camden Road, where Agnes was able to witness his gifts as a pianist:

> I must say I was most surprised with his playing. He had lovely tone, great facility, seemed able to read anything at sight with the greatest ease; yet to look at his hands – so different from the usual pianist's – it was unbelievable. He gave me the feeling of great musicianship and understanding of the music.[43]

In fact, Nicholls quickly recognised that Harty's abilities would be of enormous help her, not only as accompanist but as coach and repetiteur. 'I wrote and asked Hamilton Harty if he did such work. As a result, he came very often to the house, and my mother and my family got to know him well.'[44] At around this time, too, Harty's close friends and colleagues began to know him by the diminutive 'Hale', or more commonly 'Hay', nicknames which remained with him for the rest of his life. As Nicholls explained: 'Some people used to call him, as a joke, "Hale

---

[38] Nicholls appeared as Dido in Stanford's pioneering revival of Purcell's opera in 1895, and as Anne Page in the first English-language production of Verdi's *Falstaff* in 1897.

[39] See RCM concert programmes, 16 Dec. 1898.

[40] One of Nicholls' first major engagements was in Verdi's *Requiem* at the Bridlington Music Festival in April 1900: see *MT* 41 (1900), 394.

[41] BBC talk, 3 Oct. 1951.

[42] BBC talk, 3 Oct. 1951.

[43] BBC talk, 3 Oct. 1951.

[44] BBC talk, 3 Oct. 1951.

and Harty", and that very soon was reduced to "Hayland". But after I started calling him "Hay", everybody quickly followed suit; and ever after that, his intimate friends always called him "Hay".'[45]

Harty took full advantage of a standing invitation to dine whenever he was in Camden. He became well known to the Nicholls family, and by 1903 a close working relationship had developed between him and Agnes. She later recalled that:

> At that time I had no idea he composed, until one day he brought a song and very shyly handed it to me. It was 'The Song of Glen Dun'. I thought it lovely and put it into my programme whenever the opportunity occurred. Shortly after, he dedicated a song called 'Rose Madness' to me. Of course, I was thrilled, and it was published very soon afterwards. During the year 1903 he wrote a number of songs, many of which I sang.[46]

Nicholls and Harty appeared many times together and were in much demand by music societies across Britain. By this time, of course, Nicholls was already a well-known figure through her appearances at the Birmingham Festival (where she appeared in Bruckner's *Te Deum* under Richter's direction), and in Manchester, where she took part in a truncated concert version of *Fidelio*. What accelerated their appeal as a 'duo' was their first major collaboration at the rural setting of the twelfth Hovingham Festival in north Yorkshire, on 23 and 24 September 1903 (the festival had been founded by Canon Thomas Pemberton in 1887, and was by then considered a highlight of the English summer festival season). Nicholls took several solo parts in Verdi's *Requiem*, Mendelssohn's *Lobgesang*, a scene from Beethoven's *Fidelio* and S. S. Wesley's anthem *The Wilderness* (in its orchestral version). The festival normally concluded after the afternoon concert of the second day (24 September), but that year a further chamber concert was programmed as an experiment. It featured at its centre a vocal recital by Nicholls accompanied by Harty. Her programme included songs by Brahms, Schumann, Strauss, Weingartner, Dvořák, Grieg and Tchaikovsky, but at the end the audience were introduced to new British songs by Harty and MacCunn. Nicholls was complimented for her versatility and 'inspired singing', and Harty for carrying out his 'duties of accompanist in really masterly fashion'.[47] 'This,' as Nicholls recounted, 'meant more work together than ever'. What is more, as part of their individuality as performers, Harty would often perform the entire programme of songs from memory.[48]

After appearing in *The Apostles* in the Elgar Festival at Covent Garden on 15 March 1904 Nicholls went to America, where she sang in Bach's B minor Mass, the role of the angel in Elgar's *The Dream of Gerontius*, and in Beethoven's Ninth Symphony at the Cincinnati Summer Festival. Such was the demand for her that, soon after arriving home in England, she was on the stage at Covent

---

[45] BBC talk, 3 Oct. 1951. Harty was also known by some of friends as 'Hale'.

[46] BBC talk, 3 Oct. 1951.

[47] 'Hovingham Festival', *MT* 64 (1903), 741. Nicholls and Harty were also invited to participate in the Hovingham Festival in October 1906.

[48] BBC talk, 3 Oct. 1951.

Garden as Micaëla in Bizet's *Carmen*. At about this time she had the offer to reside in New York and to lead the choir in one of the New York churches. 'I couldn't make up my mind about it', she later recollected, 'so I journeyed over to see – but came home again. I didn't like the idea of having to appear every Sunday and lead the choir and sing solos. At the same time these American churches are splendid engagements and the authorities give one much freedom of action – but England appealed to me more at that time!'[49] One compelling reason for her to remain in England was almost certainly that her career was in the ascendant in both the concert hall and theatre. Another was surely that she and Harty decided to marry on 15 July 1904, at St Luke's Church, Kentish Town. The marriage, reported in *The Times*,[50] was intended to be a quiet affair but, in the end, as Nicholls modestly recalled: 'it caused a great sensation. Why I can't think – but it did.'[51] After their nuptials, the couple took a house at 3 Manor House, Marylebone.

Though London was Harty's principal focus, he did at intervals return to Ireland. In part this was to compose in the tranquillity of his family home at Hillsborough,[52] and in Dublin he sought the advice of Esposito on his expanding list of works.[53] One of several he probably showed to Esposito – evidenced perhaps by pencil revisions in the manuscript – was his first major attempt at an extended orchestral work – an overture, *The Exile*, Op. 2. Its exact date of completion is unknown but the autograph manuscript bears his address at Southwick Street which, together with the 'opus' designation, suggests that it was finished after Harty moved to London in 1901. The work is based on Thomas Campbell's poem *The Exile of Erin*, which had been inspired by Anthony McCann, one of several exiled United Irishmen in Hamburg whom Campbell had met during his German tour in 1800. Harty's choice of poem may not have been motivated so much by political interest, though his years in Dublin during the late 1890s would have undoubtedly made him aware of Ireland's growing nationalist ferment. Instead it seems more likely that his affinity for Campbell's verse was stimulated by his own personal predicament – an Irishman forced by circumstance to leave his home and live abroad. He was, like so many of his countrymen, part of a larger disapora. Stanford often expressed the same sentiments through the poetry of Moira O'Neill and Winifrid Letts, and most eloquently in his song *Irish Skies*. In *The Exile* a gloomy, ponderous

[49] Agnes Nicholls, 'A Vignette', *Opera* (July 1923), 26.

[50] *The Times*, 19 July 1904.

[51] BBC talk, 3 Oct. 1951.

[52] Harty's habit of returning to Hillsborough to write music was confirmed in Olive Baguley's recollections after Harty's death.

[53] The programme notes by Percy Pitt and Alfred Kalisch to the performance of Harty's Piano Quintet at the Bechstein Hall on 29 January 1905 state that Harty 'later had some lessons in composition from Signor Esposito in Dublin'. Harty's admiration for Esposito also extended to his support and promotion of his mentor's works. One of the first examples of his devotion to his master was a performance of Esposito's recently published Cello Sonata, Op. 43, at the Bechstein Hall on 9 June 1903 with Herbert Withers (cello).

introduction in C minor gives way to a swift Allegro, reminiscent stylistically of Schumann. A second subject in the flat submediant (A flat), distinctly more Irish in its pentatonicism and more relaxed tempo, sounds a note of melancholy nostalgia, a sombre mood to which Harty would return time and again in his later works. The rest of the sonata scheme is, for the most part, conventional, but the work is nevertheless remarkable for its indication of self-assurance, especially in its handling of orchestral timbres and textures which are full of romantic passion and imagination. Indeed, the more fervently emotional recapitulation of the second subject and the closing fanfare, marked 'maestoso' (surely emblematic of the United Irishman's motto 'Erin go bragh!'), confidently presage the more confident material of the 'Irish' Symphony and *With the Wild Geese*.[54]

The Exile appears to have remained unperformed, but another of Harty's instrumental works, a Fantasia for Two Pianos, Op. 6, was given a single hearing at one of the Marchesi-O'Sullivan concerts on 17 April 1902 at the Bechstein Hall. Finished in early April at Conway, probably hurriedly, it was first played by Harty and Edith Ladd, an Irish pianist who had recently assisted Esposito in the London premiere of his operetta *The Post-Bag*, at St George's Hall on 27 January.[55] Using synthetic material of Scottish and Irish derivation, intimated by the prevalence of the 'Scottish snap' rhythms, this uncomplicated and unremarkable virtuoso piece was based on the juxtaposition of a lament and a march, padded out with extended cadenza passages for both players. Harty may also have played it over with Esposito (it is strewn with pencil cuts and other alterations) who, in turn, may have been influenced to write his own Fantasia for Two Pianos and Orchestra, Op. 48, which Edith French and Annie Lord performed in Dublin on 25 February 1904.[56]

As Nicholls intimated, her first meeting with Harty initiated a series of solo songs, many of which over the next eighteen years were written for her to sing and him to accompany. They were also, of course, intended for the Ballad Concerts. Denigrating them from a distance of forty years, Harty wished to draw a veil over them: 'I even wrote a number of very bad songs myself for these concerts. Fortunately they are nearly all out of print by now, for I am thoroughly ashamed of them.'[57] Harty was, perhaps, a little harsh in his dismissal of these creations. Their quality is mixed, but among these vocal miniatures are some fine musical conceptions. A competent setting of Moira O'Neill's 'Sea Wrack' (from her *Songs of the Glens of Antrim*) heads the list of Harty's compositions – his first setting of an Irish text. The date of this song is uncertain. From Harty's autobiography there is the suggestion that he composed it while still a teenager at Hillsborough, yet this date seems odd in that Moira O'Neill's poem was not

---

[54] *The Exile* received its first performance by the Windsor Sinfonia, conducted by Robert Tucker, in Slough Parish Church on 29 September 2001, almost a century after its composition.

[55] See *MT* 18 (1902), 176; see also Dibble, *Michele Esposito*, 106–7.

[56] Dibble, *Michele Esposito*, 91.

[57] Harty, 'Autobiography'.

Example 1 *Sea Wrack*, third stanza, climax

published in *Songs of the Glens of Antrim* until 1900.[58] In which case, Harty's *Sea Wrack* was probably not composed until 1901 or 1902, at much the same time as Stanford's cycle *An Irish Idyll*, Op. 77, in 1901. It was also not published until 1905, by Boosey. A sturdy, popular ballad, ideal for the kind miscellaneous concerts and soirées Harty played for in Belfast and Dublin, the melancholy narrative achieves its climax in the quicker urgency of the third stanza. Here a tonal divergence is enacted from the tonic (C major) to D, though the peak of the phrase ('*Him* beneath the salt sea') is underpinned, not by the expected resolution to D, but by its unexpected mediant, F major (Example 1). Such unanticipated and idiosyncratic harmonic touches as this would characterise many of Harty's later works.

[58] Harty's own surviving copy of *Songs of the Glens of Antrim* (in the library of Queen's University, Belfast) is the edition published in Edinburgh in 1902, which may even suggest that it was written after he moved to London.

Another of the *Songs of the Glens of Antrim*, 'The Song of Glen Dun', became Harty's first published song. Like *Sea Wrack*, it has an Irish flavour in its use of modality and folk style. Its popular 'open air' demeanour would have been well suited to the Ballad Concerts, yet there are aspects of the otherwise jovial character of this song that belie the stereotypical: the oblique opening of the piano accompaniment (which cleverly appears at the end); the rather touching internal couplet ('Flower of the May'), which interrupts the animated march rhythms with a hushed interlude in triple metre (and a subtle modulation to the subdominant); the unexpected tonal shift to the dominant of B flat in the third verse; and, complementing the previous aspect, a further unexpected move to the dominant of E flat ('Mocher Mary, keep my love') just before the close.

The idiomatic accompaniment of *The Song of Glen Dun* is symptomatic of Harty's facility as an accompanist; indeed, all of Harty's songs reveal this aspect of his compositional skill, no more so than *Rose Madness*, a setting of words by William Lyon Bultitaft intended as a *chanson d'amour* for Nicholls. The choice of poetry also reflected a connection with home. Though English-born (in 1870), Bultitaft spent most of his life at Lisnoe, Lisburn, where he was near to his relations, the wealthy Quaker Sinton family, at Ravernet House near Hillsborough. Harty was probably well acquainted with them and with Bultitaft, who died tragically young in 1900. In 1901 Bultitaft's collected poems, *Songs on the March*, were published in Belfast and Harty clearly obtained a copy soon after.[59] The full-blooded conception of *Rose Madness*, with its major role for the pianist, is in many ways more suggestive of a miniature 'scena', while Harty's chromatic harmonic language, the interdependent dialogue between piano and voice, and the demandingly sustained nature of the vocal lines is much more reminiscent of opera. Indeed, the extrovert Wagnerian character of this song, clearly conceived for Nicholls's powerful voice, looked forward several years to the composer's most substantial work for solo voice, the *Ode to a Nightingale*.

The prominence of Harty's passionate voice is evident from the extensive piano postlude, which outlines two tangential progressions, one to the dominant of C sharp minor (Example 2), the other a *fortissimo* outburst that leads to F sharp minor; when this exhilaration is becalmed, the entry of the voice outlines, as a subtle variation, the same oblique progressions. Only with the third line of the verse ('What is the spell that this frail flower encloses?') does Harty confirm the tonic key of E major, and even then the dominant of C sharp interjects as if to underline the constantly questioning spirit of Bultitaft's verse. The restlessness of the poetry continues to be accentuated by the negation of a perfect cadence at the end of the stanza. Instead, the unsettled material of the postlude cuts in to forestall any sense of tonicisation. A second stanza, texturally altered, is also radically redirected at the point of cadence, to the dominant of C major. At this juncture the frenetic rhythmical activity is pacified, but the underlying mood is one of agitation, expressed also by the text ('Some mind-controlling power that's more than mortal'). Significantly, Harty revisits both C sharp minor and F sharp minor during the developmental phase of the third stanza; then the climax, articulated first by an 'orchestral' piano and subsequently by the voice ('To touch

---

[59] Harty's copy of Bultitaft still survives in the library at Queen's University, Belfast.

Example 2 *Rose Madness*, entry of voice, first stanza

my hand at last'), returns to the pregnant dominant of C. As in the previous
stanzas, a cadence into C is denied, this time by an underplayed and ambivalent
return to E, a key which is finally confirmed at the triumphant conclusion by a
top G sharp for the soprano and a virtuoso flourish in the accompaniment.

In his other setting of Bultitaft, *Bonfires*, which dates from October 1903,
Harty explored a more sombre, personal subject – the burning of old things
charged with the memory of former camaraderie, love and sentiment – perhaps
as a lament for the young Bultitaft and a past friendship. From the three
verses of the poem Harty created an uncomplicated ternary design, yet this
simple structure belies an impressive melodic unity based essentially on the
single rising phrase established at the beginning. Moreover, a sophisticated,
through-composed tonal dimension is evident in the fluctuation between the
tonic (E flat major), the relative (C minor) and its dominant (G) in the first two

verses, a matrix foreshadowed by the opening vocal statement and summed up in the final cadence for the piano (vi–I). The expunging of 'friendship' ('Let the old passion, in its own dull blaze / Burn out itself') is enacted at the end of the second verse by a striking passage initiated by C minor but ending on an inverted augmented sixth, replete with a resplendent top B for the singer. This harmonic device, a favourite of Harty's, provides a smooth transition to the dominant of E flat and a reprise of the opening material, though the latter part of the final verse, with its dramatic passages of declamation, is considerably modified. Nicholls often included *Bonfires* in her programmes, and it may have been the theatrical rhetoric of the vocal part and the quasi-orchestral role of the piano that persuaded Harty to orchestrate it for her to sing at the Norwich Festival in October 1905.[60]

Two other songs, of a slighter but entertaining nature, also date from 1903. *Now is the Month of Maying*, made famous by Thomas Morley's ballet of 1595 and a setting Harty knew well from his Dublin concerts with the Culwick Choral Society, was completed in March. Sung at a rapid tempo, with one of Harty's routinely demanding piano parts requiring considerable neatness and agility, the song has a quasi-bucolic air engendered by a prevailing drone. A further song dating from March 1903 was a setting of Keats's *The Devon Maid*, a humorous West Country patter song. The success of this kind of song depends much on the athleticism and characterisation of the singer, though Harty does much to encourage the coy disposition of the performer through an increasing elaboration of the accompaniment (not least the witty use of acciaccaturas) and a subtle but short-lived modulation to the submediant.

In addition to the songs, Harty added a number of short pieces for piano to his growing catalogue of miniatures, all composed in or around 1904, and all unpublished. The two pieces *Idyll* and *Arlequin et Columbine*, Op. 10, were composed at Southwick Street in January 1904. Adopting the manner of a 'song without words', the *Idyll* is nevertheless more redolent of Fauré's interpretation of Mendelssohn's invention, notably in its harmonic world and more complex polyphony. Completed a month later, *Arlequin et Columbine* is, not surprisingly, full of contrasting moods: Arlequin's eccentricities, some of them distinctly Irish, figure prominently in the outer frame (not unlike Rachmaninov's 'Polcinelle' from his *Morceaux de Fantasie*, Op. 3), but are temporarily pacified by the central, soave waltz of Colombine. A somewhat less interesting *Valse Caprice*, a concert piece, was dedicated to the Irish pianist and composer Archy Rosenthal, its more athletic Chopinesque piano writing reflecting Rosenthal's pianistic abilities. This virtuoso trend is continued in the set of three *Irish Fancies*, but these are much more sophisticated compositions and give us but a glimpse of what Harty might have written had he focused on a career as a composer and solo pianist. Though one might easily perceive the three movements as a suite, 'At Sea', a brooding, agitated, expansive seascape in B minor, is much more suggestive of a first movement of a solo sonata in terms of length and sustained writing. The opening betrays the influence of Brahms in the harmonic style and rhetoric, but Harty's

---

[60] *MT* 46 (1905), 807. Harty also orchestrated *Sea Wrack* for the same occasion. Both scores are missing.

texture is lighter and clearer (perhaps closer to Stanford or Frank Bridge), and the extended lyrical second subject in G major has a richness of voice-leading that owes something to the luscious style of Rachmaninov (whose own music at this time was becoming increasingly popular). The central movement, 'The Stream in the Glen', is a substantial sonata design whose continuity is predicated on a constant flow of delicate uninterrupted quaver movement throughout the structure, but whose 6/4 metre is continually variegated, indeed disturbed, by the introduction of subtle hemiolas. The Irish context of the last piece, 'The Spanish Stranger', is unclear. The most bravura in style, this is effectively an extended dance movement. Its exotic ambience is accentuated by its unusual 5/8 metre, showing perhaps an awareness of the 'Zortico', a Basque dance, while the 'rubato' of Harty's contrasting material (in the luxuriant flat submediant) has the languid, metrical freedom intrinsic to so many of Albéniz's impressions of the Alhambra and southern Spain.

Harty's contact with Ireland during his early years in London was not only instigated by his visits home to Hillsborough and his need to consult Esposito. We also know that he took part in concerts in Belfast and Dublin and that he was appointed official accompanist for the Feis Ceoil. The Feis's competition of new works also continued to attract him. In 1901 his two *Fantasiestücke* for piano trio were awarded a prize,[61] and, the following year his String Quartet in A minor, Op. 5, was successfully premiered.[62] The quartet was first heard at the Feis on 8 May 1902; Harty was in the audience to hear it played by his RIAM friends Darley, Griffith, Grisard and Bast. Its second and last hearing was given by four prominent London musicians, Alfred Gibson, Juliet Capron, Alfred Hobday and Helen Trust, on 22 December 1902 at a house concert at Copped Hall, Totteridge, the home of Sir Harold Edwin Boulton, an amateur poet and music-lover. Revealing a marked advance on the first quartet, this work, featuring a prominent 'autobiographical' viola part, was more fluent. The first movement in particular evinced a greater sense of technical mastery of the quartet idiom, though this is a feature common to all four movements. The lilting 'hop jig' Scherzo in 9/8 (Example 3) is fertile in its dexterous manipulation of hemiola, acting as a more vivid contrast with its trio in 2/4, while the slow movement, if a little underdeveloped, nevertheless imparts a more convincing sense of balance than its earlier counterpart, as well as a more personal and intensely lyrical emotionalism. The imaginative Finale, full of *joie de vivre*, exhibits perhaps the most intricate writing in the whole work, and the more embellished use of the slow movement's second subject as secondary material is an effective cyclic touch. The appearance of this material in the unexpected and unconventional area of the subdominant reflects Esposito's influence, but the most unusual introduction of new material (a chorale-like theme in F sharp minor) in the development and the much-truncated recapitulation reveal the entirely maverick streak of Harty's personality that had been anticipated in the corresponding movement of the first quartet.

[61] See *IT*, 9 May 1901.

[62] In addition to his Quartet in A minor, Harty also orchestrated a song by the Irish composer Alice A. Needham; it, too, was performed by the DOS.

Example 3   String Quartet in A minor, Op. 5, opening of Scherzo

Besides encountering John McCormack at the 1903 Feis, Harty was awarded a prize for his *Romance and Scherzo* for cello and piano. Engaged to perform the work at the Feis was the cellist Clyde Twelvetrees, whom Harty accompanied at the first evening concert on 18 May. At the same concert Harty also played for Gordon Cleather, a singing teacher at the RIAM, who gave an early performance of *Rose Madness*. Cleather, who had already appeared with Harty in a Dublin concert at the Antient Concert Rooms in 1902, would remain a close friend; admiration for Twelvetrees was later demonstrated by Harty's inviting him to join the Hallé Orchestra as principal cellist in 1922.

In 1902 the Feis Ceoil decided to award a prize for a symphony based on Irish folk melodies. The idea had apparently been inspired by the use of negro melodies in Dvořák's 'New World' Symphony (which had been performed in Dublin for the first time in 1901 by the Hallé Orchestra under Richter), though the more likely model was the 'Irish' Symphony of Stanford, who adjudicated the competition. The winning entry, announced in February 1902, was Esposito's 'Irish' Symphony or *Sinfonia irlandese*, Op. 50, which was first performed at the Feis on 7 May 1902 under Esposito's direction. An uneven piece lacking the subtlety and finesse of Stanford's symphony, it was described at the time, perhaps a little too eagerly, as 'a masterly work of very great power and beauty'.[63] However, the symphony was undoubtedly an important landmark in Irish composition and the Feis committee, who were delighted with the result, elected to advertise for a similar work in 1904. As Harry White has aptly posited, the Feis's espousal of this cultural policy, and the public consensus that it generated, confirmed that 'the future of Irish art music was seen to lie in recourse to the ethnic past.'[64]

Harty was almost certainly in the audience for the first hearing of Esposito's symphony, so it seems evident that he did not know it solely from his DOS audition (described above). For the 1904 competition, Alberto Randegger was the adjudicator and his choice was Harty's own 'Irish' Symphony, Op. 7. The premiere of the 'Irish' Symphony on 18 May was important for several reasons. The enthusiastic ovation his new work received from the audience was marked by applause after each movement; few Irish works had ever been accorded such an honour. More importantly, however, was Harty's own role in the performance as conductor. It was his first time on the rostrum and the realisation of an aspiration he had held since coming to London in 1901. As Agnes Nicholls remembered: 'he was a most brilliant accompanist, but his real love was conducting an orchestra. From the time I first knew him, he was constantly saying that that was his aim. Gradually, it came to him, little by little.'[65] This ambition was corroborated by the future adventurer and archaeologist Frederick Albert Mitchell-Hedges, with whom Harty shared a brief friendship. At that time Mitchell-Hedges was working as a clerk in the London stock exchange and, depressed by the experience, he would spend evenings in his local public house in Praed Street, Paddington:

> [The pub] was patronized by scores of high-spirited medical students from nearby St Mary's Hospital, and equally boisterous University men. One of my drinking companions was a full-faced, dreamy-eyed music student named Hamilton Harty. Over glasses of beer we would swap ambitions. Time and again Harty would say: 'One day I'm going to conduct my own orchestra, Mike. A fine orchestra. We'll make a grand noise, you'll see.' Then he would close his eyes, swing his arms and in a rich baritone boom out the theme of a sonata. 'A grand, proud noise, Mike. Music most beautiful and most mighty.'

[63] See Dibble *Michele Esposito*, 91–2.

[64] Harry White, *The Keeper's Recital* (Cork: Cork University Press, 1998), 114.

[65] BBC talk, 3 Oct. 1951.

He would bring his arms down in a sweeping crescendo and then: 'Whoops! Damn it, that's five glasses smashed this week. Let me buy you another, old man.' The pub's patron thought him an amiable eccentric.[66]

Such was the approbation Harty received with his 'Irish' Symphony that he was invited by Esposito and the DOS to make a return visit to conduct his work on 18 April 1905. On this occasion he not only directed the Symphony, whose individual movements were severally applauded, but also Beethoven's 'Emperor' Concerto with Esposito as soloist, and Weber's scena *Ocean, thou Mighty Monster* with Agnes Nicholls.[67] Even though he was critical of the DOS's lack of polish, Harty found the experience overwhelming: 'The first time I ever faced an orchestra was when I conducted my symphony, a strange and rather bewildering experience, for an orchestra sounds very different when one is close to it – practically part of it – to what it sounds like to the audience.[68] In keeping within the rubric of the Feis competition, Harty acknowledged the use of Irish folk tunes in each movement of the symphony, though also pointing out that additional, original material was also written in the same idiom.[69] This was perspicaciously noted by one critic at its first London performance in 1905, who drew attention to the interesting chemistry of material 'based on fine old Irish folk tunes, combined with original melodies of like character, tersely and rationally developed and admirably scored'. It was, the critic continued, a work 'replete with life and beauty.'[70] In many respects it was this personal infusion of genuine and synthetic folk melody, combined with a virtuoso handling of orchestral forces, that gave Harty's symphonic canvas such distinctiveness, coherence and panache. Although Irish tunes form an intrinsic part of the symphony's fabric, their role and quotation is not allowed to predominate, and Harty creates a fine but convincing balance of diatonic and modal in his use of melody and his broadly eclectic, European palette of harmony. Furthermore, Harty's assimilation of folk music – Irish and, as he himself admitted, Scottish (filtered, one presumes, through his Ulster upbringing) – appears to have been a particularly sensitive and personal process, for there is abundant evidence of those prolix embellishments in the ornamented rhythmical lines of his melodic writing. Some of his intricate and conspicuous woodwind scoring, almost wind-band-like, is also highly individual, while characteristic, 'heavy' octave doublings seem to be evocative of folk-instrument timbres, notably the *uilleann* pipes – the national bagpipe of Ireland, known for its sweet tone and wide range.[71]

Unfortunately the original score of 1904 has not survived, so we cannot know the extent of Harty's later revisions, but we do have the revised score of 1915; and

[66] F. A. Mitchell-Hedges, *Danger My Ally* (London: Elek Books, 1954), 48–9.

[67] *MT* 46 (1905), 405. Nicholls also appeared as soloist in the 'Liebestod' from *Tristan* under Esposito's baton.

[68] Harty, 'Autobiography'.

[69] See title page of autograph, *GB-Belqb* MS 14:12a.

[70] *MT* 16 (1905), 742.

[71] These octave doublings are particularly prevalent in the 1924 revision.

in 1924 he made further revisions, and added titles to the individual movements.[72] Though the essence of the Symphony was perhaps already self-evident from the choice of folk songs, the final version ultimately divulged the autobiographical significance of the piece as a musical impression of Hillsborough, the lake, the wonderful trees and the rich, undulating country of Co. Down and Ulster. This programme was added at the head of the score in 1927 when it was printed by Novello:

> This work is an attempt to produce a Symphony in the Irish idiom, and it has for poetical basis scenes and moods immediately connected with the North of Ireland countryside to which the composer belongs. The themes have therefore been given a characteristically Irish turn; often they are based on traditional melodies. Though the composer does not desire that his music shall be looked on as entirely 'programme music', each movement has for general poetic basis some particular scene or mood, and it is hoped that when the work is performed, the programme will contain these brief explanatory notes.[73]

Harty's comments are helpful in reminding us that, for the most part, his concept of the 'programme' is of broad visual evocations, more akin to the tableaux of Beethoven's 'Pastoral' Symphony, rather than any detailed narrative of unfolding events. The first movement, which he later called 'On the shores of Lough Neagh', is a precise articulation of this approach: 'The music seeks to recapture the atmosphere of youthful days spent near Lough Neagh, and the old legends and songs associated with them in the mind of the composer.' In conversation with the American authoress Leonora Wood Armsby, Harty elaborated on the biographical nature of the work:

> My sister and I used to attend the county fairs in Ireland and it was there that I picked up the tunes that you hear in my *Irish Symphony*. … On Fair days the town was filled with people dancing to joy tunes and penny whistles. With my tongue fastened about a bit of sticky, yellow jacket that was warranted to 'draw the teeth of ye' I followed the fakirs and the jugglers, or I hung about Fat Charlie with his cart of herrings. Somehow I managed to get into all the little side shows. It was the greatest fun. The songs I heard kept running about in my mind; I whistled them; I sang them; finally I put them on paper. All my boyhood is in the *Irish Symphony*.[74]

Keeping within the traditional confines of the nineteenth-century tradition, Harty used the familiar frame of the sonata for his first movement, enunciating the first subject in D minor with 'Avenging and Bright' (from the air *Crooghan a venee*), a tune made famous with Thomas Moore's words, and the second subject, in the relative, with 'The Croppy Boy'. This wistful air, introduced by the wind, is full of those typical Irish melodic attributes: elaborate ornamentation, a rising

[72] Autographs of both the 1915 and 1924 versions survive in the Harty archive at *GB-Belqb* (MS 14:12a and 12b). For fuller details of the revisions between the 1915 and 1924 versions, see Chapter 5.

[73] See David Greer, 'Hamilton Harty Manuscripts', *Music Review* 47(4) (1986/7), 238–52, at 242.

[74] Armsby, 'The Irish Composer-Conductor', 144.

Example 4 'Irish' Symphony in D minor, first movement, climax of second subject

sixth, and repeated notes at the cadence. As a bridge between these two generous thematic strands, which Harty genuinely develops with imaginative dexterity and colourful instrumentation, is an idea which, though it is suggestive of 'Go, My Own Darling Boy' (from John Henderson's *The Flowers of Irish Melody* of 1847), is in fact synthetic. Indeed, Harty took pains to clarify this aspect in the introduction to the 1915 revision: 'Several Irish folk-tunes are made use of in this Symphony, and in general the themes – where original – are purposely written in the same idiom. The composer asks conductors to permit themselves considerable freedom in varying the tempi – so as to preserve the characteristic unfettered spirit of most native Irish music.' This dimension of Harty's work is actually more prevalent than is the presence of the folksongs, a factor manifestly evident in the opulent extension of the second subject. Here Harty's admiration for Wagner is palpable in the accompanying voice-leading, the sequential, wave-like rise of the melody and the Tristanesque appoggiatura on the subdominant for the climax (Example 4).

The clearly defined exposition is in marked contrast to the elision of the development and recapitulation. Interestingly, Harty initiates the development in D minor with his first subject, but this reference to the tonic is fleeting as wider tonal exploration plays its part in a developmental phase more reminiscent of a rhapsody than a symphony. This rhapsodic element is nowhere more overt than at the point where the first subject is restated, at a more restrained tempo, imaginatively reharmonised, and in the 'wrong' key of A minor. This paragraph, replete at its conclusion with an quasi-improvisatory arabesque for solo clarinet, yields to an introverted reprise in D major of 'The Croppy Boy', nostalgically 'sung' by a solo violin which at the same time substantially underplays the return of the tonic. Only with the return of the Wagnerian climax and the closing phase of the movement, where the first subject is reintroduced in D minor, is the vivacious spirit of the exposition restored.

The Scherzo, entitled 'The Fair Day' was conceived by Harty as a memory of a local carnival: 'Horses and cattle – noise and dust – swearing, bargaining men. A recruiting sergeant with his gay ribbons, and the primitive village band. In the market place, old women selling ginger bread and "yellow-boy" and sweet fizzy drinks. A battered merry-go-round.' Humorous orchestral gestures, 'tuning up' on the open strings, xylophone glissandos and wind acciaccaturas, contribute to this short, light-hearted interlude of barely three minutes' music, where Harty juxtaposes the reel 'Blackberry Blossom' and the popular song 'The Girl I Left Behind Me' (also known as 'An Spailpín Fánach' or 'The Wandering Labourer' or, in England, as 'Brighton Camp'), the latter of which is presented in parallel fifths, an imitation, Harty explained, of Ulster flute bands he had heard where instruments of different pitches all played the melody together regardless of the discrepancy.[75]

For his slow movement, 'In the Antrim Hills', Harty chose as the principal idea 'Jimín Mo Mhíle Stór' to depict the 'scene in a lonely farmhouse where a wake was being held' (Example 5). Harty also quoted the words to accentuate the mood of lament:

> You maidens now pity this sorrowful moan I make;
> I am a young maiden in grief for my darling sake;
> My true lover's absence in sorrow I grieve full sore,
> And each day I lament for my Jimmy mó mhíle stór.

Like 'The Croppy Boy' of the first movement, 'Jimín Mo Mhíle Stór' bears all the typical hallmarks of the quintessential Irish melody, though, here, in addition, it also exhibits a 'double tonic' (commencing in D minor but concluding in F major), a dualistic property which Harty deftly exploits throughout the movement's simple ABAB design. The opening, for example, unequivocally states the dominant of D, and each reiteration of the melody contrives a cadence into D; but with each conclusion F major is presented as a contradiction, a key which is further accentuated by a secondary, synthetic idea (though note how D is used as an appoggiatura at the very beginning of the melody). Yet the very assertion of D is enough to create a sense of tonal dialectic. Harty's *coup de maître* occurs with the return of the secondary material in D flat – a brief but rapt moment for *con sordini* strings – before F is restored and the movement is brought to a sonorous conclusion in that key.

The lively sonata-rondo Finale, entitled 'The Twelfth of July', is heavily based, not surprisingly, on the marching fife tune 'The Boyne Water', strongly associated with the Orangemen processions which commemorate the victory of

[75] In a later programme note Harty also related this material to the recruiting sergeant in his dashing uniform, marching his recruits off to Belfast barracks to the sound of a band playing in a range of keys: ABC programme, 13 June 1934.

Example 5 'Irish' Symphony in D minor, 'Jimín Mo Mhile Stór',
opening of slow movement

William of Orange over the forces of King James II at the Battle of the Boyne in 1792. As Harty explained:

> The 12th of July is the great Protestant festival of the North of Ireland, and on this day the countryside is full of the noise of drum and fife bands playing such tunes as 'The Boyne Water', of which considerable use is made in the movement. The general gaiety and excitement of the music is interrupted by reminiscences of the lament heard in the preceding movement. The composer wishes to illustrate the impression left on his mind by once seeing a funeral procession making its slow way through the crowded streets on a certain '12th of July' in a North of Ireland village.[76]

[76] Armsby, 'The Irish Composer-Conductor', 144.

Harty once again exploits the inherent idiosyncrasy of the tune. With its strong Dorian inflection it suggests E minor at the close of its binary structure, yet all the time Harty undermines this modal centre with a final cadence in D major. An original idea in the subdominant, which bears some initial similarity to the Scots tune 'Bonie Kirsty', provides apt contrast as a second subject. Harty's rondo-sonata structure is clearly perceptible, but there are unusual departures. The second subject is restated, unusually, in the dominant before the return of the rondo theme in the tonic, while the lament from the third movement, 'Jimín Mo Mhile Stór', which forms the centrepiece of the development in B flat minor, provides the dramatic foil to the marching tune. As for the coda, Harty clearly had problems with this part of the movement, since he made substantial changes between the 1915 and 1925 versions. Perhaps this was instigated by the powerful impression of the funeral cortège (was the village Hillsborough?) to which the composer mysteriously referred in his programmatic foreword.[77]

The two Dublin performances of the Irish Symphony marked an auspicious beginning to Harty's conducting career and, perhaps associated with these first successes, the work always occupied a place of affection with the composer. It was also popular with others, such as Henry Wood, who programmed the London premiere in a Promenade Concert of 14 October 1905; Howard Halford, director of the Halford Society concerts in Birmingham, conducted the work on 30 January 1906 which 'created a great impression',[78] and it formed part of a programme of the Liverpool Philharmonic under Cowen's baton on 15 December 1906. In Dublin, where memories of the symphony were still potent, Barton McGuckin gave a further performance with the New Philharmonic Orchestra on 13 July 1907.[79]

From 1904 Harty's career as an accompanist begins to read like a catalogue of many of the finest British and Continental artists of the day. His engagements came thick and fast. He was a regular artist at all the London concert halls, and engagements from wealthy London patrons continued, some of which, in aid of public charities, reached the press. One such concert was for the Duke and Duchess of Connaught, at Lady Dickson Poynder's Mayfair residence at 8 Chesterfields Gardens to raise funds for the Great Northern Central Hospital; Harty appeared with Gervase Elwes, David Bispham and Maria Gay.[80] Another was for the Duke of Westminster at his vast Park Lane residence, Grovesnor House, for the mission to seamen;[81] but by far the most lucrative was an event arranged by Chappell on behalf of Prince and Princess Dolgorouki, Russian aristocrats close to the Tsar, who were known to entertain lavishly at their Mayfair home at 45 Upper Grosvenor Street. On this occasion Harty accompanied the

[77] For further details about the codas of the 1915 and 1924 versions, see Chapter 5.

[78] MT 47 (1906), 192.

[79] IT, 15 July 1907.

[80] The Times, 29 June 1904. Lady Dickson-Poynder was a popular society figure in aristocratic circles and became even better known after J. J. Shannon's portrait of her and her daughter was exhibited at the Royal Academy in 1905: A. L. Baldry, The Studio 35 (June 1905), 46.

[81] The Times, 20 May 1908.

soprano Mrs Emslie-Cran.[82] Such concerts, at 21 s a ticket, were only available
to the well-heeled. These 'smart' events were well paid, but irregular. More staple
fair for Harty was the Chappell Ballad Concerts at Queen's Hall. At affordable
prices, these concerts, held on Saturday afternoons, were hugely popular with
the general public. Here he came into contact with many well-established singers
such as Plunket Greene, Charles Santley, David Ffrangcon Davies, Ben Davies,
Gregory Hast, John Coates, Marie Brema, Albert Garcia, Clara Butt (and her
husband Kennerley Rumford) and Esther Palliser, noted for her performances
of Gilbert and Sullivan operettas. Taking part in these Ballad Concerts, which
Harty did until at least 1909, and in numerous concerts in the provinces, also
meant that, besides accompanying, he would often appear alongside other
artists, such as the pianists Percy Grainger, Wilhelm Backhaus, Alexander Siloti,
Ella Správka, York Bowen, Elsie Horne, Johanne Stockmarr, and Fanny Davies,
and the three young pianists Frank Merrick, Irene Scharrer and Myra Hess. The
guest pianists would appear as soloists, but the guest violinists used Harty as
their accompanist; they were invariably major virtuosi such as Kreisler, Mischa
Elman (who was a regular guest artist), the RCM professor Achille Rivarde,
Jacques Thibaud, Emile Sauret and Harold Ketèlbey (brother of the composer
Albert Ketèlbey). Perhaps the grandest of all these 'celebrity' concerts was one
organised for the League of Mercy at the Albert Hall on 30 May 1908, which was
attended by the King and Queen. On this occasion Harty appeared alongside a
majestic list of singers that included Melba, Caruso, Tosti, Santley, McCormack,
Baraldi, Davies and Scoti.[83]

As their title suggests, the Ballad Concerts were largely popular in content
and their programmes consisted essentially of items from Chappell's own
catalogue. The instrumental repertoire was well known and what 'serious' music
was included was usually interspersed with lighter 'lollipops' and 'encores';
many of the songs were written for the the individual soloists, thus guaranteeing
them a royalty. Of greater interest musically were the concerts at the Aeolian,
Bechstein and Steinway Halls. Besides appearing with well-known artists and
sharing the stage with significant ensembles such as the Nora Clench Quartet,
the Walenn Quartet and the Quatuor Capet, Harty was often there to support
newer names, some of whom were appearing in London for the first time.
His role in these concerts might be to accompany the principal performer;
alternatively, he could support artists who provided interludes for the main
soloist. In this way he accompanied singers such as Gervase Elwes, Frederic
Austin,[84] Robert Radford,[85] Kirkby Lunn, Muriel Foster, Thomas Thorpe Bates
(who appeared in early recordings of Gilbert and Sullivan), Gladys Honey,
Paul Reimers, the Polish-born Theo Lierhammer (recently appointed to the

---

[82] *The Times*, 23 Nov. 1907.

[83] See advert in *The Times*, 23 May 1908.

[84] *The Times*, 5 Apr. 1906.

[85] *The Times*, 8 Apr. 1908. This was a grand Good Friday concert at QH in which
   Harty and Radford appeared alongside Agnes Nicholls, Ben Davies and others.

RAM),[86] Marie Wadia, Pedro de Zuluetta, Rhoda von Glehn, the American sopranos Alice Esty and Arvilla Clarke, and the remarkable Mrs George Swinton.[87] There were also appearances with Agnes Nicholls, whom he would invariably accompany from memory. Described in *The Times* as 'a triumph of mind, of beauty of tone as well as of song', Harty and Nicholls evinced a 'bond of sympathy' in their recital of twenty-five songs at the Bechstein Hall on 5 April 1905.[88]

Harty's interaction with the extraordinary number of talented violinists in London also bears witness to the meteoric rise of his career within a few years of settling there.[89] Of the great Continental virtuosi, Kreisler and Elman have already been mentioned, but there were many others with whom he collaborated, such as Marie du Chastain, Irene Penso, Monique Poole, Arturo Tibaldi, the RAM professor Rowsby Woof, the Hungarian Tivadar Nachez, and the cellist Darbishire Jones. One of the most gifted violinists was the young Marie Hall, fresh from her studies in Prague under Otakar Ševčik. She and Harty had first appeared together at St James's Hall on 29 April 1903. Harty did not immediately become her regular accompanist, but by the end of 1904 he and Hall, under the aegis of the agent Sidney Harrison, toured many of Britain's major cities (with Ada Crossley, Egon Petri and Frederic Austin).[90] During the first three months of 1905 they gave three recitals at Queen's Hall in London, before making a lucrative tour of the USA and Canada between October 1905 and January 1906.[91] In front of a large audience at Queen's Hall on 7 April 1906, Hall and Harty received an ovation, Harty once again playing without music throughout the concert – probably, as the critic of the *Musical Times* remarked, 'an unprecedented feat'.[92] In playing for the fifteen-year-old prodigy Vivien Chartres at Queen's Hall

---

[86] Harty appeared with Lierhammer on several occasions. Lierhammer was a noted specialist of German lieder, and toured England with Richard Strauss (of whose songs he was a noted interpreter): see William Armstrong, 'Dr Theodor Lierhammer on the German Lied', *The Etude* 22(6) (June 1904).

[87] Swinton's first appearance as a professional was at a Broadwood concert at the Aeolian Hall on 5 April 1906. Her first solo recital, however, was not until 22 May 1906 when she appeared again at the Aeolian Hall with Harty. Percy Grainger provided solo interludes. She also sang 'Gorse' from Harty's *Three Flower Songs* at a recital at the Aeolian Hall on 6 June 1907: see *The Times*, 7 June 1907.

[88] *The Times*, 7 Apr. 1905.

[89] It was an accepted feature of recitals for violinists to select their programmes from both the concerto and chamber repertoire. There is much evidence to show that, besides the extensive repertoire of sonatas and short pieces for the violin, Harty was expected to play reduced orchestral parts of the standard concertos.

[90] For the 'Harrison' tour, see Gloucestershire Archives D11462/1/1/3.

[91] For the American tour, see See Gloucestershire Archives D11462/1/1/2.

[92] *MT* 47 (1906), 335. Harty regularly performed with Hall in London and the provinces, and also formed part of a piano trio with the cellist Ivor James, as in a performance of Parry's Piano Trio in B minor on 15 January 1908: *MT* 49 (1908), 113.

on 27 March 1906,[93] his 'restraint in preserving balance of tone' was noted.[94] Chartres's career did not flower, unlike that of the brilliant May Harrison, whom Harty accompanied on three successive occasions at the Bechstein Hall, giving the first performances in London of Debussy's *En bateau*[95] and Esposito's Violin Sonata No. 2 in E minor,[96] as well as Fauré's Sonata No. 1 in A (little known to London audiences) and shorter works by Frank Bridge and E. F. Arbós.[97]

Besides the 'hot house' of London concert life, Harty spent much of his time travelling around Britain, performing for concert societies in the larger conurbations such as Birmingham, Manchester, Bristol, Leeds, Liverpool, Hull, Wakefield, Newcastle and Glasgow, and sometimes he received invitations to perform during the major competitive festivals such as Morecambe in May 1908.[98] In these he appeared regularly with Nicholls or Plunket Greene, who were both well known for their imaginative programming. Indeed, one of the most rewarding aspects of Harty's work at this time was the opportunity to perform not only the regular canonic repertoire of vocal and chamber music, but also a good deal of music at the contemporary 'cutting edge'. Besides the lieder of Schubert and Schumann, he accompanied a great deal of Brahms's considerable output of songs (a corpus of work, incidentally, that was still little known to British audiences) as well as those of Richard Strauss, Hugo Wolf, Weingartner, and Max Reger, the songs of Sibelius, and Dvořák's *Biblical Songs*.[99] Of French song he performed the *mélodies* of Berlioz, Duparc, Debussy and Fauré. He became increasingly familiar with the Russian repertoire of songs, especially through his work with Elsie Swinton, who, with her broad command of European languages and her Russian background, impressed her audiences with her Russian-language performances of Arensky, Lyapunov, Grechaninov, Mussorgsky and Rachmaninov.[100]

Harty was truly immersed in the font of English song, too. Besides the satisfaction of having many of his own songs performed, by Nicholls,

---

[93] During the first years of the twentieth century there were great hopes that Chartres would become a major Continental virtuoso, and she was mentioned in the same breath as Elman and Huberman. An impression of her life, part fiction, part fact, was captured in *The Devourers*, a novel by her mother Annie Vivanti Chartres, which was published in 1910.

[94] *MT* 47 (1906), 334.

[95] Bechstein Hall, 23 Mar. 1908, *GB-Lam*, McCann Collection.

[96] Bechstein Hall, 30 Mar. 1908, *GB-Lam*, McCann Collection. After the London premiere of Esposito's Violin Sonata No. 2, Harrison also performed Esposito's two *Irish Rhapsodies* with Harty at the Bechstein Hall on 1 May 1908.

[97] Bechstein Hall, 6 Apr. 1908, *GB-Lam*, McCann Collection.

[98] *MT* 49 (1908), 399.

[99] Nicholls was a keen advocate of songs by Strauss and Wolf. Harty also accompanied Ernest Sharpe in his pioneering series of 'Composer Recitals', two concerts of which, on 25 October and 2 November 1906, consisted entirely of lieder by Hugo Wolf and Max Reger, respectively: see *The Times*, 3 Nov. 1906).

[100] See David Greer, *A Numerous and Fashionable Audience: The Story of Elsie Swinton* (London: Thames Publishing, 1997), 82–3, 105.

Swinton, Plunket Greene and others, he was also an important conduit in the communication of new repertoire by Holst and Vaughan Williams. An auspicious concert given at the Bechstein Hall on 2 December 1905, organised by Vaughan Williams, featured two of his songs cycles, *The House of Life* and *Songs of Travel*, sung for the first time in their entirety, as well songs by Holst.[101] There were also songs by Graham Peel, Charles Wood,[102] Quilter, Elgar, Delius, Cyril Scott (then considered something of an *enfant terrible*), the young Oxford composer and critic Ernest Walker, and a miniature cycle by William Yeates Hurlstone, soon to die in May 1906. Performing regularly with Plunket Greene also inevitably meant that the music of Parry,[103] Plunket Greene's father-in-law, and Stanford,[104] his countryman, would feature prominently, along with Somervell's cycles *Maud* and *A Shropshire Lad*. Parry paid special tribute to Agnes Nicholls (or, as the dedication reads, 'Agnes Hamilton Harty'), whom he had known as an RCM student, by dedicating his tenth set of *English Lyrics* to her. Several of these songs, sung from manuscript, were performed by her and Harty at the Bechstein Hall on 16 November 1909.[105] Through Nicholls, Harty came to know Parry well and he always retained an admiration for Parry's leadership and mission; yet, at the same time, he believed that his worldliness prejudiced his power as a composer:

> I have a personal theory – probably all wrong – that Parry was too broad and great a man to be a really first-rate musician. After all, to be a universally interested man, as he was, is better than to be a more or less narrow musician, and I can't think of any great composer whose absorption in his art did not make him a little deaf and blind to the rest of the world and its problems.[106]

---

[101] *The Times*, 5 Dec. 1904. Harty had already accompanied a number of the *Songs of Travel* with Plunket Greene at the Aeolian Hall on 3 February 1905.

[102] Charles Wood, not known for his prowess as a songwriter, nevertheless produced two remarkable settings of Whitman – *By the Bivouac's Fitful Flame* and *Ethiopa Saluting the Colours* – which Plunket Greene and Harty performed several times.

[103] Plunket Greene had his particular favourite Parry songs, which Harty accompanied on many occasions, namely 'Through the Ivory Gate' (*English Lyrics*, Set III), 'Why So Pale and Wan?' (*English Lyrics*, Set III), 'When Comes my Gwen' (*English Lyrics*, Set VI), 'Love is a Bable' (*English Lyrics*, Set VI), 'Ye Little Birds that Sit and Sing' (*English Lyrics*, Set VII), 'Follow a Shadow' (*English Lyrics*, Set VII), 'Sleep' (*English Lyrics*, Set VII), 'Dirge in Woods' (*English Lyrics*, Set VIII), and *The Laird of Cockpen*.

[104] Plunket Greene particularly favoured Stanford's *An Irish Idyll*, Op. 77, and his three 'Whitman' songs, Op. 97, which he and Harty often included in their programmes (notably 'Johneen' and 'A Fairy Lough'): see *The Times*, 13 Mar. 1908.

[105] Nicholls sang 'The Child and the Twilight', 'One Silent Night of Late', and 'From a City Window', all from *English Lyrics*, Set XI, which was not published by Novello until 1918. The set also included the popular, passionate setting of Christina Rossetti's *My Heart is Like a Singing Bird*, which would have been well adapted to Nicholl's operatic voice and Harty's pianist prowess.

[106] Charles Larcom Graves, *Hubert Parry*, 2 vols. (London: Macmillan, 1926), II.158.

Stanford, by contrast, deeply impressed the young Harty as a template for Irish art music and there is no doubt that he learned much from the older man's folk-song arrangements as well as from the craftsmanship and fluency of his songs and instrumental works.

With the success of his 'Irish' Symphony, Harty embarked on the composition of another large-scale chamber work, a Piano Quintet, which he entered for a prize advertised by the immensely wealthy Ada Lewis-Hill, a well-known patron of the arts. Mrs Lewis-Hill was renowned for her love music. She endowed numerous instrumental prizes at the RAM, and owned several valuable pianos and stringed instruments, among them several by Stradivarius. As Arthur Benjamin recollected, she 'was a London woman of fashion and wealth … who was the queen of a kind of court, with musicians attached. Zillah was one of her maids-of-honour, others being the Hungarian violinist Tivadar Nachez and W. H. Squire, the violoncellist.'[107] In fact Nachez and Squire formed part of a regular quintet ensemble which included the violist Alfred Hobday and the pianist Benno Schönberger. They would often provide music for the benevolent patroness at her evening soirées.[108] The prize for a piano quintet, which offered the princely sum of fifty guineas to its winner, essentially paid tribute to the loyal players of the quintet which had for many years entertained Mrs Lewis-Hill. From a pool of almost forty compositions – Schönberger, Mackenzie and Cowen were the adjudicators – Harty was announced the winner in January 1905.[109] The Quintet was given its first public performance soon afterwards for the 'Concert Club' at the Bechstein Hall on 29 January 1905 with Enrique Fernández Arbós (the Club's musical director), T. F. Morris, Alfred Hobday, Purcell Jones, and Harty at the piano, though the surviving programme indicates that only the first and second movements were actually given.[110] Possibly because the composer chose to revise it, the work was not performed again until 7 December 1906, when it formed part of a concert of British music given by the Concert-Goers' Club at the Langham Hotel. This, it seems, was probably its only complete hearing in public.

Harty's Quintet is a bold, big-boned, passionate work of symphonic proportions and stands happily beside those large-scale Romantic utterances of Schumann, Brahms, Dvořák, César Franck, Fauré and Stanford in the same genre.

[107] A. Benjamin, 'A Student in Kensington', *Music & Letters* 31(3) (1950), 196–207, at 197.

[108] On her death, Mrs Lewis-Hill bequeathed considerable sums of money 'to my beloved quintette of artists, in recognition of many happy evenings of music'. To Schönberger she gave £1,000 and a life annuity of £300; to Nachez £2,000 and a second Stradivarius violin (the first having been bequeathed to the RAM); to Squire £1,000 and a valuable cello; and to Hobday £500 and a valuable viola. To Mackenzie, Principal of the RAM and a close associate, she bequeathed £2,000: see *MT* 47 (1906), 811.

[109] *MT* 46 (1905), 23.

[110] See concert programme, *GB-Lcm*. The programme also noted that, although this was its first public performance, it had already been played at the home of Mrs Ada Lewis-Hill.

This is music on a grand scale, full of melodic fertility where the idiom of piano and string quartet, susceptible to hybrid treatment, is dexterously manipulated polyphonically and antiphonally. With his established reputation as a pianist, Harty gave full prominence to the piano – at times it competes with the strings like a concerto soloist. At other times it emerges and withdraws from the texture, sharing thematic material, while at moments of great poignancy it accompanies the contrapuntal fabric of the strings, providing a background for rhapsodic solo passages. Harty's concept of the first movement is largely orchestral. A rhythmically dynamic idea, presented in unison by the strings, gives way to a spacious composite theme shared among the instruments and surrounded by elaborate filigree. In a manner akin to Schubert, this extended paragraph closes in F and yields to an equally generous second subject, a pentatonic, folk-inspired melody in the subdominant, by now a common choice in the tonal organisation of Harty's sonata schemes. This extended section also closes unequivocally in B flat, but not before Harty has subjected the self-developing theme to a colourful, not to say dramatic, series of modulations which passes through the Neapolitan, B major and its dominant F sharp. A radical change of gear back to the dominant of B flat, all the while elongating the enormous arch of melody, signals the concluding phase of the second subject. Harty's capacious material also seems to exude the rhetoric of a grand concerto, not least in the way a piano cadenza punctuates the cadence. The nature of the development, though to an extent discursive, is more suggestive of the rhetorical poetry of the symphonic poem in its trading of lyrical material and scherzo. The recovery from D flat major, established at the development's climax, is impressively executed, and the restatement of the second subject, appropriately in D flat, is imaginatively handled as Harty uses the return to F, in turbulent mood, as a fresh means of thematic reworking. The restoration of the tonic is marked by triumphal piano fanfares, displaced from their normal position in the recapitulation, but this strident manner is subdued by the tranquil interjections of the string quartet which sets the tone for the reflective coda (in which the viola plays a conspicuous role on its lowest, most sonorous string).[111]

For the principal theme of his Scherzo (assigned yet again to the viola), Harty resorted once again to a synthetic pentatonicism to create an 'Irish' theme, though this time the character of his material has a striking affinity with Grainger's arrangements of popular folk melodies (Example 6). This is not only felt in the panache of the instrumentation – which is remarkably rich and vibrant, not least in the use of pizzicato – but also in the use of the vigorous diatonic harmony, quirky modulations, and countermelodies for which Grainger was renowned (in works such as *Shepherd's Hey*, *Handel in the Strand* and the Irish reel *Molly on the Shore*). Harty's structure – a beautifully crafted sonata – is also highly adroit, much skill being invested in the entertaining dialogue between

---

[111] There is evidence from surviving undated sketches that Harty made an attempt to revise the first movement of the Piano Quintet extensively. One sketch, in full score, shows a revision of the opening eight bars; a second sketch reveals an extensive revision of the opening forty bars: see Greer, 'Hamilton Harty Manuscripts', 243, 251.

Example 6 Piano Quintet in F major, Op. 12, opening of Scherzo

piano and quartet in the development, and in the playful and unexpected tonal divergencies.

If an Irish flavour is evident in the Scherzo, then it is palpable in the expressive heart of the work, the slow movement in A minor. Though no genuine Irish tune is quoted, Harty's material throughout the movement is infused with an persistent flattened seventh (of the relative, C) which pervades both the embellished arcs of the melody and the harmony. There had already been verification of elaborate melodic decoration in the 'Irish' Symphony (especially at the more extemporary points of transition between thematic subjects), but here it is even more abundantly apparent in the use of mordents, rapid scales and modal inflection. Moreover, in this context, Harty makes fertile use of the 'double tonic' phenomenon as the lengthy thematic material switches tantalisingly back and forth between A minor and C major. Concluding in C major, the first subject utilises the flattened seventh enharmonically (as A sharp) enabling, through an augmented sixth, a deft modulation to E major for the second subject. The second subject, even more so than the first, is extensively self-developing, more in the manner of Tchaikovsky's sweeping thematic paragraphs. Introduced by the viola, it is initially presented against an embroidery of countermelody at which Harty excelled, but at its grand, extrovert reprise it is even more reminiscent of the Russian, particularly in the use of the heroic 6/4, the scoring for strings in multiple octaves, and the intensity of the triplet accompaniment.

That Harty had committed himself stylistically to a Continental voice is clearly demonstrated in the 'Irish' Symphony. Though we do not know what scores his father possessed, there must have been sufficient for him to assimilate an impressive orchestral technique, one that must have been enhanced during the years of his self-communion in Dublin and early years in London. The opulence of Wagner has already been mentioned, but the 'Irish' Symphony also revealed a richness of instrumentation and a harmonic affinity that Harty must have acquired from his familiarity with Tchaikovsky's scores, which at the turn of the century were enjoying an enormous vogue, not least at the hands of conductors like Henry Wood. The romantic gestures of Harty's Symphony and, especially, the slow movement of the Piano Quintet corroborate his passion for this repertoire, and in the last movement of the Quintet this Russian predilection is confirmed both in the lively second subject (which Harty must have unconsciously gleaned from Tchaikovsky's first Piano Concerto), and in the highly unconventional episode in B flat minor that forms the centrepiece of the development. Both ideas give the finale a most burlesque character which is even more accentuated in the impetuous coda. This propensity for the exotic, as well as for vibrant instrumental colour, would feature time and time again in Harty's later work, and would also affirm his fascination for other late nineteenth-century Russians such as Mussorgsky, Lyapunov, Balakirev and Rimsky-Korsakov. The overt Continental dimension of Harty's Quintet also points to another interesting future trend in his music: while the 'Irish' Symphony also betrayed many cosmopolitan influences, the work depended a good deal on the quotation of the traditional repertoire, an imperative imposed by the rubric of the Feis; the Quintet, on the other hand, shows the self-exiled composer emancipating himself from direct citation, and at the same time bringing himself closer to the fostering of a genuine national style, one he would pursue with vigour in his orchestral works.

Henry Wood's admiration of Harty's 'Irish' Symphony made him receptive to another of Harty's orchestral works, the *Comedy Overture*, Op. 15, composed during August of 1906. It was premiered by Wood at a Promenade Concert at Queen's Hall on 24 October 1907 and was one of several novelties to appear in the concerts that season, the others by Frank Bridge, Frederic Austin and Delius. The score was subsequently revised in December 1908 before its publication by Schott in 1909. At its first hearing the overture made quite an impression:

> It proved to be one of the most successful works which this season has brought
> forth. The frank jollity of its themes and the clearness of their expression, both

as regards orchestration and formal structure, make it a delightful 'Promenade' piece – that is to say, one which tired people can enjoy at a first hearing and find refreshment in listening to. Perhaps the repetition of the material before the coda is a little long, but a fault on the side of clearness is not one of which we often have to complain nowadays. The overture was played with evident enjoyment and great spirit by the orchestra under Mr Wood.[112]

Indeed, the overture remained in the repertoire for some years. Wood often conducted it at his Promenade concerts, Esposito conducted it in Dublin in March 1911, and between 1908 and 1911 it was heard numerous times in quick succession at the Sunday Concert Society recitals, the Crystal Palace, and at the Philharmonic Societies in London and Liverpool under the baton of Wood, Cowen and Harty himself. The popularity of the work was fully justified. Though a 'light' overture in essence, like those later works of Granville Bantock, Eric Coates, Montague Phillips and Haydn Woods, it nevertheless evinced the craftsmanship and legerdemain of a master. Harty's handling of the orchestra is outstanding, as is the deft juxtaposition of humour and genuine pathos (that one also finds in Bantock's brilliant *The Pierrot of the Minute* of 1908, also dubbed a 'Comedy Overture'). Harty's busy passagework at the opening may have been inspired by the impression (rather than the detail) of Smetana's overture to *The Bartered Bride*, and the spirit of the oboe's jaunty theme is the very quintessence of English comic operetta, with the sounds of Sullivan's Savoy works lurking wittily beneath the surface. This opening theme in E flat is full of *joie d'esprit*, enhanced by the brief modulatory interpolation to C, but Harty's almost natural instinct is to move flatwise, and for the second half of his first paragraph he shifts initially to A flat, a tonal move which is accompanied by further humorous thematic ideas. This, however, proves to be temporary, for Harty is in fact circuitously preparing the way for B flat, though not before we experience one of his characteristic harmonic 'arrests' on a flat submediant (commonly used in the 'Irish' Symphony and Piano Quintet) that tantalisingly delays final resolution.[113] Harty's second group continues the trend of carefully assimilating elements of Irish music. The embellished melody is pentatonic, the harmony modal, and the use of the flattened seventh builds on the slow movement of the Piano Quintet, while the outdoor 'wind band' sonority is a sound distinctive to the composer which he retains throughout the exposition of this thematic departure (Example 7). A secondary thematic excursion, falling somewhere between Parry and Elgar in its falling sequential patterns, is taken up appropriately by the strings. This yields eventually to further development of the 'wind band' theme, and Harty's impressive skill in handling modulation to remote keys (A and D major) makes the triumphant reprise of this material in B flat most imposing. To boot, the thematic modification of the climax is both skilful and deeply moving.

[112] *The Times*, 25 Oct. 1907.
[113] Harty's frequent use of this technique, particularly his handling of augmented sixths, was probably gleaned from his study of Tchaikovsky (and to some extent the early works of Sibelius such as *Finlandia*), whose manipulation of this harmony in various inversions and contexts is particularly fecund.

Example 7 *Comedy Overture*, second subject

Un poco più moderato, non troppo rigido in tempo

The lengthy nature of the thematically copious exposition wisely instigates a truncated development of fewer than seventy bars. For the recapitulation, auspiciously prepared by a pregnant dominant for full orchestra, and a pause, the piccolo ushers in the first idea in G before an 'impatient' full orchestra stridently restores E flat with a further statement of the material inventively announced by the timpani (and accompanied wryly by whole-tone pizzicato scales). This 'Lustspiel' continues with a new sense of elation, for Harty quickly moves on to his secondary material, returning to G major, and, after one of his deeply reflective lyrical transitions, enacted so affectionately by the solo clarinet and cello quartet, the 'wind band' melody is transformed by its warmhearted reappearance in the strings in the unexpected key of D. Harty's entire second group is couched in this key, which subsequently has the effect of throwing into marked relief the return to E flat and a resumption of displaced material from the first group. Altogether, the construction and concept of Harty's overture reveals a new, refined and more confident understanding of sonata thinking, but its abundant thematic invention, stylistic cohesion and polished technique also signal a more sophisticated phase in Harty's development as a composer.

Although the orchestra was undoubtedly becoming the focus of Harty's attention, his work with Agnes Nicholls, Plunket Greene and others continued to provide a fertile environment for solo songs and, in the tradition of Stanford, Wood and Esposito, arrangements of Irish melodies. The *Three Traditional Ulster Airs* were completed in January 1905, to words by Seosamh MacCathmhaoil, and dedicated to Plunket Greene, who often sang them in recitals. The seminal stimulus to arrange these traditional airs came from a small but lively movement based in Belfast around the strong and vibrant personality of Francis Joseph Bigger, a nationalist Presbyterian lawyer with a love for Irish culture. His house at Ardrigh on the Antrim Road became a focus for linguists, artists, musicians and antiquarians who, across the religious traditions, shared an interest in the Celtic Revival and the activities of the Gaelic League. Among the many significant figures who visited his house were Roger Casement, the future Westminster MP Stephen Gwynn, playwright and future President of Ireland Douglas Hyde, the poets Padraic Colum and Joseph Campbell (also known by his *nomme de plume* Seosamh MacCathmhaoil), his artist brother John, and Herbert Hughes, a student working under Stanford at the RCM. Bigger once took the Campbell brothers and Hughes on a holiday to Donegal, where Hughes noted down folk melodies from the local singers and fiddler, including the inmates of the Dunfanaghy workhouse. Bigger then financed a publication by the name of *Songs of Uladh*, which appeared in 1904 and comprised the music collected and notated by Hughes, verses by Joseph Campbell, and woodcuts by Campbell's brother John. This was also the year of the first Feis na nGleann in Co. Antrim, a festival strongly influenced by the spirit of the Gaelic League and which celebrated the musical and literary achievements of the Ulster region as well as the practical skills of local craftsmanship. *Songs of Uladh* and the Antrim Feis were life-changing events for Hughes. He went on to found the Irish Folk Song Society with Charlotte Milligan Fox, contributed to Bigger's *Ulster Journal of Archaeology*, and worked as a music journalist for *The New Age* and the *Daily Telegraph* between 1911 and 1932. But more importantly, he also arranged a good deal of Irish traditional melody; his *My Lagan Love, Down by the Sally Gardens, I Know where I am Going, O Men from the Fields* and *She Moved through the Fair* were widely sung by Plunket Greene, Nicholls, Campbell McInnes and McCormack, and are still much admired today.[114]

Harty must have acquired a copy of *Songs of Uladh* soon after publication and was obviously inspired by the melodies and words, as is evident from the splendidly conceived arrangements of typical Irish folk-style forms in his *Traditional Airs*. 'The Blue Hills of Antrim' is an exile's lament, and 'Black Sheela of the Silver Eye' a humorous reel (with a quizzical end to the melody). But the most remarkable of the three must be 'My Lagan Love'. The rising phrase of

---

[114] That Nicholls and Harty were enthusiastic exponents of Irish folk song arrangements is evidenced by their high-profile performance of such pieces at the opening concert of the Feis Ceoil on 23 May 1905: see *IT*, 22 May 1905.

the melody's opening, with its distinctive flattened seventh, must surely have been a seminal musical image in Harty's mind, heard in his youth, for, in the 'Irish' Symphony, Piano Quintet and *Comedy Overture* it became a thumbprint, a hallmark of Harty's Irish character. Moreover, the free metrical delivery, which is almost extemporary in effect (in accordance with Harty's direction 'quasi senza tempo'), the melodic range (down to a low, attitudinising B flat), the striking Mixolydian inflections, and the manner of the vocal ornamentation are as close to *sean nós* as it is possible to be in the more formal environment of the art song (though the ornamentation might well have been gleaned from Harty's experience of Scottish folk singing, common in Ulster in the late nineteenth century, rather than *sean nós* prevalent in the Connacht and Munster areas of Ireland). The rapid figurations of elaborate embellished piano interludes, already familiar in the instrumental works, provide an apt frame and a quasi-extemporary environment. Perhaps it is this very arrangement – the 'Rosetta Stone' of Harty's Irish muse – that provides the key to his stylistic assimilation of Irish folk material. Plunket Greene also had much light to shed on *My Lagan Love* in terms of performance practice in his *Interpretation of Song*, published in 1912, and his comments on metre, ornamentation and the perception of an innate, instinctive national understanding of the art perhaps provide an insight into those very aspects that Harty instilled in his own 'Irish' melodic and harmonic style:

> Unaccompanied folk-song singing is one of the most remarkable things in music. It is the most *ad libitum* type of performance it is possible to imagine. The true singer of the people is born not made. He will drop an obvious beat here and put it in there. He will hold back a phrase to superimpose an ornament (this applies far more to Ireland, where ornament is used with an Oriental freedom, rather than to England where it is rare). He will dwell upon unaccented notes in unaccountable places. He may so juggle with the time that it may be impossible to give it a time signature. The tune itself may be so peculiar that it may demand no arbitrary key-signature! Witness the old North of Ireland tune 'My Lagan Love' (arranged by H. Hamilton Harty, poem by Seosamh MacCathmhaoil).
>
> (To the eye this looks almost like an improvisation. By the individual native singer it would probably be further ornamented *ad libitum*. In the setting it is treated hypothetically as C major, because it happens to end on C. What its time-signature is, goodness knows!) The singer may, in short, give himself a free hand, break every rule and just sing; and yet he has a rhythm of his own so strong that it sets the heart of the trained singer leaping, so subtle that it defies imitation – wholly fascinating, wholly unlearnable. It is Nature as opposed to Art. No man who has not got it in his blood, and who has not lived with it in his youth, can ever acquire it. The further he travels along the road of his art, the further he leaves that astounding sense behind.[115]

Protective of his discovery of the tune of *My Lagan Love*, Hughes was surprised to see that Harty had made his own arrangement. A Belfast music critic was more vocal in his disapproval, which provoked Bigger, somewhat

[115] Harry Plunket Greene, *Interpretation of Song* (London: Macmillan, 1912), 220–1.

precipitately, to persuade Hughes to sue Harty for breach of copyright. From the outset the case had no substance – folk song has no copyright – and was speedily dismissed. Happily, Hughes's suit was no cause of animosity between him and Harty, as his daughter recounted:

> Later Herbert and Harty met at a London party and my mother invited 'Hale' to luncheon with some friends. It all passed, she recorded, with great gaiety. The following day Harty sent Herbert a fine photograph of himself at the piano. At the top of the mount he had written 'The Lagan' with below at one end 'From H. H.' and at the other 'To H. H.' The end of an *histoire* which should never have come about. The two remained the warmest of friends.[116]

The *Traditional Airs* were published by Boosey in 1905, who also took on a further arrangement of an old Irish tune, a lively jig, to words by P. W. Joyce. The four verses of *Colleen's Wedding Song* (also known as *I'm Going to be Married on Sunday*) require dexterous enunciation from the singer and nimble delicacy from the pianist. Boosey, clearly pleased with the commercial value of Harty's vocal miniatures, became his principal publisher of songs until 1910. *Lane o' the Thrushes* was another product of a recent publication, this time of *Some Ulster Love-Songs* by Cathal Byrne and Cahir Healy in 1905. The accompaniment is based on a series of recurring figurations in emulation of the thrush's repetitive song, for the most part couched high in the piano's tessitura; only with the allusion to 'the deeper silence' does the register of the accompaniment briefly descend, ushering in an apt modulation to the flat submediant. Yet, so buoyant is the mood, that E is quickly restored together with original elevated tessitura. Nicholls often sang this with her husband,[117] and it was later a favourite of Isobel Baillie, who recorded it with Gerald Moore in 1945. For *The Ould Lad*, a rather banal homespun ballad, Harty resorted to O'Neill's *Songs of the Glens of Antrim*; it was often sung by Plunket Greene, whose voice and *persona* it no doubt suited, and it was also a favourite of the American baritone, Denis O'Sullivan.[118] More substantial were the *Three Flower Songs* which Harty dedicated to three female singers closely associated with him: 'Poppies', a slumber song in D flat whose sensuous and carefully chosen chromaticisms mask an underlying sorrow, was dedicated to his wife; the through-composed 'Mignonette', a substantial and dramatic piece, was written for Elsie Swinton; and the playful 'Gorse', spoilt by an over-mawkish text, for Muriel Foster. Besides Nicholls, who performed the *Flower Songs* with Harty at one of the Manchester Gentlemen's Concerts on 10 December 1906,[119] one of the first exponents was Mrs Henry Wood who,

---

[116] Angela Hughes, *Chelsea Footprints: A Thirties Chronicle* (London: Quartet Books, 2008), 10–11. Plunket Greene's version of events is that Hughes 'generously handed over [his Irish tunes] to his friend to set', though this may have been, with hindsight, a sanitised memory: see Harry Plunket Greene, *Charles Villiers Stanford* (London: Arnold, 1935), 177.

[117] See *The Times*, 29 Oct. 1907.

[118] See *The Times*, 17 Nov. 1906.

[119] *MT* 48 (1907), 46.

accompanied by her husband, sang them at a recital on 20 June 1907 at the Aeolian Hall.[120]

In 1907 Boosey published three more songs, all of them using Elizabethan texts. A setting of Campion's *Come, O Come, My Life's Delight*, dedicated to Lady Arthur Hill, is attractive though less passionately animated than Quilter's fine setting of a year later. *Now is the Month of Maying* attempts to recapture the 'giocoso' spirit of Morley's immortal ballet, and Harty's mixture of drones, pauses, well-contrasted dynamics (especially for the 'fa la' refrain) and sparkling accompaniment make for a thoroughly entertaining ditty. The naval ballad *Song of the Three Mariners* clearly belongs to the medium of 'saltwater' songs with its sea-shanty overtones and somewhat clichéd rhythms (such as those by Frederick Keel), though it escapes the humdrum by its humorous tonal play between G and E. A similar type of song would be explored rather more effectively by John Ireland.

Two songs clearly designed for performance at the Chappell Ballad Concerts were published by Chappell in 1908. Harold Simpson's touching love-song *Your Hand in Mine* must surely have been intended for Nicholls' soprano range, while *An Irish Love Song*, using a text by the prolific Irish author Katharine Tynan, was written for Benjamin Davies, its dedicatee and a frequent partner of Harty's at the Ballad Concerts. It was first sung at an LSO concert on 28 June 1908 at the Albert Hall by Benjamin Sewell. Like *The Ould Lad*, with which it shares the same somewhat stereotypical key (D flat), there is a rather pungent melodramatic air about the vocal line and over-saccharine accompaniment, though Harty's deployment of the flat submediant (A major) rescues the song from the commonplace. Harty soon abandoned this ethos of the 'well-crafted' ballad, though it would continue with polish and aplomb in the songs of Eric Coates and Landon Ronald. A strong indication of this change of heart can be observed in his first major collection, *Six Songs of Ireland*, which Nicholls premiered at the Bechstein Hall on 3 November 1908. Following the models of Stanford's Irish songs, Harty drew upon the familiar Hiberno-English texts of O'Neill, Byrne, Healy and Lizzie Twigg (otherwise known as Elis Ni Craoibhin, an ardent nationalist and protégée of Æ). The ambitious, pensive 'Lookin' Back' creates a stormy evocation of Antrim and the rugged seascape seen from O'Neill's 'exile' in Canada; Stanford's setting of the same text (from his *Songs of the Glens of Antrim*, Op. 174, published in 1920) is, perhaps, subtler in its mixture of wistful nostalgia and resolve. The scheme of strophic variation in 'Dreaming', which narrates the tragedy of lost love and the longing for death, provides an appropriate and effective template for the 'question and answer' dialogue of the text. Moreover, Harty's handling of chromatic harmony in association with the 'other-worldliness' of Healy's verse is effective both as accompanimental imagery and for the celestial postlude. 'A Lullaby', a traditionally benign genre, here seems sinister as expressed by the lower register of the piano in B flat minor, and the exotic images of Byrne's poem are mirrored in the brooding 'charm'. The second half of the collection is less impressive. 'Grace for Light' is an entertaining but lightweight lyric (necessary to alleviate the gloom!) and 'Flame

[120] *The Times*, 21 June 1907.

in the Skies of Sunset' is spoilt by some uncomfortable harmonic solecisms. As for 'At Sea', which in Stanford's hands is highly sophisticated (again in his *Songs from the Glens of Antrim*, Op. 174), Harty's setting is, for all its rhythmical drive, emotionally more one-dimensional. The critic of the *Guardian* considered, however, that they were among 'the best songs he [had] written. They are modern in the sense of atmosphere and the piano part is of independent musical value, but they are free from the modern fault of unvocal voice parts.'[121]

While Harty thrived as an accompanist and emerging composer, Nicholls's career positively flourished. She sang much Elgar, including *Caractacus* and, in 1906 at the Birmingham Festival, the role of the Virgin Mary in the first performance of *The Kingdom*, a work that contained some of the composer's most haunting music in 'The Sun Goeth Down'; this role, which Harty helped her learn, she virtually made her own over the next few years. Besides concert performances of *Elijah*, *Israel in Egypt* and *Hiawatha*, her operatic career remained busy with the role of Venus in *Tannhäuser*, and Richter, who placed great faith in Nicholls's ability as a Wagnerian soprano, insisted that she sing Woglinde in *Das Rheingold*, and one of the parts of the Valkyries in *Die Walküre* during the Covent Garden production of *The Ring* in 1906. Nicholls had spent much time in Europe during her time as a student at the RCM, and, after leaving the College, she had also visited opera houses in Prague, Vienna, Dresden, Munich and Berlin (though she never visited Bayreuth on account of its prohibitive cost). This acclimatised her to the style of German singing but, at the same time, she entertained serious doubts that she could achieve the same manner of delivery. Yet, Richter thought otherwise:

> I always feel I owe much to the help and encouragement of Dr Hans Richter. He liked my voice and my work, but after hearing so much opera in Germany, I came to the conclusion I could not attempt Wagner. I could not do it in the German fashion. About this time, Dr Richter was giving many excerpts from the 'Ring of the Nibelung', in concert form, and he asked me to do some for him. I told him my reasons for not doing it, but he over-ruled my objection, by telling me that Wagner had always wanted things *sung*, and as he knew him well, I imagine he was right, so I began to think about it.[122]

During the course of 1907 Nicholls sang more and more Wagner. Under Leopold Reichwein she continued to appear in *Die Walküre* and *Lohengrin*, and in *Tannhäuser* under Franz Schalk, all at Covent Garden; in these instances critics noted how her powers as an actress were also maturing.[123] At Queen's Hall she sang the role of Brünnhilde in the closing scene of *Götterdämerung*, despite clearly suffering from influenza.[124] Under Richter, who was now conducting the newly established London Symphony Orchestra, she sang in Beethoven's Ninth Symphony, and the scene 'Abscheulicher' from *Fidelio*; under Parry she sang his *De Profundis*; and under Stanford, his *Elegiac Ode*. The climax of 1907 was

[121] *MG*, 5 Nov. 1908.

[122] Nicholls, 'A Vignette', 25.

[123] *The Times*, 15 Feb. 1907.

[124] *The Times*, 22 Jan. 1907.

undoubtedly Richter's two *Ring* cycles at the Royal Opera, but Nicholls was also greatly in demand at the Gloucester Three Choirs, Cardiff, and Leeds Festivals, and Stanford was disappointed when Nicholls was indisposed for his new *Stabat Mater*, whose soprano role had been specifically conceived for her. In 1908 she was again much in demand for roles in *Elijah*, *The Kingdom*, *Messiah*, and less familiar works such as Dvořák's *Stabat Mater* and Parry's *Judith*, but all eyes were on the first production in English of *The Ring* under Richter at Covent Garden. 'I am going to sing next week at the opera after all', she wrote with some elation to Harty, 'Sieglinde in the Walküre'.[125] She also played Brünnhilde in *Götterdämmerung*.[126] The reception after the first act of *Die Walküre* was jubilant, as Nicholls remembered over fifty years later:

> When we were back in our dressing rooms there suddenly came a knock on my door, and when the dresser opened it, lo and behold there was Richter standing there with Percy Pitt. They had come to congratulate us. I could hardly believe it. It seemed incredible that such a great man as Richter should come to us to do that. I was greatly touched, and it always remains in my memory as a very moving incident.[127]

Yet, ultimately, Nicholls' first doubts about her voice's suitability for Wagner remained. 'It will probably be said', she concluded, 'that all the roles don't "lie" well for my voice, and my readings set at defiance the accepted traditions. It is all quite true, but at that time, there was no one else able to do it all in quite the same way with my experience of the stage.'[128] As the years passed she continued to sing the role of Elisabeth but, as she confessed during the war, 'I can't bear to do Brunhilde, and have escaped from her now! She is too heavy for my voice.'[129]

Nicholls's years of singing Wagner, however, marked the apogee of her career as an operatic soprano, and Harty recognised this by composing for her his one major extended solo vocal work for soprano and orchestra, a setting of Keats's *Ode to a Nightingale* for the Cardiff Festival of 1907. The choice of Keats's poem was a deliberate attempt to find a text which expressed something akin to the sentiments and philosophy of Wagnerian music drama, in particular *Tristan und Isolde*, for which Nicholls had a major reputation in the closing 'Liebestod'. Keats's ode encompassed many of those elements seminal to Wagner's diffusion of Schopenhauer and the Tristan legend: the escape from reality, the state of deep imagination (in poetry), the longing for death, the (drugged) paralysis of the pastoral dream, ecstasy in the nightingale's song (in place of the standard Romantic agency of opium), the warmth of night and dread of day, only for all

[125] Letter from Agnes Nicholls to Harty, 29 May 1908, *GB-Lam*, McCann Collection 2006.212.
[126] 'I believe,' Nicholls wrote later, 'I am correct in saying I was the first English-woman to play Brunhilde throughout "The Ring"': Nicholls, 'A Vignette', 25.
[127] *Radio Times*, 3 Oct. 1957.
[128] *Radio Times*, 3 Oct. 1957.
[129] Letter from Agnes Harty to Captain Talbot-Rice, 8 July 1918, *GB-Lam*, McCann Collection 2006.214.

of this mental transcendence to be shattered by the return to reality and the passing of an imagined world.

Harty drew on the full panoply of Wagnerian and post-Wagnerian apparatus to create his extended monologue or scena. The vocal delivery moves freely and inventively between free recitative, arioso and full lyrical set piece, while the orchestra, in true Wagnerian fashion, acts as the symphonic background and means of organic cohesion. Indeed, Harty's ambitious and masterly orchestration not only provides the key agency of unity in the work, but is vividly illustrative of mood; moreover, his dexterous orchestral technique aids a careful and colourful delineation of leitmotivs which also assists the symphonic construction of the larger structure. In this sense Harty fully understood Wagner's polyphonic methods of handling leitmotiv. His matrix of musical ideas shows a fertile variety of 'types' (i.e. some are tonally stable, while others are open-ended, transitional or modulatory) which, collectively, creates a seamless, forward-moving *gestalt*, while individual ideas retain a distinctive and descriptive power. This can be observed in the closed idea ('longing') of the opening, exclusively for orchestra, the open-ended bridge passage ('mystery'), and the transitional Bacchanalian material which is consistently associated with tonal change. Furthermore, the malleability of these ideas is enhanced by a comprehensive incorporation of late nineteenth- and early twentieth-century chromatic harmony and key symbolism, executed with Harty's particular individual thumbprints.

The musical structure that Harty brings to the eight stanzas of Keats's ode is adroitly conceived. Germane to the scheme are part of the fourth and the whole of the fifth stanzas which, for the composer, encapsulate all those facets of the poem which allude to an 'out-of-self' state of ecstasy and a transcendence over life and death. For this Harty created a set piece in C major (the key also symbolic of the 'longing' expressed in the first stanza), in effect a 'liebestod' for Nicholls, in which the lyrical aspect of the soprano soloist is given free rein. The heady nature of this section is portrayed not only by the richly melodious component but the way Harty organically extends his material first to B flat major ('I cannot see what flowers are at my feet') and then to E major, all increasingly embellished by polyphonic orchestral filigree. The effect of this passage, which concludes on a dominant pedal of E, replete with a euphoric top B for the soprano (the highest point of the vocal range in the work) and an impressive orchestral surge, is to throw into marked relief the denial of cadential resolution to E, and, in its place, the unexpected yet rapturous return of C and a restatement of the 'liebestod' melody (Example 8).

The frame around this set piece suggests a form of sonata organisation, the first three stanzas defining an expositional phase, the last three one of recapitulation. Further detailed analysis reveals a sophisticated process of thematic development: the orchestral prelude and first stanza (closely connected tonally to the 'liebestod') establish C major from the outset, as well as the essential thematic strands representing 'longing', while the second stanza, a Bacchanalian transition, is tonally fluid (passing through A flat to E flat), before arriving at the 'lament' of the third stanza ('Fade far away, dissolve, and quite forget') in F sharp minor. In stanza 6 the recapitulation of the material from the

Example 8 *Ode to a Nightingale*, 'Liebestod'

Example 8 *continued*

first stanza is fused tonally with the close of the 'liebestod', and the climax at its end ('To thy high requiem become a sod') mirrors that at the end of stanza 1. Stanza 7, though it corresponds with the transitional properties of stanza 2 (even to the point where E flat plays a prominent part in proceedings), is nevertheless an entirely recomposed paragraph which gravitates to the dominant of C. At this juncture, with the initial return of C minor (rather than major), an elegiac closure is announced where the narrator of the poem becomes aware of worldly reality. An interesting feature, too, of Harty's preparatory passage of declamation ('The same that oft times hath / Charm'd magic casements'), is the strong, unabashed allusion to the 'prayer' motive from Elgar's *The Apostles*, a work very much part of the *zeitgeist* and one especially close to Nicholls. The final stanza, which invokes the orchestral prelude (Example 9), is highly effective, for here the orchestra becomes notably articulate in its expression of the narrator's mournful demeanour. Even though the soprano has one more climactic cry of anguish on a top C ('As she is famed to do, deceiving elf'), which no doubt suited Nicholls's considerable range (and stamina), the last six valedictory lines of the final stanza are charged with a deeply affecting melancholy. The C major of the opening

Example 9 *Ode to a Nightingale*, opening

is now infected with the memory of a past elation, and yet the sparse texture conveys a despondency at the breaking of the spell ('Fled is that music – do I wake or sleep?'). And, as a final gesture of thematic, poetical and timbral unity, Harty reminds us of the lingering 'ache' in the juxtaposition of the two low flutes, a sonority used at the opening of stanza 1, and the full, sonorous orchestra.

The *Ode to a Nightingale* was given its first performance at the opening concert at Cardiff on 25 September 1907 with Nicholls singing (who had already sung in Sullivan's *Golden Legend*) and Harty conducting. The reception was enthusiastic; 'the gifted pair received every mark of approval in the unstinted applause bestowed upon their combined efforts.'[130] After the performance Elgar, who had been present at the rehearsal, wrote to Harty in praise of the 'exquisite' orchestration.[131] Harty replied:

> I am very grateful to you for writing so kindly about my 'Nightingale' and you encourage me greatly. It was particularly good of you to hear the rehearsal and I would like to tell you how much I value your words of praise. Please accept my best thanks with best greetings from us both.[132]

Soon afterwards Wood seized the opportunity to conduct the work at the last night of his Promenade Concerts at Queen's Hall on 26 October, and Harty and Nicholls were then given the chance to perform it together again at the Crystal Palace with the British Symphony Orchestra on 30 November. Nicholls sang it for a fourth time with the Hallé Orchestra under Richter on 5 December.

Passionate, indeed erotic, as the *Ode to a Nightingale* proved, and it would be easy to interpret Harty's dedication of it to his wife as an adoring love letter,

[130] *MT* 48 (1907), 726.
[131] BBC talk, 18 June 1951.
[132] Letter from Harty to Elgar, 21 Sept. 1907, Elgar Birthplace Musuem.

the marriage of Nicholls and Harty was, as the years passed, increasingly less intimate. While the couple maintained a façade of marital harmony, their house at St John's Wood reflected their independent lives, with two separate staircases dividing the house into distinct parts. From later evidence we know that Harty was by no means a dispassionate individual when it came to personal relationships, so the cause of the conjugal failure remains open to speculation. There were no children (from which we have to draw our own conclusions), and as the marriage continued the two eventually began to live more and more separately, even to the extent of separate accommodation, though as professional artists they performed together until at least the mid 1920s. Details of their relationship stayed entirely private, but one thing has remained clear: neither wished for a divorce which, one presumes, would have provoked a public scandal neither wanted. This is further borne out by the fact that Nicholls was always keen to retain her title as 'Lady Harty' after her husband was knighted, and indeed after his death. Yet, though Harty ultimately became estranged from his wife, it was through Nicholls's initial success and her connection with Richter and other conductors that her husband made that vital step into the top flight of Britain's conducting world.

Since his conducting debut with the DOS in 1904 (and his reappearance by demand in 1905), we know that Harty looked to grasp any opportunity to reach the podium. Writing in November 1931, he recalled, in spite of the plethora of major English conductors, how difficult it remained to gain experience in handling an orchestra:

> It would be an impertinence on my part to try to appraise the individual qualities of the different members of our present band of distinguished English Conductors, but any country that can claim such outstanding examples as Sir Thomas Beecham, Eugene Goossens, Albert Coates, Landon Ronald, Malcolm Sargent, Julius Harrison and Basil Cameron, to name only a few, is entitled to regard itself as not outshone by any other country in the world. This is the more striking considering how few opportunities musicians have in this country to learn to train and handle an orchestra. Some I know have gained their experience in the hard school of travelling Opera Companies, some by taking every chance offered of conducting any fortuitous collection that might by any stretch of imagination be termed an orchestra. My own simple plan was to write works for different Festivals, knowing by this means that I would be invited to conduct them, and in that way have the chance of handling a first-class orchestra.[133]

In reality Harty's 'plan' was different from the one he remembered. His commission for the Cardiff Festival did indeed lead to the direction of his own work, but after his appearances with the DOS two years earlier most of his conducting engagements were for individual concerts rather than festivals. On 5 April 1906 he conducted what was probably his first orchestral concert in London, with the pianist Winifred Christie (who later championed the Moór-Duplex piano) and the British Symphony Orchestra in a programme of César Franck's

---

[133] H. Hamilton Harty, 'The Modern Orchestra: Conductors and Conducting', The Alsop Lectureship, Session 1931–2, Lecture 5, *GB-Belqb* MS 14/29/V.

Variations symphoniques and Saint-Saëns's Second Piano Concerto in G minor. The reception was positive.[134] A second engagement took place with the same orchestra on 24 May with the young Irish violinist Madge Murphy, who had close connections with the RIAM.[135] Just before Harty's first conducting engagement at the Crystal Palace – on 30 November, where he directed performances of both his *Comedy Overture* and *Ode to a Nightingale* – Dan Godfrey, a great champion of British music, invited Harty to Bournemouth to conduct his 'Irish' Symphony. This was the first of three visits to Bournemouth that season, the second of which was to give his *Comedy Overture* in February 1908, and the third a repeat performance of the 'Irish' Symphony in April.[136] These were vital practical experiences, since Harty's ambition, to be a professional conductor, would soon be realised.

[134] *The Times*, 6 Apr. 1906.

[135] *IT*, 22 May 1906.

[136] See Stephen Lloyd, *Sir Dan Godfrey: Champion of British Composers* (London: Thames Publishing, 1995), 82.

London (2):
Composer and Conductor

I T is perhaps telling that, in the supplement to the second edition of *Grove's Dictionary of Music and Musicians*, published in the fifth volume in 1911 and compiled by its editor, J. A. Fuller Maitland, Harty appears for the first time, acknowledged for his exploits as a composer and as 'one of the best of accompanists.'[1] Certainly by 1909 Harty's reputation as a musician had become pre-eminent, which meant that he was called upon to perform a broad variety of social duties that extended beyond the purely artistic. He was asked to be judge for a competition to select a prize-winning piece for the Empire Day Concert in 1911;[2] he was called upon for Charles Harriss's Imperial Choir (a vast body of over 2,000 voices) at the Albert Hall in May 1914; with Agnes Nicholls he played for the Annual Festival Concert given by the London Sunday School Choir (also at the Albert Hall) in February 1910, and with Ysaÿe, Luisa Tetrazzini (the coloratura soprano who packed Covent Garden at her London debut in 1908), Clara Butt and Kennerley Rumford, he performed at the 'at home' given by Catherine Eckstein (wife of the millionaire Sir Friedrich Eckstein) at 18 Park Lane to receive the recently knighted and much-celebrated Sir Ernest Shackleton, the officers of the British Antarctic Expedition and 500 distinguished guests.

A further indication of Harty's growing reputation is epitomised by an unusual project initiated by the Hambourg String Quartet (which took its name from Jan Hambourg, the Russian violinist who led the ensemble) in 1908. It was their idea to commission five movements by five different composers for a *New Suite* or *English Suite*. Curiously, given the work's 'English' title, a condition was nevertheless imposed that all movements should incorporate *The Londonderry Air*, the most famous of *Irish* tunes. The Hambourg Quartet invited Frank Bridge, J. D. Davis, Eric Coates (who was a violist in the quartet at that time), York Bowen and Harty. The movements were duly produced and the work was performed at the Aeolian Hall the same year, but it was never published in its composite form. J. D. Davis's contribution later took the form of a larger work, the *Variations on the Londonderry Air*, Op. 43, while Bridge's movement was later published as *An Irish Melody* in 1915. The movements by Harty, Coates and Bowen remained in private hands; unfortunately Harty's movement, a Scherzo, only survives incomplete as a set of instrumental parts (the second violin part is missing).[3]

The catalogue of artists with whom Harty worked and who requested his assistance confirms that, within a decade of his first appearances in London, he had undoubtedly made the art, indeed the *profession*, of accompanying his own.

---

[1] J. A. Fuller Maitland, 'Harty', *Grove 2*, vol. 5 (London: Macmillan 1911), 644.

[2] *MT* 51 (1910), 46, 162.

[3] See Greer, 'Hamilton Harty Manuscripts', 242–3, 247.

Moreover, as is evident from criticisms in the press, his role was increasingly being recognised as one equal with his partner performers. In former years Harty was credited with little more than a closing comment such as 'Mr Harty accompanied', or perhaps a little more generously, 'Mr Harty accompanied throughout the recital with great skill and sympathy.'[4] But in the years before the war, his critical appraisal frequently attracted more than this. With Campbell McInnes, his participation in Schumann's *Dichterliebe* and Brahms's *Magelone Lieder* attracted unusually fulsome approbation:

> In such a programme as this the pianist's share is fully as important as the singer's, and the intimate and sympathetic playing of Mr Hamilton Harty in both the cycles was everything that it should be. Without such playing the "Dichterliebe" would lose most of its beauty, however well it were sung, for the pianist's commentary upon the poet's thought is the thing by which Schumann has transfigured Heine.[5]

His recital with the American baritone Leon Rains elicited the following remarks: 'Mr Hamilton Harty was the accompanist, and his brilliant playing of this song alone [Richard Strauss's *Der Feuerreiter*] deserved fuller recognition than his services actually gained. Throughout his playing was an important element in the success of the recital.'[6] He continued to appear with Nicholls and with Plunket Greene, though by 1914 the Irish baritone was gradually withdrawing from singing in favour of teaching (from which he also retired in 1919). His appreciation of Harty's consummate art was effusive and, not long before his death, he openly conceded the injustice that neglected accompanists were wont to suffer:

> Thank you too, old man, with all my heart for your inspiration and beautiful playing last night. Gosh! What it means to a singer. I wish old C. V. S. [Stanford] could have heard it. … You know I feel ashamed when I think of what a little fag-end of a branch any [singer] is alongside the likes o'men like you. This isn't affection – I mean it. I have an awful feeling of wanting to squirm when I think of it. It's the rank uneven justice which hands it out to the person who faces the audience. My blessing on you, old boy, for your friendship all these years. I'm rightly proud of it.[7]

Perhaps most symbolic of Harty's eminence was an invitation for him to share the accompanying at Henry Bird's Jubilee concert at Queen's Hall on 26 April 1910. Bird was, of course, an 'old timer' who was still working and had given many years' service to accompanying, especially at St James's Hall before its closure; the rich array of singers and instrumentalists – Nicholls, Hast, Rumford, Squire, Crossley, Sigmund Beel and May Harrison – bore witness to Bird's pioneering contribution.[8] Harty, dubbed 'the ablest of a younger race [of

---

[4] *The Times*, 17 Nov. 1909.

[5] *The Times*, 18 Dec. 1911.

[6] *The Times*, 28 Feb. 1912.

[7] Letter from Plunket Greene to Harty, 13 July 1935.

[8] *The Times*, 27 Apr. 1910. The *MT* also paid tribute to Bird in a feature article in its May issue, 289–90.

accompanists]', now commanded decent fees for his services. His appearances at the Bechstein, Steinway and Aeolian Halls was as regular as ever, and he enjoyed a fine assortment of clients. Some of them, like the violinists Marian Jay, Leila Willoughby and Margaret Holloway (who had not long returned from two years in St Petersburg with Leopold Auer), were young and making their way, as was Beatrice Harrison, sister of May with whom Harty had already worked. In April 1913 May and Beatrice (or 'Babe', as she was known to her friends and close colleagues) were fresh from their Continental tour. On 19 April 1913 Beatrice gave her first concert with Harty at the Bechstein Hall to great critical acclaim, especially for their interpretation of Strauss's Cello Sonata in F, Op. 6.[9] As with May, Harty would foster a close artistic relationship with her throughout his career.

The list of established artists with whom Harty worked continued to grow. On one occasion, in a programme of traditional Irish airs and arts songs at the Aeolian Hall on 17 March 1910, he shared the accompaniment of Plunket Greene with Stanford.[10] He worked with Marie Brema, Aldo Antonietti, Isolde Menges,[11] the 'Dutch nightingale' Julia Culp,[12] her compatriot Anton van Rooy (the Wagnerian bass-baritone with whom Nicholls had often sung, famous for his role as John the Baptist in Strauss's controversial opera *Salomé*)[13] and with the much-feted operatic soprano Lulu Mysz Gmeiner, highly praised by Brahms and Wolf (and the teacher of Elizabeth Schwarzkopf).[14] With Nicholls in 1909 he made what was probably his first gramophone recording, of Cowen's *Bride Song* and *At the Mid Hour of Night*, and with Alice Verlet, the Belgian coloratura soprano, he made a recording of Gounod's 'Serenade' and Delibes's *Filles du Cadiz* during the time Verlet was in London with the Thomas Beecham Opera Comique season in 1910.

Other major performers included Joseph Szigeti, Theo Lierhammer, Max Mossel, Gladys Honey, Gordon Cleather, the pianist Richard Epstein (with whom Harty featured as part of a duo),[15] and Mrs Henry Wood (Princess Olga Ouroussoff).[16] The latter he accompanied (in the company of Amy Dewhurst and William Higley) at a recital on 18 October 1909 in a programme of works by Isabel Hearne. Constantly in pain from an operation in the early 1890s, Ouroussoff, endowed with a substantial voice in the Russian tradition, continued to sing stoically, but by 1909 her condition had deteriorated considerably. Within six weeks of her recital with Harty she was removed to a nursing home, where

---

[9] See Beatrice Harrison, *The Cello and the Nightingales: The Autobiography of Beatrice Harrison*, ed. Patricia Cleveland-Pech, with a foreword by Julian Lloyd-Webber (London: John Murray, 1985), 25; see also *The Times*, 21 Apr. 1913.

[10] *MT* 51 (1910), 243.

[11] *The Times*, 9 June 1913.

[12] *The Times*, 28 Mar. 1912.

[13] *The Times*, 7 Mar. 1912.

[14] *The Times*, 7 June 1912.

[15] *The Times*, 2 June 1910.

[16] Henry J. Wood, *My Life of Music* (London: Victor Gollancz, 1938), 157.

she died on 20 December. Her husband was heartbroken.[17] Another important figure with whom Harty collaborated was the English baritone J. Campbell McInnes. Like Harty, McInnes had made an initial living from performing at after-dinner recitals for wealthy Edwardians until his career as a concert artist was established. Harty worked regularly with him during 1911, appearing with him at least six times. Though McInnes was well known for his performances of Brahms and Schumann, he was also a keen exponent of *My Lagan Love*; he also sang a great number of new English songs by Peel, Vaughan Williams, Holst and Butterworth and was soon immersed in the wave of settings of Housman's *A Shropshire Lad*. He and Harty gave the first hearing of numerous Housman songs by Peel, and, having given the first known performance of Butterworth's collection *Six Songs from 'A Shropshire Lad'* at the Oxford University Musical Club on 16 May 1911 (an event organised by Adrian Boult),[18] with Butterworth as accompanist, McInnes turned to Harty for their first London performance on 20 June at the Aeolian Hall. The critical reception was, with few exceptions, highly enthusiastic.

Often in the company of Nicholls, Harty also continued to visit music societies around Britain, not least at Bradford (where they were favoured guests of Samuel Midgley, the organiser of the Subscription Concerts),[19] Birmingham, Bristol, Burnley, Manchester, Leeds and Wakefield (where they appeared on several occasions); but Harty never forgot his past roots, and also made several visits to Ireland. In part his visits to the Irish capital were to visit Esposito, to consult him on his latest compositions, but there were also opportunities to see old friends and colleagues at the RIAM and to give occasional concerts. At the Antient Concert Rooms he supported a former RIAM student of Papini, the violinist Mary Dickenson (April 1911 and March 1912), and he made a few appearances at the Assembly Rooms in Bray (30 August 1911), the Royal Dublin Society (2 February and 20 November 1911), and Dublin's Gaiety Theatre (5 February 1912) where, nurturing Dublin's love of opera, he took part in a 'Grand Concert' featuring many operatic excerpts sung by Kirkby Lunn, Joseph O'Mara, Alice Wilna (a rising star at Covent Garden) and a new Irish celebrity, Cormac O'Shane, who had recently been asked to join Thomas Quinlan's touring opera company. The party also included Clyde Twelvetrees, a regular performer at the RDS and an RIAM professor. The fact that Harty had been secured to take part in the concert warranted particular mention in the *Irish Times*, and the concert's review paid a generous tribute to him.[20] Dublin was proud of its connection with Harty, and often feted him, whether through his folk-song arrangements, the use of his songs and instrumental miniatures as Feis competitive pieces, or the featuring of his orchestral works by the DOS. In spite of the growing political tensions, the clamour for Home Rule and the disquiet in Ulster, Harty's affection

[17] Wood, *My Life of Music*, 313.

[18] Michael Barlow, *Whom the Gods Love: The Life and Music of George Butterworth* (Exeter: Toccata Press, 1997), 57.

[19] *MT* 53 (1912), 121; see also S. Midgley, *My 70 Years' Musical Memories* (London: Novello, 1930), 39ff.

[20] *IT*, 2 and 6 Feb. 1912.

for Ireland, both north and south, remained constant and unflinching. On a sad note, one of his old Irish mentors, James George Scott, Archdeacon of Dublin, died in January 1912 and his funeral took place at Christ Church, Bray. The service was a large choral affair and for the anthem the choir exhumed Harty's youthful setting of 'I heard a voice from heaven' as an appropriate gesture of old friendship and association.[21]

During his time at Bray one of Harty's close friends was the wealthy aristocrat Sir Stanley Cochrane, a musical amateur and governor of the RIAM who lived on his estate at Woodbrook, Co. Wicklow, close to Bray and about ten miles south of Dublin. A scion of a prominent Anglo-Irish family, Cochrane was the son of Sir Henry Cochrane, founder of the highly successful company Cantrell & Cochrane, which had amassed wealth manufacturing beverages and mineral waters. After Sir Henry's death in 1904 Ernest, the eldest son, had joined the board of directors but, not wishing to be continuously resident in Ireland, he soon decided to relinquish this position to his younger brother Stanley in 1909. The result, from Stanley's point of view, was the inheritance of a substantial fortune at the age of thirty-two and the opportunity to pursue his hobbies of cricket, golf and music at Woodbrook. Indeed, Cochrane invested considerable sums of money to create excellent facilities for visiting cricket teams, including those at international level, and, as an amateur singer and follower of opera, he had built a private opera house and concert hall on his estate.[22] With this infrastructure, Cochrane was even able to persuade the local railway company to situate a station at Woodbrook for concert-goers (and cricket spectators), together with reduced ticket prices for major events. In the years immediately before the war Cochrane's concert hall became a major focus of musical activity, and its intention was to elicit a greater interest in music among the Dublin population. 'Many artists who command packed houses in London come to Dublin to appear before disheartening rows of empty seats,'[23] was the common complaint of Irish newspapers. Some blamed indifference; others, such as Esposito, attributed it to a demographic and geographical problem. But Cochrane was not to be deterred. In February 1913 he persuaded Esposito and the DOS to transfer their Sunday Orchestral Concerts to Woodbrook, where they proved so popular that another series was undertaken in May. In addition, chamber concerts became a regular fixture; Esposito and his 'Dublin Trio' gave several concerts, and Cochrane also devised a plan to feature major European pianists. Rachmaninov was announced for 7 February 1914, but was indisposed through illness. Nevertheless, Cochrane was able to secure Alfred Cortot (21 February 1914). Harty's part in Cochrane's scheme was to accompany a series of vocal recitals in early 1914. The first was a concert given on 10 January 1914 with the English tenor John Coates, famous for his Wagnerian roles with the Quinlan Opera Company, who returned with Harty to give a further concert on 28 March. No stranger to Dublin, the

[21] *IT*, 17 Jan. 1912.

[22] Such was Cochrane's enthusiasm for opera and his sense of cultural altruism that he financed a production of the *Ring* cycle in Dublin in May 1913 by a touring opera company.

[23] *IT*, 2 Feb. 1914.

soprano Kirkby Lunn (who had endeared herself to Irish audiences with her role as Norah in Stanford's *Shamus O'Brien*) gave a long and somewhat ambitious recital on 31 January of Brahms, Wolf, Strauss, Debussy and Duparc as well as some of Harty's own songs. Lunn performed before a large and ardent crowd, as did Agnes Nicholls, who gave her recital with Harty on 7 March. Billed with the hyperbole 'it is impossible to imagine a more ideal combination than that of Miss Agnes Nicholls and Mr Hamilton Harty',[24] Nicholls's recital instigated additional trains running to Woodbrook, and after 'numerous requests' she agreed to include Harty's 'celebrated song "Sea Wrack".'[25] The success of these events together with the attraction of Harty – 'one of their own' – encouraged Cochrane to consider musical events on an even more elaborate scale.

Perhaps Harty's most notable collaboration in the years before the First World War was, however, with the mezzo-soprano, Mrs George (otherwise known as Elsie) Swinton, striking images of whom have survived in sketches and a flattering full-length portrait by John Singer Sargent.[26] Harty had accompanied her at her first solo recital in May 1906 at the Aeolian Hall, and since then her career had moved on in leaps and bounds. Swinton entered the world of the provincial musical festival and became a well-seasoned oratorio singer, admired by Ethel Smyth who described her as 'my favourite vocalist',[27] and whose music she frequently performed.[28] Osbert Sitwell, an intimate friend and devotee, left the following impression:

> Her childhood had been spent in Russia [St Petersburg], and it seemed as if something of the genius of that country, of its generosity and fire, had entered into her spirit as well as into her magnificent appearance. The incomparable warmth of her voice cast a strange spell that served to keep even a fashionable audience quiet, and soon made the songs of the great Russian composers, which she had originally introduced to English audiences, both popular and modish. Moreover her beauty, as she sang, a beauty of an unusual and moving kind, inspired many celebrated artists to execute drawings and pictures of her.[29]

Swinton's prowess for singing in foreign languages, in English, French, Italian, German and Russian (languages, incidentally, that she also spoke), meant that her repertoire was unusually wide. She sang for Debussy, appeared in Paris with Ysaÿe, and was accompanied on several occasions by Fauré, with whom she also corresponded. Her career, and her home at 36 Pont Street, London, also became the subject of an extended article in *The World*, thanks to her agents Ibbs and Tillett.[30] Her circle of friends confirmed just how well connected she was in

---

[24] *IT*, 4 Mar. 1914.

[25] *IT*, 7 Mar. 1914.

[26] A full-length portrait by Sargent, dating from 1897, can be viewed in the Wirt D. Walker Collection at the Art Institute of Chicago.

[27] E. Smyth, *What Happened Next* (London: Longmans Green, 1940), 279.

[28] See Greer, *A Numerous and Fasionable Audience*, 85ff.

[29] Osbert Sitwell, *Left Hand Right Hand!* (London: The Reprint Society, 1946), 224.

[30] Sitwell, *Left Hand Right Hand!*, 96–8.

society.[31] 'She was,' wrote Osbert Sitwell, 'the most gifted of all English singers of her time, an artist of a remarkable kind.'[32] Clearly she had great presence and magnetism which had her audiences spellbound in the concert room. This remained her *forte*, for, in spite of being importuned by operatic impresarios, she turned down all invitations to take to the stage.

Harty began to work regularly with Swinton from January 1910. They toured Britain together and developed a special performing rapport that continued until the war. At a Leeds Philharmonic Society concert (with which the subscription concerts were now amalgamated) on 26 January they appeared together for the first time in a programme shared with performances of wind music. With Harty's ingress into London's orchestral world, he had befriended the wind players of the Queen's Hall Orchestra – Albert Fransella (flute), J. L. Fonteyne (oboe), Charles Draper (clarinet), Adolph Borsdorf (horn) and Edwin James (bassoon) – and, through mutual interest, founded an ensemble to explore the repertoire of music for wind and piano.[33] At Leeds Harty and his colleagues performed Beethoven's early Quintet for Piano and Wind, Op. 16, while string players augmented the wind for Schubert's Octet. Alongside these instrumental items Swinton gave a programme of mainly contemporary songs. In the evening of 3 March 1910 Harty and Swinton appeared together at the Bechstein Hall, where they performed all of Schumann's *Liederkreis*, Op. 39, four new songs by Albéniz, two songs by Lyapunov (in French translation), 'Armida's Garden' from the latest volume of Parry's *English Lyrics* (Set IX) as well as lyrics by Hubert Bath and Roger Quilter. It was regarded by the critic of the *Musical Times* as 'one of the most attractive vocal recitals of the winter season'.[34] Harty occasionally toured with his wind players, and in February 1911 he and a wind trio, Fransella (consisting of the celebrated Belgian oboist Henri di Busscher and the clarinettist Charlesworth Fawcett), gave a concert at Leinster House in Dublin for the RDS in a programme of Brahms, Goepfart, Amberg, Saint-Saëns, and two of the *Three Pieces* for oboe and piano specially composed for de Busscher by Harty himself. According to the review in the *Irish Times*, these pieces (though not specified) were given for the first time; in fact, as the critic of *The Times* remembered in reviewing Harty's orchestrations of the *Three Pieces* given in London on 7 September, two of them had been performed for the Concert-Goers' Club at the Langham Hotel on 10 November 1905, for one of their pioneering concerts of 'Music by British Composers'.[35]

[31] The Swintons soon moved to a house at 2 Hyde Park Street, where they lived until 1915. There Elsie entertained Serge Prokofiev, Karol Szymanowski, Arthur Rubinstein, Igor Stravinsky, and Paul Kochanski and his wife: Greer, *A Numerous and Fashionable Audience*, 105–6.

[32] Sitwell, *Left Hand Right Hand!*, 215.

[33] Harty's collection of music for wind and piano is preserved in the Harty Collection at Queen's University, Belfast.

[34] *MT* 51 (1910), 243.

[35] The two pieces were 'À la campagne' and 'Orientale'. The soloist was the oboist H. H. Stanislaus of the Queen's Hall Orchestra; the accompanist was unspecified but was probably Harty.

On 2 November 1911 Harty, Swinton and the wind players gave an afternoon recital at the Bechstein Hall. The programme was altogether ambitious and unusual. The instrumentalists played music by Fuhrmeister and Saint-Saëns, and, as the focal point, gave the first performance in England of Rimsky-Korsakov's Sextet (published the same year by Belaïev).[36] Such was the impact of this concert that the critic of the The Times (probably Colles) devoted an individual article to the novel subject of wind music in an attempt to develop a critique of the repertoire, and to urge Harty and his colleagues to continue their exploratory work.[37] This exhortation was fulfilled at the next concert, enthusiastically advertised, in the evening of 14 November when the 'Hamilton Harty Sextet', as it was now dubbed,[38] performed Ludwig Thuille's Sextet, Op. 6, a flute sonata by Marcello, and two of Harty's *Three Pieces* for oboe.[39] However, fascinating as this revival of wind music was, it was Swinton's performances that drew most attention. On 2 November she sang a programme of songs by Wolf and, for the first time, a group by Harty entitled *Five Irish Sketches* based entirely on poems by contemporary Irish writers. Swinton was to make these songs her own and, in a vein more serious and varied in Harty's song output, she performed them with great aplomb on numerous occasions to considerable critical acclaim. 'As the title suggests', wrote the critic of *The Times*, 'these are not songs with piano accompaniment in the ordinary sense, but duets in which the two performers are placed upon equal terms.'[40] At their second recital, on 15 November, Swinton gave a second airing of the *Irish Sketches* and complemented them with Russian songs, several of them by Mussorgsky. At a further recital, on 14 December, the Harty Sextet repeated the Thuille along with Volbach's Quintet for Piano and Wind, Op. 24, and Fonteyne played a sonata for oboe by Handel. Swinton, as if to put her stamp on the *Irish Sketches*, sang them for a third time along with more Russian songs. In addition to the *Sketches*, Harty also wrote a setting of 'The Sea Gypsy' from *More Songs from Vagabondia* (1896) by the late nineteenth-century American poet Richard Hovey. Harty's setting dates to late 1911, and is dedicated to Swinton. As an indication of his admiration for her ability, he took particular care with this song, as a letter to the singer illustrates:

Dear Mrs Swinton,

Here is the Sea Gypsy – a new copy with another one you lent me – which unfortunately got torn up in a moment of aberration! However I've mended it as well as possible – you will be pleased and gratified to notice that I have made some alterations – giving you the chance of showing your wonderful power of breath control – there are also some small alterations which I know you will find pleasure in discovering yourself! I am sorry to have to confess that my powers of altering

[36] *The Times*, 3 Nov. 1911.
[37] 'Wind Instruments in Chamber Music', *The Times*, 4 Nov. 1911.
[38] *The Times*, 15 Nov. 1911.
[39] *The Times*, 15 Nov. 1911.
[40] *The Times*, 3 Nov. 1911.

and changing the Sea Gypsy having become exhausted – the last new copy which I
send you will remain the Authorized Version – for the present anyway![41]

In January 1912 Harty accompanied Swinton during her second tour of
Holland (she had toured the Netherlands for the first time in February the
previous year); a concert in The Hague, where she sang the *Irish Sketches*, left
a favourable impression.[42] On their return, concerts with the wind ensemble
continued in various forms: one for the Burnley Vocal Society featuring them,
for example, in quintet form beside works by Mozart, Beethoven, Brahms and
Glazunov.[43] Swinton again sang songs by Harty, and the response she elicited
from her audience was animated. The critic (probably Samuel Langford) of the
Manchester Guardian recounted: 'She was extremely daring in the freedom,
vigour, and variety of style with which she sang Mr Harty's songs, and at the end
there was tumultuous applause.'[44] During 1912 and 1913 Harty and Swinton gave
a great many concerts around Britain – it was to all intents and purposes the
zenith of Swinton's career – but perhaps the apex of their collaboration was in
the late spring and early summer of 1913 when they appeared alongside the Polish
violinist Paweł Kochański. Trained in Warsaw and Brussels, and a professor of
violin at the Warsaw Conservatory between 1909 and 1911, Kochański had struck
a close working relationship with the pianist Artur Rubinstein, and together they
followed the activities of the *Młoda Polska* (*Young Poland*) movement, in which
the composer Karol Szymanowski was a leading figure. Kochański, Rubinstein
and Szymanowski congregated in London's Lisson Grove, at the musical home of
the American singer Paul Draper and his wife Muriel. Swinton interacted with
this salon in 1913 and 1914 and through her Harty was introduced to Kochański.

Harty, Swinton and Kochański together gave three concerts of 'sonatas and
songs', in which Swinton took a more retiring role. She was not for the most
part in good voice, and sang only small groups of lieder, whereas the main body
of the programme was devoted to instrumental music. At their first recital, on
24 April, Swinton sang a selection of Schubert lieder while Kochański and Harty
performed Brahms's Violin Sonata in D minor, Op. 108, and Szymanowski's
Violin Sonata, which Kochański and Rubinstein had premiered in Warsaw
in April 1909. This was its first hearing in England and, though appreciated
as 'cleverly written',[45] the work's reception was at best lukewarm. At their
second recital Swinton's execution of Heine settings by Schumann interspersed
Paderewski's Violin Sonata, Op. 13, and Harty's *Variations on a Dublin Air*,
which Kochański had premiered in London with the LSO earlier in 1913. At
their last appearance, on 10 June, it was Swinton's contribution that was more

[41] Letter from Harty to Swinton, 29 Nov. 1911. *GB-Belqb*. Three versions survive of
The Sea Gyspy. The 'authorized version' Harty sent to Swinton is largely the same
as the one published by Boosey in 1912. For further details, see Greer, 'Hamilton
Harty Manuscripts', 241, 245.

[42] *MT* 53 (1912), 338.

[43] *MT* 52 (1912), 188.

[44] *MG*, 7 Feb. 1912.

[45] *MT* 54 (1913), 391.

contemporary. Kochański chose to play Brahms's Sonata in A, Op. 100, and Beethoven's 'Kreutzer' Sonata, while she sang lieder by Brahms, a new setting by Harty of Walt Whitman's *By the Bivouac's Fitful Flame*, and *Adieu, Sweet Amaryllis*, attributed to John Dowland and supposedly transcribed by Harty 'from an old manuscript in the possession of John Broadley Esq. of Bristol'. As Greer has elucidated in some detail, no setting of these words survives by Dowland, nor can Broadley's manuscript be traced; Harty's so-called 'transcription' is all that exists, and it is probably by Harty himself, intended to be a pastiche not unlike those of Kreisler.[46] Nevertheless, the 'Dowland' song was much admired and to its audience it must have seemed like an authentic voice from the sixteenth century, even though it is more than evident that the harmonic syntax is of modern provenance.[47]

While Harty and Swinton worked closely together between 1912 and 1913 they saw a good deal of each other, for Harty was often at 2 Hyde Park Street rehearsing and socialising. The house, from Swinton's point of view, was also empty; her husband George Swinton was frequently away on business, and only the youngest child, Mary, was at home.[48] As a gregarious type, she enjoyed the company of others and was stimulated by the presence and conversation of other musicians. During this period Harty undoubtedly filled this void, and there is no doubt that he and Swinton cemented a close friendship. Indeed, it may have amounted to more than this. Harty himself was locked in an unhappy marriage and probably craved affection and intimacy; Swinton, too, was lonely and clearly enjoyed Harty's attention and intelligence. As two young, physically attractive people, the liaison was probably quite conspicuous; tongues wagged and gossip reached the ears of Swinton's friends, including Sargent, a close confidante. What is more, Swinton no longer advertised herself as 'Mrs George Swinton' but as 'Elsie Swinton', a change, as Greer has suggested, that was open to misinterpretation.[49] The matter seems to have come to a head with a lavish party that the Swintons gave at their home in June 1913 which was attended by an impressive list of aristocrats, the Archbishop of Canterbury, and senior officers from the military. Harty and Kochański were asked to perform, and, most significantly, so was Nicholls. It was surely intended as public gesture of denial to all the speculation and rumours and one of conjugal unity.

But what is perhaps a more regrettable conclusion to this affair is that, after this event, and the three recitals with Kochański, all connections between Swinton and Harty ceased forever.[50] It was a sorry outcome to a most fruitful artistic association, but, as Greer has suggested, Swinton's career was in decline

---

[46] See David Greer, 'A Dowland Curiosity', *The Lute* 27 (1987), 42–4.

[47] Greer, *A Numerous and Fashionable Audience*, 106.

[48] Harty furnished a simple song for Mary Swinton called *Nursie* ('My nursie hates a rainy day'), which has survived. See Greer, *A Numerous and Fashionable Audience*, 110–11.

[49] Greer, *A Numerous and Fashionable Audience*, 111.

[50] Greer, *A Numerous and Fashionable Audience*, 112.

by the end of 1913, and by 1914 she had virtually ceased to sing altogether.[51] As Sitwell noted:

> As a singer, however, not the least remarkable thing in her career was her decision to leave the concert platform in the plenitude of her powers and with her vitality undiminished. Her sense of the theatre, so evident in her singing, made her determined to avoid the inevitable anti-climax of a declining voice, a gesture of sacrifice to her art which is, indeed, all too rare among singers.[52]

Harty, on the other hand, did continue to tour with his sextet until the war; Nicholls filled the void created by Swinton's absence and she carried on the trend of promoting Harty's own songs and Irish arrangements.[53]

Harty's production of songs between 1909 and 1914 continued to be abundant. Settings of seventeenth-century poems, published in 1909, such as *Song of the Constant Lover* (Suckling) and *Tell Me Not, Sweet, Thou Art Unkind* (Lovelace), and *When Summer Comes*, to a text by the popular Edwardian poet Harold Simpson, were written for consumption at the Chappell Ballad Concerts which were still providing Harty with a valuable source of income. Two other songs, *Homeward* (a further setting of Simpson dedicated to the English baritone Robert Radford)[54] and *The Sea Gypsy*, are also evocative of the 'ballad' culture', yet both also evince an increasing sophistication. An esoteric handling of chromaticism lifts *The Sea Gypsy* out of banality, notably in the central section where, aptly underpinning the more erotic sentiment of the text ('For the Islands of Desire'), Harty reaches the flat submediant from which the recovery to E flat is achieved with a deft mastery. *Homeward*, with its robust synthetic folk melody – there is a more than passing affinity with the opening song of Vaughan Williams's *Songs of Travel* – reveals a more interesting exploration of modality where a somewhat unstable C minor is undermined by a refrain strongly inflected by F minor. This sense of modal duality is prolonged in the last verse and refrain where the corresponding major modes are brought into conflict (note the persistent B flat pedal at the opening, which creates a tension with the melody in C major). Indeed, in this song, with its numerous passages of unusual progressions, Harty's harmonic language is far from conventional.

The more serious demeanour of *Homeward* was also symptomatic of Harty's more earnest approach to song composition. By 1910 audiences at the Bechstein and Aeolian Halls were more accustomed to song recitals of more challenging

---

[51] Greer, *A Numerous and Fashionable Audience*, 113.

[52] Sitwell, *Left Hand Right Hand!*, 224–5.

[53] *IT*, 6 Jan. 1914. This details a charity concert in Dublin in which Harty, Nicholls and the Sextet appeared.

[54] Radford was also the recipient of another (presumably popular) song by Harty, *The Ballad of Falmouth Town*, which has since disappeared. It was first sung by Radford at a concert given by the Royal Amateur Orchestral Society at Queen's Hall on 20 April 1910: see *The Times*, 21 Apr. 1910. There is also mention of Nicholls singing 'two ballads' at a concert of the Bristol Choral Society on 6 April 1910, but these are not specifically identified: see *MT* 51 (1910), 321.

repertoire. The songs of Wolf, Strauss, Reger, Debussy, Duparc and Fauré were common fare, as was the blooming of a new, distinctive English genre, signalled particularly by the advent of Vaughan Williams's Housman cycle *On Wenlock Edge*, first performed at the Aeolian Hall on 15 November 1909. It was at this very juncture that Harty's songs shifted away from the one-dimensional model of the ballad to something more intricate, inventive and emotionally complex. *By the Sea*, an unpublished song 'written for some particular person whose name I have forgotten' (as Harty wrote on the title page of the manuscript), has a simple stanzaic structure, but its melodic character and harmonic idiom are much more typical of his orchestral voice (the accompaniment of the second verse is markedly orchestral in texture), as is the decorative filigree and homespun Irish disposition of the rhythmical figurations. A folk-like spirit, replete with the physical 'swing', permeates *Scythe Song*. Fashioned in the mould of those traditional songs based on repetitive actions, Harty's nimble accompaniment of arpeggiated decoration cleverly simulates the back-and-forth motion of the scythe, itself a symbol of hazy June days seen through the eyes of a waking girl. The two verses are simple enough in their tonal scheme – tonic, dominant and subdominant – but it is the more sensuous, chromatic progressions of the cadence, where the voice coyly rises a semitone to the tonic, that gives the song special character – that and the delicious 'scherzando' of the postlude, where Harty's Irish fingerprint of the flattened seventh locates the song somewhere in an Ulster cornfield.

Although the *Ode to a Nightingale* must count as the high point of Harty's extensive collaboration with Nicholls, their work together in London recitals and provincial music societies also produced the little-known and unpublished set of three songs entitled *Three Sea Prayers from the Greek Anthology* which are dated, respectively, 13, 14 and 15 October 1909 and were taken from the recently published revision of J. W. Mackail's *Select Epigrams from the Greek Anthology* (1906). These three musically substantial items were first given by Nicholls and Harty at a recital at the Bechstein Hall on 16 November 1909 (along with three new songs by Parry: *Nightfall in Winter, One Silent Light of Late* and *From a City Window*). The first, 'To the Gods of Harbour and Headland', was by Antiphilus. Cast in A major, the expressive mood is marked by melancholy introspection, the characteristic opening progression harking back to the rich romanticism of the slow movement of the Second String Quartet. Yet the dense, chromatic voice-leading of much of the song is suggestive of Harty's interest in Richard Strauss and of that composer's post-Wagnerian language of immensely elaborate polyphony. Indeed, there is something of the orchestra in Harty's piano, but the languid trills, impressionistic washes of sound, and carefully situated moments of sumptuous texture are nevertheless appositely calculated for accompaniment at the keyboard. Leonid of Tarentum's 'Saved by Faith' is a graceful scherzo in F, whose whimsicality (personified throughout by a matrix of lower chromatic neighbour notes) is derived from the 'little boat's' faith in the gods and their ability to see it safely from one port to another. Harty's gossamer accompaniment, another of his most idiomatic creations, is a model of invention, particularly in the capricious coda. The last song of the set, 'To Apollo of Leucas' by Philippus, continues the trend of exploration, not least in its extensive use of chromatic harmony. Conceived on a grand scale – the piano accompaniment is an immense undertaking – the song has an almost operatic swagger, its long, architectural, prose-like lines suggestive of the strenuous vocal declamation of the Wagnerian music drama so closely associated with Nicholls's capacious vocal technique (Example 10). Indeed, Harty had at first envisaged the final climax of a top A, held for four bars, but eventually considered (rightly) that the gesture was excessive. (It was eventually reduced to half a bar and a short piano postlude.)

Critical reception of these unusual pieces was mixed. The songs elicited praise from the critic of *The Times* for being 'strong, melodious, and written with a fine feeling for climax', especially 'To Apollo', which was, incidentally, perceived as being Harty's 'first step (on paper at any rate) in the direction of the modern French school'.[55] But the *Times* critic was less enthusiastic about the choice of poetry, largely because it elicited a version which was unfamiliar:

> ... if the Anthology is to be used in this way, it must be used with discrimination, and neither Philippus's prayer to Phoebus, nor Antiphilus's prayer to the gods of the harbour and headland are really suitable for music, and even the epigram of Leonidas of Tarentum about the little boat is not really lyrical. Besides even if one avoids the gnomic, reflective, and declamatory poems and chooses only the epigrams of Meleager, or the lyrical writers, they should be set in verse and not in prose, not even in Mr Mackail's, for although prose may be lyrical it cannot be lyrical in the same way or convey the same sort of impression as the verse original.[56]

By contrast, the critic of the *Guardian* perceived them as 'fine studies in atmosphere' showing great imagination, finding criticism only in that with contemporary songs 'the interest is almost always in the piano part rather than the voice. But when the piano is played as Mr Harty plays it, that is not as much to be regretted as it would be in ordinary circumstances. Indeed his playing was as perfect in the way as Miss Nicholls's singing.'[57]

The *Three Prayers* are preludial to an even more impressive corpus of songs that Harty wrote during the years immediately before the First World War. His *Five Irish Sketches* (written for Swinton and, according to the *Observer*, styled by the composer 'duets for voice and piano' owing to their substantial piano parts),[58] and two others – *A Rann of Wandering* and *A Wake Feast* – again using texts by Irish authors, are among his most fertile inventions for voice and piano. All seven were eventually published individually by Novello in 1913 and 1914. Three of the *Irish Sketches* drew texts from Padraic Colum's collection of poems *Wild Earth*, which had been published in 1907. It is unlikely that Harty

[55] *The Times*, 17 Nov. 1909.
[56] *The Times*, 17 Nov. 1909.
[57] *MG*, 18 Nov. 1909.
[58] *The Observer*, 5 Nov. 1911.

Example 10 *Three Sea Prayers from the Greek Anthology* (iii),
'To Apollo of Leucas', conclusion

Oct 15th 1909

new Colum personally at this time,[59] but his continuing interest in the poetry of
Seosamh MacCathmhaoil (whose popular collection of poems, *The Mountainy
Singer*, Harty had obtained after its publication in 1909) suggests that he retained
a major interest in F. J. Bigger's 'salon' in Belfast with which Colum, born in

[59] A letter from Harty to Colum of 9 August 1914 (*US-NYp*, Berg Collection)
suggests that a proposed rendezvous in Dublin may have been the first time they
met.

Co. Longford, had a close connection.[60] By 1911, when Harty had completed the songs for Swinton to perform (he had acquired his own copy of *Wild Earth* when it was published in a later edition of 1909),[61] Colum had acquired a reputation as a playwright for the Irish Literary Theatre and the Abbey Theatre, as well as for his potent nationalist views, articulated politically in his first play *The Saxon Shillin'* of 1902, and culturally through his membership of the Gaelic League and his links with nationalist writers such as Yeats, Lady Gregory, Thomas McDonagh and Æ, not to mention a close association with James Joyce. His play *Thomas Muskerry*, of 1910, also attracted negative criticism for its gloomy, pessimistic portrayal of Irish life. There is something of this Ibsenite darkness in 'A Drover', which tells of the hardship of an Irish farmer driving his cattle to Meath across the harsh, boggy country of the counties of Leitrim and Longford (well-known to the poet), yet a comparison with the life of a soldier, who has seen much of the world, nevertheless suggests that freedom, however poor, is better than the tyranny of the 'captain's commands'.

This austerity is reflected in the rugged, ponderous nature of Harty's marching rhythms in the prelude to his song, and the strange, ascetic harmonic progressions, full of chromatic interpolations and augmented triads, aptly conjure up a world of endless toil and physical fatigue. The part-stanzaic impression of Harty's structure, engendered by repeated recurrences of the opening material in C minor ('To Meath of the pastures') underscores this sense of drudgery, but Harty's organisation of Colum's nine verses is conceived as a bipartite structure in which the first five verses form the initial section, and the last four a shorter second. Even more striking are the conclusions to each section. In the first, at the crucial point of the poet's comparison ('O! farmer, strong farmer / You can spend at the fair'), Harty shifts cleverly to F major, and, ending the verse in this tonality, heightens the song's underlying sense of questioning. Reverting initially to the grim tread of the C minor material ('O! the smell of the beasts') at the beginning of the second section, Harty's repeated move to F ('O! strong men with your best'), replete with a violent outburst ('I could quiet your herds / With my words') marked 'wild' by the composer, would seem to suggest a similar conclusion, yet this time it is truncated to form a transition to C major where a becalmed, softer, Elgarian diatonicism evokes the promise of a better life. Such a tonal move would ordinarily close off the musical structure, but Harty's *coup de maître* resides in a most unexpected additional modulation

---

[60] Harty's copy of *The Mountainy Singer* survives at *GB-Belqb*.

[61] Harty's copy of Colum's *Wild Earth* can be found at *GB-Belqb*. Perhaps fuelled by the desire to write more songs during this pre-war period, Harty clearly showed a considerable appetite for Irish poetry and literature from both sides of the political divide. Besides his volumes of Campbell and Colum, he obtained copies of Emily Lawless's *With the Wild Geese* (1902), McDonagh's *April and May with Other Verses* (1903), O'Byrne's *The Lane o' the Thrushes* (1905), Moira O'Neill's *The Ould Lad* (1906), Alice Milligan's *Hero Lays* (1908), Helen Lanyon's *The Hill o'Dreams and Other Verses* (1909), W. B. Yeats's *The Wind Among the Reeds* (1911), J. M. Synge's *The Well of the Saints* (1912), W. M. Letts's *Songs from Leinster* (1914), and James Stephens's *Songs from the Clay* (1915). All are now housed at *GB-Belqb*.

to E ('But you'll think of scant croppings / Harsh with salt from the sea.'), an extraordinary and apposite gesture which symbolises that deeper spiritual relationship between the farmer and his land, and, for all its abrasive harshness, the sense of identity and belonging.

'Across the Door' is an altogether more erotic utterance which narrates, from a woman's perspective, how she is symbolically carried across the threshold, an act highly emblematic of the first experience of carnal love and the loss of virginity. The through-composed structure of Harty's song narrates these events with striking clarity. The first part, replete with 'open-string' drones and a fiddle tune, portrays the simple pleasures of the dance. In marked contrast, the second part, which is approached by way of a series of mystical chromatic progressions, embarks from the dominant of F sharp, a world away from the C major of the dance floor. As a sensuous portrayal of Colum's erotically charged lines ('Ah! strange were the dim, wide meadows'), this distant tonality is accompanied by descending parallel seventh chords, thoroughly reminiscent of Debussy, and the harmonic reference to this composer becomes even more intense with the colourful return to C via its sensuous and hushed dominant ninth. The highly suggestive climax, again on the dominant of C ('And they making *cry*!'), is further intensified by the piano's dissonant, chromatic elaboration which, in its textural placing for the hands, is distinctly evocative of Ravel. Harty's thoroughly pregnant dominant harmony is then powerfully resolved in the last ten bars where, in returning to the composer's more familiar late nineteenth-century Romantic palette, the sense of longing and sexual pleasure (and not a little nostalgia – Harty marks the closing bars 'Sadly') is somewhat redolent of *The Ode to a Nightingale* in its sense of languorous delight. Interestingly, Bax's setting of the same text in his *Five Irish Songs* of 1921 adopts a very similar rhetorical formula, the only difference residing in his denser chromatic harmony and the somewhat quizzical closing harmonic gesture of an unresolved dominant ninth.

The third setting of Colum, 'A Cradle Song', recounts the tale of the shepherds at the nativity and their entrance to the humble stable. It is a text that has now become familiar, principally through its setting by Herbert Hughes in his *Songs of Connacht* of 1913 (a collection of nine songs to poems by Colum), Arnold Bax's sumptuous setting in *Three Irish Songs* (all settings of Colum) of 1922, and by the much later 'carol' setting of Arnold Cooke (*O Men from the Fields*) written for Oxford University Press's hugely successful *Carols for Choirs* of 1961. Harty's song appears to have been the first composed, and in keeping with the simple nature of the genre of Irish 'hush song', it follows an uncomplicated stanzaic design (eliding Colum's four verses into two). Yet Harty's skilful handling of the largely diatonic fabric allows the tonality to fluctuate between A (the final tonic) and D. This relationship is enshrined in the plagal opening of the song, and the significance of D minor is accentuated by its use at the close of each stanza. Yet, in each case, it is nevertheless a passing tonality, a fact radiantly emphasised by the final plagal cadence and *tierce de Picardie* in A, whose effect is nothing short of transcendental.

For the last two remaining songs from the *Irish Sketches* Harty resorted to authors he knew well already. Emily Lawless's grim poem *A Stranger's Grave*, is set 'in a graveyard upon Inishmaan, dedicated to unbaptised babies' where, nearby, 'an unknown drowned man lies buried'. The backdrop of Inishmaan (or Inis Meáin in the Irish) was well known to Lawless, who, 'discovering' the island well before Synge, spent much time in the small Irish-speaking community of the middle of the three main Aran islands, as is evident from her important proto-feminist novel *Grania*, of 1892. The atmosphere of lament in Harty's interpretation is utterly desolate, for at the heart of Lawless's bleak verse are both tragic sentiments of infant mortality and the loneliness of anonymous death. Cast in G minor, the text is interspersed by a plaintive, modal chorale (one that looks forward many years to *The Children of Lir*) which sets the mournful, quasi-religious tone. A further frame is created by the refrain, 'Little feet too young and soft to walk', which heads and closes the song, and whose lines, characterised by an almost folk-like declamation, are coloured by a solemn vein of Neapolitan harmony. The two verses, one agitated to reflect the windswept landscape, the other (in C) in more tender mood, share a common refrain ('O plotting brain and restless heart of mine') which reverts to G minor and which, like the outer refrains, is similarly inflected with Neapolitan colour. This is a powerful, original miniature essay with an equally interesting and varied musical structure, one that is enhanced by Harty's rich harmonic resources and, to judge by the moving recording made of the song by the eighty-year-old Isobel Baillie in 1974, its vivid, pictorial accompaniment. As for Moira O'Neill's 'The Rachray Man', it would appear, at first glance, to be an entertaining and lively 'hop jig' in much the same tradition as other Irish 'patter' songs of the period; but a closer look reveals – below the 'rueful humour' which Swinton no doubt portrayed with her usual élan – a darker tale of a woman destined for marriage (and a hard life) on the desolate Rathlin Island (off the coast of Ulster and the northernmost point of Northern Ireland), but determined to escape it in spite of the social and personal consequences.

In addition to the *Irish Sketches*, which drew critical acclaim from the press, Harty produced three other songs of earnest demeanour between 1912 and 1914. His love affair with Colum's *Wild Earth* continued with *A Rann of Wandering*, a rather simpler song of largely unchanging strophes, with a text extolling the joys of the open air, of country life and the popular Irish celebration of St Bride's Day (the beginning of spring). Important here is the controlled, lyrical disposition of the melody and its gradual upward trend to the climax on F sharp in the mediant (D major), an event which, each time, points to important words in the poem ('the *fires* will be piled high' in verse 1, and, even more notably, 'and my *heart* was ever lifted' in verse 2). Harty's introspective interpretation contrasts markedly with Bax's (from *Three Irish Songs*), where there is a much greater air of personal confidence in the broad march-like rhythms and muscular harmony.

More in the vein of Lawless's *A Stranger's Grave* is *The Wake Feast*, another thoroughly Irish subject, but in the poem of the Omagh-born poetess and playwright Alice Milligan, there is no hint of festivity, only the anguished cry of a farm labourer, and his undeclared, secret love for, as the poem's subtitle reads, 'a young girl dead'. A common theme in Irish poetry (take O'Neill's *Denny's Daughter*, which explores the same sense of loss), it is nevertheless expressed here with a particularly acute bitterness, a mood captured in the threnody-like monotony of the piano accompaniment, the free, speech-like declamation stipulated by the composer, and the descending chromatic lines, redolent of old baroque laments, while the musical construction of the song, which contrasts suffering in the D minor of the first three verses with the tenderness of D major in the fourth ('She was my secret love'), deftly elides the material of both sections in the last two verses.

One other song, *By the Bivouac's Fitful Flame*, a setting of Whitman's poem from *Leaves of Grass*, stands apart from the strongly Irish disposition of so much of Harty's choice of poetry, and reflects the composer's passion for the American's work.[62] Published in 1912, it was first sung by Swinton the following year (see above) and was one of several Whitman works, inspired by the American Civil War, that occupied the composer at this time. Indeed, one senses that this song was in some way a 'study' for Harty's large-scale Whitman essays, which manifested themselves in choral form with orchestra. Certainly, *By the Bivouac's Fitful Flame* reveals a quite different sub-genre of song style-forms, its emphasis on drama suggesting instead a miniature 'scena' with the piano mimicking an orchestral accompaniment. The dramatic nature of the song's ternary structure is enhanced both by the solemn, chorale-like material which functions as a bold frame for the more tonally fluid central paragraph (itself a skilful manipulation of a prolongation of an augmented sixth on B), and by the variation of Harty's vocal delivery which, in keeping with the freedom of Whitman's prose, fluctuates between lyricism and declamation. Harty's drama, moreover, is not stereotypically characterised by strident, extrovert gestures; rather, conversely, the stress is placed on an 'internal' mood of reflection and mystery, conveyed by restrained dynamics and the underplaying of structural events such as the controlled reprise ('While wind in procession thoughts') and the hushed conclusion.

The incipient success of conducting in London and Bournemouth, as well as directing the *Ode to a Nightingale* in Cardiff, undoubtedly fuelled Harty's desire to reinforce his connections with London's orchestral world. As he intimated many years later, one means of gaining experience on the rostrum was through the performance of his own works, and a golden opportunity presented itself with the production of a newly completed Violin Concerto written for the sixteen-year-old prodigy Joseph Szigeti. Szigeti had recently come to England – his first major foreign tour – after his studies with Jenő Hubay in Budapest, and, having established his residence with a benevolent, music-loving couple in Surrey, he proceeded to participate in many of London's chamber concerts. Harty came down to Surrey on several occasions in order to rehearse the Concerto with Szigeti.[63] For the young Hungarian virtuoso it was the first time

[62] Harty also produced a song with words by Riccardo Stephens, *To the King*, for piano and organ obbligato during the Coronation year of 1911. It was published by Chappell, but Harty had a low opinion of the piece and later requested its withdrawal from the catalogue.

[63] Joseph Szigeti, *With Strings Attached: Reminiscences and Reflections* (London: Cassell, 1949), 77.

he had collaborated with a living composer – there would be countless more – and he was clearly proud of the dedication 'To Joska Szigeti, in Friendship' which marked this important stage in his career. Szigeti recalled his first encounters with Harty during their preparations for the Concerto's first performance:

> Harty was then – around 1908 – England's premier accompanist; and my working at his manuscript concerto, with him at the piano coaxing out of his instrument all the orchestral colour which he had dreamed into his score, was probably decisive in forming what a long-suffering and excellent pianistic partner of mine later on termed my 'expensive tastes' in accompanying.
>
> This concerto, which I played a number of times in London, and elsewhere under Sir Henry Wood, Sir Landon Ronald, and others, gradually found its way into the repertory of other violinists too, mostly Anglo-Saxons. I had the somewhat 'paternal' – or, rather, 'godfatherly' – satisfaction of hearing the still disarmingly charming work, more than a quarter of a century after my introducing it, in an excellent broadcast performance by the BBC Symphony Orchestra under Sir Adrian Boult, with Paul Beard as soloist. Some years later, in January, 1944, to be precise, it had its first New York performance – thirty-five years after I had premièred it – at Mishel Piastro's recital, with piano accompaniment.
>
> It was the first new work I carried across the Channel, playing it in Budapest and also in Cologne under Fritz Steinbach, the famous Brahms interpreter.[64]

The Concerto was in fact premiered by Maria de Chastain, who played it at Bournemouth under Harty's direction on 18 March 1909 in the same programme as the much admired 'Irish' Symphony.[65] Szigeti's London premiere took place a few days later, on 24 March at Queen's Hall in one of Landon Ronald's New Symphony Orchestra concerts (which also featured Elgar's still novel First Symphony). The reception was encouraging:

> Mr Harty has so many ideas of good quality, and such skill and ingenuity in developing them, that there is no need for him to meddle with the accepted forms, and his work is accordingly clear, straightforward, and interesting from beginning to end. There is a pleasant flavour of the more romantic side of Irish music in the beautiful slow movement, and the subject of the last movement starts as if an imitation of an Irish jig were intended; this soon yields to something of greater musical importance and an earnestness that is in keeping with the style of the opening movement, a solid and admirably constructed piece of work. There are all sorts of clever touches in the scoring, but throughout we are never diverted from the design of the concerto by any orchestral tricks, such as are beloved by those whose invention is apt to run dry. There is a burlesque cadenza to introduce the last movement, from which a player more sure of himself and his audience will probably extract even more fun than M. Szigeti realized. The composer conducted a capital performance, and, with the soloist, was recalled many times.[66]

As Szigeti intimated, he performed the Harty Concerto numerous times. Two movements from the work featured in a recital (with Harty) at the Bechstein

---

[64] Szigeti, *With Strings Attached*, 108.
[65] Lloyd, *Sir Dan Godfrey*, 86.
[66] *The Times*, 25 Mar. 1909.

Hall in May 1909,[67] but its major launch took place with its appearance with Szigeti and Henry Wood at a Promenade Concert on 31 August, where, amid criticism of a lack of strong melodic material, the last movement was singled out as the most distinctive of the three for its Irish inflections.[68]

That Harty's terms of reference for his own violin concerto were those of the great German canon of Beethoven, Mendelssohn, Bruch and Brahms is indisputable, as is the shadow of Tchaikovsky's effulgent contribution to the genre. They, and less well-known Romantic concertos such as Dvořák's, Stanford's (given by Kreisler at Leeds in 1904), Glazunov's (premiered in London by Elman in 1906) or Mackenzie's fine Bruch-inspired work (which Harty played as accompanist),[69] were familiar repertoire to him, along with their rhetorical chemistry of lyricism and virtuoso display. Moreover, during its composition in 1908, with Szigeti as close advisor, this style of concerto was by no means in decline, as Elgar's Violin Concerto of 1910 attests, and it was the style of concerto, promulgated by Kreisler, Elman, Kubelik and others, that the Edwardian public knew and associated with the genre. As the critic of the *Observer* remarked:

> The work in question is frankly a violinist's concerto, which means that the musical material plays a subordinate part to technical writing for the instrument. If the work had been written by Vieuxtemps, every violinist would probably have it in his or her repertoire. The Rondo finale is the sort of thing that might have been written by Wieniawski: only it is much better done by Mr Harty.[70]

Harty's response may have been traditional, even conventional, in its approach to form and gesture, but his execution of its constituent parts was carried out with great panache and professionalism. The orchestral accompaniment, colourful, varied and beautifully balanced, has much that is original and creative in detail. In addition, while the solo writing exploits the range and sonority of the violin with a fresh and convincing elegance, there is also a somewhat unusual and distinctive 'Irish' nuance (and an oblique allusion to Irish fiddle-playing) which is engendered by an assimilation of dance characteristics (notably the reel), melodic decoration, modal progressions and a touch of bucolic 'abandon', all of which subtly adds an exotic tint to the broader European context of the style and syntax. In fact, the structural design of Harty's concerto reveals a work very much geared to the soloist rather than to the more probing symphonic conception of Brahms or Elgar, where the orchestra plays such an intrinsic musical role. This can be observed in the somewhat truncated developmental phases of the outer movements. Instead Harty relies heavily on the character of his 'closed forms' within his sonata schemes – that is, self-contained, voluptuous melodic paragraphs which are dominated by self-developing thematic processes. The lyrical second subject, in particular, is treated with great flair, especially on its return in the tonic major accompanied by muted strings. It was a feature of

[67] *The Times*, 7 May 1909.
[68] *The Times*, 2 Sept. 1909.
[69] *The Times*, 18 Feb. 1907.
[70] *The Observer*, 28 Mar. 1909.

the first movement much admired by Delius, who heard it broadcast in 1932: 'I heard your concerto ... for the first time and it seemed to me superbly played by Mr Barker. After a first hearing the first movement especially appealed to me with its touchingly beautiful second subject.'[71] Yet arguably the finest and most musically coherent and stylistically original movement of the concerto is the sweeping architecture of the 'Molto lento'. Here Harty exploits the lower strings (sul G and sul D) of the violin with much skill, and the delicate nuances of the divided violas and basses, 'con sordini', combined with the rubato of the probing, dark melody and decorative quintuplets, provide a telling pathos to the extended theme (Example 11). Moreover, after a brief Rimsky-like departure at the beginning of the central section, Harty carries his initial melodic expansion to even greater registral and expressive heights, interrupting it only with an eccentric transition back to the recapitulation, one that seems almost parenthetical in its role within the larger structure (a practice he may have gleaned from Elgar). The tranquil recapitulation derives its effect principally from Harty's deft scoring, but perhaps the most adroit touch is left for the closing bars where, in invoking the original low timbre of the solo violin, the composer seals the impression of the movement's broad arc-like shape.

Harty's love-affair with the violin continued in 1910 with his first significant arrangement of Handel, a venerated figure from his Hillsborough days to whom he would return again and again throughout his life as the subject of instrumental 'embellishment'. That year Schott published four pieces – 'Rigaudon', 'Arietta', 'Hornpipe' and 'Passacaglia' – which proved highly popular as recital 'lollipops' at the London Ballad Concerts at the Albert Hall and were a particular favourite of the violinist Isolde Menges. In 1920 Harty added three further movements – 'Polonaise', 'Siciliano' and 'Allegro giocoso'. These chamber arrangements naturally suited Harty's position as accompanist, but later, as his career became entirely occupied with the conductor's rostrum, he returned to this suite of pieces to arrange the 'Polonaise' (taken from Handel's Concerto Grosso, Op. 6 No. 3), the 'Arietta' (an arrangement of the aria 'Si che lieta goderò' from the opera *Rodrigo* and the 'Passacaglia' (the Passacaille from the last part of the overture to *Rodrigo*) for a variety of imaginative orchestrations which were published by Boosey and Hawkes in 1932.

In 1910 a number of new opportunities for Harty to pursue his goal as a conductor presented themselves. A concert given by the pre-eminent Belgian cellist Jean Gerardy, at Queen's Hall of 6 May, provided an opening to conduct a string orchestra made up of members of the Queen's Hall Orchestra,[72] and he directed similar forces at the Bechstein Hall for the violinist Henriette Schmidt in a performance of Haydn's Violin Concerto in G on 3 June.[73] These chances in London were important, but perhaps Harty's greatest advance in fortune came with the offer from Landon Ronald to share the conducting of an orchestra made up of London players for the Birmingham Promenade Concerts at the city's Theatre Royal. This was a month-long series of concerts organised

[71] Letter from Delius to Harty, 26 Feb. 1932, *GB-Belqb*.

[72] *The Times*, 9 May 1910.

[73] *The Times*, 4 June 1910.

Example 11 Violin Concerto, opening of second movement

by the Birmingham-based violinist Max Mossel,[74] intended to bring more live professional orchestral music to Birmingham and to rival those concerts of Wood in the capital. To begin with there was some hostility to the concerts from

[74] Harty, who had appeared with Mossel in Broadwood Concerts in London, retained a happy working relationship with him in Birmingham concerts, notably in Mossel's highly regarded 'Drawing Room' concerts at the Grosvenor Room, Grand Hotel, with Nicholls: see *MT* 52 (1911), 258.

local musicians, and attendance was mixed, save for the last concert which was sold out.[75] Nevertheless, the series enjoyed a certain financial success and the eighteen concerts divided between Ronald and Harty (which ran from 23 May until 11 June) drew approbation from critics, including the recently signed up music columnist of the *Birmingham Post*, Ernest Newman, as did the seventy-strong 'scratch' band (which included the clarinettist Charles Draper and a very young Archie Camden on the bassoon) and the solo violinists, among them Mossel, Antonietti and Szigeti.[76] The concert repertoire also, for the first time, gave Harty a period of time to establish an air of self-confidence. There was, rather like Wood's Promenade Concerts, a vein of popularity in the amount of Beethoven, Tchaikovsky and Wagner that filled the programmes, but there were novelties in the shape of Parry's recently revised Fourth Symphony (which Parry directed), Dukas's *L'Apprenti sorcier*, Debussy's *L'Après-midi d'un faune*, Harty's own 'Irish' Symphony, Bantock's *The Pierrot of the Minute*, the tone poem *The Mystic Trumpeter* by the American Frederick Converse, and an entire programme of Elgar's works, conducted by the composer. Although Ronald thought the concerts might cease,[77] Mossel mustered a guarantee fund for the following year, which offered a further opportunity for Harty, as assistant (and accompanist) to Ronald, to consolidate his experience and also to acquaint himself with an even more ambitious programme of new works by British composers. Among the concerts was a special choral one for Coronation Day.[78] As Ronald commented:

> The programme soon developed from being mostly popular to comprising all the best classical and modern music. Gradually and surely the concerts drew bigger and bigger audiences, and they were at the zenith when the World War broke out and they automatically ceased. I have never spent happier times in my life than I did during those three weeks every year conducting Promenade concerts at Birmingham, surrounded as I was by friends … loving the work and loving my public.[79]

Harty would continue to conduct for the Birmingham concerts until the outbreak of war.

His other main chance to conduct in 1910 was through a second commission from the Cardiff Festival. On this occasion he completed a purely orchestral work, the tone poem (or, to use Harty's exact subtitle 'Poem for Orchestra') *With the Wild Geese*, based, once again, on Emily Lawless's eponymous collection of poems of 1902. In many ways this work sought to expand on the theme of exile which had inspired Harty's first major orchestral essay. This is evident from the two poems in Lawless's collection which the composer quoted at the head of his autograph manuscript and the published score of 1912, which had a brief preface. In this short preamble Harty detailed the significance of the 'Wild Geese,' a

[75] Ronald, *Myself and Others*, 47–50.

[76] *MT* 51 (1910), 447. Camden had joined the Hallé Orchestra in 1906.

[77] Ronald, *Myself and Others*, 50.

[78] *MT* 52 (1911), 473.

[79] Ronald, *Myself and Others*, 52–3.

disparate band of soldiers of the Irish Jacobite army who, after the Williamite War in Ireland, were allowed to leave for France after the Battle of Aughrim and the surrender of Limerick in 1691 (an event that is popularly known in Ireland as the 'Flight of the Wild Geese').[80] As part of the French army, the Irish regiments distinguished themselves at the Battle of Fontenoy in 1745 (during the War of the Austrian Succession), and took a substantial share of the battle's high casualties. Afterwards legend has it that the Irish dead arose and sailed home all through the night to their beloved country, a myth which is effectively framed by the quotation of Lawless's two poems *Before the Battle; Night* and *After the Battle; Early Dawn, Clare Coast*. The 'action' described in Lawless's texts to a large extent dictate the programme.

Though programmatic in spirit, Harty's structure is essentially a sonata. With the exception of the open-ended introduction, the constituent parts of the sonata scheme are, however, distinctly 'closed' in design and mark off the programmatic events with clarity and vividness. The opening of *With the Wild Geese* must be one of the most impressive and moving statements of any Romantic tone poem. A bold, noble fanfare, articulated by a strong yet oblique set of diatonic progressions, sets the scene, which is vibrantly contrasted with a 'wind-swept' sequential series of progressions supporting one of many synthetic strains of Irish melody (Example 12). This reveals an orchestral palette of tremendous dexterity and skill, and a symphonic fluency heavily influenced by the self-developing precedent of Tchaikovsky (notably *Romeo and Juliet*), features which distinguish this orchestral essay as a thoroughly mature example of Harty's ability as an orchestral composer. The rallying 'cry of exile' established in the introduction – representing, according to Harty's own programme note, the soldiers' farewell to Ireland – is answered by the 'weary march' mentioned at the very beginning of Lawless's first poem ('Oh bad the march, the weary march, beneath these alien skies') – a depiction of the life of the Irish soldier abroad. Cast in E minor, this is the first of several self-contained sections. The antecedent part of the march theme (presented appropriately on 'fife-like' flutes and piccolo) is derived from a glossary of well-tried 'Irish' melodic components, but the consequent part is much more spacious and rhythmically varied, its chromatic progressions reflecting something of Harty's assimilation of Tchaikovskian harmony (especially the abundant use of augmented sixths) and that composer's preference for autonomous paragraphs of extended melodic treatment. E minor yields to an episode (effectively the second subject) in C major which attempts, with its lyrical outpouring, to capture the exiles' nostalgic memories of Ireland ('Oh little Corca Bascinn, the wild, the bleak, the fair!'). This is another 'Irish' song, a homespun air, which Harty develops into a fully blown symphonic essay. Moreover, its orchestral colours by now bear

---

[80] Lawless's poems are more specific in identifying the men of Corca Bascinn and the Clare Brigade. The term 'Wild Geese' refers more generally in Irish history to soldiers who fought in continental Europe during the sixteenth, seventeenth and eighteenth centuries for several nations. Recruitment for foreign armies ceased in 1745 after an Irish detachment from the French army was used to support the Jacobite rebellion in Scotland.

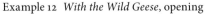

Example 12 *With the Wild Geese*, opening

Harty's firm stylistic imprint, namely the initial cor anglais solo with strings and harp, the elaborate wind filigree, the characteristic doublings of flute, oboe and clarinet, and the use of the brass and wind 'chorale' (so distinctive in the *Comedy Overture*).

At the conclusion of the well-defined exposition Harty makes reference briefly to the 'march' theme, now in C minor, which concludes with a trumpet solo signalling the bugle's 'lights out'. This is followed by a new thematic episode in A flat marked 'quasi un Nottorno' in place of the regular development, portraying the night before the battle and the passionate, restless dreams of the soldiers ('Vain dream, and foolish waking, we shall never see Clare'). Like the material of the Piano Quintet's slow movement, this 'Irish' melody, introduced on a solo viola (surely another biographical touch) and oboe, makes fertile use of the flattened seventh as part of its singing phrases, particularly in the bass clarinet's final gesture at the end; and much of the melodic decoration is suggestive of the *sean nós* tradition (Example 13). Equally effective, too, is Harty's use of melodic sequence (reminiscent perhaps of the 'cry of exile' of the opening), the chamber-music intimacy of the scoring, and the affecting use of countermelody in the trumpet. In the half-light of morning Harty paints an impression of ghostly mists with the bass clarinet and horns, before the return of the waking 'bugle' call, now more strident in the expectation of battle; in the charge that follows, Harty skilfully effects a return to E minor for a bolder reprise of the march theme. More tonally fluid and thematically developed than before, the first subject portrays the clamour and confusion of battle. As the fighting ceases, a cry of anguish is declaimed by a solo clarinet as it announces the second subject, couched unexpectedly in D major. In this more wistful version, rescored for strings and replete with 'parenthetical' comments from the wind, Harty skilfully uses the need to return to the tonic, E major, to introduce a sequence of modulations, each indicated by grandiose Straussian 6/4 chords. At the same time, the original spirit of yearning is now transformed into one of exhilaration as the spirits of the soldiers return homewards to Co. Clare, a triumphal scene ultimately reserved for the seascape of the coda (in keeping with Lawless's second poem), where the 'rallying cry' of the opening is recalled in a Tchaikovskian paean of liberation and joy.

With the Wild Geese was first performed at Cardiff on 23 September 1910 and was an instant success, one critic observing the noble Irish sentiment as a feature which '[marked] it apart from all that Mr Bernard Shaw tears to tatters in the first act of "John Bull's other Island".'[81] It was also commended by the *Manchester Guardian*, which praised Harty's 'spirited and authoritative conducting' as well as the lucidity of the score. 'It is a work', the critic affirmed, 'which ought not to be relegated to the shelf on which so many novelties repose.'[82] Only a few weeks after its premiere the tone poem was given by the Liverpool Philharmonic Society on 8 November conducted by Cowen; Harty, who was present, received an ovation. Then, on 20 March 1911, the work was included in a programme given by the LSO, an orchestra which had been founded by Hans Richter, its principal conductor, in 1904. Through the offices of Agnes Nicholls, who was of course close to Richter as a performer and colleague, Harty was given the opportunity to conduct his own work. It was an auspicious occasion, for not only did it mark the beginning of Harty's long and profitable association with the LSO, but it also signalled an important transition from a senior conductor to a junior, for

[81] *MT* 51 (1910), 719.

[82] *MG*, 21 March 1911.

Example 13 *With the Wild Geese*, 'quasi un Notturno'

Richter was soon to retire from the concert platform.[83] Harty maintained that, through Richter, who lent him his own scores of Wagner's works, he developed his own knowledge, love and devotion to the German's masterpieces.[84] Moreover, Harty found himself for the first time rubbing shoulders with such other prominent conductors as Beecham, Elgar, Nikisch, Safonov and Koussevitzky.

In terms of his reputation and career as a composer and conductor, the period between 1911 and 1914 represented an important tipping-point, one that was also assisted by his being taken under the wing of London's most prestigious agents, Ibbs and Tillett. Besides his appearance with the LSO, Harty was invited to Bournemouth again, this time to direct *With the Wild Geese* on 11 May. Godfrey evidently admired Harty's work, and had recently revived his Violin Concerto with the violinist Grace Triggs during the season of 1910–11. Shortly before this Harty was called upon by the LSO to conduct an unusual programme of music by the Polish pianist and composer Jules Wertheim, which included his Symphony in E minor and the Rhapsody for Piano and Orchestra. More auspicious, however, at this point was the announcement that, along with Elgar, Mackenzie, Parry, German, Wood and Coleridge-Taylor, Harty was selected to conduct one of the nine concerts with the LSO scheduled for the Festival of Empire at the Crystal Palace. The 'Irish Day' on 4 July included his own *Comedy Overture*, but there were also songs by Stanford, sung by Plunket Greene and O'Mara, Stanford's *Irish Rhapsody* No. 1 (a work Harty greatly admired and would conduct many times), and Sullivan's overture *Di ballo* and the suite from *The Merchant of Venice*. This concert undoubtedly helped to secure his increasing stature as a conductor of national standing.

On 7 September 1911 Harty's *Three Pieces* for oboe were first performed in their orchestrations by the composer at a Promenade Concert under Wood's direction, played by de Busscher, an important pioneer in the development of oboe repertoire, well-known for his singing tone, warm vibrato, expressive phrasing and delicate fingerwork, and a major influence on the young Léon Goossens. The first of the pieces, 'Orientale', presents a haunting, Caucasian picture influenced by sounds of Mussorgsky and Rimsky-Korsakov (composers relatively little known to the London public at that time), a sound world enhanced by the striking juxtaposition of G minor and B flat minor triads at the opening, and by the florid, modal oboe triplet figurations strongly reminiscent of *Scheherazade*, a work which had recently been popularised in Michael Fokine's choreography with the London debut of the Russian Ballet in June under Beecham's baton.[85] Already featuring in the Finale of his Piano Quintet, this was a style that Harty would return to on several occasions in his orchestral and theatre music. A central section in the tonic major (G major), more rustic in character and more

[83] The programme of the LSO concert actually announced Richter's retirement at the concert on 20 March 1911, though Richter gave two further concerts before he stood down on 10 April.

[84] *Melbourne Herald*, 23 May 1934.

[85] J. Lucas, *Thomas Beecham: An Obsession with Music* (Woodbridge: Boydell Press, 2008), 77–8.

eccentric in its arresting series of modulations, exploits the oboe as mimetic of the old shawm in a lively bucolic dance redolent perhaps of d'Indy or Déodat de Sévérac. The French spirit continues in 'Chansonette', a piece in which Harty clearly exploited de Busscher's ability to sustain long phrases with an expressive sense of 'cantabile',[86] and in the graceful 'À la campagne', a simple ternary dance requiring some dexterity in the pastoral 'trio musette', evocative perhaps of an idealised rural Brittany.

Harty began 1912 with another important appearance with the LSO. With Richter's retirement, the orchestra appointed Elgar as their principal conductor, but among the guest conductors (Safonov, Mengelberg, Steinbach and Doret) there was also room for Harty to conduct *With the Wild Geese* for a second time on 29 January 1912. This performance came only a few weeks before the realisation of another important commission, the incidental music to the play *Proud Maisie* by the well-known barrister and politician Edward G. Hemmerde, which opened at the Aldwych Theatre on 12 March.[87] The play, a romance written in verse, is a tragedy set during the 1745 Jacobite Rebellion at Pitcour Castle, based on the 'Proud Maisie' of Walter Scott's well-known poem. During a 'revel' at the castle Bonny Prince Charlie appears to fuel the fervour of those sponsoring the rebellion. Neil McAlpine, a stalwart supporter of King George, raises a solitary dissenting voice, only to be denounced as a Hanoverian spy by young Guy, Lord Monteith, Lady Maisie's brother; he challenges McAlpine, an able swordsman, to a duel. However, a major complication arose because of Maisie's love for McAlpine. Divided cruelly between love and duty, she loved McAlpine but could not bring herself to marry a traitor to her cause. Hearing of the duel, Lord Pitcour forbade his son to fight and locked the gates of the castle to prevent him from leaving, but Maisie, eager to maintain the honour of her brother, donned the kilt in imitation of her brother, scaled the walls of the castle and died in the ensuing duel. McAlpine, discovering the true identity of his victim, chose to take his own life and fell beside her.

Harty provided appropriate 'Caledonian' music for the play (an idiom with which, by his own admission, he was familiar from his boyhood) and furnished several substantial and carefully composed items. While the pentatonic material of the overture may remind us of pages from MacCunn's *The Land of the Mountain and the Flood*, Harty's effort is much more enterprising, especially in the tonally fluid restatement of the first subject which travels from G major, via B flat, F, and A flat, to E major, before the tonic, A major, is re-established for the lyrical secondary idea. The first of the two *entr'actes* is a lyrical rondo, using a gentle hymn-like section in A major for strings (rhythmically akin to the famous melody from Schubert's *Rosamunde*) as the central theme, and containing luxuriant episodes which surely depict the conflicted love of Maisie and McAlpine. For the second *entr'acte*, an attractive contrast of lively Scottish

---

[86] While the orchestrations of 'Orientale' and 'À la campagne' have survived, the score of 'Chansonette' is missing.

[87] It is not clear whether Harty conducted his incidental score to *Proud Maisie*, though it was customary for the composer to conduct at least the first night of the production before the 'in house' conductor took over.

dances, Harty found himself working within an idiom already familiar from the Scherzo of his 'Irish' Symphony. Two miniatures, a courtly 'Minuetto' used in Act II and a drinking song called 'The White Cockade', come before a third *entr'acte* which takes the form of a funeral march in C minor, an impressive, brooding piece accentuated by the initial scoring for divided violas, cellos and basses. Harty also took the opportunity to recall music from the overture in the trio in A flat; while in the Interlude between the first two scenes of Act IV, thematic resonances of his earlier tone poem permeate music of striking passion and nobility.

Proud Maisie ran until 19 May 1912. A curious period piece rich in dialect, the play's romantic setting held a certain fascination for its audience, particularly with Alexandra Carlisle in the role of Lady Maisie. The critic of *The Times* glibly described Harty's score as 'conventionally Caledonian',[88] yet this underestimated the quality of the orchestral music which, though indebted to *With the Wild Geese*, has much to rival it in terms of its more subtle assimilation of the folk idiom into an entirely Continental romantic idiom. After the play closed Esposito conducted two of the *entr'actes* (unspecified) with the DOS in Dublin on 20 October 1912,[89] and the overture was recorded for BBC Radio 3 in December 1985 by the Ulster Orchestra under Yannis Daras. Much of the score, however, merits a hearing in the form of concert suite.

Three more works, two of them with a distinctively Irish flavour, were composed by Harty in 1912. A dance-like work for orchestra in C minor dated 'May 14 1912' survives complete in short score but was clearly abandoned by a dissatisfied composer.[90] An *Irish Fantasy* for violin and piano was written for and dedicated to his Irish friend and Professor of Violin at the RIAM P. J. Griffith, who performed it on 8 December at the Antient Concert Rooms during one of Esposito's Sunday Orchestral Concerts.[91] The third work, also for violin, completed on 1 September 1912, was his *Variations on a Dublin Air* (also known as *Variations on an Irish Air*). An orchestral introduction deploys an idea which Harty had originally employed in the opening bars of the first movement of his *Irish* Symphony, though this is contrasted by a much more doleful presentation of the Irish melody in which the wistful character of the solo violin is effectively exploited. The theme of the work is a well-known traditional Irish melody *The Pretty Milkmaid Milking her Cow* (also known as *The Valley Lay Smiling before Me*), an eighteenth-century ballad whose main English source is attributed to Thomas Moore's *Irish Melodies*. The melody, in ABA form, is presented in D minor in a slow tempo, though characterised by moments of rubato and spasmodic changes of tempo. The seven variations that follow are arranged with imaginative dexterity and in many ways constitute a miniature suite or 'serenade' of character pieces in their manipulation of tempo and rhetoric. The first two

[88] *The Times*, 13 Mar. 1912.

[89] *MT* 53 (1912), 740.

[90] Greer, 'Hamilton Harty Manuscripts', 251. See also *The Children of Lir* in Chapter 8.

[91] *IT*, 9 Dec. 1912. The *Irish Fantasy* was later recorded by Edith Kelly-Lange for HMV (B2419) in April 1927.

variations are faster in tempo – the first a scherzando in 9/8 aping a hop-jig, the second a rhythmically more dynamic reel – and constitute a first movement in the tonic. The more introspective third variation, in the submediant, B flat major, and marked 'Andantino', retains the ternary design of the theme, but includes a subtly crafted flatwise shift as part of the warmer emotional temperament engendered by the violin's Bruch-like lyrical demeanour. The delicate fourth variation, in B flat minor, is effectively an aphoristic scherzo, its creative hemiolas revealing a Brahmsian influence. To this variation Harty originally appended an orchestral fugato (in effect an additional eighth variation), but he marked a cut in the manuscript score (though when this was observed is not clear).[92] D minor is restored for Variation 5 which, as an elegant waltz, provides apt contrast with the initial dance movements and the succeeding Lento of Variation 6 in the tonic major. As the emotional climax of the work, and the one ultimately the most characteristic of the composer, this is cleverly underplayed by the sense of chamber intimacy (akin to the central song of *With the Wild Geese*), spawned by the medium of delicate contrapuntal lines provided by solo cello, horn and clarinet. Effective too is the role of the Lento as a prelude to the most extended movement of all, the Finale which, besides recalling the introduction, also apes the sense of 'concerto', with a cadenza (Variation 7) in D minor at the conclusion (which also acts as a counterweight to the cadenza-like material of the opening).

The *Variations* were first performed by Paweł Kochański with the LSO under Harty's baton, at Queen's Hall on 10 February 1913. A few months later Kochański played them a second time at the Bechstein Hall on 5 May with Harty at the piano. The critical reception was mixed. *The Times* was benevolent: 'There is a candour about Mr Hamilton Harty's music which earns good will.'[93] Only the violin cadenza was thought weak and out of place. However, the critic of the *Manchester Guardian* was unsympathetic to the idiom:

> ... to any modern the form of variations suggests exploitation of every resource of colour which can be got from the orchestra. To set a violinist to dominate the orchestra implies the shifting of the centre of interest from an instrument of almost unlimited variety of effects to an instrument in which the effects are strictly limited. For this reason one fears that these Variations will hardly have the success their careful and tasteful workmanship deserves.[94]

The Observer, on the other hand, was full of approbation for the way in which Harty had confounded the perceived contradiction of modernism, variation and folksong:

> It is really not the business of the young modern composer to entangle his creative abilities with the fallacious subtleties of primitive tune. The folk-song as an incentive to original or satisfactory composition has proven its uselessness

---

[92] The first performance, on 10 February 1913, did include the fugal movement, as is clear from the review in *The Times*, 11 February 1913.

[93] *The Times*, 6 May 1913.

[94] *MG*, 11 Feb. 1913.

time after time, and Mr Harty is clever and brilliant enough to discard such adventitious assistance to his creative talent'[95]

The performance of the *Variations* with the LSO was an important event, for it was in effect the first concert of *core* repertoire – Bach's Orchestral Suite No. 3, Strauss's *Don Juan* and Beethoven's Seventh Symphony – that Harty had undertaken. For many, Harty was still a familiar face as a guest conductor of his own music, and this impression would linger for some years, even though, by this stage, his orchestral works were being taken up avidly by professional and amateur orchestras throughout the land.[96]

Nevertheless, at the very point when Harty's conducting career seemed about to flourish, the LSO, at their Annual General Meeting in July 1913, announced that both the Elgar and Harty concerts had made a loss for the orchestra, so the directors had resolved to look elsewhere. Harty did make a request for another engagement, but this was turned down.[97] This was undoubtedly a setback for him, for, although he did continue to work with players from the LSO, it would be several years before he would again be engaged by the orchestra for their own concert seasons in London. Other welcome engagements did, however, present themselves. Mary Dickenson, the Irish violinist from the RIAM with whom Harty had worked in the past, appeared with the National Symphony Orchestra at Queen's Hall in a programme of Bruch's *Scottish Fantasy*, Saint-Saëns's *Rondo capriccioso* and Beethoven's Violin Concerto. On 7 March he conducted *With the Wild Geese* with the Hallé Orchestra in a programme otherwise undertaken by the orchestra's principal conductor Michael Balling, and in May he was invited up to Aberdeen to direct the instrumental part (which included Bach's Suite No. 2 in B minor and the string serenades by Elgar and Dvořák) of a concert staged by Professor Charles Sanford Terry's competitive festival.[98]

In August 1913, in connection with Stanley Cochrane's musical initiative at Woodbrook in Co. Wicklow, Harty was able to organise a week's tour for

[95] *The Observer*, 16 Feb. 1913. There is evidence from Harty's surviving sketches that he had designs on arranging the *Variations on a Dublin Air* for cello and orchestra, probably for W. H. Squire, to whom he had dedicated his early 'Two Pieces for Cello and Piano', *Waldesstille* and *Der Schmetterling*, of 1907. A short score exists of the opening forty-two bars at *GB-Belqb*: see Greer, 'Hamilton Harty Manuscripts', 243, 249.

[96] During 1912 the exposure of Harty's orchestral works expanded exponentially. *With the Wild Geese* was programmed in the last of Balfour Gardiner's concerts of music by younger British composers on 1 May with the New Symphony Orchestra (under Gardiner himself). Harty conducted the work at Bournemouth, and it was eagerly taken up by the amateur Strolling Players under John Ivemey in December. *A Comedy Overture* also remained a favourite of Henry Wood, who continued to conduct it at his Promenade Concerts, while Edgar Bainton, Principal of the Newcastle Conservatory, introduced it to the Newcastle Philharmonic Society, another enthusiastic amateur organisation.

[97] Hubert Foss and Noel Goodwin, *London Symphony: Portrait of an Orchestra* (London: The Naldrett Press, 1954), 75.

[98] *MT School Music Review Supplement* (July 1913), 3.

fifty-two players from the LSO to give a series of daily concerts.[99] Held between
11 and 16 August, six concerts took place at Woodbrook which featuresd not only
the orchestra but an array of distinguished soloists. The music of Wagner and
Tchaikovsky, two composers who always assured substantial audiences, were the
focus of two concerts,[100] while the others were given over to programmes of a
more contemporary nature. Having already conducted Strauss's *Don Juan* with
the orchestra, Harty included it along with Debussy's *L'Après-midi d'un faune* as
well as his own 'Irish' Symphony.[101] There were also several major core concertos:
Victor Love, one of Esposito's star pupils, played Rachmaninov's Second Piano
Concerto, W. H. Reed (leader of the LSO and a close associate of Elgar's)
appeared in Saint-Saëns's Third Violin Concerto, and the nineteen-year-old
violinist Isolde Menges, with whom Harty had recently worked in London, gave
performances of the Tchaikovsky and Mendelssohn Violin Concertos. Nicholls
and O'Mara also took parts as vocal soloists. Harty elicited lavish praise from
the Irish press. It was a rare opportunity for what the *Irish Times* affirmed to
be 'the best orchestra in the world' (even though the band was actually under
strength),[102] but in Harty, a son of Ireland, 'one was in the presence of a master
mind, full of grand conceptions and unflinching aims.'[103]

As an indication of Harty's established status as a composer, he received a
commission from Leeds to write a choral work for the 1913 festival. After the
1910 festival Stanford, who had been musical director of the last four, resigned
after it was made clear to him that the conducting of the 1913 festival would
be shared. Nikisch, Hugh Allen and Elgar were chosen as the three principal
conductors, and, knowing Elgar's interest in Harty's music, it may well have been
at his prompting that Harty was offered the commission. The poem ultimately
selected by Harty was Whitman's 'Mystic Trumpeter', a poem taken from the
American's *Whispers of Heavenly Death*. The score was completed in April 1913,
and the composer adjudged it his best effort yet. The title page of the manuscript
of the piano score bears a presentation note from Harty to Elsie Swinton: 'Dear
Elsie – I send you this original piano score of my best work, with my most
grateful thanks for your help in its composition.'[104] The choice of Whitman's
poetry clearly articulated Harty's considerable enthusiasm for the American's
verse at that time, as is also indicated by his setting of 'By the Bivouac's Fitful
Flame' (also from *Drum Taps*), of which Swinton was the prime executant.
Of course, Whitman had for many years been a favoured poet among British
composers, inspiring the composition of Stanford's *Elegiac Ode* (1884), Charles

[99] This Irish tour is briefly mentioned in Foss and Goodwin, *London Symphony*, 74,
but not in connection with Harty.

[100] *IT*, 13 Aug. 1913.

[101] *IT*, 15 Aug. 1913.

[102] *IT*, 12 Aug. 1913.

[103] *IT*, 14 Aug. 1913.

[104] *The Mystic Trumpeter*, manuscript of the vocal score, *GB-Belqb*; see also Greer,
'Hamilton Harty Manuscripts', 245. What type of assistance Swinton provided
is not clear, but it may well have been in the solo vocal writing, which is a major
feature of distinction in the work.

Wood's impressive setting of 'Ethiopia Saluting the Colours' (1898), Delius's *Sea Drift* and Vaughan Williams's two choral works *Toward the Unknown Region* and *A Sea Symphony*, commissioned for the Leeds Festivals of 1907 and 1910, respectively, so Harty's choral essay boldly continued the trend. Moreover, his decision to set 'The Mystic Trumpeter' had already been pre-empted by Holst in his rather Wagnerian scena for soprano and orchestra (first performed in 1905 and revised in 1912) and by Frederick Converse's tone poem of 1904, which received its British premiere at the Cardiff Festival in 1907 (and which Harty may well have heard at the premiere of his own *Ode to a Nightingale*).

It is possible, however, that 'The Mystic Trumpeter' was not Harty's initial choice of Whitman's poetry. Dated 13 July 1912, an unpublished piano score of a setting of Whitman's 'Come Up from the Fields, Father' (again from *Drum Taps*) survives which Harty styled a 'Ballad for Chorus and Orchestra'. The work does not appear to have been orchestrated and it has never been performed. In all likelihood Harty withdrew it because he was dissatisfied with it, or, again, he may have considered it too short, or even perhaps that its solemnity was unsuitable for the Leeds commission.[105] Nevertheless there is merit in Harty's discarded creation. Whitman's poem has a deeply affecting narrative in its pastoral, autumnal scene of a farm in rural Ohio, removed from the carnage of the Civil War. The drama begins immediately, as the father, tilling the land, is called up to the house to read a letter 'from our dear Pete'. The mother and daughters also collect at the front door as the letter is opened, to find, with terrible realisation, that it is written in another hand. Pete has been severely wounded and is in hospital. Though the letter expresses hope of his recovery, Whitman's tone abruptly turns darker, for 'while they stand at home at the door he is dead already.' The last portion of the poem is devoted to the solitary grief of the mother as she wakes fitfully from sleep 'to follow, to seek, to be with her dear dead son.'

To portray the abundance of the rural landscape Harty opens his ballad buoyantly in C major, yet there is a pregnant sense of foreboding with the arrival of the letter, subtly engendered by a temporary modulation to A flat in the second stanza ('Above all, lo, the sky so calm'). This tonal change subsequently renders the return to C major that much more effective as Harty portrays the mother hurrying to the door, an action which more ominously ushers in F minor ('Fast as she can she hurries'). At this fulcrum of the narrative, with the reading of the letter, Harty attempts to achieve commensurate tension with the rapid fluctuation of tempos. This occurs twice, concluding with portentous unison octaves on C for chorus ('gunshot wound in the breast, cavalry skirmish, taken to hospital, / At present low, but will be better soon'). The lament that follows commences in F minor, where, to depict the anguish of the mother, Harty makes telling use of the unaccompanied chorus, and the transformed reprise of the chorus's opening material is tenderly transformed by a shift to A flat. For the

---

[105] It is also possible that Harty tried his hand at a further Whitman text, for GB-Belqb holds sketches of *A Dirge for Two Veretans* for chorus and orchestra in short score. These are undated, but they may have been a further attempt for the Leeds commission; see also Greer, 'Hamilton Harty Manuscripts', 249.

final part of the work, however, Harty restores C, first in the minor to convey the picture of a tragic funeral cortège, and finally, with a powerful, heroic sense of longing, to the major, though, even with the closing choral gesture ('to be with her dear dead son') the cadence is quizzically held up before the orchestra alone establishes the tonic with a C major that embodies a very different emotion from the outset. It is as if Harty himself, in accordance with the poem's inner meaning, was moved to provide the final interpretation – one of hopeless waste and scarring loss.

Dedicated to his Irish friend Stanley Cochrane, *The Mystic Trumpeter* was Harty's only large-scale choral work. It was conceived as a setting of seven of the eight stanzas of Whitman's poem (Harty omitted stanza six) and, in a similar vein to Delius's *Sea Drift*, the forces used were a solo baritone, chorus and orchestra. The poem itself is a typical expression of Whitman's humanism and of the philosophical movement of transcendentalism he inherited from his fellow American writers such as Emerson, Thoreau and Hawthorne. Also at its heart is Whitman's vision of man's immortal soul in a constant state of spiritual change and progress, in which, most essentially, democracy and human love are enshrined. One of the most attractive elements of *The Mystic Trumpeter* is the fact that Whitman uses the 'symbol' of the trumpet, with all its metaphorical appendages of fanfare, clarity, exhilaration, war and awakening, as an extension of the musician, or, as is more specifically expressed in stanza 2, the composer ('Some dead composer – haply thy pensive life / Was fill'd with aspirations high – unform'd ideals'). With the exception of stanza 2, where this idealism is expressed by the chorus, all the other stanzas commence with a reference to the trumpeter, most commonly in the form of an exhortation ('Blow, trumpeter, free and clear – I follow thee').

The entire structure of *The Mystic Trumpeter* is framed by the tonality of C major. This is the key of the outer two stanzas and of the emotional heart of the work, stanza 5. Secondary tonalities are established in stanza 3 (A flat major), stanza 4 (F major) and stanza 6 (F minor). All such tonalities had figured prominently in *Come Up from the Fields, Father*, which perhaps emphasises that this work had been a preliminary attempt in 1912. The first major statement of the work, in C major, joins the texts of stanzas 1 and 2 into a larger exposition. The structure embarks with an arresting passage of declamation for the solo baritone in which the sequential chromatic theme ('Hark! some wild trumpeter – some strange musician') is outlined vocally, accompanied by symbolic muted trumpets and horns which 'vibrate[s] capricious tunes'. This thematic idea is keenly taken up by the orchestra, which is established early on as the principal force of momentum in the work. In this sense Harty was adopting a technique he had already learned in *Ode to a Nightingale*. A secondary statement, of new material by the chorus ('Come nearer, bodiless one'), in a largely homophonic texture, also establishes a mode of expression from which Harty rarely strayed. His chorus speaks with 'one voice' where harmony and texture provide nuance and meaning to Whitman's free verse. In this way his treatment of the chorus is more an enhanced style of partsong, not unlike Delius's treatment in works such as *Sea Drift* and the later *Songs of Sunset*. The chorus concludes its reflection on the initial statement of the solo baritone questioningly by avoiding the platitude of the cadence. This is ultimately provided by the orchestra, which reiterates the baritone's opening motive in a serene coda, but this is shattered by the bold entrance of the chorus in stanza 3, which is characterised by a fanfare idea, a telling shift to A flat, and the general luxuriant *schwung* of the Straussian orchestral gestures. Its central section, by contrast, is more tranquil and introduces another sequential idea, this time based on a series of suspensions which depict nature's tenderness ('I scent the moist air and the *roses*'). The reprise of the first section is markedly altered and musically developed, but perhaps the most affecting part is how Harty appends the material of his secondary paragraph to the strident fanfare by restating it, sonata-like, at the conclusion in a wonderfully romantic, sensuous vision ('Floating and basking upon Heaven's lake') apportioned partly to the orchestra and partly to the chorus.

Whitman's text in stanza 4 looks back to the music of the middle ages, to old pageants, tournaments and the monasteries. Harty furnishes us with a ternary dance movement, the outer parts distinguished by a polonaise rhythm, the trio by a mimesis of 'old' harmony to portray the advancing procession of monks (this also being a further and more intense transformation of the sequential suspensions of stanza 3). The transitional passage of declamation for solo baritone that follows heightens our awareness once again of the potent Wagnerian role of the orchestra, as well as Harty's highly polished technique of flexible word-setting, the free nature of Whitman's poetry finding a happy abode in the irregular periodicity of Harty's vocal lines, supported by a tonally fluid harmonic background. The climax of this section, which embraces the first two-and-a-half lines of the stanza, is on the quintessential word '*Love*'. Here Harty took the trouble not only to mark the word in italics in the vocal score, but also to place it at the head of a cadence into C major which itself encapsulates one of the work's central meanings ('*Love*, that is pulse of all'). What follows is a powerful tripartite monologue in which soloist and orchestra weave an elaborate and melodious polyphony strongly reminiscent of Wagner in *Die Meistersinger* and *Parsifal* especially through the conspicuous agency of diatonicism (Example 14). Indeed, one critic remarked at the Leeds premiere that the 'music glows less with passion than with poetry, of the type of the "Preislied".'[106] Even so, Harty's full assimilation of *Tristan* allowed him to manipulate the pedal point with consummate skill, a feature which is executed at the reprise ('Love, that is all the earth to lovers') and with even greater dissonance and tension at the final cadence (replete with its own startling interruption on the dominant of A).

The antithesis to this expression of ecstasy – the stark realisation of human suffering – is conveyed by a funeral march in F minor for stanza 6, linked by a choral transition which makes a deft reductive reference to the opening motive of stanza 1. Furthermore, the march also provides a useful counterbalance to the dance of stanza 4 in F major whose own transition from stanza 3 invokes a march-like rhythm ('Blow again, trumpeter! And for my sensuous eyes'). The structure of stanza 6, like so many of the simple yet direct forms of each

[106] *MT* 54 (1913), 744.

Example 14 *The Mystic Trumpeter*, climax of baritone monologue

stanza in Harty's design, is a closed ternary scheme which chillingly establishes F minor by way of its choral medium of ponderous, dark octaves and strident declamation. The stanza ends dejectedly ('all lost! the foe victorious!'), but in the true spirit of Whitman's transcendentalism the indomitable human spirit awakes with a rapturous outburst ('Yet 'mid the ruins Pride colossal stands'), marking a decisive return to C major. For the final stanza, in which Whitman invokes a hymn 'to the universal God from universal man', Harty responds with his own hymn-like material, replete with appropriate fanfares, in the form of a dialogue between baritone and chorus. This imposing event, besides being an opportunity to summon, in transformed manner, the noble material of stanza 5 ('Rouse up my slow belief'), is used as a prelude to the Finale ('O glad, exulting, culminating song!). Here Harty creates a thrilling choral paean in which the exhilaration of C major is contrasted with the central 'dance' in A flat, recalling the tonality of stanza 3 ('A reborn race'). Almost waltz-like, this heady, bacchanalian section, initiated by the solo baritone (his last, elated utterance), is taken up by the increasingly spirited chorus whose bounding energy is encapsulated by the climactic return to C major (through the characteristic agency of an augmented sixth) and the restatement, now 'animato', of the paean material. So keen was Harty to express a sentiment of virtual abandon at this stage of the work – the final thirteen bars, marked 'più allegro', are so fast as to be chaotic – he chose at a very late stage to replace the cries of 'joy' (eight bars before cue 48), conventionally written as pitched notes in the manuscripts of both the full score and vocal score, with headless notes so that they would be shouted unrestrainedly.[107]

The Mystic Trumpeter shared its Thursday-night concert of 2 October 1913 with the premiere of *Falstaff* by Elgar, who conducted the entire programme save for Harty's work. At the end of the performance Harty was enthusiastically acclaimed, as was Thorpe Bates who undertook the solo baritone part. The general critical reception was positive. Harty was praised for his sense of clarity and directness, not to mention his imaginative use of the orchestra. *The Times* acknowledged his sincerity and picturesque treatment, though was less enamoured of the conclusion. The *Manchester Guardian* considered that Harty had 'already outstripped most of those who only a few years ago were his equals in merit', though no names were mentioned.[108] It was also noted that the audience found Harty's composition instantly appealing and it 'gained the greater immediate popularity' over Elgar's challenging orchestral masterpiece.[109] Critics also observed that the chorus was deeply enthusiastic about the work, and anxious to express this during the applause;[110] indeed, one suspects that it was this aspect of the work that generated its many performances in the years that followed. As the critic of the *Musical Times* remarked: 'The composer pursues his path in the open, and appeals to choralists, choral-trainers and audiences who have a taste for open-air music.'[111] Perhaps more precisely, what choruses particularly appreciated was the substantial and vivid effect of the vocal writing, given its relative simplicity. After Leeds *The Mystic Trumpeter*

---

[107] These headless notes appear only in the vocal score published by Novello: see Greer, 'Hamilton Harty Manuscripts', 242.

[108] *MG*, 6 Oct. 1913.

[109] *The Times*, 3 Oct. 1913.

[110] *The Times*, 3 Oct. 1913; see also *MT* 54 (1913), 744.

[111] *MT* 54 (1913), 744.

was taken up avidly by choral societies across Britain. Cowen conducted it in Liverpool on 10 February 1914 and a week later it was performed by the Cardiff Musical Society. There were performances in Edinburgh (25 March) and Bristol (22 April) before Harty himself was asked to direct a performance at the Westmorland Festival with the Hallé Orchestra. In May the work received its first American performance at the Chicago and North Shore Festival, and Harty directed it again at Woodbrook on 6 August with the baritone Robert Radford and members of the LSO.

After the triumph at Leeds Harty launched himself into another new conducting experience, this time of opera. Under the aegis of the impresario Raymond Rôze (son of the renowned soprano Marie Rôze), who produced several performances of his own opera *Jeanne d'Arc* at Covent Garden in early November, Harty was signed up to conduct productions of Wagner's *Tristan und Isolde* and Bizet's *Carmen*. *Tristan* opened on 8 November amid considerable interest from the press, not least because the part of Tristan was taken by John Coates and the part of Isolde by Marta Wittowska. 'Although new to the work of operatic conducting, he [Harty] was able to express a great deal, and to show that with the necessary experience he would have no difficulty in attaining distinction in this branch of his art.'[112] This positive response was echoed by the *Manchester Guardian*:

> The success of Mr Hamilton Harty at Covent Garden last night ought to have a far-reaching effect on our musical conditions, for once again he proved conclusively that some valuable talent has been neglected in the past through the unwillingness of managers and of the public to use its own judgment. No-one wishes that the coming of the English conductor should mean the absence of men like Nikisch and Steinbach or any other man who has reached the highest excellence. But it would be a grave thing for English music if men like Mr Hamilton Harty were allowed to continue their career as accompanists, or, as Mr Roze calls them, masters of music, without being given the chance to use their unquestionable talents for the higher branches of musical activity. Last night Mr Harty had a far more trying task than he ever had before. The conductor of opera must possess qualities which are not absolutely essential to the conductor of concert music. The last has ample time to prepare his score and to influence his band. The length of opera, on the other hand, demands, above all else, a quick eye, rapid summing up of the situation, and personal magnetism which makes itself felt through all obstacles – distance, for instance, as the influence of the conductor is realized much more easily by those who are in his immediate vicinity than those who are at the back of the stage, and of course the weight of numbers, as a full choir being of one mind, will always impose its will on a weak conductor. Mr Harty controlled all his forces admirably, and his reading of the score had all the fine impulse, the vitality one noted in his readings of concert music. He has a most enviable temperament, which seems to lead him naturally to the right thing.[113]

The Times, too, though critical of Harty's 'stiffness and [lack] of warmth',

[112] *MT* 54 (1913), 806.
[113] *MG*, 10 Nov. 1913.

described the performance as 'creditable'.[114] But while the *Musical Times* described his conducting of *Carmen* on its opening night of 29 November as 'spirited and perceptive', *The Times* was by no means so charitable. At best the orchestral playing was 'heavy and untidy', and Harty's 'rigid beat and inflexible *tempi*' in the *entr'actes* 'petrified their delicate and fragile phrases and made them sound like quotations from some forgotten German score.'[115]

The opportunity to conduct opera at Covent Garden coincided, significantly enough, with Harty's desire to compose an opera himself. He had for some time been contemplating the idea of writing a work with a strong Irish theme and for this he entered into correspondence with Padraic Colum, whose poetry had earlier inspired him in the composition of the *Five Irish Sketches* for Elsie Swinton. What is clear from the outset is that he wanted to make use of an early, tragic episode in Irish history, a fact he explained to Colum in a long letter of October 1913:

> The story I wanted to base an opera libretto upon is the story of the Lynches of Galway – which is already perhaps known to you. You will find it in the Histories of Ireland I expect. At all events it is given in Murray's Handbook of Ireland page 240. When I was in Galway I made some enquiries round about the 'Claddagh', and the story is implicitly believed there. In fact there is a stone at the back of St Nicholas Church [which] has this inscription. 'This memorial of the stern and unbending justice of the chief magistrate of this city, James Lynch Fitzstephen, elected mayor AD 1493 who condemned and executed his own guilty son, Walter, on this spot has been restored etc etc'. The main facts of the story – that James Lynch was owner of a fleet of ships trading from Galway with Spain – and that his son Walter was a wild and reckless youth much admired and loved by his townspeople – and that he committed murder, his victim being connected in some way with his father's aristocratic Spanish friends – are similar in all the versions of the story I have seen or heard – and of course, the final tragedy that, to his father's dismay, he gave himself up to justice – and was tried – and as it was impossible to find another willing to act the part of executioner – hanged by his own father – is a matter of history.[116]

Harty was happy to leave the details of the libretto to Colum, but he nevertheless had a definite operatic perspective of the scenario, action, *mise en scène* and *dramatis personae* which he was keen to lay before his potential librettist:

> I imagine the 1st Act to take place at early morning at a quay in some Spanish town from which the ship was to sail that morning – carrying not only her cargo of Spanish goods – but also the affianced bride – of the captain. I imagined that Walter – intending to say goodbye to Dolores, with whom he had fallen in love – had yet been unable to let the ship sail without him, as he had at first intended – and overcome by his longing – had at the last moment taken a flying leap on board as the boat had already left the quay.

[114] *The Times*, 10 Nov. 1913.
[115] *The Times*, 1 Dec. 1913.
[116] Letter from Harty to Colum, 11 Oct. 1913, *US-NYp*, Berg Collection.

Act II At sea – near the Aran Islands – the night before the ship wd [*sic*] make Galway – Dolores in terror – feeling the approaching tragedy – sailor's songs and doings and a general swell of the sea – Walter has let himself go and Dolores – though in love with him – is yet trying to act up her ideas of right – various events lead up to a quarrel between Walter and the captain and Walter kills the captain.

Act III In James Lynch's house (I imagine a long low room with Spanish leather chairs and long table with a great window opening on the square but covered by a curtain). James Lynch has tried his son and sentenced him – but no-one can be found to carry out the sentence – and the mob are gathered outside and threatening riot and violence if Walter is not released to them – James Lynch is forced by his stern puritanical mind to carry out the sentence himself – and does so – on his own balcony in sight of the townspeople.

The principal characters wd be:

Walter Lynch – Tenor

James Lynch (his father) – Bass

The Captain – Baritone

Dolores – Soprano

Her Nurse – Contralto

Warders – soldiers – messengers and sailors etc.[117]

This operatic perspective was needed because Harty had already conceived of a work that would be full of colour, movement and contrast, with enough room for psychological exploration of the main characters:

The details wd of course be very much your affair – but the broad lines of the story appeal to me most strongly – offering to me as they do – in the first act – so much colour in the contrast between the Spanish senoritas and the Irish sailors – and the 2nd act so much to my mind in the feeling of the sea over everything. Then the final scene with the terrible study of James Lynch – and his struggle and gradual acceptance of what he conceives to be his duty. I can only hope that the story will appeal to you as it does to me and that I may induce you to accept a commission to write a libretto for me on these lines.[118]

Harty was anxious to begin work as soon as possible. 'Of course as soon as the main lines were settled – I cd get on with the 1st act while you were doing the rest', he insisted to Colum.[119] But Colum, though he liked the basis of the story, was keen to restore it to its original form rather than retain Harty's elaborated version. Harty, on the other hand, was adamant that his adaptation would enhance the operatic dimension since it would necessitate fast-moving action and sentiment. Significantly, with the very two operas he was rehearsing at Covent Garden – *Tristan* and *Carmen* – his attitude to successful dramaturgy had hardened:

---

[117] Letter from Harty to Colum, 11 Oct. 1913.

[118] Letter from Harty to Colum, 11 Oct. 1913.

[119] Letter from Harty to Colum, 11 Oct. 1913.

1 Harty at the piano, aged 16 (1896)

2 Willam Harty (with his wife Annie seated centre) with the St Cecilia Society, Lisburn

3 Harty and Agnes Nicholls

4 Agnes Nicholls Harty as Isolde

5 Michele Esposito

6 Lieutenant Harty, Royal Navy, *c.* 1917

7 Harty with the Hallé Orchestra in the Manchester Free Trade Hall, 1923–4

8 Complimentary dinner given by Harty for the Hallé Orchestra, December 1923

9 Harty with his Honorary DMus, Manchester University, 1925

10 Harty with Esposito and members of the Hallé Orchestra, Dublin, 1926

11 Harty on the S.S. *President Roosevelt*, 1936

12 Harty at the Hollywood Bowl

13 Harty conducting Mendelssohn's *Elijah*, Sydney Town Hall, 20 June 1934

14 Harty on the carillon at Sydney University, June 1934

15 Harty, late 1930s

16 The interior of Harty's flat at Hove, *c.* 1940

17 Harty, a last photo (1940)

On the other hand, colour and action are so necessary to a good opera that I took the liberty of changing the scene and detail for my own purposes. The most successful opera from all standpoints ever written is 'Carmen' – and there is not a page in which this constant change of colour and feeling does not give the composer his great chance. For the same reason – much of the great Wagnerian dramas are hopeless and must eventually fail – picturesque staging and a swift changing action interest not only the audience but the composer.[120]

Harty's recourse was to provide an even more detailed account of the story, scene by scene, in which he attempted to reach a compromise between his conception and Colum's. 'If you could possibly see eye to eye with me in the broad lines of this', he wrote to Colum, 'I shd be very happy as it appeals to me strongly from a musical point of view.'[121] For the commission Harty suggested a fee of £50 with some manœuvre for additional royalties. More importantly, though, Harty believed that Colum was the ideal man for this new enterprise:

> I cannot tell you how strongly this story draws me, and I know of no-one who wd satisfy me so completely as a colleague, as yourself. I am at present very much engaged at Covent Garden Opera but later on hope to be in Ireland when we might meet – and talk. But if you are pleased – I hope you will be able to write as soon and completely as possible.[122]

Little progress took place over the next eight months, for it was not until June 1914 that Harty took up his pen to Colum again. The delay, as Harty explained, was because he had been unwell for some time. 'Presently I am going away for a voyage, which will I hope make me quite fit again, and I expect to be in harness again in the early autumn.'[123] He was still keen to make progress with the opera and come to some agreement with Colum about the general scenario, one he laid out in some detail in his letter. There was also a problem with Colum's commission fee. Because of his illness, Harty's income had been appreciably curtailed:

> I am afraid that I am not in a position to do as you wish. You see – unfortunately I am far from being well-off. When the libretto is finished, I will do as at first arranged and send you the sum agreed on – but I don't want you to leave over your other work. As I explained to you – it will still be some time before I am in a position to work hard – and there shd be plenty of time for the libretto to be put together. I have not a copy of the 'Carmen' libretto handy – but will send you a copy of the opera in a day or two. … You mustn't mind the stilted English translation – the action's the thing – and brevity – I am sure – is to be aimed at in both words and music.[124]

[120] Letter from Harty to Colum, 19 Oct. 1913, *US-NYp*, Berg Collection.

[121] Letter from Harty to Colum, 19 Oct. 1913.

[122] Letter from Harty to Colum, 19 Oct. 1913.

[123] Letter from Harty to Colum, 11 June 1914, *US-NYp*, Berg Collection. It is not clear whether Harty did make his voyage since, by August, he was conducting at Woodbrook.

[124] Letter from Harty to Colum, 13 June 1914, *US-NYp*, Berg Collection.

Harty and Colum were in contact again in August 1914, this time with the possibility of a meeting in Dublin, where they hoped to discuss further ideas.[125] However, plans for the opera evidently never went any further. This may have been due to the outbreak of war, or, perhaps, the imperative of a new commission for the Norwich Festival in the autumn. But Harty's enthusiasm for the genre was never wholehearted. Beecham once explained that he had offered Harty an important position in the Beecham Opera Company, but recognised that the Irishman's 'interests and inclinations were entirely with the symphony orchestra'.[126] In fact, by the time the First World War was over, Harty was openly critical of opera's artistic possibilities. In an interview for the *Musical Times* in 1920 he commented, in characteristically bald terms, that opera held a limited attraction for him. Given his wife's major achievements on the stage, it represented a surprising and major divergence in their interests:

> Opera seems to me a form of art in which clumsy attempts are made at defining the indefinable suggestions of music. Or else one in which the author of a plot and his actors are hampered by the music which prolongs their gestures and action to absurdity and obscures the sense of their words. The sound apologia for opera is on the lines that it induces into listening to music many people who are not musical enough to listen to love it for its own sake without the accessories of operatic acting and operatic scenery – such as they are! Is it possible today not to see that Wagner deluded himself when he thought he was making a new and supreme art harmony out of half a dozen arts? When we hear Wagnerian opera we put up with a lot – for the sake of the music. Who for instance wants actually to see Isolda waving her scarf in signal to Tristan? The music is telling us of that, and also of the fluttering of Isolda's heart. The action here is as superfluous as that objectionable habit of some people at concerts when they start humming on recognizing a favourite theme. Sometimes Wagner's staginess tends to make ridiculous scenes which, left to the music, would be amply significant. Take, for instance, that supper-party in Hunding's hut (first Act of 'The Valkyrie'). The music tells us that the two Volsungs are stealing enraptured glances each from other. But the Bayreuth tradition also insists that the actors shall stare transfixedly, and stare they always do in the most aggressive way, though under Hunding's very nose. The apprehensive and throbbing music has told us of their feelings and of Hunding's suspicion. But the behaviour of the actors is always such as more than to confirm any suspicion, and you feel that Hunding would be more than justified in turning the stranger out into the storm straightaway.
>
> Operatic scenery affects me similarly. The Prelude to Act 3 of 'Tristan' has painted the sea so well that it is always a descent to be shown the scenic artist's attempt at it a minute or two later. The subject might be run to earth in those operas where music is at its most grandiose, and the scene precipitates itself from the merely banal into something near the grotesque. The last scene of 'The Twilight of the Gods' is a classic example.[127]

---

[125] See letter from Harty to Colum, 9 Aug. 1914, *US-NYp*, Berg Collection.

[126] Michael Kennedy, *The Hallé Tradition: A Century of Music* (Manchester: Manchester University Press, 1960), 202.

[127] [Colles], 'Hamilton Harty', 229.

Harty held this view all his life. In 1926, when it was suggested that the Manchester audiences lacked perception or sufficient musicality because the city did not have regular opera or a bespoke opera house, he was equally contentious in his letter to the *Manchester Guardian*. Just as before, Wagner was the focus of his argument:

> Many people take the attitude that if Manchester will not support opera it must be that her citizens are not sufficiently musical. Is this a justifiable conclusion? Sometimes I wonder if the lack of support is not caused by a precisely opposite reason. From a strictly musical point of view a good deal of opera music sounds better on the concert platform than in the theatre. This is especially true as regards Wagner. One reason is that the ordinary English theatre is not constructed in such a way as to provide sufficient room for a large orchestra such as is required, for instance, in the operas of Wagner and Strauss. And then a good many people feel that, if music is beautiful in itself, it is worth devoting all one's attention to it without being distracted by action on the stage and make-believe scenery, which are, after all, only very clumsy expedients to translate what the music itself conveys perfectly to those of whom I speak. There are many people who derive more pleasure from reading Shakespeare's plays than from seeing them acted, but it would be absurd to say that because of this they do not appreciate his genius; and in the same way it is unfair to hint, as I have heard hinted, that because the people in this city did not crowd the recent opera performances of the BNO Company it is a reflection on their musical intelligence.[128]

And in 1927, when Beecham was attempting to set up his so-called 'Imperial League of Opera', Harty, who was interviewed on the subject, reiterated his dislike of the idiom: 'Personally … I am not particularly interested in opera, as I think it is an unsuccessful fusion of two or more arts, and I shall always think so.'[129]

Shortly after his operatic debut at Covent Garden Harty was invited by the Liverpool Philharmonic on 23 January 1914 to conduct *With the Wild Geese* in a programme which also included his *The Wake Feast* and *A Rann of Wandering* and some Irish songs by Herbert Hughes sung by Agnes Nicholls (with Harty at the piano). Bach's Suite No. 2 for Flute and Orchestra, a work Harty had already conducted, was played by V. L. Needham (the principal flautist of the Hallé), and Rachmaninov performed his Piano Concerto No. 2. Another of Harty's important appearances, this time with the Hallé Orchestra, was at the Westmorland Festival on 23 April where he directed *The Mystic Trumpeter*. He was also invited over to Woodbrook a second time by Cochrane between 3 and 8 August with members of the LSO. In Dublin this aroused particular anticipation because this time Harty and Cochrane invited Esposito to share the rostrum. Moreover, the programme of six concerts featured more music by both men.[130] In the first concert, on 3 August, Esposito conducted his *Irish* Suite, and he appeared as soloist in his Piano Concerto No. 2 the following evening. Harty

[128] Letter from Harty to *MG*, 1 Feb. 1926.

[129] *MG*, 15 Nov. 1927.

[130] *IT*, 12 May 1914.

conducted *The Mystic Trumpeter* with Robert Radford as soloist on 6 August, and *With the Wild Geese* formed part of the last programme. Harty and Esposito were lionised by the Irish public, and for Esposito it must have seemed like a climax to the enormous efforts he had devoted towards music-making in the Irish capital. Yet, while the Woodbrook festival was under way, Germany invaded Belgium, which brought Britain into the war against the Central Powers. The economic disruption brought about by the European conflagration would have immeasurable consequences on music across the continent. In Ireland, Esposito's activities would soon be curtailed. As for Harty, at an important juncture of his conducting career, the need to be assertive and expeditious was imperative since orchestras, concert halls and festivals would soon be forced to consider their role against the new and menacing backdrop of the war.

The War Years and After

WITH the outbreak of war, Harty, like so many other active musicians, gave time to charitable concerts for the YMCA, the Belgian Relief Fund and the Red Cross. This replaced, to some extent, a decline in his professional work as an accompanist. Fortunately engagements for orchestral concerts continued to be buoyant. In Manchester, major changes in musical personnel had arisen because of hostilities. Michael Balling, the Hallé Orchestra's permanent conductor, had gone to Bavaria after the Westmorland Festival for rehearsals at Bayreuth, and was at Partenkirchen when war was announced. Gustav Behrens, a prominent member of the Hallé's Board of Management, knew that it would be impossible for Balling to return.[1] In order to assist the orchestra a host of conductors – Beecham, Verbrugghen, Safonov, Cowen, Ronald, Bantock, Elgar and Harty – offered their services (some without honorarium), which meant that the Hallé Concerts, the Promenade Concerts and the Gentlemen's Concerts were all able to able to announce 'business as usual'.

Harty appeared at the Promenade Concerts in October and November and caught the eye of Samuel Langford, a particularly incisive critic for the *Manchester Guardian*:

> A certain liveliness is characteristic of the concerts given under Mr Hamilton Harty's conductorship. It is not that he lacks in any way the control or repose of style necessary for fine interpretations; on the contrary, he possesses these qualities in a supreme degree, and his readings have the plasticity of the true creative musician. But he has warmth, and likes liveliness for its own sake.[2]

For the concert in question (on 31 October), Harty directed Elgar's *Cockaigne* Overture and Tchaikovsky's Fourth Symphony, full-blooded Romantic works in which Langford sensed Harty's affinity: 'Elgar's "Cockaigne" Overture, which is a work of boisterous fancy, through which the blood runs nevertheless rather coldly, becomes twice itself in Mr Harty's hands, from the extra infusion of life which he imparts. We have never heard this piece given so finely as at the close of Saturday's concert.' Langford also felt that Harty's interpretation of Tchaikovsky's work had 'more life and warmth than Elgar's recent reading', a vitality which was also reflected in the overture to *The Marriage of Figaro* and the Scherzo from Mendelssohn's incidental music to *A Midsummer Night's Dream*. Langford was also present at a further Promenade Concert in Manchester on 14 November, when Harty appeared along with Nicholls who, with her husband at the piano, sang *By the Bivouac's Fitful Flame* to an appreciative audience. In addition to movements from Saint-Saëns's *Algerian* Suite and Schubert's 'Unfinished' Symphony (in which he gave what Langford described as 'one of the

[1] Kennedy, *The Hallé Tradition*, 188.
[2] *MG*, 2 Nov. 1914.

most exquisite readings we have ever heard' of the second movement),[3] Harty conducted his *Comedy Overture* for the first time in Manchester.

Among the conurbations of Yorkshire, Bradford elected to reduce its subscription concerts (three of which were served by the Hallé) because of the war. The Bradford Permanent Orchestra, founded in 1892 and a well-established organisation with a tradition of established conductors, decided to continue with its five concerts. For these Harty and Julian Clifford were appointed to share the rostrum. Harty undertook two of the concerts. At the first, on 24 October, he directed performances of Mozart's 'Jupiter' Symphony, his *Comedy Overture* and the prelude to *Parsifal*, among other works. At the second he introduced *With the Wild Geese* for the first time to his Bradford audience (though, by all accounts, the orchestra found the score demanding),[4] and the following year, on 10 March 1915, the Bradford Old Choral Society chose to perform *The Mystic Trumpeter*, securing Harty to conduct it.[5]

Engagements in the provinces proved to be a vital means of gaining experience and expertise for Harty, as well as accumulating a broader portfolio of repertoire. In 1915 his association with Manchester grew closer with a concert for the Hallé Orchestra on 28 January 1915. Langford continued to sing the praises of the Irish conductor. The programme was well chosen to show his technical advantages. 'Few conductors', Langford proclaimed, 'can endow music with a more stirring life.'[6] In accordance with Behrens's assurance to the orchestra's guarantors that the concert programmes would be 'as attractive as possible, avoiding all heavy and depressing works',[7] Harty directed a series of spirited classics: Beethoven's Seventh Symphony, Tchaikovsky's Violin Concerto (with Isolde Menges), Smetana's overture to *The Bartered Bride* and Elgar's *Cockaigne*, the only unusual work being Lyadov's tableau *Baba-Yaga*. During the months of February and March 1915 there were three other welcome orchestral engagements in Manchester. Two were for the Saturday Promenade Concerts on 27 February and 13 March, the former in place of Bantock who was indisposed through illness. At the beginning of his critique of this concert Langford was keen to note how Harty was maturing: 'Mr Hamilton Harty ... again showed that he is coming on apace as a conductor, and that as the players get familiar with his methods his active musical temperament helps more and more to ensure liveliness and even brilliance.'[8] The programme was made up of Wagner, Rimsky-Korsakov's *Capriccio espagnol*, and Berlioz's march from *The Damnation of Faust*. Just as Lyadov's *Baba-Yaga* had signalled Harty's interest in Russian music in his January programme, so did the Rimsky here, along with Berlioz, a composer whom Harty would continually and unapologetically champion from this early point in his conducting career onwards. The imaginative nature of Harty's past

[3] *MG*, 16 Nov. 1914.

[4] *MT* 56 (1915), 49.

[5] *MT* 56 (1915), 238.

[6] *MG*, 29 Jan. 1915.

[7] Kennedy, *The Hallé Tradition*, 188.

[8] *MG*, 1 Mar. 1915.

Promenade Concerts, in which a more serious note had been struck with whole symphonies rather than individual movements, provoked Langford to express his disappointment at the more blatantly 'popular' programme of 13 March, where shorter orchestral and operatic works, often in the form of excerpts, by Grieg, Stanford, Svendsen, Verdi and Brahms predominated. At an intervening concert on 15 February for the Manchester Gentlemen's Concerts at the Midland Hall, Langford extolled Harty's vigorous interpretation of Schumann's Second Symphony: 'As would be expected, Mr Harty adopted the liveliest possible reading of the work, and if occasionally solemnity was sacrificed, the over-reiterated rhythms were less tiresome than in more serious readings, and Mr Harty's zest for them seemed as inexhaustible as the composer's.'[9] In addition, Harty characteristically included Berlioz's *Le Carnaval romain*, Dvořák's Serenade for Strings, and, as a symbol of his admiration and support for the work of his mentor, the *Irish* Suite by Esposito.

The general opinion in Manchester was that Harty and Verbrugghen had acquitted themselves with flying colours at the Promenade Concerts and that their re-engagement for the 1915–16 series was to be welcomed. As for the Hallé, Beecham was still very much in the ascendant, but the prevailing view was that to entrust all the concerts to one man was inadvisable. 'This is the age of the specialist, in art as in other professions and businesses', the *Musical Times* commented, 'and the public want, and will have, the best of all sorts. Everything seems to point to Manchester having at least four young modern conductors of outstanding ability playing regularly to her audiences next winter – Beecham, Harty, Verbrugghen, and Wood (the order, be it noted, is alphabetical).'[10]

Harty's London appearances at the Bechstein and Aeolian Halls as an accompanist were somewhat less numerous as his engagements as a conductor increased, but during the months of May and June there was a flurry as he appeared with Albert Sammons at Leighton House (13 May) in violin sonatas by Beethoven and Franck, Isolde Menges in a series of three concerts (18 May, 3 and 10 June) in performances of violin sonatas by Brahms and Schumann,[11] with Sammons and the London String Quartet (5 June) in Vaughan Williams's Phantasy Quintet, and May Harrison (16 June) in Delius's recently composed Violin Sonata No. 1, over which, according to Harrison, he 'spent hours editing and correcting the piano part'.[12] Moreover, Harty and Nicholls were invited to appear as part of a Festival of British Music in May, in which they took part in

---

[9] *MG*, 16 Feb. 1915.

[10] *MT* 56 (1915), 235.

[11] Harty's work with Menges also extended to some early recordings in 1915 of Brahms's Hungarian Dance No. 7 (arr. Joachim) and Benjamin Godard's *Six Morceaux*. He also recorded Elgar's miniature, *Rosemary*, in a version for cello and piano with Squire in 1916.

[12] After Harty's painstaking work on the manuscript, 'with joy and gratitude Delius carried it off then and there from the artists' room to send it direct to the publishers; but by some extraordinary chance, the wrong part got published, and … Harty's wonderful work was irretrievably lost': May Harrison, 'Delius', in *A Delius Companion*, ed. C. Redwood (London: John Calder, 1976), 101–6, at 102.

the second of three concerts on 13 May at Queen's Hall; in the same programme Nicholls sang Bantock's 'The Wilderness and the Solitary Place' from his oratorio *Christ in the Wilderness*, and Emil Młynarski, one of four conductors of the festival, directed the LSO in *With the Wild Geese*.

In the closing months of 1914 Harty's compositional activities met with disappointment. The Norwich Festival, one of many choral institutions to be a casualty of the war, had commissioned an orchestral work from him, and a symphonic poem, *The Tinker's Wedding*, had been announced in March in *The Times* along with new works by Bax, Balfour Gardiner and the revision of Parry's *A Vision of Life*.[13] Greer has pointed out that we are unable to be sure about which of the many surviving sketches could be this work, but we do know that Harty had sketched some of it, for there is a double sheet of manuscript paper on which he wrote 'Sketches for the Tinker's Wedding'; this probably acted as a cover to keep all his sketches together.[14] Although this composition did not come to fruition, Harty did turn his attention to his old 'Irish' Symphony which, owing to the popularity of his *Comedy Overture* and *With the Wild Geese*, he had not aired with the public for some time. As mentioned in Chapter 2, the 1915 version of the 'Irish' Symphony bore no titles for the individual movements (these were added in 1924), nor did it have an introduction (added in 1927 for the printed version). Revised in December 1915,[15] this version received at least two performances under Harty's direction during 1916, one in Leeds,[16] and the other in Bournemouth, where it had always been popular.[17]

Before Harty embarked on the revision of the 'Irish' Symphony, he produced a short work for harp, *Spring Fancies*, a set of two preludes. Although the work bears no dedication, it was probably written for the distinguished harpist Miriam Timothy. The first, a lively miniature, in A flat, is a study in parallel harmonies, clearly influenced by Debussy, though largely deferring to the French composer's earlier style of the 1890s, where the tonal frame is still clearly discernible.[18] A ternary structure, the first part is dominated by strings of parallel sevenths whose harmonic rationale is defined at strategic moments by punctuative functional progressions. In the central paragraph this 'seventh' colour is distilled into a slower, more lyrical effusion redolent of Debussy's two *Arabesques*, while the harp-writing has much to suggest that Harty had learned his lessons thoroughly

---

[13] *The Times*, 9 Mar. 1914.

[14] Greer, 'Hamilton Harty Manuscripts', 243. But see also David Greer, 'The Composition of *The Children of Lir*', in *Musicology in Ireland*, ed. G. Gillen and H. White, Irish Musical Studies 1 (Dublin: Irish Academic Press, 1990), 74–98, at 97, n. 14.

[15] The autograph manuscript of the 1915 version (*GB-Belqb*) shows that the revision of the Finale was completed on 11 December 1915, the second movement on 17 December, and the first movement on 29 December.

[16] R. Warren, 'Orchestral Music', in *Hamilton Harty: His Life and Music*, ed. David Greer (Belfast: Blackstaff Press, 1978), 89–115, at 93.

[17] Lloyd, *Sir Dan Godfrey*, 119; see also *MT* 57 (1916), 252.

[18] This piece was performed by the Hallé harpist Charles Collier in Manchester on 19 October 1918.

from other masters of the instrument such as Hasselmans and Ravel. The second *étude*-like piece, in the more idiomatic key of C flat, is more reminiscent of the nineteenth century, of such composers as Delibes and Massenet, with its more traditional style of melody and florid accompaniment. *Spring Fancies* was later recorded by Timothy's most eminent pupil, Sidonie Goossens, on the HMV label in 1928.[19]

Alongside *Spring Fancies* was a short work called *In Ireland*, subtitled 'A Fantasy for Flute, Harp and Piano', which Harty completed in February 1915. This was dedicated to Timothy, but was probably intended for the well-known flautist Albert Fransella, already familiar to Harty both as an orchestral and chamber musician and with whom Harty had often worked in his sextet of pre-war years.[20] Harty appended a short statement in parentheses at the head of the score – 'In a Dublin street at dusk, two wandering street musicians are playing' – clearly suggesting a romantic tableau or fantasy (as the subtitle implies) of an Irish itinerant flautist (or, more likely, a tin-whistle player) and harpist. Commencing with a long, quasi-improvised section for the flute in its highest register (where the extended, elegiac melody's sense of metre – 9/8 – is also deliberately obscure), the atmosphere is tinged with a passionate melancholy, perhaps engendered by the shadow of war. This mournful material frames a livelier reel in A minor (cast in a transposed Dorian mode) which acts as a secondary thematic and tonal foil, and Harty's 'fantasy-like' treatment of it is effectively a set of variegated repetitions shared between piano and soloist, including a canonic one towards the end. Significantly, this variegational tendency becomes an important *topos* for the rest of the work, for the 'Vivace' in E minor that follows, also a reel, is a variant of the initial threnody; while the slower, contrasting section, again in A minor, is a further variant on the secondary material, in many ways recalling the doleful mood of the opening. In effect, furthermore, Harty, in this second ternary form, has subtly reversed the roles of the first.

By far the largest creative undertaking of 1915 was Harty's agreement to provide a considerable amount of incidental music for James Bernard Fagan's play *The Sing of Shiraz*, which, according to correspondence from Fagan, would remunerate Harty to the tune of £100 for every performance.[21] In the event, it appears that the play was never staged, so Harty may not have received a penny for his trouble, yet from the music he produced (on a much more ambitious scale than for *Proud Maisie*), the venture was clearly an elaborate one in which Fagan

[19] HMV B1753.

[20] Miriam Timothy, a founder member of the LSO and a longstanding member of that orchestra, developed a reputation for the performance of rarified chamber repertoire with Fransella and the violist W. Waldo Warner. In February 1917 these performers gave the British premiere of Debussy's late Sonata for flute, viola and harp at the Aeolian Hall; seven weeks later, at the same venue, they performed Bax's *Elegiac Trio*, composed for them in 1916. In later years, at the Hamilton Harty Chamber Concerts in Manchester, *In Ireland* was often played by the Hallé's principal flautist, John Lingard, with Harty accompanying.

[21] Greer (ed.), *Hamilton Harty: His Life and Music*, 75.

envisaged a colourful and sensual spectacle having much in common with the *One Thousand and One Nights* (often known as the *Arabian Nights*), probably of Persian origin.

There is no existing evidence to confirm that Fagan, a Belfast-born actor, producer and playwright, was known to Harty before their collaboration, but their shared cultural background suggests that their common heritage might well have brought them together. Fagan, six years older than Harty, had become well known in theatre circles as a dramatist in the years before the war, and his 1904 play *The Prayer of the Sword* achieved some renown, not least through its incidental music by Franco Leoni, as did his 1909 translation of Eugène Brieux's play *La Foi*, with music by Saint-Saëns. His play *Bella Donna* also found its way into an eponymous silent film of 1915, by which time Fagan had returned to the stage as an actor. At the outbreak of war Fagan attempted to make his mark with a patriotic play, *The Fourth of August*, at the Coliseum, but it was later, in 1917, with Brieux's controversial play *Damaged Goods* (on the taboo subject of syphilis) that his skills as a producer became more established. What became of *The Singer of Shiraz*, described as 'A Persian Romance in Three Acts', is unknown. Unmentioned in accounts of Fagan's life, it may have been derailed by the onset of war. Fagan's intentions may have been for a production in the winter of 1915 or the spring of 1916, for Harty completed all thirteen items of music (consisting of eight preludes to individual scenes and five songs) in a fevered period of compositional activity between 29 July and 18 August 1915. Such industry must have taken place in the belief that the play would materialise. Yet, even though Fagan's play survives in typescript, there is no record of a production.

The story of *The Singer of Shiraz* centres around a Circassian slave girl, Murwarid, who possesses a beautiful, haunting voice. Her song is heard by the bored Sultan of Shiraz, Shahriman, who sends his vizier, Mahmud Ben-Sabah, and the chief of his seraglio, Shacabac, to seek her out. Murwarid's dulcet tones are also heard by Bahr-ul-din, a poet, who is intrigued that she sings his verse. By playing her song on his pipe, Bahr-ul-din forces Murwarid to open the window to reveal herself; she lowers her veil and the two fall in love. However, their bond is frustrated by her owner Baktyar, a jewel merchant who takes Murwarid to be sold at the slave market. Bahr-ul-din outbids Shacabac and frees Murwarid. They marry, but in order to raise a vast sum to pay his debt to Baktyar, Bahr-ul-din must sell his house and goods. But before this can happen, Mahmud bursts in and declares that Murwarid must be delivered to the Sultan. Bahr-ul-din is also banished from the kingdom and forbidden to return.

In Act II Murwarid mesmerises the court with her singing, but she is melancholy. Meanwhile Bahr-ul-din, who has spent his time as a healer, plans his return. He arrives back in Shiraz disguised as an Indian sage, and offers to heal the Sultan. In Act III Bahr-ul-din is discovered and imprisoned as a traitor, but his escape is aided by Murwarid, who also declares to the Sultan that, as Bahr-ul-din's wife, she was abducted unlawfully. The Sultan grants her freedom, pardons Bahr-ul-din, but refuses to retract his banishment. At the end of the play, through the melody that united them, Bahr-ul-din and Murwarid come together triumphantly as man and wife.

Harty had already evinced a certain affinity with the music of the Russians in his earlier Piano Quintet and the 'Orientale' movement in his trilogy of oboe pieces, but Fagan's play provided a much more ambitious outlet for him to experiment with the exotic scales essayed by Mussorgsky, Rimsky-Korsakov and Borodin. In addition to an overture, Fagan wanted music for almost every scene, and since the play centred round the haunting sounds of a female singer, Harty was also required to provide no fewer than five songs for Murwarid, a role which clearly demanded an actress with unusual vocal dexterity. Bahr-ul-din's pipe likewise necessitated the presence of a proficient flautist. The quality of Harty's music is impressive. Beautifully scored for 'pit' forces (two flutes, oboe, clarinet, bassoon, two horns, trumpet, trombone, harp, percussion and strings), there is a colourful dexterity to the instrumentation and, fired by the exotic ambience of the play, Harty clearly felt no inclination to be parsimonious with his invention. The overture in G minor, though a shorter, abridged sonata scheme, juxtaposes an eastern dance with a more luxuriant secondary section full of wistful, Rimsky-like thematic material reminiscent of *Scheherazade*, an enchanting paragraph that settles in D flat major, the most romantic of late nineteenth-century keys. The first song, 'O moon arise', sung offstage during Act I Scene 1, enshrines Murwarid's melody and Bahr-ul-din's pipe extemporisations (played on an obbligato flute using material derived from the secondary material of the overture with harp accompaniment). Imaginatively couched in 5/4 metre, its irregularity enhances its extemporary impression, and Harty's more animated second verse, ultimately a variation on the first, serves to strengthen the perception of a more through-composed structure, one that more adeptly expresses the aspirations of the singer.

While the first two items reflect a more familiar 'eastern' musical paradigm, the short yet remarkable Prelude to Act I Scene 2, for flute and strings, has an inner intensity with shifting, experimental harmonies and a deeply melancholy, Borodinesque theme (Example 15). Clearly, Harty was constrained by dramaturgical expedients, and it is a shame that he was unable to develop this music more ambitiously. For the Prelude to Act I Scene 3 Harty returned to the familiar sounds of *Sheherezade* and provided an attractive slow dance that might well have found its home in a Russian classical ballet, the solo violin and cello recalling the delicate *pas de deux* of Tchaikovsky's classical masterpieces. Belonging to the same scene, the song 'The Bee hath Stolen the Secret of the Rose' has a more popular character in its simple strophic design and repetitive interludes, but Harty's pentatonic melody has real charm, as does the cadential 'sigh' to each verse. The dramatic interlude 'The Slave Market', a short orchestral piece used at the beginning of Act I Scene 4, was used again by Harty in Act III to heighten the sense of drama. (In the former, Murwarid is to be sold; in the latter, Bahr-ul-din, beard shaven, is in prison.)

In Act II the focal points of the first scene, in Shacabac's seraglio, are two songs for Murwarid. Delicately orchestrated, 'O Sultan of the Shadowy Courts of Sleep' expresses Murwarid's longing for her exiled love, assisted by the warbling of a nightingale; though brief, 'O Wind of Dawn', for clarinet and strings, is a surprisingly moving coda to the scene as Murwarid's yearning seems to

Example 15 *The Singer of Shiraz*, opening of Prelude to Act I Scene 2

overtake her. For the beginning of Act II Scene 2 Harty used another exotic dance to capture the house of Mir Anjoo, where Bahr-ul-din had taken refuge in exile, and this is complemented by a further dance-like episode for the opening of Scene 3. Ideally suited to the genre of the 'suite', both pieces have a lighter element to their textures and deportment. The last and most substantial of the songs, 'Lo! All the Garden Sleepeth', draws its material from the Prelude. Here Murwarid, with her winning voice, sings to the weary Sultan, just before the entry of Bahr-ul-din in disguise. For the denouements in Act III Harty took the opportunity to recall material from earlier scenes. For the Prelude to Scene 1 he provided an orchestral reworking of 'The Bee hath Stolen the Secret of the Rose', now in the guise of a more extended character piece; and for the beginning of Scene 2, as mentioned above, the prelude of Act I Scene 4 is redeployed to depict the abject conditions of the imprisoned Bahr-ul-din. For the last of the orchestral preludes, to Act III Scene 3, a reworking of the first song, 'O Moon Arise', is fashioned into a tripartite structure in which the central paragraph witnesses a reprise of the emotional prelude to Act I Scene 2, now in a much more opulent and somewhat plangent orchestration.

Though Fagan's failure to stage *The Singer of Shiraz* must have been a severe disappointment to Harty, there is some evidence that he attempted to bring together some of the movements into an orchestral suite. Hoping to interest the LSO in the idea, he wrote in October to the Board of Directors. The response by the Board seemed positive: 'Request from Mr H H asking the Board to include his new orchestral suite in one of next season's Symphony Concerts was considered, and it was agreed that Mr Beecham be consulted with a view to including it in one of his programmes.'[22] There is no evidence, however, that Beecham ever performed it. On 19 November, while assisting the renowned teacher and pianist Mathilde Verne in performances of Beethoven's Piano Concerto No. 3 and Schumann's *Introduction and Allegro* for piano and orchestra, Harty conducted members of the LSO in orchestral works by Bach, Debussy and Stanford, and in two so-called 'sketches' for small orchestra – *Night in the Desert* (probably the Prelude to Act I Scene 2) and *In the Bazaar* (perhaps the overture) – which *The Times* noted were being heard for the first time.[23] In addition, as part of the Leinster Chapter's local meeting of the Incorporated Society of Musicians in Dublin's Aberdeen Hall, Esposito conducted his newly formed string orchestra and 'a charming arrangement of a Persian love-song' by Harty on 21 December.[24] Again, this must have been one of the vocal items from the play, but which one is unspecified. After that Harty seems to have shelved the material, though he clearly did not forget about it, for after the war his work on *The Singer of Shiraz* would be recast in a new orchestral work whose programme would contain numerous parallels with Fagan's eastern romance.

In the autumn of 1915 Harty hoped that he might restore his links with the LSO. He knew many of its players well and was anxious to re-establish himself with the London orchestras. The LSO, however, was struggling to survive because of the exigencies of wartime. To their rescue came Beecham who, after conducting the orchestra at two invitation concerts in the 1914–15 series, was appointed principal conductor by the Directors for the 1915–16 series. The arrangement was highly advantageous to Beecham, who was able to choose concert dates convenient to him, and such was the accommodating atmosphere of the experience that he felt moved to assist the orchestra financially, a most welcome gesture since a worrying overdraft loomed over the orchestra's activities

[22] LSO Minute Book 1915–20, 12 Oct. 1915, 45.

[23] *The Times*, 20 Dec. 1915.

[24] *MT* 57 (1916), 108.

until the end of the war.[25] With only average attendances at the LSO concerts, Harty wrote in November 1915 suggesting that if larger works were performed, audiences would grow. Given the orchestra's financial constraints, this was the last thing the Directors wanted to hear, and the secretary was instructed to write back informing Harty that 'the Board were not of his opinion as the experience of the past had taught them otherwise, and furthermore the Board were not in a position to employ a large orchestra which the inclusion of big works would entail.'[26]

Though there was little prospect of conducting the LSO, Harty was able to share the rostrum with Beecham at a Promenade Concert on 9 October where he conducted *With the Wild Geese* to much acclaim (while Beecham's performance of Balakirev's *Thamar* fell flat).[27] But, apart from occasional chamber concerts (including a notable one on 25 November with the London String Quartet), London offered little opportunity at this time and Harty once again looked to Manchester, where he was active in the city's own Promenade Concerts shared with Beecham, Ronald, R. J. Forbes, and R. R. Wilson. He also he resumed his duties as one of the conductors of the Bradford Permanent Orchestra.

In early October Harty began his appearances in Manchester with a concert of Schumann's Fourth Symphony, a work he always favoured, and as a contrast he also directed Debussy's *L'Après-midi d'un faune*, the Prelude to *Die Meistersinger*, and *With the Wild Geese*; Agnes Nicholls was also there to assist with solo vocal pieces. A few days later he was engaged at the Manchester Vocal Society to accompany Madame Stanley Knowles in an interesting programme of Russian songs (somewhat reminiscent of those he had performed with Swinton) as well as items by Delius, Pfitzner, Smyth and Cyril Scott. During the earlier part of his career as an accompanist Harty had always been keen to promote new British music, but with the heightened national consciousness of the war, and his own acute desire to see justice done to indigenous composers, this programme highlighted his adherence to the cause.[28] Early in the new year Harty was again at the piano to accompany a party of singers, which included Nicholls and Austin, and the violinist Sammons at the third series of Percy Harrison Concerts. It was, according to Langford, the best-attended concert since the war began, partly owing to the eminence of the performers, but also to the distinctive content of the programme. In particular Langford was effusive about Harty's accompanimental art and the individual conception of his songs for Nicholls's voice:

> If anything could reconcile us to the substitution of the pianoforte for the orchestra it would be the presence of Mr Hamilton Harty at the pianoforte. He is

---

[25] Foss and Goodwin, *London Symphony*, 80–81.

[26] LSO Minutes Books, 9 Nov. 1915, 53. A series of Sunday Afternoon Concerts was also put forward by the LSO in 1915 with Harty as the conductor and Julian Clifford as his assistant. Because of his war duties Harty was initially unable to take these on: Foss and Goodwin, *London Symphony*, 85, 89.

[27] *MT* 56 (1915), 678.

[28] See *MG*, 25 Sept. 1915.

never merely a pianist or an accompanist, but is always a maker of music, and he imparts the breath of life to all the music in which he takes part. Miss Nicholls was also present, and sang as only she among English singers can sing. When we hear her sing Mr Harty's songs, with him at the piano, we begin to understand why he writes accompaniments which run like the sea, and how the great gaps which often lie between the towering voice and the swift current of the played notes are meant to be spanned. These songs are not themselves until the right singer and the right player are there.[29]

Shortly after his success at the Harrison Concerts, Harty made a second appearance at the Promenade Concerts on 13 January 1916. In fact the concert had been subject to some rearrangement because Beecham had been called away on a politico-musical mission to Rome at the invitation of Count San Martino, president of the Accademia di Santa Cecilia, a visit fully endorsed by the British government, which wanted to encourage the much-bruised Italy (after her costly military efforts in the Dolomites against Austria) to keep her nerve.[30] In the first half Bantock conducted Part I of his *Omar Kháyyam* and Harty was forced, at short notice, to cobble together a programme which again included *L'Après-midi*. By all accounts, the performance was magnificent: 'a Corot-like haze enveloped the whole work, and you positively felt (rather than heard) the atmosphere of heat and languorous ease.'[31] At Bradford on 4 December 1915 Harty continued to widen his repertoire. Besides conducting Beethoven's Fifth Symphony and Mozart's Violin Concerto in A with Arthur Catterall, leader of the Hallé, he introduced the novelty of an orchestral suite – *The Shoes that were Danced to Pieces* – taken from a ballet by the Sheffield-born composer Dora Bright, who had collaborated closely with the ballerina Adeline Genée. For his second concert at Bradford on 18 March, Harty directed Tchaikovsky's Fourth Symphony and Stanford's Irish Rhapsody No. 1, works which remained standard fare throughout his conducting career. Indeed, Harty always loved Tchaikovsky's symphonies and greatly admired the 'Pathétique', which he directed along with Berlioz's 'Queen Mab' Scherzo, Dvořák's Symphonic Variations and Wagner's *Faust* Overture at a return appearance at the Edinburgh Orchestral Concerts in January. Such a programme confirmed his allegiance and devotion to the late Romantic masters.

In the early months of 1916 there were more concerts in Manchester, and as a useful supplement to his income – there being little accompanying work available apart from three recitals with Menges at the Aeolian Hall in February – he took employment at the Kingsway Theatre as the pianist in the hundredth performance of *L'Enfant prodigue* (a revival of the celebrated pantomime by Michel Carré with music by André Wormers) and was engaged for the rest of the run.[32] The Royal Manchester College of Music (RNCM) also engaged him

---

[29] *MG*, 26 Jan. 1916.

[30] See Lucas, *Thomas Beecham*, 127ff.

[31] *MT* 57 (1916), 111.

[32] *The Times*, 27 Mar. 1916.

as one of their external examiners, along with Robert Radford.[33] In May, for the Shakespeare tercentenary celebrations at the Theatre Royal, Drury Lane, which were directed by Parry and Mackenzie in the presence of the king and queen, he was guest conductor with his *Comedy Overture*. He was also engaged by the LSO to take part in the concerts for Women's Tribute Week in June and July at Covent Garden, though these would prove to be the last of his conducting engagements for 1916.

With stalemate on the Western Front, the forever rising casualties, and the need for more men in uniform, the Prime Minister Herbert Asquith felt compelled to introduce compulsory military attestation of men in January of that year. After the Military Service Act received royal assent, single men between the ages of eighteen and forty-one were liable to be called for military service. In May the Act was extended to married men, and this included the thirty-six-year-old Harty, who elected to volunteer for the Royal Navy. After presenting himself for duty in June 1916 he was assigned to the Royal Naval Volunteer Reserve (RNVR) and underwent training at the shore establishment of HMS Victory VI until the end of July.[34] There, besides basic training, he learned signalling and other technical skills for military life at sea. From there, given his special aptitudes for sound, he was given special duties at Hawkscraig Hydrophone Experimental Station at Aberdour in Fife, Scotland, at the rank of sub-lieutenant. In December he applied for promotion to lieutenant. This was initially refused, though with the assurance that it would reconsidered after one year's seniority. In April 1917 his military record notes that he was on transfer to HMS Tarlair, where he was again working with hydrophonic detection of submarines. He was based there until his commission was terminated on health grounds on 22 May 1918, having been promoted to lieutenant in September 1917.[35] From the scant evidence we have of Harty's time in the navy, it seems that he enjoyed the experience and the camaraderie of military life and discipline. Recognising his musicianship, the Navy was quick to put his aural aptitudes to work:

> The notable talent of Lieutenant Hamilton Harty RNVR ... was enlisted to tune the equipment and match pairs of hydrophones. Anybody with a musical ear was an asset to underwater sound research, but one man deserves immortality, not so much for possessing perfect pitch, but for checking it with a precisely tuned cranium. Sir Richard Paget was convinced by 1916 that the key to hydrophone design was to establish propeller frequencies. Accordingly he arranged to be suspended by his legs over the side of a boat in the Solent while a submarine circled him. After a suitable period submerged (and before he actually drowned) this devoted scientist was hauled up humming the notes he had heard whereupon, safely back in the boat, he related them to the standard G-sharp which he obtained by tapping his skull with a metal rod.[36]

[33] *MG*, 19 May 1916.

[34] Agnes Nicholls recalled that during the war she 'learned to cook' in Scotland, where she was 'canteening' for the navy: Nicholls, 'A Vignette', 26.

[35] National Register of Archives, ADM 337/122.

[36] R. Compton-Hall, *Submarines at War, 1914–1918* (Penzance: Periscope Publishing, 2004), 92.

During an interview in Australia in 1934, conducted during a rehearsal in Sydney, Harty recalled some of his work with the hydrophone station:

> The hydrophone service was one of the 'hush' services of the Admiralty and called for skilled tonal development by the listener, a kind of discriminating and musical A.B., who could distinguish the throb of a ship's engine from the more rhythmic and subdued beat of the Diesel engines of the submarine.
>
> The listener worked in a room surrounded by delicate instruments, not unlike the operator in the wireless room of a ship.
>
> A cable, either from the shore or running out from the survey ship, picked up the vibrations, magnified them and sent them to the discerning ear of the listener.
>
> Still, we accounted for many submarines during the war, and, if not successful in sending them to their doom, warned ships of their proximity.[37]

Harty, so the broadcaster and writer Eric Gillett maintained, retained a deep love of the sea, and this in turn engendered a deep desire to travel. 'In the last war', Gillett recalled, 'Harty commanded a trawler in the North Sea and this gave him some of the pleasantest memories of his life. He had a tremendous admiration for the men of the Merchant Navy, and there was scarcely a book written by them or about them that he had not read.'[38]

The Navy was generous to Harty in allowing him some flexibility to conduct during his period of duty in the North Sea. He was given leave to undertake several concerts with the Hallé in Manchester and the LSO in 1917, which included both their concerts at Queen's Hall and at the Palladium for the Sunday League. In January 1917 Emil Młynarski was due to conduct the fourth, fifth and sixth orchestral concerts of the LSO's winter season, but owing to an incomplete recovery from a recent illness, and passport difficulties in Moscow, he was unable fulfil his contract. Consequently Harty was asked if he could undertake the fourth concert at short notice. In an act of single-mindedness, Harty agreed, but on the basis that Młynarski's programme be almost entirely altered. Only Beethoven's Fourth Piano Concerto, with Irene Scharrer, remained unchanged; otherwise, Harty insisted on Berlioz's overture *Benvenuto Cellini*, Wagner's *Siegfried Idyll* and Dvořák's Ninth Symphony. The LSO acquiesced.[39] With this arranged, the LSO met again on 2 February and unanimously agreed to invite Harty to conduct the fifth and sixth concerts on 5 and 19 March.[40] On the former occasion Harty directed Glazunov's Sixth Symphony (whose works had a certain following in London, not least by Stanford), which was well received; at the latter Harty directed de Greef's Piano Concerto with the composer as soloist, which was heard for the time in England. More significantly, a major change to the programme was Bantock's 'Hebridean' Symphony which took the place of Brahms's Second Symphony. The adjustment came about because the critic of the *Pall Mall Gazette* had taken umbrage at the concert series as a whole, labelling it a 'German Festival'. At first the LSO Directors considered

---

[37] *The Sun*, 6 June 1934.
[38] Typescript of BBC talk by Eric Gillett, 19 Feb. 1943, *GB-Mcm*, Man.Mus.49.
[39] LSO Minute Book 1915–20, 11 Jan. 1917, 132.
[40] LSO Minute Book 1915–20, 11 Jan. 1917, 135.

legal action for malicious libel, but Counsel's advice was to ignore it. With Elgar's *Cockaigne* Overture opening the concert, a sufficiently more British programme was presented to the audience.[41] At the Palladium Harty worked with an impressive array of artists, including Sammons in Lalo's *Symphonie espagnol* (Sammons's fame had been ignited at the beginning of the war when he undertook Elgar's Violin Concerto at short notice after Kreisler, a member of the Austrian army, had to withdraw), de Greef, Robert Radford, Myra Hess, and the Lancashire pianist Tyrer Anderson. In fact, Harty worked particularly closely with Anderson in the years immediately after the war. Anderson, who had been a scholarship student at the RMCM, served throughout the war in the British Army before making his debut with Beecham at a Promenade Concert in 1919. Harty, impressed with his talents, engaged him on many occasions as soloist in concertos by Grieg, Tchaikovsky and Rachmaninov, for which Anderson became well known during the 1920s.

For the 1916–17 Manchester Promenade season Harty was announced with Beecham, Ronald, Młynarski, Harrison and Goossens.[42] Among the more unusual repertoire, he conducted Chabrier's *Spanish Rhapsody* (28 October), and in the new year, on 10 February 1917, he conducted his revised 'Irish' Symphony in a concert which largely consisted of operatic numbers with the Manchester Beecham Operatic Chorus. At a concert on 10 March he appeared along with his wife and Arthur Catterall in a programme which featured Berlioz's overture *Benvenuto Cellini*, Sullivan's *Di ballo* and *L'Après-midi*, though, for the first time, in Schubert's 'Unfinished' Symphony Langford found room for criticism:

> That Mr Harty is both a romantic composer and an interpreter of poetic power is beyond question. But there are some definite elements of romance to which his vividness seems alien. In Schubert's 'Unfinished' Symphony the essence of the music seems to be not its sadness, its tenderness, its melody, or its immediate power, but the suggestion that all beauty is fleeting. The most essential feature of its interpretation seems, therefore, to be a rhythm which has no stay, or which lingers only so much as is required to give a pensive tinge to the passing of the melody. The sort of expressive ritardando which Mr Harty imparted to the opening unison passage, and even the very warmth of the expression indulged, frequently tend rather to make this illusion of swiftly-passing beauty impossible.[43]

In the early months of 1918 Harty was able to continue his arrangements with the Hallé and directed the orchestra in Berlioz's *Beatrice and Benedict*, Elgar's *Enigma* Variations and Tchaikovsky's Fifth Symphony (23 February), though in the event, he somewhat unexpectedly changed the programme to introduce the unfamiliar Second Symphony by Borodin.[44]

[41] See Foss and Goodwin, *London Symphony*, 88.

[42] *MG*, 4 Oct. 1916. Classified advertisements described Harty 'who will travel especially from his naval duties "somewhere" in Scotland to conduct this concert': *MG*, 27 Oct. 1916).

[43] *MG*, 12 Mar. 1917.

[44] *MG*, 25 Feb. 1918.

Though Harty acquitted himself honourably in the RNVR, with 'excellent abilities and diligence', he was discharged from naval duties in May 1918 owing to poor health; in fact, we know from a letter Nicholls wrote to Captain Harry Talbot-Rice of the Welsh Guards that her husband had suffered a collapse: 'Do come see us some time if you are anywhere near Lords? My husband is just discharged from the Navy owing to a nervous breakdown, but he is already better and hopes to take up his work again in the autumn.'[45] Quite what the reasons for Harty's breakdown were is unknown. It may have been the constant pressure of military life and responsibility mixed with trying to keep his musical career going, or poor health, or even the knowledge that his father's health was fragile.

But once out of the Navy, Harty seems to have recovered rapidly, for as his wife predicted, he was able to resume his career with renewed vigour. In fact, by July, he was already accepting engagements. One was to examine composition and the orchestra at the RCM. Parry, who had been much impressed by Harty's abilities as an accompanist, not least in the performances of his *English Lyrics* dedicated to Agnes Nicholls, was equally taken by Harty's energy and insight at the RCM examinations:

Hamilton Harty arrived to examine composition and orchestra. Seemed well qualified for both. In the absence of Stanford he conducted the orchestra, and quite astonishingly well. He put energy and warmth into them they had never known before. Elastic tempi, vivid points. It was delightful to see. The utmost opposite of C V S. And they took it in thoroughly. If he was conductor he would make a sensation.[46]

In July Harty also wrote to the LSO Board of Directors rather boldly to announce that 'he could not share the conducting of the Sunday Afternoon Concerts at the Palladium with any other conductor, and that he must have a voice in the selection of the programmes.'[47] Although the Board refused initially to grant Harty his request – they reserved the right to employ other conductors periodically in the interests of the orchestra – they eventually acceded to his wishes. It was an early indication of Harty's tendency towards autocracy, and from the following account it is clear that negotiations between him and the Directors were not always without discord:

It was agreed that Mr H H be invited to conduct the whole of the Sunday afternoon concerts during the present season and on the question of programmes it was agreed that the Board should meet once a month to definitely fix programmes and that Mr Harty be invited to attend each meeting to assist and thereby avoid any

[45] Letter from Agnes Harty to Captain Talbot-Rice, 8 July 1918, *GB-Lam*, McCann Collection, 2006.214. There is an indication from Harty's military record that he intended to resign his commission in May 1918 but that this was not accepted (this part of the record is crossed out). It may well have been at this stage that Harty's nervous condition reached breaking point.

[46] Diary of Sir Hubert Parry, 16 July 1918, *GB-ShP*.

[47] LSO Minute Book 1915–20, 8 July 1918, 174.

friction in future, and that should Mr Harty fail to attend, he must abide by the arranged programmes in his absence.[48]

Securing regular work with the LSO and the Sunday League Concerts was an important *coup* for Harty. Able to choose much of his own repertoire, he was free to mix up standard classical works with new pieces, as well as to establish a growing reputation for his love of certain composers, notably Tchaikovsky, Berlioz and Mozart. Tchaikovsky and Wagner, without doubt, were assured box office successes so that concerts such as those on 26 October and 19 December 1919 (all-Tchaikovsky affairs) and 22 November 1919 (all Wagner) filled the hall, as did those which featured the favourite piano concertos of Grieg and Rachmaninov. Critical acclaim for his Wagner interpretations was also such that his stature as a conductor was steadily being compared with the top rank:

> Mr Harty has not shrunk from exposing himself to comparisons with the greatest conductors, whether in miscellaneous bills or in all-Wagner or all-Russian programmes. It helps in measuring progress when it is remembered that half-a-dozen years ago an evening of the big Wagner or big Russian was only successfully attempted by one or at most two English conductors. Harty's Wagner has the unmistakable feeling for vastness and sublimity. There is more of the Richter nobility and grandeur than of the Beecham galvanic qualities. In the climaxes the stately, irresistible, overpowering advance of the ocean flood rather than the rush and tumult of wild waters. The latter is more exciting, and very exhilarating, but the former has greater enduring quality and consequently is more satisfying. Except for the absence of a fuller body of string-tone, one need never expect to hear a more truly superb *finale* of 'Götterdämmerung' than the Harty reading and his wife singing Brünnhilde.[49]

Harty enjoyed a good rapport with the LSO players and occasionally worked with them outside the forum of Queen's Hall. One such concert was an appearance with the Finnish baritone George Pawlo, who sang with the LSO under Harty at the Wigmore Hall on 8 November 1918 in music by Elgar and Holst, with orchestral interludes that included music by Delius and the inevitable Berlioz.[50] With the LSO there were also opportunities to experiment with rare works such as Cowen's forgotten Piano Concerto (30 March 1919) and *A Phantasy of Life and Love* (11 January 1920), and W. H. Reed's Violin Concerto in A minor (27 April 1919), and with newer productions such as Respighi's *Fountains of Rome* (11 November 1919), completed in 1918, and Howells's *Puck's Minuet* (19 October 1919), written in 1917 as part of two pieces for small orchestra (the second being *Merry Eye*). In fact Harty was highly enthusiastic about Howells's miniature and first introduced it with the LSO at Queen's Hall on 4 March 1919. Unfortunately Howells was not well enough to attend his premiere:

[48] LSO Minute Book 1915–20, 16 Dec. 1918, 182.

[49] *MT* 59 (1918), 521.

[50] Harty's appearance with Pawlo was in fact part of a series of concerts at the Wigmore Hall between September and December 1918, which unusually featured 'Anglo-Finnish' art songs with a particular emphasis on Sibelius and Palmgren: see *MG*, 24 Aug. 1918.

I am sorry that illness kept you away last night because your charming piece had a great success – indeed I was obliged to repeat it. It sounded delightful and the L.S.O. played it perfectly. Simple as it is, I think the beautiful way it is made makes it quite a little classic. I hope to perform it at Manchester Ap:5th – also at my Sunday Concerts here. Have you written any work of about 12–15 minutes for orchestra? I shd. be glad to know of it – you know I am as keen as anything on British music that is really good and interesting and wd. do a great deal to further it – but I can't stand the usual stuff we get so much of. Either heavy dull pretentious music or Ravel & Debussy 10 years too late. I am sure this way of 'British' music is useless if we don't weed out the bad from the good in a very ruthless way. Many compliments on your 'minuet' and I hope your indisposition is only temporary.[51]

Harty honoured his promise to perform *Puck's Minuet* with the Hallé (and he also performed it in Leeds in December 1919), but he was keen to cajole Howells, at that time seen as a man of real promise, to write a work of greater substance. His eagerness to promote British music would be a recurring feature of his mission as a conductor – which was consistent, of course, with the performance of his own music – but he was deeply sceptical about the wave of Francophilia that had seized many of the younger native composers. Moreover, as this letter shows unambiguously, Harty was not someone to mince his words, an honest trait that endeared him to his friends and some of his colleagues, but was also apt to generate controversy, not least when his own ideas were either inconsistent or not clearly thought through. In a second letter to Howells, whose music he evidently admired, he was no less forthright than in his first:

You will see that your 'minuet' besides pleasing the audience (which is excellent) was greeted with approval by the entire press (which wd. be alarming if it were not for the fact that the critics are – for the most part – ignorant and uneducated & simply follow the crowd). One time I heard some pieces for strings at the college – there was a beautiful slow movement, an elegy I think – Was this the string suite you refer to? I thought this particular piece was on a very high level if I may say so.

You will think I am narrow – but I don't like the name of your suite 'The B's'! It sounds to me rather like the RCM and Grove's Dictionary – and I shd. prepare myself for jokes at the expense of Bach, Beethoven etc. Excuse my frankness – From an orchestral point of view – what is badly needed is work of medium length – with a central interest – not a suite – but a poem of 12–15 minutes – Failing this a symphony of 30 minutes – are you in sympathy with these ideas? Perhaps you will feel inclined to write something in either form.[52]

From Howells there were other major orchestral works, but he rejected Harty's suggestion for a symphony. This task ultimately fell to others to fulfil.

While work with the LSO increased substantially, Harty returned to familiar haunts for other conducting engagements. The Manchester Promenade season, more ambitious than before, announced that Harty would take on at least fourteen concerts during the four weeks of concerts between 30 September and 26 October, as well as two others jointly with Beecham. This was on account

[51] Letter from Harty to Howells, 5 Mar. 1919, *GB-Lcm*.
[52] Letter from Harty to Howells, 10 Mar. 1919, *GB-Lcm*.

of the Manchester Opera Company's (founded by Beecham) being on tour in Scotland, which meant that Pitt, Goossens and Harrison could only appear once each during the season.[53] For all its punishing schedule of concerts, this was a golden opportunity for Harty to undertake an extended period of concert 'exposure' which Langford considered commensurate with his rising fame and fortune, and with his ability to develop as a conductor of stature in the wake of Nikisch and Richter:

> Mr Hamilton Harty has fairly won a second time by his own merits the success of the Promenade Concerts, which was won first by a galaxy of brilliant conductors last year. The actual musical success of his conducting has increased almost from night to night as the players have adapted themselves to the rapidity and complexity which are a valuable part of his quality and style but are a difficulty of his method. It will be understood that nowhere except in the full current of the music can the action of the conductor find an absolutely simultaneous response in that of the players. Granted, therefore, all the rhythmical and musical genius requisite for the conductor's art, there remains still the intractable difficulty of conveying by anticipatory suggestion every vital departure that is to be made in the interpretation of the music. It is well known how diligently Nikisch laboured with his permanent orchestras and in the minute control of his own movements to arrive at an understanding with his players. ... It is as notorious how by an extreme simplicity of style Richter achieved the same certainty.[54]

This season also enabled him to expand his repertoire with an impressive catalogue of works such as Ravel's *Rhapsodie espagnole* and Pitt's new *English Rhapsody* (9 October), Stravinsky's *Firebird* Suite (11 October), Somervell's suite *Thomas the Rhymer* (16 October), the choral dances from Borodin's *Prince Igor* and the coronation scene from Mussorgsky's *Boris Godunov* (18 October), Ravel's *Introduction and Allegro* (19 October), Esposito's *Neapolitan* Suite (22 October), Stravinsky's *Danse infernale* (23 October) and a revival of his own Violin Concerto with Bessie Rawlins (6 October), who also took the work to Bournemouth.[55] On 24 October Harty was called away from Manchester having heard that his father was gravely ill (probably with the influenza epidemic that was just beginning to grip Manchester); his place was taken by Julius Harrison.[56] But by 26 October Harty had returned to Manchester in order to appear with Beecham as pianists in Bach's Double Concerto for Two Pianos. The item proved an immense success and the last movement was encored.[57] But Harty's time in Manchester was curtailed by the need to return to Hillsborough

---

[53] C. B. Rees, *One Hundred Years of the Hallé* (London: MacGibbon & Kee, 1957), 57. Beecham was to have conducted a concert performance of Berlioz's *Damnation of Faust* on 8 October at the Promenade Concerts, but was unable to get back from Glasgow, so Harty stepped into the breach at the last moment. It was, of course, a work he loved and knew intimately.

[54] *MG*, 21 Oct. 1918.

[55] *MT* 59 (1918), 564.

[56] *MG*, 25 Oct. 1918.

[57] Lucas, *Thomas Beecham* 144.

for, shortly afterwards, his father began to fail seriously, and by 1 November he
was dead. It affected his son deeply.

In addition to the Promenade Concerts, Harty was engaged to conduct three
of the concerts in the 1918–19 Hallé season. With the cessation of hostilities on
the Western Front, the concert of 14 November was rapidly altered to reflect the
mood of the moment. Harty conducted Mackenzie's overture *Britannia*, Parry's
Blest Pair of Sirens (a work he otherwise rarely conducted), Bizet's *La Patrie*,
Tchaikovsky's *Francesca da Rimini* and Elgar's *Pomp and Circumstance* March
No. 1, which was accompanied by a vocal rendition of the trio melody as 'Land
of Hope and Glory'. Langford was unimpressed by the expression of unbridled
patriotism, but the audience, who joined with soloist Gladys Roberts in the
refrain, were in no mood to feel sympathy with the enemy.[58] In December Harty
made a second appearance to conduct *With the Wild Geese*, excerpts from the
Firebird, Berlioz's *Carnaval romain*, and Beethoven's Violin Concerto with Daisy
Kennedy (the Australian-born violinist who had married the virtuoso pianist
Benno Moiseiwitsch in 1914) in a performance Langford considered equal to
that of Lady Hallé.[59] More auspiciously, in terms of public attention, Harty
undertook the traditional Christmas performance of *Messiah* by the Hallé on 19
December, in place of Beecham, who was ill. Adhering to Beecham's plan of cuts,
reorderings and transpositions, Harty also conformed to the tradition of placing
the 'Hallelujah' chorus at the conclusion. The *Musical Times* commented: 'Never
before (and possibly never again) shall we experience that peculiar sense of
fitness in moving the "Hallelujah" chorus to the end of the work, where its blend
of solemnity, sublimity, and jubilation voiced the feelings universally uppermost
in popular thought.'[60] It was also an occasion when he met the young English
bass Norman Allin, who by that time had become a well-established oratorio
singer. The two men became great friends and often took their holidays abroad
together. As Allin recalled:

> I first met Hay professionally, and a personal friendship began that lasted until his
> death. We had many holidays together on the Continent. A favourite rendezvous
> was Barbizon, where we used to take long walks during the day in the forests, and
> became gourmets at night, sampling the food and wines of the country with gusto.

> He was of medium height, broad-shouldered, well built – slight stoop, iron-
> grey hair brushed front to back, a bewitching smile, with laughing eyes alternating
> with a solemn countenance and wrinkled brow; very loyal in his friendships, but
> would never suffer fools gladly and would not hesitate to let you see it. He had
> a splendid sense of humour – his stories were short and to the point. At other
> times, he was pessimistic and full of gloomy forebodings; not always talkative and
> sometimes would walk for miles and say just nothing.[61]

---

[58] *MG*, 15 Nov. 1918.

[59] *MG*, 9 Dec. 1918; *MT* 60 (1919), 87.

[60] *MT* 60 (1919), 87.

[61] BBC talk, 3 Oct. 1951.

Beecham's last-minute absences incensed the Hallé Directors,[62] and there were several other occasions when Harty was requested to stand in for him. On 22 March Beecham had to remain in London when he was supposed to have given a notable performance of Holbrooke's symphonic poem *Ulalume*. Harty took over the concert and also introduced Martucci's *Noveletta*, Op. 82, to the Manchester public for the first time. This particular bent for late nineteenth- and early twentieth-century Italian music stemmed from his admiration for Esposito, who was still active as a musician at the RIAM in Dublin, though much of the lively music-making in the Irish capital had ceased since 1915, including the activities of the DOS. At the concert on 22 March notice was given that Harty would also take the place of Beecham in Bach's Mass in B minor. Though this was slightly more time than the critic of the *Musical Times* declared,[63] it was still a short period for Harty to learn the score. This, however, he did with aplomb, and he benefited from the experience at a further performance which Beecham was unable to undertake, this time with the Birmingham Festival Choir on 3 April.[64] Such an ability to assimilate complex works undoubtedly caught the eye of the orchestras and orchestral boards, who were, after all, on the look-out for new figures of artistic authority. However, Harty scored his greatest success with the Hallé on 5 April, when he conducted Berlioz's *Symphonie fantastique* to great acclaim, a work that had not been heard at Manchester since 1911. 'This ... predilection of his', wrote the critic of the *Musical Times*, 'is very strongly marked'.[65] Indeed, it was a work with which Harty would closely identify throughout his life, and one which stood at the forefront of his championship of the French composer. Surviving books from his personal library on Berlioz reveal that he was well aware of modern scholarship.[66] In his own programme notes to the work, Harty, whose heart was in the concert hall rather than the theatre, found an ideal admixture in the illustrative genius of the Frenchman and his affinity for literature:

> But if Berlioz has always had his detractors, he has also inspired warmest admiration in the hearts of those who really appreciated his aims and intentions. His music has always excited the fiercest controversy – it does still, though many years have passed since the death of the composer. About no musician probably has so much been written, both for and against; every year fresh books appear dealing with his life and compositions. Nevertheless the last word remains to be said and Berlioz's ultimate niche in the temple of music has yet to be assigned. Berlioz was first of all a 'literary musician'. His music is almost entirely programme music. He sought to translate into sound literary and pictorial ideas. His gods were not so much Bach and Beethoven as Virgil and Shakespeare, and the magical charm of his music consists to a great extent in the manner in which he translated and

[62] Lucas, *Thomas Beecham*, 148.

[63] *MT* 60 (1919), 243.

[64] *MT* 60 (1919), 239.

[65] *MT* 60 (1919), 243.

[66] Harty's extant copies of Berlioz literature by A. Ernst, A. Boschot, J.-G. Prodhomme and T. S. Wotton show that he was familiar with much of the current scholarship.

illumined ideas which already existed in another form. Occasionally indeed, especially in his operas, he deliberately sacrifices the merely musical effect in order to be more sincerely truthful to the particular scene or emotion he is illustrating.[67]

Such was Harty's reputation for conducting Berlioz, and especially the *Symphonie fantastique*, that he drew special admiration from his fellow conductors. As Rees remembered of Boult:

> On more than one train journey Sir Adrian Boult has enthused to me about the Hallé Orchestra's performances, under Harty, of the 'Fantastic' Symphony. 'Whenever I had a chance,' he said, 'I would always rush off to Manchester to hear it': and these conversations, it may be added, occurred years after Harty had left Manchester, and indeed after he died. How alive the memory of those interpretations must have stayed in the mind – and in the mind of another eminent conductor at that.[68]

From time to time during the war Harty was able to accept engagements as accompanist with the Welsh violinist Tessie Thomas, the Polish virtuoso Bronisław Huberman, and the New Zealand soprano Stella McLean at the Aeolian Hall, though, because of the deteriorating economic circumstances, these tended to be sporadic. In the years directly after the war Harty continued, albeit more selectively, to earn part of his living in this way. He befriended the violinist Katie Goldsmith, who was a keen exponent of his Violin Concerto.[69] He was particularly close to the Harrison sisters and took part in many of their Wigmore Hall concerts in 1918 and 1919, not least in the propagation of new chamber music.[70] On 31 October 1918 he and Beatrice Harrison gave the premiere of Delius's Cello Sonata, and repeated their performance on 11 January 1919. On 11 November 1918 he accompanied May Harrison in another performance of Delius's First Violin Sonata. Such events sealed the close association of the Harrison sisters and Harty with Delius's music. They had a similar connection with Stanford, too, continued by Margaret Harrison's first appearance at the Wigmore Hall on 6 December 1918, in Debussy's Sonata (which had recently appeared in 1917) and, with sister Beatrice, in Stanford's new *Irish Concertino*.[71] Harty accompanied them again in February 1919 in a chamber performance of Brahms's Double Concerto, and in June 1919 in Ravel's Piano Trio. Ravel's Trio (completed at the beginning of the war) and Delius's Cello Sonata were new to London audiences. Also new was the series of chamber works which Elgar had

---

[67] Harty's programme note is pasted into the preliminary pages of his own copy of the score (held at *GB-Belqb*).

[68] Rees, *One Hundred Years of the Hallé*, 61.

[69] Goldsmith and Harty performed the Concerto at the Wigmore Hall on 8 February 1919. Later that year Goldsmith championed the work with Harty and the LSO on 14 June, and with Wood and the New Queen's Hall Orchestra on 28 August.

[70] The Bechstein Hall, which was seized as enemy property during the war, was reopened as the Wigmore Hall in 1917.

[71] Harty also appeared with Murray Lambert at the Wigmore Hall in a new Violin Sonata by Stanford on 7 May 1919.

written towards the end of the war. W. H. Reed, leader of the LSO, gave the first performance at the Aeolian Hall with Ronald on 21 March 1919. This was then followed with some excitement by Catterall and Harty, who received special mention in the press for their forthcoming performance at the Houldsworth Hall, Manchester, on 15 April 1919. Langford, who was there to witness an enthusiastic audience, found most to praise in the first movement: 'The general handling of this movement was most admirable, and, indeed, the warmth of Mr Catterall's playing and the musicianly vigour and electric current of Mr Harty's general style ensured the work a most happy introduction.'[72]

In addition, Harty also continued to make a living conducting semi-professional orchestras in Leeds and Newcastle, where, like the programmes of the Palladium Concerts, the repertoire was essentially popular. With Tyrer Anderson they performed concertos by Grieg, MacDowell and Rachmaninov, and Harty occasionally conducted his own works such as the *Comedy Overture*. As a celebration of the end of the war Agnes Nicholls sang in a performance of Bach's *Magnificat* as a counterpart to *The Mystic Trumpeter* given by Leeds Philharmonic Society under Bairstow in March 1919, and, early the following year, in the same city, Harty conducted the first performance of his *Fantasy Scenes (from an Eastern Romance)*, completed in 1919 and later published in Dublin by the publishing company C. E.[73] This work had grown out of the abortive experience of *The Singer of Shiraz* which had remained unperformed from 1915. Rather than construct a suite from the existing pieces from the play, Harty elected to write a new work with his own programme (he provided his own notes in the score), deploying some of the music from his original theatre score and, at the same time, shaping his four short balletic movements around a story – the 'Eastern Romance' – that followed recognisably similar lines to Fagan's play. The first movement, 'The Laughing Juggler', depicts Mohammed the juggler, who has been commanded to attend an audience with the Sultan. While before the Sultan, he catches sight of the beautiful Zuleika, the Sultan's favourite dancing girl, and attempts to imbue his jesting words with veiled messages of love. A lively scherzo full of gossamer scoring for wind, the movement's outer sections are somewhat reminiscent of Chabrier's light, colourful canvases. The trio, on the other hand, has a more familiar Russian flavour, and many of the elaborate triplet figurations Harty drew from the *Shiraz* Prelude to Act I Scene 1. 'A Dancer's Reverie' effectively pays tribute to the Scherzo of Tchaikovsky's Fourth Symphony in its extended use of pizzicato. Zuleika, who reclines alone by a fountain in the palace courtyard at dusk, dwells on the immediate memories of her encounter at a distance with the juggler, her wilder romantic thoughts conveyed by the more wayward trio (which refers to the corresponding section of the first movement). 'Lonely in Moonlight', to all intents and purposes the

---

[72] *MG*, 16 Apr. 1919.

[73] C. E. were the initials for Esposito and Cochrane, who founded a music publishing company in Dublin in 1915 largely to promulgate Esposito's pedagogic editions of piano music by other composers, as well as his own music. Besides Harty's *Fantasy Scenes*, Esposito oversaw the publication of the full scores of his protégé's Violin Concerto and Piano Concerto: Dibble, *Michele Esposito*, 156.

slow movement of the suite, is a truncated reworking of the Prelude to Act I Scene 2 of *The Singer of Shiraz*, using an orchestration of solo horn, strings and harp that seems strikingly suggestive of the slow movement of Borodin's Second Symphony, a work Harty knew well. The melody is the juggler's simple love song for Zuleika. The lively Finale to the suite, 'In the Slave Market', portrays the Sultan's discovery of the love of Mohammed and Zuleika. Mohammed has been banished, while Zuleika is to be sold at the slave market. Yet all attempts to buy Zuleika are outbid by a stranger who proves to be the juggler disguised as a merchant. The lovers then escape from the city to freedom. The central paragraph, which clearly depicts the exotic surroundings of the slave market, again uses the opening material of the Prelude to Act I Scene 1 from *Shiraz*, though with a number of more imaginative orchestral decorations.

In early 1919 Harty came together with the LSO at Queen's Hall to raise money for Russian women and children who were in distress owing to the civil war between the White and Red Armies.[74] He was then engaged for a second concert at the same venue with violinist Louis Godowsky, who played concertos by Brahms and Paganini. His relationship with the LSO Directors had remained reasonably cordial though, frustrated that his Palladium Concerts were unrehearsed, he had asked for 'occasional rehearsals', a request granted on the premise that funds were available.[75] However, after the Palladium series, it was not clear what the LSO wanted to do, and by March 1920, when Harty wrote requesting information about the next Palladium series, the Directors replied that no decision had yet been made.[76] In fact, during the 1919–20 series of Sunday League concerts, proceeds fell well short of predictions so that the Directors felt it necessary to cut down on the number of prominent soloists.[77] At this stage Harty must have thought that his future with the LSO seemed precarious.

But while work with the LSO looked less certain, his association with the Hallé grew ever closer. In October 1919 he made visits with the orchestra to Glasgow, Edinburgh and Newcastle,[78] while his connections with the semi-professional orchestras in Leeds and Newcastle strengthened his bond with the north. In Manchester, as in previous seasons, Harty shared conducting engagements with Goossens, Beecham and Albert Coates, who, having recently escaped the Bolshevik regime in Russia (where the appalling living conditions had made him ill),[79] had been appointed chief conductor of the LSO. Harty again conducted Berlioz's *Faust* on 22 December (a work which Langford pointed out had strong links with Manchester after Sir Charles Hallé premiered it there in January 1882)[80] and, on 11 December, he directed Respighi's *Fountains of Rome* for the first time in the city and Mozart's Symphony No. 40 with a

[74] *The Times*, 26 Feb. 1919.

[75] LSO Minute Book 1915–20, 14 Aug. 1919, 207.

[76] LSO Minute Book 1915–20, 29 Mar. 1920, 236.

[77] Foss and Goodwin, *London Symphony*, 100.

[78] *MT* 60 (1919), 707.

[79] Rees, *100 Years of the Hallé*, 57.

[80] *MG*, 24 Nov. 1919.

much-reduced orchestra, and also accompanied Nicholls in songs by Elgar (from the recent *Starlight Express*), Walker, and Kennedy-Fraser. His last concert before the Christmas vacation took place on 18 December in a programme which imparted much of his musical personality. Three French works – Grétry's overture *The Village Trial*, Dukas's immutable *L'Apprenti sorcier*, and Berlioz's *Symphonie fantastique* – confirmed Harty's devotion to French music of the nineteenth century, but it was the interpretation of Berlioz's masterpiece which shone brightly. As Langford noted: 'Mr Hamilton Harty has a special faculty in his interpretation, and he does a special service whenever he gives this master's music.'[81] In addition, Harty included two of Esposito's arrangements for small orchestra of the eighteenth-century Italians Rossi and Marcello, and a novelty to Mancunians was Delius's Violin Concerto with Albert Sammons (its dedicatee), though the unconventional nature of this one-movement structure was clearly not entirely amenable to either critics or audience. As Langford noted: 'The body of the work will at least need knowing to be generally acceptable.'[82]

Circumstances at the Hallé were in serious state of flux. Beecham, who had done so much generously to subsidise music in Manchester out of his own resources (and he never took a fee in all the time he conducted during the war),[83] now faced major financial problems of his own. Indeed, his operatic ventures had generated such interest and popularity that he had offered to build a new opera house after the war if the city could find a suitable site for it. But, in view of his pecuniary position, all this died a prompt death in 1919. Municipal aid had not been forthcoming in 1918 – the city had much greater social and infrastructural problems of its own – and the Directors, concerned that guarantors would not or could not countenance an increase in the commitments, foresaw a crisis worse than had been the case in 1914 when war threatened to bring the Hallé to its knees. The orchestral players, after years on half-pay, agitated to be remunerated on a concert-by-concert basis and looked for a substantial increase in their rate of pay, not least because the war had brought considerable inflation to the cost of living; and with the cessation of the Promenade Concerts (after the Directors had agreed that the Hallé would play for the Brand Lane Concerts, a rival concert series), a number of more militant players filed for damages on the grounds of loss of engagements (though they were ultimately unsuccessful in their legal case). This animus acted like a contagion across the orchestra and negotiations for revised salaries festered during the summer. Added to this, not all those who had served in uniform decided to return to their former positions in the orchestra. By the beginning of the 1919–20 season in October the orchestra found itself seriously depleted, even though it had managed to retain some of its core players, notably Arthur Catterall (leader), E. S. Redfern (flute), Harry Mortimer (first clarinet), Archie Camden (first bassoon) and Wilhelm Gezink (timpanist). In light of these difficulties, with Beecham and Coates committed elsewhere, and the impossibility of re-appointing Michael Balling or any other

---

[81] *MG*, 19 Dec. 1919.

[82] *MG*, 19 Dec. 1919.

[83] Kennedy, *The Hallé Tradition*, 201.

German or Austrian, the Directors called a meeting with Beecham and Coates at Christmas. Beecham outlined his advice in his autobiography, *A Mingled Chime*:

> I notified the various concert organizations with which I had been connected since 1914 of my inability to continue my association with them, and in the case of the Hallé Society counseled the appointment of a permanent conductor who would be willing to settle in the town. During the war the orchestra had been kept together with great difficulty, losing member after member every month, and had thus taken on a shape almost as impermanent as that of Proteus himself. What it needed badly was the control of a resident musician who would give all his time to the rebuilding of its badly shattered constitution, and the committee, accepting my advice, appointed Hamilton Harty.[84]

Coates was of the same mind, so Harty was approached. It was an offer that would change his life forever, and one that brought to fruition the prophecy of the young, impecunious pianist of Paddington of 1901.

[84] Thomas Beecham, *A Mingled Chime* (London: Hutchinson & Co., 1944; repr. 1987), 176.

Fig. 1 The first movement of Harty's transcription of Handel's *Water Music*

The Hallé Years

Harty's contract (which he always accepted as a gentleman's agreement)[1] was initially a fee of 650 guineas (about £30,000 by today's money) for thirty concerts, and for each additional concert, 25 guineas. The Manchester season, it was agreed, would consist of eighteen concerts, the traditional performance of *Messiah* at Christmas, and a concert for the orchestra's Pension Fund.[2] It was also agreed that Harty would be free to continue his engagements with other orchestras in London, Leeds and elsewhere (which included a new appointment as a joint conductor at the North Staffordshire Choral Society),[3] provided they did not impinge on his Manchester commitments. Harty also agreed to move his residence to the city, a factor which would add weight to the impression of 'permanence' (as well as satisfying those members who disliked the system of guest conductors) while also providing stability to the longer-term planning of the orchestra. Moreover, the Board's appointment of Harty, whose artistic sympathies lay entirely with orchestral music, also meant that musical emphasis in the city would now be placed on the concert hall rather than the opera house (which, for some members, was perceived as a disruptive influence on the traditionally 'private' ethos of the Hallé). Beecham expressed his satisfaction at the new arrangement, but the Board was still anxious about the broader financial aspects of the orchestra's accounts. The players wanted a fifty percent increase in their fees, and, besides the conductor's fee, the cost of visiting artists was now also much higher. Fortunately, by July 1920 new fees were agreed (giving a wage bill of £166 6s 6d per concert), and subscription rates for concert-goers were raised, albeit reluctantly.[4]

Knowledge of Harty's appointment soon leaked out so that by the end of January the press were ready to comment, especially about Harty's commitment to the Hallé as a concert orchestra:

> Mr Hamilton Harty has been offered and has accepted the post of official conductor of the Hallé Concerts. Mr Harty, now in his forty-first year – he was born in County Down, Ireland, on December 4, 1879, – is already well known in Manchester as a composer as well as a conductor. His first appearance here was at a Hallé Concert in 1913, when he conducted one of his own compositions. Since then he has frequently conducted at the Hallé Concerts and the Promenade Concerts. Like Sir Henry Wood, Mr Harty has devoted himself entirely to concert work, and has taken no part in the operatic movement. He is considered the best of British accompanists.
>
> It is the new conductor's intention to live near Manchester.[5]

[1] See *GB-Mha*, HS/1/6/2.

[2] Kennedy, *The Hallé Tradition*, 202.

[3] *MT* 61 (1920), 403.

[4] Kennedy, *The Hallé Tradition*, 213.

[5] *MG*, 27 Jan. 1920.

This largely factual article was supported by a more detailed endorsement by Beecham in February. There was, of course, no mention of Beecham's insolvency, but at the report of the twentieth annual meeting of Hallé Concert Society the Directors were anxious to make public Beecham's belief that the Society now had a bright future. Gustav Behrens, the Society's secretary, declared openly that it was the commonly held view that, under the system of guest conductors, music had suffered in Manchester. It was therefore, with the approval of both Beecham (who was retained for the time being as the orchestra's musical advisor, and with whom Harty would remain in close contact) and Coates that Harty's appointment had been expedited, and 'the executive could have made no better choice'.[6] Moreover, it was clearly stated that the new Hallé season would 'revert to pre-war conditions',[7] and would take place, without interruption, in the concert hall. Beecham concluded his letter to the Society with the following optimistic prognosis:

> One of your former musical directors – Dr Richter – once said that Mozart was a composer with a great future. May I echo this seeming paradox and say I believe the Hallé Concerts Society has a great future? Everywhere today throughout the North of England we have evidence today of growing devotion to serious music. It is true that the aspirations on the part of this growing public are at present somewhat indefinite and ill directed, but here is exactly where a resident conductor of an orchestra like yours can be of unlimited service. There is any amount of fresh ground to be broken and new areas to be cultivated. This task can be accomplished only by a man who is willing to come to Manchester, and remain there and devote himself to it.
>
> As your musical advisor it is with more than a little satisfaction that I look back on the last five years. In the autumn of 1914 the outlook was dark and depressing. Your Society, like many others, might easily have gone down and with difficulty have been lifted up again. But in spite of a hundred difficulties we kept our flag flying, and today I hear with the greatest gratification that the ship is riding safely at anchor in a smooth harbour.
>
> Let me be frank and tell you it was not always easy or cheerful for me to come to Manchester during the worst days and play as frequently as I then did to attenuated and over-anxious audiences, but one of the reasons why I have lessened the number of my appearances during the last eighteen months is that I have felt that the worst was over and the solidity of the Society was unimpaired. From what I hear from everyone around me I have no doubt at all that the Society will in a very short time be restored to that position of unquestioned prosperity and prestige that it enjoyed before the war broke out.[8]

Harty had a number of concerts with the Hallé to honour before his new contract began in October 1920. In March, on request, he gave a repeat performance of *The Fountains of Rome*, Stanford's *Songs of the Sea* and excerpts from Berlioz's *Faust*, but the main item of the programme was the first hearing

---

[6] *MG*, 17 Feb. 1920; see also Behren's statement, *GB-Mha*, HS/1/8/21.

[7] *MG*, 17 Feb. 1920.

[8] *MG*, 17 Feb. 1920.

in Manchester of his *Mystic Trumpeter* with Robert Radford. It was received cordially, though Langford, by now well-used to Harty's style of conducting and composition, was cooler than usual. Whitman's text, he professed, did not excite Harty to profundity in the same way it had Delius in *Sea Drift*:

> There is very little here of the of the poignant insight which is both vision and fidelity to nature, and which gave such a rich harvest of musical feeling in the 'Sea Drift' of Delius. Mr Harty has to soar very much on his own wings, and from the opening attempts a type of expression which the poem does little enough to support except in manner. The weakness of Mr Harty's music is that, like so many exalted compositions, it has little plasticity or graphic power.[9]

All the same, this was a useful return to a work Harty had not conducted for several years, and excellent preparation for a second performance which he was invited to direct for the London Choral Society on 24 April at the Albert Hall.[10] A final Hallé concert, in which Harty had to replace Albert Coates, again at short notice, wound up the series with a deliberately popular programme intended to fill every seat, featuring excerpts from *Parsifal* and *Tannhäuser* and Tchaikovsky's 'Pathétique' Symphony.

After doubts about his future with the LSO, Harty's association with the orchestra continued healthily in 1920. The Sunday League concerts at the Palladium were indeed in serious financial trouble. Losing money heavily, the orchestra decided to suspend the concerts in November 1920, and, after consultation with Boult, they were reorganised under his direction. After their next annual general meeting the Directors resolved to bring the series to an end.[11] The LSO was, nevertheless, unwilling to dispense with the popular concert altogether, and instead asked Harty to conduct a series of afternoon concerts (eleven in all) at the Albert Hall as part of the London Ballad Concerts (under the aegis of Boosey). Although these concerts tended to veer on the lighter side of the repertoire, Harty was keen, whenever possible, to introduce new British works to his audience. These included Eric Coates's *Miniature Suite* (6 November 1920), Quilter's suite from *As You Like It* (8 January 1921),[12] and his own *Fantasy Scenes (from an Eastern Romance)* (20 November 1920). These concerts were, however, in direct competition with the Queen's Hall Symphony Concerts, and after a year, with dwindling box office receipts, it was sensibly adduced that the series was no longer viable.

Harty's eagerness to promote new British works continued in harness with his association with the LSO's London season of concerts in 1920. On 27 January he gave the premiere of Bantock's *Overture to a Greek Tragedy* and directed a

---

[9] *MG*, 26 Mar. 1920.

[10] On this occasion, Harty shared the platform with Frederick Bridge (the RCS's chief conductor), an ageing Stanford (who conducted his *The Voyage of Maeldune* and *The Songs of the Fleet*), and Hubert Bath (who directed his *A Dream Poem: The Visions of Hannele*).

[11] Foss and Goodwin, *London Symphony*, 100.

[12] Quilter's music had yet to be used for the London Old Vic's production in the forthcoming October.

rare revival (with Tyrer Anderson) of Mackenzie's *Scottish* Concerto written originally for Paderewski. A further rarity in this concert was Anderson playing Arensky's Concerto in F minor. Anderson appeared regularly with Harty at this time, and at their next concert together with the LSO he performed another two concertos by Tchaikovsky and Liszt. Yet it was Harty's brilliance that was noted by the critic:

> The real interest of the evening lay in Mr Harty's conducting. He said to the thing 'Go'; and it went. If he was accompanying, he had everybody on the alert not to miss a point. If he was introducing a new work like Ducasse's 'Sarabande' bristling with new points, or one not so new like Ravel's 'Rhapsodie Espagnole', as witty and as tiring to read as G. K. Chesterton, he kept his head.[13]

With the violinist Murray Lambert and the New Queen's Hall Orchestra, Harty became acquainted with the Glazunov Violin Concerto (23 March 1920) and juxtaposed this Russian work with the first London performance of his *Fantasy Scenes (from an Eastern Romance)*. 'It is notable for the variety of colour the composer has been able to obtain with the use of limited means', remarked one critic, who also added that it 'was the first occasion in the history of music that an orchestral piece has been recorded on the gramophone before its first public performance.'[14] This referred to a recording with Columbia, with whom Harty was working ever more closely. He made no recordings in 1918 because of his naval duties and his breakdown in health, but in 1919 recording began again with alacrity, and, as Columbia were keen to publicise,[15] was contracted exclusively to the company. With the violinist Daisy Kennedy Harty made numerous recordings of chamber works by Beethoven, Schumann, Brahms, Grieg and Saint-Saëns, and he also made a number with Isolde Menges; with his growing stature as a conductor, Columbia engaged him regularly to make orchestral recordings, and more specifically extracts from popular operas, many of them with the most eminent singers of the day.[16] These included his friend Norman Allin, Clara Butt (who recorded Elgar's 'Where Corals Lie'[17] and Cowen's 'The Better Land'),[18] the Australian soprano Elsa Stralia, and the tenors Hubert Eisdell, Tom Burke and Frank Mullings. Stralia and Mullings between them recorded a considerable amount of operatic favourites by Handel, Mozart, Wagner, Verdi, Puccini and Mascagni, all under Harty's direction with 'scratch' orchestras, and much of it during the summer months when orchestral players

---

[13] *The Times*, 5 Feb. 1920.

[14] *MT* 61 (1921), 314. The Columbia recording of the *Fantasy Scenes* (C. 753–4) dates from 1919, but the critic may not have been aware of the work's premiere at Leeds in the previous January.

[15] *The Times*, 1 Sept. 1920.

[16] For more detailed reference to Harty's full panoply of recordings, see John Hunt, *More Musical Knights: Harty, Mackerras, Rattle, Pritchard* (London: John Hunt, 1997; repr. edn 2009), 7–70, and Niss, C., 'The Recordings of Sir Hamilton Harty', *Le Grand Baton*, issue no. 61, vol. 23(2) (1990), 16–37

[17] C. 7246.

[18] C. 7260.

were earning their fees in provincial town halls, seaside piers, or, in this case, for the gramophone companies.

News of Harty's appointment gained national attention when a biographical article about him was published in the April edition of the *Musical Times*. Through this agency, details of Harty's life were presented to the public, but perhaps more importantly, Harty was able to set his own agenda by laying emphasis on those elements of his background and training which he considered significant. A principal factor, articulated at the very beginning of the article, was Harty the 'autodidact' and 'an independent', engendered by his father's unbelief in the value of academic teaching. Such descriptions had the potential to present Harty as a 'free spirit', untrammelled by the restrictive, doctrinaire, even blinkered outlooks of the conservatoires and universities. Elgar had done just such a thing in his biography for the *Musical Times* in 1900.[19] Shaw, the iconoclast, with his anti-academic, anti-clerical and anti-institutional standpoint, had endorsed the same mindset, and Delius was in the process of creating his similarly autodidactic image, with the help of his confidante Philip Heseltine. As the article enunciated:

> Such a few years ago would have appeared impossible qualifications in a conductor of the Hallé Orchestra. The last-named would in itself have been pretty well fatal to a candidate for the appointment, quite apart from autodidactic independence. But there has been a European war; and Mr Hamilton Harty, ungarlanded with the laurels of Leipsic, Bayreuth, or Berlin, steps into the hieratic succession of Herren Hallé, Richter, and Balling.[20]

In addition to describing Harty's background at Hillsborough (which, like his much later autobiography, was not entirely accurate), the article mentioned his undeniable prowess as the 'prince of accompanists'. His ability to talk intelligently and garrulously about music and other subjects was attributed to his Irish birthright, and there was mention of his marriage to Agnes Nicholls, though of course no allusion was made to the 'convenience' of their relationship. One suspects perhaps that Harty, though in the ascendant, still needed the professional alliance of his wife, and, anyway, the last thing he needed at this time was the scandal of a divorce.

Similarly, Harty's political views were underplayed: 'Hamilton Harty is Irish to the core, but is not a musical nationalist.'[21] No doubt these words were chosen with some care. In April 1920 the struggle for Irish independence was at its height. Royal Irish Constabulary barracks were being burned to the ground, and many institutions connected with the judiciary, customs and the Inland Revenue – symbols of the crown – were in crisis because of their subversion by the IRA. Violence by one side was answered clumsily with reprisals by the other, all of which appalled the Irish public, but heavy-handed actions on the part of the British government through the military bolstering of the RIC by the infamous 'Black and Tans' only inflamed public sensibilities. Unfortunately

[19] See 'Edward Elgar', *MT* 41 (1900), 641–8.

[20] [Colles], 'Hamilton Harty', 227.

[21] [Colles], 'Hamilton Harty', 227.

lessons had not been learned since the execution of Irish nationalist rebels after the Easter Uprising of 1916. Stanford, an unrepentant southern Unionist, was entirely candid about his views on Irish Home Rule, but what Harty truly thought about the Irish political question he never expressed, at least not in public. 'Personally', he once declared, 'I have never regarded myself as other than a British musician with an Irish accent.'[22] Clearly his Anglican roots in Ulster remained a powerful part of his make-up which led him to identify with his British heritage, But Harty was part of many Irish families who were divided by the border, for he had numerous relatives in the newly established Irish Free State with whom he kept in close contact; and there were his friends – such as John McCormack, Esposito's children,[23] Padraig Colum and John Larchet – who had gladly embraced the new regime. Surviving books from his private library, poetry by Thomas McDonagh and Patrick Pearse, and Dan Breen's *My Fight for Irish Freedom* of 1924, suggest that he did make an effort to understand the motives of the nationalists with whom he still felt some element of kinship, one borne out by the letter of commiseration he later expressed to Eamon de Valera on the loss of his son in 1936.[24] There was, of course, the abiding attachment to his mentor, Esposito, which brought him frequently to the Irish capital for consultation. But quite evidently Harty wished to contribute something more substantial to musical life, both north and south of the new border. After the establishment of the Irish Free State and the province of Northern Ireland in 1921 Harty's actions spoke louder than words. He acted as adjudicator not only at the Dublin Feis,[25] but at others in Sligo and Londonderry; as conductor of the Hallé he made a special point of taking the orchestra to Belfast and Dublin; he actively took part in assisting the institutions of both the Free State (notably Radio Telefís Éireann) and Ulster, and he keenly encouraged the pursuit of Irish composition. Such deeds suggested a deep-seated 'Irish' identity that, in many ways, transcended the politics of his day.

The *Musical Times* article also gave Harty an opportunity to lay down some artistic markers of his own. He flattered the Manchester audience for its open receptivity, at the expense of closed-minded Londoners, particularly in view of his controversial devotion to the music of Hector Berlioz:

> One of the pleasures of the musician at Manchester is in the subtlety of the audiences there. Yes, they are not only keen but also subtle. The difference is immense between them and Londoners, who so often seem to be listening with closed minds. A London audience is often simply not to be won, but sits in apathy as much as to say that as a sufficient impression of such and such a composer, or such and such a work had been formed years ago, no fresh one is desirable. I should despair of charming London with Berlioz in the way in which Manchester has lately been charmed. This leaning of theirs towards

[22] In H. Hamilton Harty, 'The Discouragement of English Music', *GB-Belqb*.

[23] Dibble, *Michele Esposito*, 156ff.

[24] See the letter from de Valera to Harty, Feb. 1936, *GB-Belqb*.

[25] The Feis also instituted the 'Hamilton Harty Cup' for the performance of a piano concerto.

Berlioz suits me, because Berlioz is one of the gods of my idolatry. We shall be having quite a lot Berlioz at Manchester next winter – 'Fantastic' again, and 'The Damnation of Faust' complete, 'Harold in Italy', and portions of his opera, 'The Trojans'.[26]

Harty then proceeded to give some account of his own musical preferences. His attraction to symphonic and choral music, to the detriment of opera, has already been mentioned (although, as we have seen and will see, his antipathy to opera was essentially in the *theatre*, not in the concert hall or recording studio). Again he returned to Berlioz, and to Mozart (a more unconventional choice given the pre-war Richter-led zeal for Beethoven) as 'intuitive composers', a revealing description perhaps of Harty's own 'intuitive', indeed 'instinctive', autodidactic situation:

Berlioz and Mozart are my private deities. I cannot always make people see what ground they have in common, yet it is clear to me that they are the two great intuitive composers as distinguished from the great logical ones. Of course all great composers must have intuition, but most have had to eke theirs out with logic, while intuition hardly ever seems to have failed my two heroes. And it is intuition that I count as the supreme thing in music. Call it heart as against head if you will. In Berlioz, as in Mozart, you are always coming upon a beautiful, fresh-sprung melodic line such as no amount of head-work could have suggested. In Wagner, much as I love his music, I feel sometimes a mechanical process at work which makes me rate him below Berlioz.[27]

In César Franck he found a weakness in the mystical style, even though later he would champion the Symphony in D minor; in Brahms's output he was selective, preferring the 'grey, level serenity of such works as the "Requiem",' yet with the Hallé he did much not only to rehabilitate the composer's symphonies but also to convince his detractors that he was not a nineteenth-century conservative.[28] For the music of Skryabin he predicted a short vogue (which must have rankled Albert Coates, who had been promulgating the Russian's orchestral music enthusiastically with the LSO and the Hallé). Yet it was towards 'logic' or cerebral music that Harty directed his severest criticism:

This logic that can go on for ever, though intuition fail, is the source of all the dull, pretentious music of the ancients and of the terrible cleverness of the moderns. But I think the modern logicians have the better of it, because they are not so preternaturally solemn. Logic if tolerable must tend towards comedy, and such composers as Stravinsky and Ravel (whom I admire greatly) are all that is witty. Save us from the composers who argue solemnly![29]

Cleaving to his touchstone of intuition, Harty retained a deep suspicion of new – or what he deemed 'clever' – methods of composition. Although he admitted to an admiration of Stravinsky, this was largely reserved for the

[26] [Colles], 'Hamilton Harty', 228.

[27] [Colles], 'Hamilton Harty', 228–9.

[28] [Colles], 'Hamilton Harty', 229.

[29] [Colles], 'Hamilton Harty', 229.

composer's earlier Russian period; Ravel's later experiments were also ignored. In terms of British music, he was open to the Romantic language of Bantock, Bax and, later Walton, whose music he conducted with enthusiasm (as witnessed by his programmes with the Hallé and later with the LSO), and he was receptive to the folk-song-led works of Vaughan Williams, Holst, Moeran and Grainger. However, he clearly considered Vaughan Williams's and Holst's later fascinations with synthetic modes, bitonality and polytonality to venture into areas that were artificial and empty, and that risked alienating the audiences who were the life-blood of a professional orchestra's existence:

> Meanwhile, so many clever musicians are writing in England that it is strange no English music is being made – I mean music that naturally strikes one as English. It is all the stranger because the English countryside has a nature so much its own, and yet I can think of no music clearly inspired by it – unless, perhaps, some of Dr Vaughan Williams's earlier work. What is the reason? Do we musicians live too much in towns, or aren't we patriotic enough?[30]

Harty's views were also typical of the more conventional nationalist attitude towards music of the early 1920s, when to be openly anti-German, and to see stylistic salvation in nationalism and folk music, was the popularly held consensus. But his belief in this maxim, albeit naïve by today's standards, was also based on a powerful secondary factor, that Britain in general needed to learn to respect its own musicians and to see them as *equals* of their continental European counterparts. Until this happened, he believed, Britain would always be hampered by a systemic malady. In this he was uncompromising, and it was a view he retained pugnaciously throughout his professional career:

> I think a country's first duty is to be national, in music as in everything else. It will be time enough to talk of being international when English people have learned to be as interested in their own composers and executants as they are in those of other countries, and when our composers have learned the trick of translating into music scenes and emotions typically English.[31]

After the difficulties over remuneration to the Hallé's orchestral players had been settled, Behrens requested with some urgency that Harty should come to Manchester in August 1920 to finalise details for the forthcoming season. In addition, with the assistance of Adolph Brodsky, Principal of the RMCM, recruitment of new players was effected to replace those who had rejected the Directors' new contract.[32] This, in itself, was no simple business. With inflation after the war, average incomes for instrumentalists had dwindled substantially and the cost of living and personal taxes had risen. In 1920, with the transference of the railways into private hands and the increase in train fares, this placed an additional burden on the modestly paid musician. Mindful of the pressure that this placed on players for the Hallé and elsewhere, who had to travel not

[30] [Colles], 'Hamilton Harty', 229.
[31] Hamilton Harty, as quoted in Sydney Grew, 'National Music and the Folk-Song', *Musical Quarterly* 7(2), 172–85, at 174, n. 1.
[32] Kennedy, *The Hallé Tradition*, 213.

only to Manchester but also to other cities such as Sheffield and Bradford (which were regular venues), Leeds, Newcastle, Hanley, and Nottingham (where Harty was conductor of the Sacred Harmonic Society), Harty wrote a long and forceful letter to the *Musical Times*, based in part on the memory of his earliest experiences:

> The increased charges in railway travel are going to hit musicians of all kinds harder than almost any trade or profession. Before the present increase it was difficult to make anything out of an ordinary fee when the engagement involved a lengthy railway journey; but now it is a hopeless business. And if it is hard on artists with a recognised position, how much more so on those who are still little known, and who have to make their name by accepting, at a purely nominal fee, engagements which will give them an opportunity of appearing under good conditions. You know already that is impossible for a beginner – even when talented – to secure a good position in London musical circles until an apprenticeship has been served and experience gained in the provinces.[33]

Harty also complained of the hardship caused to musicians who had to travel several times a week to secure their work (unlike actors and variety artists, he argued, who, with fare concessions, had only to make one journey). Inevitably, he then turned his attention to the Hallé:

> As conductor of the Hallé Manchester Orchestra I am concerned not only as regards myself, but as regards all artists who will come from London etc. to perform for us; and there are also the numerous occasions on which I take the Orchestra to different towns. Does it not seem just that we of the musical profession should enjoy the same privilege as the members of the music-hall entertainment? It is true that there are certain conditions which they must fulfil, such as travelling in parties of not less than five; but those conditions could easily be adjusted to suit our case.[34]

Harty came to the conclusion that musicians could not apply the same pressure as those from the acting profession because there was no union or society to represent them. In consequence, he urged the newly formed British Music Society (of which he was President of the Manchester branch), which claimed at least to represent a large cross-section of the profession, to negotiate with the Minister of Transport, Sir Eric Geddes, for equality with the theatrical profession.

Besides the initiative on fare concessions for musicians, Harty was also an ardent supporter of municipal subsidy, and he took over the orchestra at a time when debate about aid from the Manchester Corporation had been enthusiastically revived. It was also a matter of great interest to the press since, if such a scheme was to be accepted, it would be an important model for other municipalities throughout the country.[35] The Manchester branch of the British Music Society also weighed in during September 1920 to discuss the viability

---

[33] Letter to the Editor, *MT* 61 (1920), 701.

[34] *MT* 61 (1920), 701.

[35] *The Times*, 25 Sept. 1920.

of a municipal orchestra. In November they put forward the notion of the
Hallé taking part in a series of Municipal Concerts in various halls around
the city, where modest admission prices would allow schoolchildren and the
working class to avail themselves of one of Manchester's greatest cultural assets.
Comparisons with Birmingham and Glasgow were usefully made, and Harty
lent his support, but the matter was shelved for the time being.[36]

As Rees put it, Harty's impact on the Hallé was immediate.[37] He made it
known publically that he considered the orchestra 'the alertest of bands', with the
finest wind section in the country, and Catterall, its leader, the best of Britain's
native violinists. He also acknowledged that, with the regime of constant guest
conductors, the orchestra had invested too much time adjusting to one artistic
personality after another, unlike the times under Hallé, Richter and Balling. But
Harty was no stranger to the orchestra. 'I have no apprehensions, for I know
that though there is no possible bluffing of such a first-rate orchestra, and no
bullying', he conceded, 'they can be got to do anything if one will explain
himself quietly and rationally.'[38] Archie Camden, the first bassoon, was one of
many to welcome Harty's appointment:

> In 1920, Hamilton Harty was invited to become the conductor of the Hallé
> Orchestra – an appointment which was inspired – and the orchestra settled down
> to prove this, during an era for the Hallé unsurpassed in musical achievement.
> Not since Richter's day had there been a logical and regular series of performances
> where a feeling of 'belonging' to a planned purpose, under a firm and brilliant
> director, gave the necessary impetus to interpretation and performance, and
> ensured the essential cohesion which makes a great many individuals play
> as one. Such was the great gift of Hamilton Harty: an ability to inspire other
> musicians with his own burning enthusiasm and musical insight, and this without
> showmanship and gimmicks. A man of great understanding and humility, he was
> first and foremost a dedicated musician.
>
> Harty came to us at a time when he was greatly needed. After the war and
> the long period of change and uncertainty, the orchestra was licking its wounds
> and looking for help to get into condition again. Nothing is so demoralising to
> an orchestra, I think, as changes of personnel, new faces and no hand on the tiller.
> Harty brought everything he had to this daunting task, and soon we began to
> respond by giving a new dimension to playing, interpretation, and team-work.[39]

Harty, as his commentators remarked, had a charming personality both on
and off the rostrum; he enjoyed a drink (especially Irish whiskey), a cigarette,
night-long card games (he was a capable poker player, as Moiseiwitch found
out to his cost), good food, dinner parties, and club life.[40] As Barker related,

---

[36] Rees, *One Hundred Years of the Hallé*, 59–60.

[37] Rees, *One Hundred Years of the Hallé*, 58.

[38] [Colles], 'Hamilton Harty', 228.

[39] Archie Camden, *Blow by Blow: The Memories of a Musical Rogue and Vagabond* (London: Thames Publishing, 1982), 85.

[40] Harty was a member of the Devonshire Club in St James's Street and often used the facility while he was at Manchester and after. He was also a frequent member

'supper after the Thursday's Hallé concert became a rite.'[41] His down-to-earth manner appealed to his players (or 'boys' as he would often informally address them), and he cultivated a form of egalitarianism within the orchestra where all its members, while respecting the authority of their 'leader', felt as though they were indispensable 'fellow artists', idealists, and 'co-operators in a musical enterprise'.[42] In a letter to Philip Heseltine Harty let drop the following comments: 'The young men of the Orchestra are quite romantic – strange, in Manchester. Their hearts are very flinty coal, but once you set it alight, it burns hotly enough!'[43]

One thing Camden refrained from mentioning early on in Harty's regime was his decision to dispense with the female instrumentalists who had come to the aid of the orchestra when vacancies had multiplied during the war, especially after conscription. It was a clumsy policy based on a flimsy rationale that 'unity of style' could not be obtained by an orchestra of men and women and 'that it was difficult to arrange accommodation for women when the orchestra went on its travels'.[44] The latter argument may have had some possible practical significance, but in the wake of the women's suffrage debate Harty's decision could not stand unchallenged; for Ethel Smyth, guardian of the rights of women in the musical world, it was red rag to a bull. Letters to the newspapers see-sawed between the two in November 1920. Smyth's reasons ranged from the sensible to the fanciful. The most obvious was equality of treatment and the social advantage: '... how dull is a party of all men, and how dull is a party of all women. I never thought for a second women would be turned out of an orchestra. Sir Henry Wood told me he would rather give up his post than turn women out of his orchestra.'[45] But it was on Harty's feeble assertion of 'unity of style', that she really turned her guns:

> I never heard such unutterable rubbish in my life. ... Women suffragists remember all the pitiful arguments put forward against women having the vote, and Mr Harty's arguments are just in the same line, but really that 'unity of style' argument is a little too thin for the present day. 'Unity of style'! What a phrase! Like all cant phrases, it cannot be subjected to strict analysis. Let anyone repeat it to himself twice very slowly and ask himself what it means, and he will see its emptiness. Such a vamped-up excuse ... would not take any grown-up person in.[46]

Unfortunately Smyth chose not to leave the her argument there, but proceeded to introduce an additional humbug of her own:

of London's Music Club, where he attended many formal dinners and events in celebration of the achievements of fellow musicians such as Albert Coates and Walter Damrosch.

[41] BBC talk, 18 June 1951.
[42] Rees, *100 Years of the Hallé*, 59.
[43] Letter from Harty to Heseltine, 9 Jan. 1926.
[44] *MG*, 21 Nov. 1920.
[45] *MG*, 24 Nov. 1920.
[46] *MG*, 24 Nov. 1920.

Dr Smyth recurred to what she had said about the value of women in an orchestra, and what the performance gains in tone, dash, and soul. Their emotions lie nearer the surface, and they bring a warmth and glow into the work. They have, she holds, much more spirituality than men, and at the same time they are more precise. They are less disposed to tinker with a subject; they like to get to the bottom of it, and they are very conscientious.[47]

But Harty was not to be deterred and, notwithstanding its vagueness, adhered stubbornly to his decision. With a certain sardonic demeanour, he seized on Smyth's own blunder:

I have read Dr Ethel Smyth's interesting remarks in to-day's 'Manchester Guardian'. I have an adequate respect for Dr Smyth's opinions on musical matters, but is natural that I should have still more respect for my own. I think most people will know what is meant by 'unity of style' in orchestral playing, even though the phrase may annoy Dr Smyth. Orchestral players will know what is meant in any case. It is not a case of whether women orchestral players are or are not superior to men; there may be varying opinions on this subject. Dr Smyth, for instance, thinks they are, but there are many others with an equal right to an authoritative opinion who totally disagree with her. The great object of the Hallé Committee at the start of the season was to get together as good and efficient a body of players as possible. The orchestra is now, I consider, a much finer organisation than it has been for some years. This is not only my own opinion, but the general impression, I am told, of all those who have heard the orchestra this season. Finally, if I must be attacked by anyone, I should prefer it to be by women rather than by men – and I should always be unable to see the justice of dispensing with men players, whose work is perfectly satisfactory to me, just because Dr Smyth thinks women players have more spirituality and precision. (That is her opinion, but it is not by any means mine.)

I trust this explanation will be considered sufficient by those who are interested in the subject, and that Dr Smyth may be induced to turn her attention to the other orchestras in England which can offer her an equal opportunity for criticism.[48]

With the privileged position of being permanent conductor of the orchestra, Harty saw it as his mission to nurture his players. This he did socially, but on the rostrum it was done by unobtrusive yet telling encouragement and approval. As Camden recounted:

Harty was immensely conscious of his players as people. Particularly fine playing from his wind soloists would bring that gentle smile and a little nod in the player's direction; a lovely string passage well played brought the same response. An approaching difficult passage for a rather unexperienced player would bring an extra-well-defined beat to help, but he himself would not appear to be listening or noticing the passage; probably he would be intently watching someone elsewhere. He was always courteous and understanding to his players and took endless pains with those whose temperament needed this.[49]

[47] *MG*, 24 Nov. 1920.
[48] *MG*, 25 Nov. 1920.
[49] Camden, *Blow by Blow*, 86.

As will be demonstrated, Harty's imposing personality engendered admiration but also loyalty from many of his players, even when more favourable pecuniary terms existed elsewhere. Camden, for one, remained utterly devoted to Harty and only moved on from the Hallé after Harty himself left in 1933. It was the same with the oboist Alec Whittaker:

> Alec came to the Hallé while Harty was the conductor who at once saw the potential that was there. He would draw the most beautiful music from Alec and his oboe with deft care and gentle persuasion. He would say: 'Alec, can we have that with just a little more feeling on the *crescendo*?' He would describe the curve with his hands. Alec would feel it immediately and the sound that came out was exactly what Harty wanted. In this way, Alec grew almost to anticipate Harty's requirements. He hung on every word, and Harty's smile and congratulatory remarks brought the most wonderful music from this temperamental player. 'Alec's playing like an angel' was the word that went round. So he was. When he left the orchestra and Harty he found life very different and could never adjust to other conductors. 'Not a patch on Sir Hamilton', he would say. He could not find the means within himself if he were not *en rapport* with the conductor.[50]

In this way Harty generated his own form of collective discipline and unity of purpose, but one which lacked the rigid regimentation that, for example, Furtwängler or Karajan exercised with the Berlin Philharmonic. It has, nevertheless, been suggested that he did not insist on uniform bowing,[51] a charge refuted by Leonard Hirsch (who played both first and second violin in the orchestra), though he always believed that this was less important than the coherence of the score.[52] Rather than hum or sing a phrase, he would whistle it with flawless intonation and pitch.[53] He developed a wide glossary of unostentatious gestures through a subtle use of his left hand, so as to cover a quite legendary range of nuances and dynamics. Harry Mortimer, who joined the Hallé as third trumpet in 1927, referred to Harty's penchant for 'rubato' as 'Hartification', a description he believed encapsulated the distinctive sound and character of the conductor's interpretations.[54] As John Russell, the librarian of the Henry Watson Music Library, recalled:

> One prominent feature was an upraised and extended left hand in a constant urge to reduce *pianissimo* to the merest whisper, and a softly sibilated 'S'sh'. It has been said by members of the orchestra that 'he "S'shed" and "S'shed" until we ceased to play, and still he went on "S'shing",' but that is only an overstatement designed to show Harty's concern with tone gradation.[55]

[50] Camden, *Blow by Blow*, 86.

[51] See John F. Russell, 'Hamilton Harty', *Music & Letters* 22(3) (1941), 216–24, at 214.

[52] Hirsch, 'Memories of Sir Hamilton', 68.

[53] Michael Kennedy, *The Hallé, 1858–1983: A History of the Orchestra* (Manchester: Manchester University Press, 1982), 16.

[54] *A Child of Lir*: BBC Radio 3 centenary broadcast, written and presented by Bernard Keeffe, 4 Dec. 1979.

[55] Russell, 'Hamilton Harty', 219.

Such physical gestures also extended to his facial movements. Russell only half-believed that such a thing was possible:

> The notion that Harty used his eyes to evoke the more subtle nuances is not so far-fetched as it may appear on the surface – bearing in mind the limited possibility of such glances being always perceived in the hurly-burly of performance. Perhaps the idea arose from his mobile face, which so readily mirrored his emotions. It was no uncommon thing for tears to flow when he was profoundly moved by the music – this happened in such works as the slow movement of the third Brahms symphony.[56]

Yet Harty's legerdemain was confirmed by the young John Amis, whose first evening orchestral concert as a boy was one conducted by Harty:

> My first ballet was *Petrushka*; my first concert was a Robert Mayer Children's Concert conducted by Dr Malcolm Sargent at the Central Hall, Westminster, and my first evening concert was conducted by Sir Hamilton Harty. I remember complaining to my father that the whole thing was a swindle because Harty was not throwing himself about as Sargent had done – nor did he seem to be doing much elementary time-beating. Seeing that there were some empty seats behind the orchestra, and seeing this was my first visit to Queen's Hall, my father suggested that we should take a look at the orchestra from behind, where we would be facing the conductor and be able to see exactly what he was, or was not, doing. This was a most sensible idea because we could then observe that Hamilton Harty was doing it all with his *eyes* plus rather sparse gestures with his hands. The work was Brahms's Fourth Symphony which I knew well from our piano duetting. So I was able to appreciate how Harty got his results, and how just with a look he could produce a thrilling fortissimo or an even more thrilling pianissimo.[57]

This extraordinary *rapport* which Harty was able to develop with his orchestra undoubtedly stemmed from the cumulative effect of working with them day in and day out. But with the amiable relationship also came the potential for controversy and friction that had been nascently witnessed with the LSO. Harty's was a complex personality, and alongside the cordial public figure was a man who, as permanent conductor, wanted to take full control of the artistic side of the orchestra's work. That included taking part in the training of the chorus. Harty proceeded to make clear that he wanted a more substantial role in an area that had traditionally been the preserve of the chorus master:

> In my work I shall come in touch too with various choral societies, and here a thorny problem exists which to my mind has hardly been satisfactorily handled in the past. The problem concerns the relations of the choirmaster who trains the singers and the conductor who directs the public performance. If performances of the larger and more modern choral works are to be brought nearer adequacy, the conductor must in future have more say in the preparation of the choir.[58]

---

[56] Russell, 'Hamilton Harty', 219.

[57] J. Amis, *A Miscellany: My Life, My Music* (London: Faber & Faber, 1985), 34.

[58] [Colles], 'Hamilton Harty', 228.

Similarly, with his exclusive contract with Columbia (with whom he was also an artistic advisor), he wanted to direct most if not all the Hallé's business affairs, including control over what and when the orchestra recorded. At first this seemed to make sound commercial sense but, in time, the Directors and some of the orchestral players came to feel that their role was subordinate to Harty's more egotistical aims.[59]

Harty began his first concert series in Manchester on 14 October 1920 with a popular programme. In doing this, he put down a significant artistic marker. Conscious of making allies of the Manchester public, he wanted to create a culture that would appeal to a broad range of the city's population, with one eye on the financial survival of the orchestra:

> My ideal at Manchester will be to have no music played simply because it is new – or because old – or because it is familiar or because not, or just because it was composed in England or in Jugo-Slavia, or in the Isle of Man. I hope to arrange programmes based on worth. I do not believe in too great a proportion of a concert being in strange, novel idioms. I hope to have something new at each concert, and also at each a solid proportion of music that can be enjoyed without the learning of a new language every week.[60]

The programme opened with the Prelude to *Die Meistersinger* and concluded with Beethoven's Seventh Symphony. In between, Harty inserted Strauss's *Don Juan* and Weber's aria 'Ocean, thou Mighty Monster' with Nicholls. The piano was also wheeled out for him to accompany Nicholls in two negro spirituals and the 'Ballatella' from Leoncavallo's *Pagliacci*. As Rees related:

> the Hallé Concerts became notable also for Harty's appearance at the piano in the role of accompanist. These were memorable in every way, and it is not going too far to say that those who never heard him in this role or as a chamber-music performer have been denied the opportunity of appreciating the most consistently brilliant aspect of his great gifts.[61]

Langford added to the general consensus: 'Mr Harty accompanied at the pianoforte, and such a means of accompaniment might be thought a mild disadvantage. Yet he made the unpromising task such a *tour de force* of brilliant execution and shining fancy that the pianoforte became the very centre and force of the triumph.'[62]

During much of the 1920–21 season Harty navigated himself through familiar repertoire to consolidate his audiences. With Brahms's Second Symphony and Tchaikovsky's *Romeo and Juliet* he introduced Glazunov's Violin Concerto with Menges (whom he had accompanied some months past in Medtner's unfamiliar Violin Sonata No. 1 in London) as well as Bantock's *Chinese Songs* with Mullings on 21 October. Glazunov was also on the menu a week later, on 28 October, with his early symphonic poem *Stenka Razin* along with Elgar's *Enigma* Variations

---

[59] Kennedy, *The Hallé, 1858–1983*, 17.

[60] [Colles], 'Hamilton Harty', 229.

[61] Rees, *100 Years of the Hallé*, 60.

[62] *MG*, 15 Oct. 1920.

and Berlioz's *Beatrice and Benedict*, but the programme ultimately focused on the introduction of the brilliant nineteen-year-old Jascha Heifetz to Manchester (months after his English debut at Queen's Hall in May), in Tchaikovsky's Violin Concerto and in miniatures where Harty obliged with piano accompaniment. Three other prominent virtuosos figured during the season: Alfred Cortot performed Rachmaninov's Third Piano Concerto (18 November 1920); Busoni returned after a two-year gap to appear in Mozart's Concerto in E flat, K449 and his *Indian Fantasy* (21 February 1921); and Albert Sammons played in Brahms's Violin Concerto (17 February 1921). Harty's love of Strauss's orchestral music – his readings of which were in some quarters considered superior to Richter's – manifested itself in performances of *Til Eulenspiegel* (18 November) and *Tod und Verklärung* (6 January 1921). In stark contrast to the lavish forces demanded by these works, Mozart's G minor Symphony was given with a much reduced band, a form of delivery Harty always adopted for this music, though, eccentrically, he was never moved to adopt a similar practice in the music of Handel; for successive performances of *Messiah* at Christmas, he happily embraced the well-used supplementary scoring traditional to interpretations of the time.

Besides giving yet another performance of Berlioz's *Faust* on 25 November 1920 and a Wagner night to appeal to a large audience (strangely preceded, to commemorate Armistice, by Sullivan's overture *In Memoriam*), Harty was keen to continue Manchester's attachment to opera on his own terms by giving concert performances of Act I of *Die Walküre* with Nicholls (in her celebrated role as Brünnhilde), Mullings and Radford, and a full concert performance of *Carmen* with Astra Desmond in the principle role. Such a performance provided a change of diet for the Hallé Chorus and it also lent variety to the season's programme. Harty gained praise enough from Langford for his innovation:

> Hamilton Harty deserves the highest praise both for his fastidious and animated reading of the score and for the control of its details. Miss Desmond's Carmen possibly gained as much as it lost by the concert adaptation, for it was strong rather in the purity of its vocalism and in an intellectual dramatic intention than in the natural abandonment of mood which is the dramatic Carmen.[63]

Among the novelties of the season were the first English performance of Stravinsky's early *Scherzo fantastique* (21 January 1921), Julius Harrison's *Worcestershire* Suite, two pieces by Bax – his new symphonic poem *November Woods* (18 November 1920), which Harty had premiered in London for the Philharmonic Society at Queen's Hall two days earlier, and *In a Vodka Shop*, which had been rearranged for orchestra for use as an interlude during Diaghilev's Russian ballet season in 1919 – and ballet scores by Pizzetti (*La Pisanella*) and Eric Fogg (*The Golden Butterfly*), which both appeared in a programme on 24 February, the former continuing Harty's trend of introducing contemporary Italian orchestral music to Manchester. Catterall, who had appeared with the principal cellist W. Warburton in Delius's Double Concerto (6 January 1921), gave the Manchester audience their first hearing of Harty's newly revised and published Violin Concerto on 3 March 1921 after the composer

---

[63] *MG*, 8 Nov. 1920.

and violinist had collaborated in a performance at Liverpool's Philharmonic Society two days before. In London, two months earlier, the concerto had been aired by Murray Lambert (though no mention was made of the new version), but the reception was distinctly cool, largely on account of what was perceived as a somewhat dated idiom. By comparison, both Liverpool and Manchester ignored this factor and were greatly pleased with the work, Langford finding much to commend in the poetic slow movement: 'In the slow movement … especially, where he attempts the feat of writing an accompaniment which shall leave the solo part aloft, while colouring its emotion with soft, low harmonies, Mr Harty's choice of notes and instruments has been so fastidious that a rare originality of feeling is found.'[64]

More significant, however, than the revision of his Concerto was Harty's presentation of his transcriptions (as they were billed) of select movements from Handel's *Water Music* which appeared for the first time at the Hallé Concerts on 18 November 1920.[65] Although its reception was at first unremarkable, the arrangement would soon capture the imagination of a very wide public indeed, and for many listeners Handel's much-loved music would be best known in Harty's arrangement for decades to come. Six movements were freely selected from Handel's two suites, which the latter composed for the royal occasion of 1715; five were taken from the Suite in F major, and one, the last, from the Suite in D major (linked tonally by the fifth movement in D minor). All were arranged for 'modern orchestra' – strings, double wind, four horns and trumpets, with the omission of heavy brass – yet many of the effects, such as reserving the last movement for trumpeters (in keeping with the very baroque key), had a strong eighteenth-century resonance, and Harty remained close to the original musical material throughout. Of course, the four horns and the colourful wind writing provided a powerful romantic aura. For the first airing at Manchester only three of the movements were heard (in the following order): the 'Hornpipe', 'Air' and 'Bourée', though in its final form these constituted the fourth, second and third movements respectively. For the first movement Harty omitted the initial French overture, launching, like the first movement of a symphony, into an Allegro particularly arresting for the opening repartee of horns and strings. The famous 'Air', originally the sixth movement of Handel's scheme, is notable for the scoring of its coda for muted horns – a delicious, imaginative and, indeed, haunting effect – while the trio in F minor, a thoroughly successful interpolation, was taken from the seventh movement. The 'Bourée' and 'Hornpipe' form, as Raymond Warren has suggested,[66] an attractive scherzo-like amalgam at the centre from which the tonality turns to D minor for the 'Andante espressivo', a plangent conduit to the grandiose finale in D major.

Published in 1922, Harty's *Suite from Handel's 'Water Music'* was the first of several arrangements Harty made of a composer whose greatness had been

---

[64] *MG*, 4 Mar. 1921.

[65] The pieces were later featured at a concert with the CBSO at the Birmingham Town Hall with Harty as guest conductor on 15 December 1920, and at the Royal Philharmonic Society (Queen's Hall) under Harty the following day.

[66] Greer, *Hamilton Harty: His Life and Music*, 104.

instilled in him when he was a boy at Hillsborough. In fact, by making these orchestrations, Harty was tapping into the already well-established tradition of making eighteenth-century transcriptions for modern orchestra (by then a familiar concept and an accepted part of civilised urban life in Britain and elsewhere). Among the tradition's other exponents were Harty's mentor Esposito (whose transcriptions he had already begun to perform with the Hallé and LSO) and Respighi (his *Ancient Airs and Dances No. 1* of 1917), as well as conductors such as Henry Wood and Leopold Stokowski, renowned for their showpiece orchestrations of Bach. Furthermore, by transcribing Handel, who was very much 'national property', Harty's name became synonymous with something intrinsically *national*. Vindication of this fact surely came with the inclusion of Harty's suite in Henry Wood's celebratory concert for the royal wedding of Princess Mary on 5 March 1922 at Queen's Hall.

At the close of the season Behrens announced at the Hallé Society's annual general meeting that the accounts showed a loss of £333, which was regrettable in light of the Society's engagement of a permanent conductor for the first time since the beginning of the war. Moreover, Behrens recognised that Harty, with his desire to be involved in all the orchestra's financial affairs, had made economies wherever necessary (though it was not mentioned that he had put aside a request for a stipendary increase), and with the conductor's initiative the orchestra had begun to make its first recordings with Columbia, an activity which brought in much-needed earnings.[67] It was with some relief that the Committee had been able persuade the orchestra to accept slightly lower rates of pay in line with London orchestras, since, besides creating a strain on the orchestra's finances, the higher cost of concert-giving often meant that engagements outside Manchester were being lost. Given the still somewhat precarious nature of the orchestra's finances, the Committee, at Harty's recommendation, appointed Olive Baguley as secretary and R. B. Hesselgrave as choral secretary to keep a keen eye on financial incomings and outgoings, thereby giving a more business-like edge to the Society's management.[68] There was also an appeal for more guarantors and for an increase in the number of subscribers, who would be able to enjoy a slight increase in the number of concerts (to twenty) for next season,[69] a season, Harty promised, that would build on the type of programming and artists of the previous series.

Now that the Hallé had a permanent conductor, the Committee wanted to avoid the culture of guest conductors altogether, a policy which suited Harty's more autocratic leanings. Edward Clark, who initiated his own orchestral concerts in London to explore new British and Continental works, was on the look-out for additional engagements, but discovered in correspondence with Harty that Manchester no longer offered such opportunities:

[67] Among the first recordings made by the Hallé under Harty were Berlioz's *Marche hongroise* and a cut version of Debussy's *L'Après-midi d'un faune*, made in December 1920 (C. L1405).

[68] Kennedy, *The Hallé Tradition*, 219.

[69] *MG*, 12 May 1921.

When we met at Queen's Hall, there was every probability that I cd not fulfil all my Manchester concerts – owing to other engagements on the same dates. Since then, however, things have been arranged in such a way that as far as I know, I shall be in Manchester when required. Besides this, at the last general meeting of my Committee, when the subject of guest conductors was introduced, this met with little approval and for this reason it was felt that having a permanent conductor, they wd prefer the concerts to be directed entirely by him.

I am rather sorry about this – for various reasons, but have an idea that later on the subject may be re-opened; in which case I will immediately communicate with you.[70]

Nevertheless, Harty himself was keen to maintain his links with London's principal orchestras (and, for the time being, he still maintained his home at Grove End Road in St John's Wood). In February he gave a further concert for the Philharmonic Society which featured Frederic Lamond in Beethoven's 'Emperor' Concerto and Debussy's *La Mer* and conducted the LSO in a programme which featured two of Esposito's arrangements of Rossi and Marcello, two pieces by the Irish composer G. O'Connor Morris, and, 'by request', Harty's Violin Concerto with Murray Lambert. At the end of the following month, he, Ronald and Wood and the entire orchestra took part *gratis* in a 'Warrior's Day' concert for Earl Haig's fund for ex-servicemen at Queen's Hall, and, with the influence of the British Music Society at its apogee, he shared the podium with Walter Damrosch in a programme of British and American works at the Society's Congress in June.

In both 1920 and 1921 Harty accepted Esposito's invitation to adjudicate the piano classes at the Feis, events which strengthened their already close bond. During the summer of 1921 Harty spent much of his time in Italy, staying with the Espositos at their home at Fiesole, near Florence. In 1920 Esposito's Russian wife Natalia decided, for reasons unclear, to move to Italy, and, soon afterwards, the rest of her children moved to join her, leaving behind her aging husband, who was still active as a piano professor at the RIAM in Dublin. Only during the summer holidays could Esposito then find the opportunity to see his family again and this he did during the 1920s before he moved permanently to Fiesole in 1928.[71] In addition to the quiet haven of Italy, which took Harty away completely from the vicissitudes of Manchester's hubbub, he also found a retreat in the Lake District, at a remote house at Lambrigg Foot, near Kendal, in what used to be Westmorland. It was the home of an elderly couple, Billy and Louise Farrer (to whom Harty dedicated his 'Irish' Symphony), who enjoyed books and music, but especially country life, shooting and dogs. As he described some years later:

In the old-fashioned country home there has always been a little green suite given over to me. Always kept ready, though sometimes I can't go there for many many months. And whenever I see a weekend or so free, I have slipped up there and been quite out of the world, and alone in the hills and on the moors, sometimes with

[70] Letter from Hart to Edward Clark, 8 Sept. 1921, *GB-Lbl* 52256.
[71] See Dibble, *Michele Esposito*, 160ff.

Billy and his gun and dogs, oftener quite alone the whole day. It is the only place in the world I can be alone and undisturbed.[72]

This hide-away he disclosed to virtually no one, for it was a haven of peace where he could work without interruption.

For the 1921–2 season the Hallé was joined by Clyde Twelvetrees as the orchestra's principal cellist. Well-known to Harty, he had been a professor of cello at the RIAM for some years and was a close colleague of Esposito in chamber music and the DOS. His arrival, however, was something of a novelty, for the Hallé underwent virtually no change in its personnel, a fact which signified a growing sense of stability among the orchestral ranks. Moreover, through the permanence of Harty's appointment, the orchestra had already begun to enjoy a reputation as the country's finest ensemble. This was indirectly endorsed by Newman after hearing Harty conduct the LSO – a poor comparison – at Queen's Hall on 1 November 1921: 'Unfortunately neither the orchestra – on this occasion – nor the pianist [Margaret Collins] was worthy of the conductor. Some of the orchestral playing was so thoroughly bad that even insufficient rehearsal cannot excuse it.'[73]

Harty's musical programme at Manchester largely followed the aesthetic *dictum* of his first season, though the number of orchestral concerts was increased to the pre-war total of twenty (including two consecutive nights for *Messiah* at Christmas), with four operatic nights. In addition, which earned a telegram of congratulation from Beecham, it was decided, in connection with the Beecham Operatic Chorus, to stage an opera festival at the city's Opera House in October 1921, an innovation that was widely welcomed, especially since further festivals were announced for future years.[74] Although it was generally known that Harty disliked opera, he nonetheless offered to conduct Gounod's *Faust* and *Carmen*, and at the performances he distinguished himself. As Langford noted, it was Harty's first appearance as an operatic conductor in Manchester, and in Gounod's opera he 'was the greatest success of the whole. He has not been much associated with opera, and he has been credited, and even credited himself, with some dislike for it. But he was extraordinarily successful in keeping the rhythm alive throughout a work that is often made dreary.'[75] He seemed similarly at ease in *Carmen*, a work he knew well,[76] so that, with an increased audience, all augured well for future operatic performances.

Before the main concert series began in early November, Harty and the Hallé responded to an appeal from the Lord Mayor to give their services free for a concert on 23 October 1921 in aid of the city's unemployed.[77] The gesture only served to enhance the orchestra's reputation and, in good time, could not

---

[72] Letter from Harty to Lorie Bolland, 8 Aug. 1934 (in possession of Christopher Bolland; henceforth CB).

[73] *MG*, 2 Nov. 1921.

[74] *MG*, 18 Oct. 1921.

[75] *MG*, 18 Oct. 1921.

[76] *MG*, 19 Oct. 1921.

[77] *MG*, 13 Oct. 1921.

but help endear its application to the City Corporation for a subvention. In Bradford, a city where Harty was affectionately remembered for the Permanent Orchestra concerts, he renewed his popularity through regular visits with the Hallé. On 26 October he was invited to the city to celebrate the centenary of the Bradford Old Choral Society, who had decided to mark the occasion with a visit from its most famous musical son, Frederick Delius, and a performance of *Sea Drift* with Frederick Ranalow. It was Harty's first meeting with the composer whose music he greatly admired. Unfortunately the Bradford audience was less enamoured:

> Mr Hamilton Harty last night secured one of the finest performances of 'Sea Drift' which have so far been given. The audience, which has been fed far too much on standard works, did not show a due appreciation either of the work or the fine singing of Society's chorus in it. Probably it is true that the work is more notable in the poetic than in the technical sense, but it is indeed a beautiful work, and the day will come when a later Bradford will pride itself more on it than the Bradford of today seems able to do ... Mr Harty subdued the orchestra most admirably while keeping the greatness and sea-surge of the music always in being.[78]

The first concert of the Manchester season commenced by affirming Harty's passion for Strauss. His incidental music *Der Bürger als Edelmann* (for Molière's play *Le Bourgeois Gentilhomme*), which the composer revised as a ballet in 1918 (3 November 1921), had not been heard in England hitherto.[79] A performance of the melodrama based on Tennyson's *Enoch Arden* (19 January 1922) was also included as a tribute to Strauss, who was due to appear at the Brand Lane Concerts on 21 January 1922.[80] Popular concerts continued, with a Wagner night (26 January 1922); another devoted entirely to the music of Beethoven, represented principally by a 'voyage' from the First Symphony to the Ninth Symphony interspersed by *Egmont* and Agnes Nicholls in 'Thou Monstrous Fiend' from *Fidelio* (2 March 1922); and another to Russian music, featuring Rimsky's *Scheherazade* (8 December 1921). But, though the concerts may have lacked a sharper contemporary edge, to Harty's credit they evinced a remarkable diversity of repertoire and artists. Among the pianists was the Polish (soon to be American) Josef Hofmann – described as 'the Rubinstein of modern times' – in Rubinstein's Fourth Piano Concerto (24 November 1921); Alexander Siloti, who had recently fled the Bolshevik regime in Russia for England, appeared in Tchaikovsky's First Piano Concerto (8 December 1921), and Frederick Dawson in Delius's Piano Concerto (9 February 1922). Casals performed Schumann's Cello Concerto in A minor (10 November 1921); the young Russian violinist Toscha Seidel (who had received approbatory reviews during his American tour) gave a fine interpretation of Brahms's Violin Concerto; and Catterall (who had to stand

---

[78] *MG*, 27 Oct. 1921.

[79] Harty later recorded Strauss's work with the Hallé for Columbia in October 1923, along with *Siegfried's Funeral Music* (C. L1522).

[80] Strauss conducted the Hallé in *Don Juan* and *Til Eulenspiegel* at this concert and professed himself so pleased with the orchestra's playing that he offered little comment. See also Hirsch 'Memories of Sir Hamilton', 68–9.

in for an indisposed Jacques Thibaud) played Bruch's Concerto in G minor in what was to have been a largely French programme (9 March 1922). Native soloists were also given a fair hearing. Harty's Violin Concerto was heard with Catterall, Glazunov's with Murray Lambert, and Twelvetrees played in *Don Quixote*. Needless to say, Harty accompanied them all with a celebrated array of singers: Vladimir Rosing (the brilliant Russian bass whom Shaw described with Chaliapin as 'the two most extraordinary singers of the twentieth-century'),[81] Nicholls, Kirkby Lunn (who sang Elgar's *Sea Pictures*), and Bella Baillie (now known as Isabel Baillie),[82] who gave her debut in the offstage solo part of Casella's symphonic suite *Le Couvent sur l'eau* from his ballet *Il convento veneziano* (17 November 1921, the first performance in Manchester).

Baillie recalled in her biography how Harty, having heard her sing a recital at the Houldsworth Hall, remembered her clear voice and delivered 'a piece of manuscript through the post' with an invitation to sing at a forthcoming Hallé concert:

> It was the barcarolle, *The Convent on the Water*, from Alfredo Casella's symphonic suite *The Venetian Convent*, a movement containing a wordless soprano part which at that time appeared to my ears very avant-garde owing to its complex intervals and clustered chromaticisms. Harty had long displayed an interest in contemporary Italian music though he was not, I think, overimpressed by the musical content of this work. The suite contained music rescued by the composer from his ballet of the same name written for and rejected by Diaghilev. Casella also later admitted in his autobiography *Music in My Time* that *The Venetian Convent* was not one of his 'happier' works.
>
> But there I was with a copy of this strange music staring me in the face. 'Well, here it is', I thought, 'I'll just have to learn it.' I went to the rehearsal totally confident that I knew every note of a very challenging manuscript. It was a confidence which instantly evaporated when I discovered that I had to sing from the back of the stage of the Free Trade Hall, some thirty yards or so from the conductor. All hopes of receiving some reassuring guidance from a position close to the conductor were totally dashed. So, from my eyrie near the organ console I joined the orchestral players and furiously counted the bars. Thus I made my Hallé debut on 17 November 1921. Later that night I was due to sing at a banquet held in the Midland Hotel just a few yards away from the Free Trade Hall. As Harry [her husband] escorted me to the hotel he remained ominously mute; obviously my first Hallé concert was to be my last. My feelings were confirmed when to my question 'Well, what was it like?', came the reply, 'Oh, it was *awful!*' I entered the hotel with a very heavy heart but who should enter the lift with us but Hamilton Harty who, at that time, was living at the Midland. He came forward, congratulated me, and informed me that it would not be long before he could give me something really rewarding to do from a singer's point of view.[83]

[81] George Bernard Shaw, *The Perfect Wagnerite* (London: Constable & Co., 1923), 132.

[82] Bella Baillie was persuaded by Harty to alter her first name to Isobel on the grounds that it was more marketable: Isobel Baillie, *Never Sing Louder than Lovely* (London: Hutchinson, 1982), 28.

[83] Baillie, *Never Sing Louder than Lovely*, 27.

A similar congratulation came from Langford in the *Manchester Guardian*, who complimented Baillie on her 'clarity ... and purity of intonation'.[84] In the following December Harty, true to his word, gave Baillie a further opportunity in *Messiah* at Manchester (which also proved to be the first broadcast of the work).

In addition to the 'discovery' of Baillie, Harty cultivated a close friendship with Camden. During his first season with the orchestra, and with his special love of Mozart, he asked Camden if he had ever played Mozart's Bassoon Concerto. Camden was not familiar with the work but was especially delighted when he was asked to play it during the 1921–2 season, though it was necessary for them to collaborate in the composition of the cadenzas. 'During the ensuing summer [of 1921]', Camden recalled, 'I looked at the concerto. It was by no means an easy work, and I wondered how any bassoon player in Mozart's time had managed it with the more primitive instruments that they had then – few keys and more chancy notes.'[85] The cadenzas, according to Camden, were written in a light-hearted vein and even contained several short passages from *the Marriage of Figaro* and *The Magic Flute*, but after one critic believed that they had been written by Mozart himself, trying out, at the age of eighteen (the year of the concerto), themes of his future operas, new ones were written. Much to Camden's delight, after he performed the concerto on 16 March 1922, he learned that a 'Signor Raspi' had given it at the thirteenth Hallé concert in 1858, but since then it had completely dropped out of the repertoire.[86]

Among the new works to Mancunian ears were Ravel's *La Valse* (15 December 1921), Casella's ballet and Holst's *The Planets* (23 February 1922), which had not long had its first complete public hearing under Coates with the LSO in November 1920. There was room, of course, for the *Water Music*,[87] and Elgar's transcription of Bach's Fugue in C minor (10 November 1921), which Goossens had premiered in London three weeks earlier. Harty continued his exploration of Italian music in Bossi's suite *Goldoniani* (24 November 1921) and an all-Italian concert (23 March 1922) which featured Martucci's *Giga* and Respighi's *Fountains of Rome*, though the concert was ultimately a tribute to the sixty-seven-year-old Esposito who, besides being represented by his overture *Otello* (which Harty had performed with the LSO in November of the previous year), appeared as soloist in Mozart's Concerto in E flat, k271, as well as his own *Ballades*. 'As an Italian player of rank', Langford affirmed, 'Mr Esposito may be said to have been more closely in touch with Mozartian tradition than we in England can be. ... His playing in the lovely fugitive notes at the close of the slow movement was of

---

[84] *MG*, 18 Nov. 1921. Harty later arranged a test recording for Baillie with Columbia in February 1926, when he accompanied her in Wakefield Cadman's *At Dawning*. It was not issued on 78 rpm, but later it appeared on 33{1/3} rpm in 1974 with RLS.

[85] Camden, *Blow by Blow*, 87.

[86] Camden, *Blow by Blow*, 93.

[87] It is not clear whether this performance was of the three movements of the premiere in 1920. It is clear, however, that the suite was peformed in its complete set of six movements for the wedding concert for Princess Mary on 5 March 1922: *The Times*, 6 Mar. 1922.

surpassing beauty.'[88] British music also enjoyed a modest gesture in Delius's *Brigg Fair*, Elgar's *The Apostles*, Bantock's much-favoured *Omar Khayyám*,[89] the Holst suite, and Harty's *With the Wild Geese*. And to supplement the considered success of performing *Carmen* and *I Pagliacci* in concert form, Harty began his series of operas with Saint-Saëns's *Samson and Delilah* (19 November 1921) and closed with excerpts from Mussorgsky's *Boris Godunov*, Borodin's *Prince Igor* and Glinka's *Life for the Tsar* (11 March 1922).

Having established himself as a major figure in Manchester's musical life, Harty took a close interest in the city's cultural welfare, especially in the progress of the RMCM, where he frequently adjudicated. He appealed in particular for better accompanists and improved wind players with a view that, one day, the Hallé might be composed entirely of local players, 'a self-contained musical centre, independent of outside help'.[90] Often, in the company of Nicholls, he entered into the wider spirit of the city's music-making, giving recitals for the Rochdale Chamber Music Society, the Bowden Chamber Concerts and the Tuesday Midday Concerts (where Harty revived his interest in music for wind and piano), while he collaborated with Catterall in a series of 'Sonata' programmes at the Memorial Hall and the inauguration of the Manchester Chamber Concerts with the Catterall Quartet in December 1922. As Langford remarked, his luminosity as an accompanist had not deserted him: 'he revels in many notes and yet it is in the brilliant and poignant use of every single note that he so far excels every other player.'[91]

After the Hallé season in Manchester was over, Harty took the orchestra to the Westmorland Festival in April where he conducted *Hiawatha's Wedding Feast* and *The Death of Minnehaha* with his old friend Plunket Greene in the principal role. He also fulfilled engagements as adjudicator at the Dublin Feis and Buxton Festival in May. After that he travelled again to Esposito's villa in Fiesole for a summer of solitude. There he composed his Piano Concerto in B minor which, dedicated in homage to his mentor, was published by C. E. Publishers in 1923. It was given its first performance, with Harty as soloist, at a concert of the Leeds Philharmonic on 22 November 1922 before, in typical fashion, Godfrey invited him to play it at Bournemouth on 28 December.[92]

The Concerto was the first large-scale work Harty had attempted since *With the Wild Geese* of 1910, and in that time it is discernible from the work's more fluid chromatic style that his language had undergone some harmonic advance.

---

[88] *MG*, 24 Mar. 1922.

[89] The orchestral parts of Bantock's work failed to arrive in time for this performance, so, as Langford described, Harty had an opportunity 'to display his remarkable abilities as a musician in an improvised piano accompaniment to the work' from the full score, while an astonished orchestra remained on the platform: *MG*, 2 Dec. 1921. See also Hirsch, 'Memories of Sir Hamilton', 69. The same performance was also afflicted by an unwell Mullings having to leave the platform.

[90] *MG*, 3 Dec. 1921.

[91] *MG*, 13 Oct. 1921.

[92] See Lloyd, *Sir Dan Godfrey*, 155.

The concerto clearly still cleaved to the Romantic tradition, notably to the voluptuous and epic style established by Rubinstein, Scharwenka and especially Rachmaninov, and Harty had of course imbibed Rachmaninov's grand style at first hand with the world's finest pianists (including Rachmaninov himself). Indeed, his choice of a brooding B minor no doubt emulated Rachmaninov's use of minor keys in his Second and Third Concertos. There is a surely a gestural similarity to Rachmaninov's Second Concerto in the way that Harty obliquely opens his first movement on the chord of the supertonic seventh with a flourish for the piano before the well-defined cadence into the tonic. There is also something of Rachmaninov in the manner of the first subject, where melodic interest is given almost entirely to the orchestra while the piano provides rich accompanimental figuration. This orchestral dominance continues throughout the voluptuous transition and introduction (by the woodwind) of the second subject, before the piano finally asserts itself as the principal agency of lyricism. And, without labouring the comparison with Rachmaninov, Harty had clearly learned from the Russian how to create a dialogue between orchestra and soloist, through a matrix of countermelodies and skilful voice-leading within the 'inner' voices of the harmony (the piano's left–hand figurations of the second subject are a particular case in point). Such devices undoubtedly appealed to Harty's own propensity for embellishment, of which there is much in the elaborate wind writing familiar from his earlier orchestral works. The developmental phase of the first movement, where Harty's more Irish accent is observable, is largely lyrical, which allows the virtuoso cadenza (as a conduit to the recapitulation) to stand out. Harty's transformation of his second subject in the recapitulation is also magically executed, for here he combines elements of poetical tranquillity (again in the style of a free cadenza) with an heroic conclusion, making reference to the initial flourish that began the movement.

The second movement, which begins with a languid introduction and a quasi-improvised Irish gesture for the clarinet, builds on the luxuriant Romantic style of the first. Here the interest lies not only in the presentation of the affecting sequential phrases of the elegiac melody, but also in the counterpoint of the 'alto' line and its dissonant interactions with the upper figuration of the left hand (Example 16). An orchestral repeat of the melody proceeds to accentuate this contrapuntal interplay in a dialogue between strings and wind which recalls similar gestures in the 'Irish' Symphony. By contrast, the movement's more fluid central section, more reminiscent of Brahms, is turbulent, allowing the piano some room for technical fireworks. It is, however, with the serene reprise of the first section (introduced deftly by a short flute cadenza), and a beautifully understated and unexpected progression back to the tonic (E major) that Harty achieves his greatest emotional impact. Again, much of Harty's wonderfully judged effect is created by his manipulation of orchestral timbres – gentle woodwind doubling of the melody, sustained strings, a counterpoint for solo violin and cello, and the distant chime of a bell, while the piano is placed in a higher register that seems to enhance its plangent voice. A final, 'flat seventh' gesture in the clarinet reminds us of Harty's roots, and in the last movement this element finally comes to the fore in the spirit of an Irish reel, set against an

Example 16 Piano Concerto in B minor, second movement, entry of piano

orchestral background of a jig. In his programme note for its performance at
the Hallé Concerts in 1923, Harty even went so far as to describe it as redolent of
'an Irish tavern with drinking, dancing and general gaiety'. The second subject,
in 6/4 metre and couched in Harty's favoured subdominant, returns us to the
Romantic world of the first and second movements with a melody of majestic
proportions, though not without a veiled passing allusion to the Irish melody *The
Wearing of the Green* in the horns. In fact, the Irish demeanour of this movement
is never far away for, in the poignant link to the epic restatement of the second
subject, synthetic strains of Irish melody inhabit the tender passage of string-
writing, while *The Wearing of the Green* is given greater prominence in a coda
that also seems to allude to the second subject of the Finale to Rachmaninov's
Second Concerto.

On returning to Manchester after the summer break Harty once again
provoked controversy in a speech he gave to the Manchester Luncheon Club

on 2 October. There he took the opportunity to reiterate his views expressed in the *Musical Times* article of 1920, asserting that the English required a greater patriotism to appreciate their own music, as did native composers, whom he considered mostly 'bad and insincere'. When challenged as to why he had not produced more English music at Manchester, he retorted that younger English composers still lacked 'the trick of saying really English things in English, instead of saying foreign things in broken French, German and Russian'. He declared that in England 'since Purcell we have had only one distinguished composer, Sir Arthur Sullivan', and that Elgar's work, notwithstanding his present-day standing, seemed to him 'the music of a great religious mystic'.[93] It was an argument riddled with contradictions, inconsistencies (not least because Harty's own music owed so much to Continental styles), and his own prejudices against what he perceived as contrived, modern compositional methods. The talk was reported widely and it received a bristling rejoinder from the young, rebellious Arthur Bliss in his paper 'Some Aspects of the Present Musical Situation', for the Royal Musical Association in March 1923. Bliss, who at this time was considered a firebrand owing to his associations with Ravel, Stravinsky and European Neo-Classicism,[94] aimed his invective at both Stanford (whose own recent paper for the RMA had also criticised contemporary musical developments)[95] and Harty. To Harty his attack was stinging, not least in his veiled condemnation of the Irishman's own music and conservatism:

> This trick of labelling English composers and of pigeon-holing them, each with a ticket stamped with a foreign name, has led another Irishman to say that there is no English music of the present day. It is all copied from abroad, and, so I understand, is ugly and bad. But what are Mr Harty's credentials for passing judgment on English music? He is an Irishman, who picked up Richter's baton at the Hallé concerts, and whose programmes do not show a great knowledge of contemporary work, but in fact reflect the conservatism of the stronghold in which they are given. He is in short an eminent conductor who is carrying on the German Classic tradition in Manchester with great success, and whose exuberance, of not a very venturesome order, leads him to composition of a charming nature not unlike that of his great model, Arthur Sullivan. But he must not condemn all other composers for not being like Arthur Sullivan. We can't all be as serious as the Sullivans of 'In memoriam' and 'The Golden Legend', and as for the Gilbert and Sullivan Operas, well! where is the Gilbert of to-day?[96]

Bliss's comments were echoed by a number of journals, and it would not be long before the charge of conservatism would be aimed at Harty from closer to home.

In the meantime, however, Harty's close management of the Hallé had, at the end of the 1922–3 season, generated a profit of £30 – an achievement in a

---

[93] *MT* 63 (1922), 774.

[94] See E. Evans, 'Arthur Bliss', *MT* 64 (1923), 20–23, 95–9.

[95] See Charles Villiers Stanford, 'Some Recent Tendencies in Composition', *PRMA* 47 (1920–1), 39–53.

[96] Arthur Bliss, 'Aspects of the Present Musical Situation', *PRMA* 49 (1922–3), 59–77, at 67.

time of economic depression which earned praise in the young Adrian Boult's paper for the RMA 'The Orchestral Problem of the Future'.[97] Boult's praise for Manchester as a model for financial prudence effectively strengthened Harty's own 'safe' artistic policy for the orchestra, as he explained in a letter to Behrens from Fiesole:

> Miss Baguley has told me that a guarantor – Mr Murray – enquires why the Mass of Stanford [his new Mass 'Via Victrix'] has not been included in our scheme of concerts during the Hallé season, and as I have not only a great regard for Sir Charles Stanford, but also a wish to meet the views and wishes of our guarantors as far as possible, I am writing to explain that it is purely financial reasons which make the inclusion of the work in question difficult and unwise.
>
> Until we have such a body of support at our concerts that will enable us to give any works we choose without regard to their popularity, I feel obliged to include only such works as may be reasonably assured of drawing a good house. Eventually I have the greatest hopes that the Society will be in a stronger financial position, such a position as will allow us to forget the box office sometimes, but for the moment I feel that though of course all the music we perform must be of the highest class, we cannot afford to take many risks with works of a large calibre which are new to our public.
>
> This policy has, as you know, been arrived at by the Hallé Committee in consultation with myself, and so far has proved successful, but I shd like it to be known that my musical sympathies are altogether with those who wish for the performance of such works as the Mass of Stanford, and that the policy we pursue is one that I hope will eventually place us in the position of being able to produce many such works. Our prospectus for next season contains several orchestral works of Stanford.[98]

With an increased number of concerts to give in Manchester and elsewhere in the midlands and the north during the 1922–3 season – which amounted to an unprecedented sixty-eight in all – Harty gave no concerts in London and moved his accommodation to the Clarendon Club, on the corner of Mosley Street overlooking St Peter's Square in the heart of Manchester. Before the Hallé concerts got under way, he undertook the direction of *Samson and Delilah*, one of the productions of the British National Opera Company (BNOC), on 30 September at the Opera House. Neville Cardus, at that time a theatre critic for the *Manchester Guardian* as well as its cricket correspondent, hailed Harty's attempt to give 'plastic energy to the essentially undramatic music of Saint-Saëns' as 'miraculous'.[99] The following week he conducted the double bill of Debussy's *The Prodigal Son* and *I Pagliacci*.

[97] See Adrian Boult, 'The Orchestral Problem of the Future', *PRMA* 49 (1922–3), 39–57, at 48.

[98] Letter from Harty to Behrens, 7 Aug. 1922, *GB-Mha*.

[99] *MG*, 30 Sept. 1922. During 1922 the question of opera in Manchester had experienced untold confusion. There was the prospect of the Carl Rosa Opera Company coming to Manchester, where Harty would take musical control with the assistance of the Hallé orchestra. However, negotiations with Carl Rosa foundered after difficulties over scheduling with the visit of the BNOC.

As far as the Hallé programme was concerned, it was a matter of consolidating the successes of the previous season and to return a profit. Besides the usual Wagner evening, *Messiah*, the Mass in B minor, *The Dream of Gerontius* and the Berlioz favourites, Harty directed the latter's *Te Deum* and *Harold in Italy* and he was hailed the finest interpreter of Strauss after his authoritative direction of *Ein Heldenleben*. Guilhermina Suggia, the Portuguese cellist and pupil of Casals, performed Schumann's Concerto (26 October 1922) and Casals himself returned to play Lalo's Cello Concerto (7 December 1922); Harold Bauer played Franck's *Variations symphoniques* and a Mozart concerto (16 November 1922), Sapellnikoff gave Liszt's First Concerto (14 December 1922) and Busoni performed Saint-Saëns Fourth Concerto; the French violinist Renée Chemet gave Lalo's *Symphonie espagnole*. There were first performances in Manchester of Dukas's ballet *La Peri* (22 February 1923), Martucci's *Tarantelle* (16 November 1922) and Respighi's *La Boutique fantasque* (9 November 1922), a revival of Stravinsky's *Petroushka* (23 November 1922) and a second performance of Strauss's *Le Bourgeois Gentilhomme* (16 November 1922). Among the British works were Elgar's *In the South* and *Dream Children*, and John Ireland's *The Forgotten Rite* was given an airing, but Vaughan Williams was represented only by his *Wasps* Overture (8 March 1923) and Holst by his early *Somerset Rhapsody* (8 March 1923).

On 25 January 1923 Harty directed the first performance of a second Handel orchestration, this time of a 'Concerto for Orchestra with Organ' with the choral director Harold Dawber as the organist. The work is a strange hybrid arrangement of the second of three Handel concertos (Concerto 'B' in Chrysander's *Händel-Gesellschaft*, which was incorporated into *Music for the Royal Fireworks*), in which the original Handel movements are reordered. The work was not published until 1934 by Universal. It was often billed by Harty as a popular filler in his orchestral programmes, and was used as a thoroughly practical *pièce d'occasion*. The climax of the season was, however, the very last concert on 15 March 1923 when Harty, who was after all so well known to Manchester audiences for his abilities as an accompanist, appeared as soloist in his Piano Concerto under the baton of Thomas Beecham. Harty was greeted with an ovation when he stepped onto the platform. Soon after, he took the Hallé to Dublin where, at the Theatre Royal, the city's 'musical son' was lionised by the audience and press to such an extent that a special feature article was produced about him in the *Irish Times*. As the journalist recollected, it was well nigh ten years since the city had last witnessed his powers and appearance, and in that time he had noticeably aged:

> ... most of musical Dublin ought to retain a fairly vivid impression of Mr Hamilton Harty, the conductor – a tall figure, a fine head, a crop of grey hair; in the distance not unlike Mr W. B. Yeats (but has anybody ever seen Mr Yeats in a 'morning coat'?). That is the outward impression of Mr Harty which I received the other day. I have a fainter recollection of a young man at Woodbrook some years before the war, slimmer, and the hair blacker, and more of a 'mop'.[100]

---

[100] *IT*, 14 Apr. 1923.

In May 1923 Harty continued his association with, and support of, the BNOC for their second season at Covent Garden. On 16 May he again directed *Samson and Delilah* and was applauded by the critics for his control of the orchestra. On 23 May he took up the baton in *The Marriage of Figaro* with Nicholls (who was made CBE in the king's birthday honours list) in the role of the Countess. Both received plaudits from *The Times*, but the somewhat flat performance was considered one of 'uninspired carefulness'.[101] One critic lamented that it was a pity Harty could not be the permanent conductor of the company, but acknowledged that his interest in the operatic stage remained guarded.[102] Nevertheless, Harty continued to pursue opera as if he had something to prove, directing three works in a week in Manchester – *The Marriage of Figaro* and *Die Walküre* (both for the BNOC on 23 and 26 October) and Mascagni's *Cavalleria rusticana* at the Brand Lane Concerts (27 October).

Before spending the summer in Fiesole, Harty and Behrens were happy to announce to the Hallé Society that a larger profit of £168 had been made during the past season. With a sense of increased confidence in the Society's future, Harty felt bold enough to request both an increase in the size of the orchestra and more rehearsals, even if this placed a greater pressure on the Society's guarantors. He also sensed that there might be room for a little more enterprise in the orchestra's repertoire, as he told Behrens:

> I do feel we have come to a point where a certain amount of progression is expected of us, and that the public, who are at present well disposed towards us, may lose faith unless we seek to justify the increased support they have given the concerts.
>
> It is not my desire to rush wildly into extravagance – far from it – but I do think we ought to make it plain at the general meeting that our general policy for the next season will be to provide music of a still better character and that this will probably result in a call being made upon the guarantors.[103]

There was also pressure to shorten the programmes, to discourage encores (a practice Richter had forbidden) and to increase the number of concerts outside Manchester; this would have the mutual benefit of reaching more audiences and creating additional employment for the players.[104] In addition, the Society was also building pressure on the City Corporation for a municipal grant, notably on educational grounds, in order to appeal to a wider range of the city's population. This would finally come to fruition in 1924.

During the 1923–4 season Manchester enjoyed the reappearance of the pianists Cortot, Casals, Hofmann, Hambourg, Busoni and Moiseiwitch. Among the string players, the young Hungarian violinist Jelly D'Arányi played the Tchaikovsky Concerto and Beatrice Harrison played Dvořák's Cello Concerto (10 January 1924). Two unfamiliar Mozart works caught the eye – the Concerto for Flute and Harp and the *Echo* Nocturne – and though Beecham was initially advertised to conduct Strauss's *Alpine* Symphony on 15 November, the task

---

[101] *The Times*, 26 May 1923.

[102] *The Times*, 18 and 25 July 1923.

[103] Letter from Harty to Behrens, 7 June 1923, *GB-Mha*.

[104] *MG*, 26 June 1923.

eventually fell to Harty whose interpretation Langford extolled, commenting that 'the concert did something to bring back memories of the great days of Richter's first presence among us.'[105] To some annoyance among the subscribers, Harty changed a number of concert programmes after they had been publicised, a habit in which he increasingly indulged and which provoked letters of complaint to the Society and the press. For example, a new edition of Bizet's *La Jolie Fille de Perth* was due for its first hearing in Manchester on 10 January, but this was cancelled in favour of an orchestral programme which featured Saint-Saëns's *Carnival of the Animals* (the first hearing in Manchester after its recent publication) and Respighi's *Ancient Airs and Dances*. Besides the familiar Berlioz overtures, Harty introduced the composer's *Symphonie funèbre et triomphale* to Manchester (13 December 1923) for the first time, in collaboration with the Stephens Military Band (though without the optional chorus). A Whitman evening brought Vaughan Williams to the city to hear *A Sea Symphony*, which was coupled appropriately with Harty's *The Mystic Trumpeter* (1 November 1923). Again Harty seemed keen to avoid Vaughan Williams's later music, as was also the case with Holst who was represented by his earlier suite *Beni Mora* of 1909.

Further novelties to the audience were the 'Adagietto' from Mahler's Fifth Symphony (Harty's first public performance of the composer), Bax's *The Garden of Fand* (28 February 1924), and E. J. Moeran's First Rhapsody which had been introduced at Bournemouth by Godfrey. Moeran's music, with its strong Irish flavour, appealed to Harty, and the two men's acquaintance led to the suggestion from Harty that Moeran should write a symphony for him and the orchestra. Unfortunately, as Moeran neared completion of the work in 1924 (which was subsequently announced in the Hallé's season of 1925–6),[106] he withdrew it; it would be late 1934 before he resumed work on it. In his own Piano Concerto Harty took up the baton with Myra Hess as soloist (14 February 1924), and to continue his bent for the transcription of Handel he conducted his orchestration of *Music for the Royal Fireworks* for the first time on 25 October 1923, having announced it at the Society's summer AGM (incidentally, the performance gained in context from the first hearing in Manchester of Elgar's own transcription of Handel's Overture in D minor). Dispensing with flutes and clarinets, Harty explained at the front of his score that the instrumentation – for two oboes, two bassoons, four horns, three trumpets, side drum, timpani and strings – was 'more or less in accord with the indication of Handel's published score, though certain instruments have been added here and there, in order to gain a fuller effect to modern ears, without, however, departing in any way from Handel's essential framework'. For his transcription Harty selected only four movements from Handel's original, beginning with the French Overture but leaving out the final Lentement. The two inner movements (the 'Alla Siciliana' and 'Bourée') reversed Handel's original order, and the final, regal 'Menuetto', Handel's sixth movement, used Handel's fifth as a central trio. Of particularly magical effect is the 'Alla Siciliana' (originally called 'La Paix' by Handel). Scored for muted strings alone, its contrast between the ensemble for divided violas and cellos and the full string sound lends a profound Romantic glow to the slow dance, especially at the affectingly sonorous final cadence.

Two performances of *Messiah* took place at Christmas. At the second, marking the 100th performance of the work by the Society, four members from each of the many local choral societies were invited to take part. Harty's sense of public service also extended to the festivals at Blackpool and Alderley Edge, a well-attended lecture at the National Library for the Blind, a concert for 2,500 children from Manchester, Salford, Stockport and Stretford, and the inauguration of his own chamber concerts (known as the 'Hamilton Harty Chamber Concerts'), where part of his mission was to encourage the careers of younger players from the orchestra. All this served to amplify both music's standing with the City Corporation and the orchestra's wider relevance to the community. Recordings for Columbia also promoted Harty and the Hallé and invariably reflected works that had featured in the main season at the Free Trade Hall such as the Bach Double Violin Concerto (with Catterall and Bridge), extracts from *Die Meistersinger* and *Parsifal*, Dvořák's 'New World' Symphony, and further movements from Strauss's *Le Bourgeois Gentilhomme*. But a much more radical form of promulgation was also looming in the form of BBC broadcasts. News that Harty had already agreed to take part in broadcast concerts began to circulate in the early months of 1924 and was welcomed by the Society.[107] The first of these broadcasts was a Royal Philharmonic Society concert relayed from London's Central Hall by the 2LO station on 9 April 1924; the programme consisted of Respighi, Beethoven, Berlioz and Wagner.

The Hallé Society announced a loss of £258 for the 1923–4 season, but surpluses from the previous years obviated a financial appeal to the guarantors. Behrens retired from his role as secretary and his position was filled by W. W. Grommé, who had been a member of the Committee since 1913. One of the happiest announcements was a series of six municipal concerts in collaboration with the City Corporation at 'popular prices' with seats specially reserved for children, while a second announcement publicised the outcome of negotiations between the BBC and the Society for ten concerts of the 1924–5 season to be broadcast from the Manchester station 2ZY. On a more acrimonious note, Catterall and Harty, who had worked so closely together with the orchestra and in chamber music, fell out, and it was widely held that Harty had begun his own series of chamber music as the resentment between them escalated. The rancour spread to the Committee and Harty, refusing to employ Catterall as a soloist during the 1923–4 season, was overruled.[108] Some of the disagreement stemmed from Catterall's questioning of Harty's readings, which some of the orchestra shared (especially about Harty's treatment of Beethoven), but the Committee knew that it could not question its conductor on matters of interpretation. As a result, Catterall resigned early in 1925 and his position was filled by another Brodsky pupil, Alfred Barker.

In 1924 Harty gave a paper for the Manchester Organists' Association on 'Modern Composers and Modern Composition'. Published in full in the

---

[107] *MG*, 13 Feb. 1924.

[108] Kennedy, *The Hallé Tradition*, 222.

Musical Times, Harty attempted not only to build on his previous controversial comments, but also to seek to justify them in the light of his career as a conductor. He reiterated his disappointment at the contemporary situation of musical creativity:

> I think we have been passing through a very empty, unprofitable time in the history of musical composition … [and we have] tried to formulate for ourselves some kind of standard, some sort of mental measuring-rod, by which to appraise not only those stars whose light has paled, but the new ones which are constantly appearing over the horizon.[109]

Harty's point was not without value; the traditional school of criticism had been challenged by a fracturing of musical styles, and old criteria no longer seemed relevant to the new experiments and schemes of post-war composition. Courting derision, Harty cited his own yardsticks: '1. Music must be beautiful in shape; 2. Melody must be the first reason for its existence; 3. What appeals only to the brain cannot live; 4. It is the emotional quality of music which gives its value, and the nobler the emotion aroused, the greater the music.'[110] These were, in the main, reformulations of past aesthetic judgments, but with the added assertion that 'the race of musical giants [had] finished with Wagner and Brahms.' Harty then proceeded to list a number of post-Wagnerian names – Grieg, Dvořák, Tchaikovsky, Strauss, Elgar, Debussy, Ravel, Puccini, Skryabin, Stravinsky; he appraised each in terms of 'greatness', but found weaknesses too, especially in Skryabin and Stravinsky (citing the *Poem of Ecstasy* and *The Rite of Spring*) whom he found decadent and unhealthy. 'Sensuality, hysteria, brutality, are qualities which cannot exist in great art, and I know of nothing really decadent which has lived in music.' Quite wrongly, Harty predicted no future for either work. In the end, he returned to his hobby-horses of intuition and instinct, his antipathy to cleverness, and his resolution to stand up to those who made a virtue of modernism. 'As for myself', he declared uncompromisingly, 'no matter how old-fashioned, no matter how out-of-date, even weak and sentimental, it may sound to some – I am content to take my stand with those who value honesty more than cleverness, for I am convinced that in this there lies the guiding principle of all that is enduring in our art.'[111] Harty then placed his trust in the educational force of recorded music and the advent of broadcasting, and indirectly praised the autocratic *dictum* of Lord Reith at the BBC in his vocation to 'educate, inform, entertain'.

For all the criticism that was mounting about Harty's conservatism, he could not be criticised for the continuing breadth of variety that he brought annually to the Hallé's seasons, or for his continued efforts to support the BNOC;[112] or for the extraordinary energy he poured into the Columbia recordings he

[109] H. Hamilton Harty, 'Modern Composers and Modern Composition', *MT* 65 (1924), 328–332, at 328.

[110] Harty, 'Modern Composers and Modern Composition', 328.

[111] Harty, 'Modern Composers and Modern Composition', 331.

[112] Harty conducted a performance of Gounod's *Faust* during the BNOC's visit to Manchester in March 1924, but was indisposed for both *Cavalleria Rusticana* and

made, many of them with the Hallé, during the course of 1924 and 1925. The concert programme in Manchester for 1924–5 included Delius's *Eventyr* (30 October 1924), Howells's *Pastoral Rhapsody* (22 January 1925), De Falla's *Night in the Garden of Spain* with Artur Rubinstein (13 November 1924), Honegger's *Pacific 231* (23 October 1924), Moeran's *In the Mountain Country* (27 November 1924) and Vaughan Williams's *A Norfolk Rhapsody*. The promotion of Italian composers also continued with Set II of Respighi's *Ancient Airs and Dances* and Casella's rhapsody *Italia*. The main theme of the programme, however, was 'the Symphony', though, as Langord commented somewhat wryly, its choice of composers ignored Sibelius, Bruckner, Mahler and Reger, thereby chiming 'almost entirely', with what was a delightful criticism, in so far as it went, given by Mr Harty of modern composers in Manchester during the spring.'[113] Elgar's First Symphony was revived after a gap of nine years, but the principle focus was the four symphonies of Brahms, for whom Harty had developed a major reputation (somewhat contrary to his earlier published impressions) that even superseded Richter's. As one critic put it: 'I venture to single out Hamilton Harty's Brahms Symphony readings as having all the elements of greatness.'[114]

Harty's belief in Brahms's music had changed many minds when Brahms was still considered a strangely backward, classical composer of the late nineteenth century. As he explained to Brodsky (who had complimented him on his interpretations):

> I feel that I would like to tell you how much your kind remarks about the Brahms Symphony [No. 4] last Thursday meant to me. I don't look for anything in the way of public praise or appreciation but I always look on you as the one who understands what Brahms tried to express in his music, and to think that I gave you some pleasure and satisfaction means more to me than I can express.
>
> His music touches me deeply, almost to tears, when I conduct it, and I am gratified to think that sometimes I may be privileged to convey a little of his divine feeling to others – that is quite enough for any artist to experience.[115]

To Walter Legge, however, who greatly admired Harty's personal affinity for Berlioz, the kinship for Brahms's symphonic music seemed to jar:

> His [Harty's] mind has much in common with Berlioz's. Berlioz loves the vivid, the exciting, and he wrote hyperbole. His criticisms, essays, and letters are vehement and eloquent; what a normally pulsed man would call large, Berlioz called colossal, stupendous, and pyramidal. He felt life like that. Harty gives the impression that he feels music in that way, so that one wonders why a comparatively low-pulsed

I Pagliacci at Covent Garden for the BNOC in the presence of the King and Queen on 9 April.

[113] *MG*, 2 Aug. 1924.

[114] *MT* 66 (1925), 69. Harty's admiration for Brahms is also evident in a lecture he gave at the Royal College of Organists in February 1929 on Brahms's *Variations on a Theme of Haydn*, the set work for analysis for the FRCO (*GB-Belqb*). The lecture was printed in the RCO Calendar for 1929–30, 111–15.

[115] Letter from Harty to Brodsky, 19 Jan. 1924, *GB-Mcm*.

composer like Brahms features so frequently on his programmes. Harty's fire, his eloquence, his persuasiveness, his charm are wasted on Brahms.[116]

One of Harty's triumphs in 1924 was the Hallé's three visits to London's Queen's Hall, planned in collaboration with the Columbia Gramophone Company, which were widely acclaimed by the critics. The orchestra had not visited the capital since 1913. The first appearance, on 28 October, drew praise for Harty's reading of Brahms's Fourth Symphony. 'We have rarely heard Brahms so fully presented', wrote the critic of *The Times*. Harty wrote of his success to Esposito (two of whose arrangements of early music had been in the programme), whose reply was jubilant:

My dear Hay,
I am so delighted with your letter which I was waiting for with eagerness. Bravo! and with the Brahms No. 4! I remarked in the leaflet that only one critic dared say the truth that the band is *your* making and they had never heard that symphony performed in such a way as to understand it. The work is a hard-nut for performers and public and you ought to be thankful to the band and take your rightful share in the success. Whatever Strauss may think, if the instrument is not reliable the conductor cannot do full justice to a complicated masterpiece. You have got the instrument and the genius to make use of it. I never doubted. It always amazes me to see how the so-called critics believe in their own superior knowledge: they not only know everything but also what a composer or a performer ought to do. What fun if they were presented with the Score of this Brahms No. 4 and an orchestra and invited to conduct!?[117]

A second concert, on 11 November, featured Berlioz, Tchaikovsky, Elgar and Strauss's *Ein Heldenleben* (in which Catterall was much complimented on his solos). At the third, on 25 November, Harty paraded the *Symphonie fantastique*, the work for which he become renowned, together with the *Music to the Royal Fireworks*, the Mozart Bassoon Concerto (with Camden), and Delius's *Brigg Fair*. The accolade from the *Musical Times* paid glowing tribute to Harty and his orchestra:

When all is summed up, by far the finest orchestral playing we have this season enjoyed in London has been that of the Hallé band under Mr Hamilton Harty. The treatment of the Berlioz 'Fantastic' Symphony at the concert on November 25 was perfect. This is a big word to use, but there is no other available. A public that cannot recognize the beauty of well-shaped phrasing, of living rhythm, of balance of instrument with instrument, and blend of strings, wood, and brass, as sections and with one another, of continuity (or what I have called above 'all-thoroughness'), of precision in attack, and of the other qualities, small and big, which the Hallé and Hamilton Harty give us, is incapable of realizing that in them it possesses exponents of the very highest class.
    If the Hallé Orchestra came from abroad it would have to be praised as having

[116] *MG*, 23 Nov. 1934; see also A. Sanders (ed.), *Walter Legge: Words and Music* (London: Duckworth, 1998), 19.
[117] Letter from Esposito to Harty, 2 Nov. 1924, *GB-Belqb*.

given us the best we have heard for a long time, and the fact that its members are our own kin need not restrain us.[118]

Although by this time Harty had become very much an adopted Mancunian, he was still deeply aware of his Ulster roots. This was evident from a simple but charming arrangement he made for strings and harp of *The Londonderry Air*, which was recorded with the Hallé by Columbia in March 1924. But more substantial was Harty's return to the score of his 'Irish' Symphony for a further revision. The odd fact, however, about its publicity in Manchester, London and the musical journals, was that it was billed as 'new' and 'written that summer'. In the programme note Harty supplied for the Hallé performance on 13 November 1924 he claimed that 'some of the themes have been used previously by the composer in a youthful Symphony which gained the prize given by the Feis Ceoil, or Irish Music Festival, about twenty years ago'; in fact, a good deal of the actual composed material remained much as it was in the version revised in 1915.

Though the work was very enthusiastically received by orchestra and audience, Langford was more ambivalent in his response:

> His symphony was both brilliantly played and received with the greatest enthusiasm. ... The one doubt is whether he should have the order of merit as a composer or as the expert arranger of national melody. No standard symphony, we think, stands so completely on national melody as does this Irish Symphony. There is the example of Stanford, which comes nearest the case, but Stanford had other obsessions besides that of Irish melody, and this preoccupation of mind with a noble emulation of workmanship compelled him to do more spadework and more original work than Mr Harty in this symphony has done.
>
> ... It is a defect in the essence of the symphony, considered as a great work or a work of ambition, that it goes so little beyond the obvious character of the melodies used. ... It needs, let us say, something distinctly personal added to the something distinctly national. This essential is where Mr Harty's symphony, and his music generally, somewhat fails us.[119]

Though such criticism was perceptive on the question of nationalism and the limitations of folk-song in a symphonic context (one that Constant Lambert was enunciate only too clearly in *Music Ho!* some years later), it was perhaps a little unjust in that Harty's score contained a good deal of his own material (especially in the first movement), and its more general criticism of Harty's music served to fuel a growing individual rancour against Langford.

The 1924 revision of the 'Irish' Symphony differed from the 1915 version in several respects. Apart from the titles to the individual movements (along with the prefatory programme notes which Harty added at the head of the score at its publication in 1927),[120] and the expansion of the percussion section, Harty's

---

[118] *MT* 66 (1925), 62.

[119] *MG*, 14 Nov. 1924.

[120] It should be noted, however, that Harty did provide some 'colourful' descriptions in his accompanying programme notes, as evident from Frank Howes, 'A Note on Harty's 'Irish' Symphony', *MT* 66 (1925), 223–4.

changes to the orchestration were extensive, and often meant reassigning material to quite different instrumental timbres. In the Wagnerian material of the first movement's second group of themes the passagework in Harty's characteristic wind doublings is relatively simple in the 1915 version; in that of 1924 it is considerably more elaborate, presaging the composer's later style, and, indeed, looking forward to a similar orchestral sonority in the complex wind passagework of *The Children of Lir*. In addition, though much of the material remained the same, numerous musical details were altered, or sometimes quite markedly recomposed; some bars were cut to tighten the structure, or new rhythmical figurations were introduced to heighten the effect. In the first movement, for example, the transition to D major for the second subject was modified (the hushed clarinet solo was new, as was the chamber-like concept of the scoring with solo violin) and the coda substantially reworked. Similarly, the coda of the slow movement was altered (including the xylophone glissandos) and became much more richly orchestrated for divided strings. In the Finale, besides major reassignments of material from strings to wind, or vice-versa, Harty made major changes to the conclusion, an obvious one being the last grand 'memory' of the slow movement presented in the horns (whereas the 1915 version ended 'vivace', without interruption). These changes, at the hand of a more experienced musician, may well have emboldened Harty to announce that the symphony was, after all, 'new', though as Greer has pointed out, on at least one other occasion he claimed that the 1906 *Comedy Overture* had been composed during an American tour of the 1930s.[121]

On 16 January 1925 Harty conducted his 'Irish' Symphony to a packed Ulster Hall in Belfast, where he received a triple encore. He then took the orchestra on to Dublin, where he made a point of featuring Stanford's First Irish Rhapsody, a performance which commemorated his great Dublin-born compatriot who had died in March 1924. Harty extended his commiserations to the composer's widow, asking if he might cherish a manuscript of one of his works. Jenny Stanford replied:

> No words can say how deeply your letter has touched me. Your appreciation and love of my husband's music is very beautiful and I realized the other evening when I listened to your perfect rendering of the Rhapsody, how very very real it was. I will be delighted to give you a piece of his music, but I am afraid it cannot be just yet, as we have not been able to tackle things up to the present.[122]

From Dublin Harty swiftly travelled to London where, on 21 January, he conducted his *Royal Fireworks* transcription and his 'Irish' Symphony with the Royal Albert Hall Orchestra at Queen's Hall, an event which provoked Frank Howes to produce an article on the symphony in the March edition of the *Musical Times*.[123] It is not known how well the people of Bournemouth remembered the 1915 version, but it was given there as a 'new' work at the eight-day festival on 18 April (with an attentive Moeran in the audience).

[121] See Greer, 'Hamilton Harty Manuscripts', 242.
[122] Letter from Jenny Stanford to Harty, n.d., *GB-Belqb*.
[123] Howes, 'A Note on Harty's 'Irish' Symphony'.

It is perhaps an indication of the eminent artistic position Harty had created for himself at Manchester that he was showered with honours from the RCM (FRCM in 1924), Trinity College, Dublin (MusD, awarded 26 June 1925), Manchester University (DMus, 1926) and the Royal College of Organists (Honorary Vice-President). In 1925 he received a knighthood. The RIAM, for whom he had acted as external examiner for the piano students in 1924, organised a special reception for him at which the Governor General, members of the RIAM Council, eminent professors such as Esposito (who was now a Commendatore) and his daughter attended, together with students who gave a recital of his music, including his Piano Concerto in a version for two pianos.[124] The folk of Hillsborough rejoiced at the news of his national accolades, and a few days after the Dublin ceremony, Harty travelled north to his hometown to give an organ recital in a packed St Malachi's Church.

Over the next two years Harty attempted to settle down more permanently in Manchester. Having taken accommodation at the Clarendon Club or the Midland Hotel, while maintaining the house in St John's Wood, he set up home (from all accounts, without his wife) at 3 Rusholme Gardens, just off the Wilmslow Road. His work pattern changed little. During the concert season he was entirely devoted to the Hallé, and from time to time he took engagements in London, notably with the Royal Choral Society – he gave a memorable performance of *The Dream Gerontius* with them in February 1925 and 1926 – and he began to accept more work from the Liverpool Philharmonic. Though he now had no professional dealings with the LSO, the orchestra was keen for him to be involved in their twenty-first-birthday celebrations on 25 June 1925, when a special concert took place with a dinner afterwards at the Hotel Cecil. Beecham presided. On his right were Allen, Elgar, McEwen, Coates, Pitt, Goossens, Bax, Austin and Kennedy Scott; on his left were Cowen, Ronald, Boosey, German, Radford, Squire and Tertis.[125] During the summer months Harty accepted engagements from the increasingly popular seaside-town municipal orchestras in Eastbourne, Hastings, Torquay and Bournemouth. There was also time for composition and orchestration, albeit limited. After the production of two poignant unpublished songs, *My Thoughts of You* (1920) and the nostalgic *Carnlough Bay* (1921), he published a set of four songs in 1926, returning to the Irish texts of Moira O'Neill and Elizabeth Shane in *Antrim and Donegal*, an area the composer adored. Particularly striking is the turbulent first song 'The Two Houses', a spaciously conceived structure which is notable for its extended postlude for the piano. The 'Hush Song' was a genre in which Harty excelled, and this somnolent miniature is no exception, while the lively finale, 'Herrin's in the Bay', replete with a self-quotation from *Sea Wrack* in the piano, evokes the windswept seascape of Ulster's northern coast.

Clearly delighted by the impact and popularity of his Handel transcriptions, Harty produced the *Polonaise, Arietta and Passacaglia*, probably during the summer of 1926. These movements had, of course, been arranged some years earlier for violin and piano (see Chapter 3). Scored unostentatiously for double

---

[124] *IT*, 27 June 1925.

[125] Foss and Goodwin, *London Symphony*, 113.

wind (and piccolo), two horns, timpani and strings, it was first introduced at Manchester on 4 November 1926. After the delicately poised instrumentation of the 'Polonaise', the 'Arietta' is arranged with reduced forces. Conceived for two antiphonal sets of strings, one marked '*p*', 'vibrato' and 'molto espressivo', the other '*pp*', 'con sordino' and 'senza espressione, lontano', and haunting lines for solo flute, it is one Harty's most subtle examples of his finesse as an orchestrator. As a fitting finale, the 'Passacaglia', scored for fuller forces together with three trumpets and optional contrabassoon, is a magnificently colourful, Romantic recreation of Handel's variations, though, owing to the enormous popularity of his transcriptions of the *Water Music* and *Royal Fireworks*, this brilliant arrangement remained much less well known.

From Liverpool, Manchester and London, Harty enthusiastically took up the mantle of broadcasting, and as the technology of concert relay progressed steadily, orchestral concerts from these centres were able to be heard across the country rather than purely in their localities. This all-embracing spirit was accentuated by the BBC's introduction of 'National Concerts' (employing no fewer than 150 players from the Wireless Orchestra and the Covent Garden opera orchestra), in which Harty participated both from the Albert Hall and, with the Hallé, from the Free Trade Hall. Reith also appointed him to act as advisor for the broadcasting of music in the Irish Free State.[126] Matters between the orchestral players, the Musicians' Union and BBC were, however, far from settled. In the summer of 1926 Harty had the unhappy duty of announcing at the Society's AGM that, even though fees from the BBC for broadcasts had assisted with the orchestra's healthy balance sheet, the Society and the BBC had been unable to agree to the demands from the Musicians' Union for an extra broadcasting fee for each player. While Harty did not wish to enter the controversy on either side, he did nonetheless indirectly stress to the players that, in receiving fees larger than those in other orchestras, their additional demands might kill the very means of their livelihood:

> The Hallé Society is like an aged and overworked goose which does its very best to produce as many golden eggs as its interior mechanism will allow, but too many inexpert attempts to increase the size of the eggs and the rate of delivery will only result in the speedy death of the exhausted and bewildered bird. With all respect to the aims and ideals of the Musicians' Union and its members, I wish to say something to them which is between an appeal and a warning – 'Leave the orchestral societies alone, especially the Hallé Society, or before long you will force them out of existence and they will cease to be a source of profit to anyone at all'.[127]

Harty's zeal for recording exclusively with Columbia, for whom he continued his advisory role, remained as potent as ever. Here, too, technology was moving ahead in leaps and bounds as Columbia developed a much improved form of electrical recording, studios were larger, and the range of frequencies obtainable on recordings, especially for the bass, was improving constantly.

[126] *The Times*, 5 Oct. 1925.
[127] *MG*, 23 June 1926.

In 1926 Harty resigned from the Manchester advisory committee for the BNOC on the grounds that he had no time available for the company, and took the opportunity to stress his long-held view that much opera, for him, sounded better on the concert platform than in the theatre (a point he tried to make by giving *Carmen* at the Manchester Hippodrome with the Beecham Opera Chorus on 6 December 1926). His love of such music without the encumbrance of the stage was further supported by the number of recordings of operatic extracts he continued to make for Columbia. Moreover, Harty felt, perhaps with his own interests in mind, that a permanent base for opera in Manchester was more desirable than a touring group (see Chapter 3), though there was little sympathy for his views, not least from his old friend Frederic Austin, the BNOC's artistic director.[128] Believing that the BNOC had little future in the provinces after Beecham had considered founding his more London-centric 'Imperial League of Opera', Harty satirically commented that 'it [was] dying of T.B.'[129]

In September 1926 Harty gave another address – 'A Musical Renaissance' – to the National Union of Organists Association (which later became the Incorporated Association of Organists).[130] Among the somewhat disparate threads of his speech was a call for the use of church buildings for concert use, given that church attendance was dwindling and a proper 'sacred' use for them might be the performance of good music. Harty's decision then to lambast the growing partiality for jazz (which he described as 'sensual, noisy and incredibly stupid')[131] was, frankly, intemperate, but it seems that these opportunities to speak publically were a means of venting his spleen, particularly on subjects about which he held strong, if irrationally prejudicial, views. Yet for all his distaste, Harty would still give the first public performance as pianist of a jazz-inspired work like Constant Lambert's *The Rio Grande*, and delight in the sounds of George Gershwin's *An American in Paris*. Such were the conundrums of this complex and autocratic personality. On English music he remained incorrigibly resolute, yet in a letter to Philip Heseltine, who sent his orchestral carols and *Serenade* for scrutiny, he was kind and complimentary: 'Thank you for your Christmas remembrance. I have not had time to look at the Serenade but the carols are awfully good and beautifully done, if you will allow me to say so.'[132] Heseltine thoroughly endorsed Harty's devotion to Berlioz, and put forward the idea of using ophicleides in the *Symphonie fantastique*. Harty's rejoinder was one of intrigue: 'I will make enquiries as to whether my tubas are willing to tackle the ophicleides. I have never heard this instrument but can understand that many of the effects of Berlioz' Orchestration require it.'[133]

---

[128] *MG*, 6 Mar. 1926. Austin also disagreed with Harty's preference for 'concert' opera.

[129] Neville Cardus, *Autobiography* (Collins: London, 1947), 248.

[130] See *MT* 67 (1927), 924; also *The Times* and *MG*, 1 Sept. 1926.

[131] *MT* 67 (1927), 924. Although Harty was antipathetical to jazz, he was not, as Camden alluded, against all forms of popular and light music. On one occasion he entertained several friends to Noel Coward's new musical *Bitter Sweet*: Camden, *Blow by Blow*, 113.

[132] Letter from Harty to Heseltine, 9 Jan. 1926.

[133] Letter from Harty to Heseltine, 16 Aug. 1926.

It cannot be denied that Harty and the Hallé were on top of the world as Britain's leading national orchestra, and this was unanimously attributed to the virtue of employing a permanent conductor and eschewing the system of deputies that still beleaguered the London orchestras.[134] The extent to which the orchestra was universally admired can be measured from a letter sent by the Italian baritone Cesare Formichi after his appearance in operatic extracts by Bizet, Giordano and Puccini:

> I wish to express to you my sincere appreciation and admiration of your wonderful leading of the Orchestra on the occasion of my concert in Manchester.
>
> I would very much appreciate it if this letter could be published, as proof of my high opinion of your Orchestra, which I can say is one of the best I have ever heard.
>
> Marvellous rhythm, exceptional combination, perfect sound, are the vital characteristics of your musical ensemble, to which your valuable leadership gives the highest merit.
>
> It will always be a happy thought for me to recall my success in Manchester, where I have had the pleasure to meet a most enthusiastic public.[135]

Grommé announced, in light of this success and the general health of the orchestra's finances, that Harty's contract had been renewed 'for a series of years'.[136] Well-known faces returned in the likes of Casals, Cassadó, Suggia, Rubinstein, Backhaus and Cortot, who gave a rare performance of Fauré's *Ballade* for piano and orchestra (29 October 1925); and on one rare occasion Harty and the orchestra took part in an interesting experiment performing Saint-Saëns's Second Piano Concerto with a Duo-Art Pianolo reproducing a performance by Bauer (4 November 1925). There was some modest sign that Harty was prepared to be a little more accommodating in his attitude towards contemporary works. Novelties such as Glazunov's Serenade (28 October 1926), Respighi's *Pines of Rome* (18 February 1926) and Bax's *The Happy Forest* (21 January 1926) were familiar territory, as were Chausson's Symphony (25 November 1926) and the early twentieth-century items of Ravel's second *Daphnis and Chloë* suite (29 October 1925) and Roussel's *Le Festin d'araignée* (3 March 1927), but it was more unusual to see Bartók's *Danse suite* (14 January 1926) and Ibert's recently composed *Escales* (17 February 1927). On 18 and 25 February 1926, respectively, Harty revived Sibelius's *En Saga* and Second Symphony, both of which baffled Langford who failed to appreciate the merits of the Finn's work. There was also a revival of Elgar's Second Symphony, for which Harty had a special affinity; by Harty's invitation, Elgar conducted it himself at a concert entirely of his own works (20 January 1927), which included his old friend Brodsky who played the Violin Concerto. Bantock's *Song of Songs*, commissioned by the Hallé Society, had its premiere on 10 March 1927, and symbolised a long and rich friendship between conductor and composer:

[134] *MG*, 4 June 1927.

[135] Letter from Formichi to Harty, 5 Mar. 1926, *GB-Belqb*.

[136] *MG*, 23 June 1926.

My dear old O'Harty,

I am not going to attempt the impossible task of trying to express what is on my mind. No man ever did a kindlier act or a more heroic deed than you have done. You have given me new life and new hopes, and opened the door of all future desires. Your knowledge of, and sympathy for my work touched me deeply, dear friend, the more so, because I am as helpless as a mendicant Dervish to offer you anything in return, except a prayer of Allah for your everlasting welfare and happiness.[137]

Other English works enjoyed a belated first hearing in Manchester: Butterworth's rhapsody *A Shropshire Lad* (18 November 1926) and Vaughan Williams's *The Lark Ascending* with Jelly D'Arányi (3 February 1927). Yet with another of Vaughan Williams's works, *A Pastoral Symphony*, Harty courted controversy when he decided to replace it, at short notice, with Bantock's *Hebridean* Symphony.[138] Complaints issued forth to the *Manchester Guardian*, which forced a somewhat disingenuous rejoinder from Harty:

A letter from 'Musicus' in to-day's 'Manchester Guardian' makes some complaints regarding the Hallé programmes. It is very difficult to carry out a series of twenty-one concerts without making some alterations; but I should like to assure 'Musicus' that such alterations are not merely the result of caprice. The Elgar Symphony will be given as announced, as well as the Symphony of Moeran [postponed for reasons beyond Harty's control] and other new works. The 'Sinfonia Domestica' of Strauss, which was to have been given next Thursday, has been transferred (as already announced) to March 18, so that it may receive the extra rehearsal which its complexity demands.

The object of the Hallé Committee, in conjunction with myself, is to give good music which will at the same time make the widest possible appeal. In the end, after careful consideration and rehearsal, the Pastoral Symphony of Vaughan Williams was not felt to fall quite in this category. It was therefore thought better to delete it.[139]

Harty had already cancelled a performance of Beethoven's *Missa solemnis* in favour of Bach's *Mass in B Minor* which provoked several letters to the press, as did the replacement of Strauss's *Sinfonia domestica* with Schubert's Ninth Symphony (on the grounds that it bored the orchestra),[140] but the abandonment

[137] Letter from Bantock to Harty, 12 March 1927, *GB-Belqb*.

[138] Harty had earlier run into trouble with Vaughan Williams's Symphony. It was publicised at the end of 1924 that he would conduct the work along with Howells's new Second Piano Concerto and works by Bax, Ireland and Berners at the last concert of the Royal Philharmonic Society on 27 April 1925. Harty later withdrew, and the concert was instead conducted by Malcolm Sargent.

[139] Letter from Harty to the Editor, *MG* 8 Dec. 1925.

[140] *The Times*, 7 Aug. 1926. In the event Harty cancelled the Strauss for a second time for the concert on 18 March 1926, and replaced it with Brahms's Fourth Symphony. This forced Langford to remark that the Hallé Committee 'had gone a little needlessly beyond its province', even though he expressed sympathy with the decision that there was not enough rehearsal time to bring the work up to standard: *MG*, 19 Mar. 1926).

of Vaughan Williams's symphony was seen as patronising.[141] 'Why should the pace of musical appreciation be set by the laggards', Musicus replied, 'rather than by artists like Sir Hamilton Harty, who can speed the laggards up? Richter came to England when the public as a body still disliked Wagner's music. His remedy was obvious; he performed that music until everybody liked it.'[142]

But Harty was ultimately at his best in his beloved Berlioz. On 12 November 1925 he conducted an all-Berlioz programme which began with the *Grand Messe des morts*, an appropriate work for Armistice Day. Owing to the longstanding presence of the tuba player Harry Barlow, who was one of the most respected brass players in the north of England, and a major supporter of the region's brass band culture, Harty was able to prevail on Barlow's 'Besses-o-th'-Barn' Band to provide the supplementary brass for Berlioz's gargantuan instrumentation.[143] The occasion, of such musical importance nationally, brought to Manchester not only the London critics but also some from Paris, astonished at the enterprise of its conductor. Covered by the national press, it left an indelible impression on the sizeable audience which encouraged Harty and the Hallé Society to repeat the work on 11 November 1926. Such was the success of this epically dramatic choral work that the BBC requested Harty to broadcast it as one of the BBC National Concerts at the Albert Hall on 20 January 1927, with an orchestra of 200 (using players from the northern brass bands and the Hallé chorus). 'The performance calls for nothing but the highest praise', wrote the critic of *The Times*; 'the orchestra played superbly throughout under Sir Hamilton Harty, whose understanding of Berlioz's music can hardly be surpassed in England.'[144] There were many letters of congratulation. H. L. Gordon from *Musical Opinion* was unequivocal in his approbation:

> I have not had such a thrill like that of last night for years. It <u>was</u> fine and a very great feat. The tone-quality and technique of the chorus were such as I had nearly forgotten existed. I could have jumped on my seat and yelled after the Mass. My neighbour (Ormond Anderton) protested that a Mass ought to inspire more sober feelings, but he is too sophisticated to delight in the sensations of an exalted barbarian.[145]

Another letter was from a more insistent Heseltine with his ophicleides:

> I feel I must write and thank you for the wonderful experience of Thursday night's performance. It is more than fifteen years since I last heard the 'Requiem', very inadequately done, in Germany – so that your magnificent rendering was a real revelation of the work to me, and I am sure to hundreds of others. It is impossible to appreciate Berlioz properly from mere study of his scores – in fact, his music seems to me to be more difficult than any other to 'realize' from the printed page,

---

[141] *MT* 67 (1926), 65; see also *The Times*, 7 Aug. 1926.

[142] Letter from 'Musicus' to the Editor, *MG* 10 Dec. 1925.

[143] The presence of the additional brass also induced to Harty to give the first English performance of Glazunov's *The Kremlin*.

[144] *The Times*, 21 Jan. 1927.

[145] Letter from H. L. Gordon to Harty, 21 Jan. 1926, *GB-Belqb*.

since his art is so utterly his own, unique down to the smallest detail. And so fine performances are an absolute necessity to our understanding of him – and as great a necessity to musicians as to the general public. You have laid us all under a debt of deep gratitude to you by your splendid work in restoring Berlioz to his rightful place among the greatest masters of music. May you go on from strength to strength in your noble campaign!

I have been going through the original French edition of the full score. This ought certainly to be reprinted – together with many other of the first editions, for Weingartner has made some quite unwarrantable alterations in several works.

At the end of the 'Hosanna' the four ophicleides, <u>without</u> the trombones doubling them, must have sounded amazing. As they are nearly always doubled elsewhere, either in the octave or in unison, this passage must have been intended as a special effect.

A Grenadier Guards bandsman told me the other day that two members of the band learned the ophicleide some years ago and played it at, I think, the Military Tournament – or it may have been some historical pageant. If you ever feel inclined to try the instrument in performance, these men could probably manage the parts. I still have my ophicleide which is always at your disposal; and if more than one should be wanted, I know there are two at least at Potters', in West Street, Cambridge Circus. But one would probably be hard put to it to find an '<u>Ophicleide monster avec pistons</u>' at this time of day![146]

Although Harty was always to be known for his electric performances of the *Symphonie fantastique*, it was with the *Grand Messe des morts* that he gained true national adulation. The Hallé performances of the Mass undoubtedly represented some of his greatest triumphs so far in his conducting career, but his years with the Hallé had yet to reach their zenith.

[146] Letter from Heseltine to Harty, 21 Jan. 1927, *GB-Belqb*.

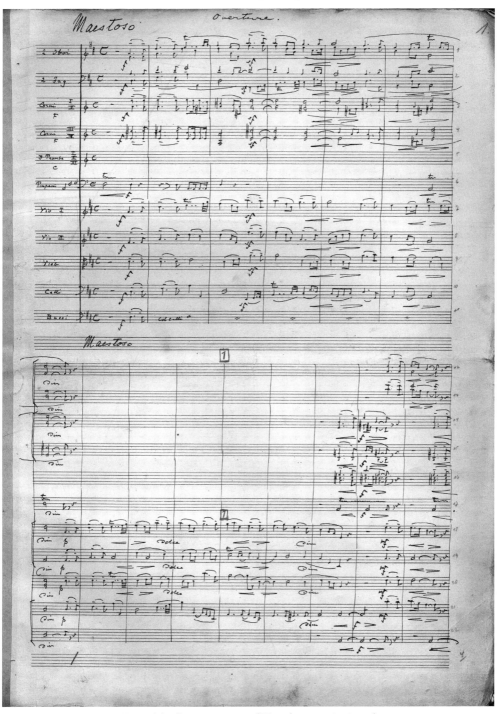

Fig. 2 The first movement of Harty's transcription of
Handel's *Music for the Royal Fireworks*

Apogee: From Hallé to the LSO

I N May 1927 Manchester mourned the passing of Langford, who had followed the progress of the Hallé since the days of Richter. Harty was reputed to have stayed away from the funeral. 'Why should I go to the funeral of that – market gardener?', was his anecdotal reply (making reference to Langford's predilection, like that of his father, for horticulture).[1] Langford's place was taken by Neville Cardus, who was already well known to readers of the *Manchester Guardian* for his imaginative prose and his columns on cricket and the theatre. His admiration for Langford's work was considerable, and as a tribute to his former colleague he edited a selection of his reviews for publication in 1929.[2] Cardus, untrained in music, but whose emotional, untechnical responses appealed to his audience, had already reviewed a number of Harty's opera productions for the *Manchester Guardian*, so he was familiar with Harty's style of programming. After the concert series for 1927–8 had been announced, Cardus weighed in with pointed criticism:

> unless the arrangements for the season now announced do not reveal everything, next March will find most of us as wise as we are to-day about Stravinsky's 'Le Sacre du Printemps', about the Five Orchestral Pieces of Schönberg, about Holst's 'Hymn of Jesus', Vaughan Williams's 'Pastoral' Symphony, Delius's 'A Mass of Life', Arnold Bax, Béla Bartók and Honegger. ... In Manchester it is sometimes hard to hear all the crackling of the flames under the melting-pot, as it boils prodigiously from hour to hour.[3]

This, and Cardus's criticisms of Harty's readings, led to a letter from Harty to C. P. Scott, the editor of the *Manchester Guardian*. As Cardus related in his *Autobiography*:

> I fell foul of Hamilton Harty almost as soon as I was given the reins of office and almost before Langford's ashes were cold; he wrote to C. P. Scott and asked if 'this young man presumes to be a better conductor than myself'. Scott replied that he hardly thought so but in any case he engaged me to write about concerts, not to conduct them: a simple but sufficient answer.[4]

Cardus was unjustified in citing Bax and Delius, whose works Harty had performed on numerous occasions, but the issue of Bartók, Schoenberg, Vaughan Williams and Holst (not least the cancelled performances) was more sensitive. There was the exciting prospect of hearing Mahler's Fourth Symphony, a concert performance of *Fidelio* (a new venture for Harty), and the *Siegfried*

---

[1] Kennedy, *The Hallé Tradition*, 220.

[2] See Samuel Langford, *Musical Criticisms*, ed. Neville Cardus (London: Oxford University Press, 1929).

[3] *MG*, 24 Sept. 1927.

[4] Cardus, *Autobiography*, 221.

Idyll in Wagner's original chamber instrumentation during the forthcoming season, but otherwise the list of unfamiliar works – Ernest Bryson's Second Symphony (which had been postponed from the previous season, again at short notice), two works by Respighi, his *Concerto Gregoriano* (played by Catterall) and the overture *Belfagor*, and de Falla's *Three-Cornered Hat* – seemed strangely restricted. Cardus congratulated Harty on his introduction of Mahler's music,[5] but he was sardonically incisive in his disapproval of Harty's tempos in Beethoven. Indeed the relationship between the two men blew hot and cold. Cardus greatly admired Harty and his achievements in Manchester:

> He [Harty] made an approach to me shortly after Langford's death. I liked and admired him; he invited me to lunch at his club and he expressed the hope that we would work together for the good of music in Manchester. He did not, he assured me, object to criticism so long as it was constructive. A blessed phrase this; and usually it means that a criticism is regarded as 'constructive', by the subject of it, if it is favourable.[6]

But Cardus was not to be cowed, nor was he deliberately negative or vindictive. He considered Harty's interpretation of Berlioz's *Romeo and Juliet* to be 'amongst the finest things ever done at a Hallé concert',[7] but he delivered a particularly adverse assessment of Harty's performance of the slow movement of Beethoven's Ninth Symphony on 15 March 1928:

> … in the adagio – which is any conductor's severest trial – his tempo was extraordinarily dilatory. During the performance I chanced to be sitting next to one of those curious individuals who 'follow' music at concerts with a score; and at the end of each movement he marked down the length of time taken playing it, to a second. This man informed me that Sir Hamilton had beaten, in the adagio of the Ninth, the record held for thirty years by Hans Richter against all comers. Knowing that every conductor rightly dislikes an estimate of his tempo by a literal time-test, I mentioned in my notice next day that Harty had established a new record for slowness in the adagio of the Ninth Symphony, and I named the minutes and the seconds to a fraction. Harty sent me a furious letter; he deplored that a music critic on a responsible journal should demean himself by attending a Hallé Concert 'accompanied by a stop-watch'. Such mechanical aids, he added, might well be legitimate and helpful to a critic of Lancashire's batting at Old Trafford [this was a palpable hit]; but he submitted that Beethoven and himself deserved a judgment based on musical knowledge and feeling, not measured by a 'mechanical time-test'.[8]

Cardus gracefully accepted the ironic rejoinder, but provided a similar retort by reassuring Harty that, if he attended another performance of the Ninth under

[5] See Neville Cardus, *Talking of Music* (London: Collins, 1957), 34, 52.

[6] Cardus, *Autobiography*, 221.

[7] *MG*, 2 Dec. 1927.

[8] Cardus, *Autobiography*, 222. Cardus was slightly over-elaborate in his account, for his review in *MG* stated 'With Richter, who was no "speed-merchant", this adagio played for less than a quarter of an hour; last night it dawdled for more than eighteen minutes.'

his direction, 'I shall bring with me – less for critical purposes than for those of personal convenience – not a stop-watch but an alarm clock.'[9]

During 1927, the centenary of Beethoven's death, the composer was on everyone's mind including Harty's. As part of the wave of articles and newspaper columns that appeared that year, he contributed a paper entitled 'Beethoven's Orchestra: A Conductor's Reflection' to *Music & Letters*. Based largely on his years of practical experience of conducting the composer's orchestral music, it contributed to a discourse that had been current since the time of Wagner, though it had gained particular momentum since Felix Weingartner's *Ratschläge für Aufführungen der Symphonien Beethovens* (*On the Performance of Beethoven's Symphonies*) of 1907. Weingartner had advocated alterations to Beethoven's instrumentation in which Harty, influenced by his own innate sensitivities as an orchestrator, was in complete sympathy; but did these changes go far enough? The nub of Harty's argument was his assertion that 'without some radical change, either by the reduction of the strings or by an increase of wind instruments, it [was] impossible to give performances which are really satisfactory.'[10] This pertained, essentially as he saw it, to those symphonies of 'immense, dramatic conception', the Third, Fifth, Seventh and Ninth. Harty insisted on retaining the large body of strings – feeling that this was entirely appropriate to the power of Beethoven's gestures – so the outer movements of these works (and one or two inner movements, such as the funeral march from the 'Eroica' and the scherzos of the Fifth and Ninth), he contended, called for reinforcement in the woodwind and horns; for solo passages this might be a question of discretion for the conductor. Harty proceeded to put this into practice with the Hallé.

Beethoven was one of many composers Harty recorded with Columbia in 1926 and 1927. In March 1926 he did the Mozart Bassoon Concerto with Camden – a first, since the company had not made any woodwind records[11]. This took up five sides of three records (at 78 rpm), but there was some doubt about what could occupy the sixth. For a nominal fee from Columbia, Camden volunteered a transcription of Jean-Baptiste Senaillé's 'Allegro spiritoso' whose character suited the bassoon. Little did he know at the time that it would become a best-seller internationally:

> I produced this, we timed it and 'Can you arrange that with string accompaniment by tomorrow?' I was asked. By sitting up half the night it was done. Sir Hamilton gave some additional suggestions and we varied the pitch of the three 'verses' to bring out the three different registers (three different octaves) of the bassoon. All done in a day: five sides of the concerto and of the Senaillé, and parts copied, too! Listening to that recording now it may seem rather strange. At the time it was considered quite a tour-de-force and the Senaillé became well known and was often called my 'signature tune'.
>
> Because of the uncertain future success of this recording I was offered a fairly nominal fee outright – the Senaillé to be 'thrown in'. This I accepted – to discover

[9] Cardus, *Autobiography*, 222.

[10] Hamilton H. Harty, 'Beethoven's Orchestra: A Conductor's Reflections', *Music & Letters* 8(2) (1927), 172–7, at 174.

[11] Camden, *Blow by Blow*, 109.

later just what a success this unknown instrument's discs had become. Harty came back from America and said all the bassoonists, and most of the woodwind players, had got it. The same story kept coming back to me from other parts of the world, the Senaillé had acquired quite a public of its own, and (I was told officially) had the greatest sales in America and – Japan![12]

Besides this success, Harty recorded his own *With the Wild Geese*, Haydn's 'Clock' Symphony, Dvořák's 'New World', excerpts from Berlioz's *Faust* and *Romeo and Juliet*, Saint-Saëns's Cello Concerto in A minor with his old friend Squire, and a considerable quantity of operatic excerpts with Formichi. This brought the Hallé additional and much-needed revenue, for, without the broadcasting fees from the BBC, the orchestra found itself with a deficit of £712 at the end of the season. This necessitated a call on the guarantors which provoked criticism from one of its body, the Dean of Durham (although his grievance was sternly met with the retort that he had not been called on to assist for six years). Moreover, for the 1927–8 season, the financial prognosis was more optimistic since negotiations for BBC broadcasts were successfully resolved.

The face of the Hallé had undergone some small changes since Catterall's departure. After a year with Bridge as leader, his place was taken by a Brodsky pupil, Alfred Barker, with the second violins being led by another of Brodsky's pupils, the Dublin-born Leonard Hirsch (with whose quartet Harty had often appeared); elsewhere the personnel remained loyally committed to the orchestra and Harty's ethos. The orchestra was as peripatetic as ever, giving concerts in Burton, Buxton, Bradford, Bolton and Derby, invariably with a great international soloists such as Suggia, Moiseiwitch, Cassadó, or the great Australian Wagnerian soprano Florence Austral. In January 1928 Harty was invited by the BBC to bring the Hallé to London. Queen's Hall was packed to the brim for a concert of Mozart, Beethoven and Wagner. The critic of *The Times* provided a rapturous review: 'There is nothing vicious in the tone of this northern orchestra: it cuts clean as a razor',[13] and though the London critic of the *Manchester Guardian* (not Cardus on this occasion) found fault with Harty's interpretation of Mozart's G minor Symphony, his verdict of Beethoven's Fifth Symphony (which was duly reinforced by Harty's added horns and woodwind) and the Wagner excerpts was ecstatic: 'The balance of the Hallé Orchestra', he averred, 'is superior to anything here.'[14] When the orchestra made a return visit in March for the *Symphonie fantastique* they received an equally euphoric response.

The orchestra were also no strangers to Dublin, where Harty clearly had a special loyalty. Since the war, and with political change, the Irish Free State had not enjoyed the same regularity of professional orchestral music as it had under Esposito and the DOS. In February 1926 Harty accompanied his principal wind and string players from the Hallé to Dublin to give a number of concerts at

[12] Camden, *Blow by Blow*, 111.

[13] *The Times*, 14 Jan. 1928.

[14] *MG*, 14 Jan. 1928. It is perhaps one of the tragedies of Harty's career as a major interpreter of the *Symphonie fantastique* that he never recorded it.

the RDS in their new accommodation at Ballsbridge and were greeted by large audiences. An endearing photograph taken at the time shows Harty with his arm affectionately round that of his old Italian master, whose *Neapolitan Suite* Harty conducted as a tribute. After returning to the Irish capital again in October to attend an assembly in Mills Hall at the unveiling of Sarah Harrison's portrait of Esposito, Harty brought his 'chamber orchestra' to the RDS for a second time in February 1927. During this visit the conductor and players were invited to Cochrane's home at Woodbrook for a concert. Hirsch, who was among the party, vividly recalled the occasion:

> The following day, we had another treat in store – we were to give a concert at Woodbrook, the home of Sir Stanley Cochrane, about ten miles outside Dublin. Harty had a surprise up his sleeve for us, but he did not reveal it until we arrived at the house: there to greet us was the famous Count John McCormack. The mansion house at Woodbrook provided a magnificent setting for that evening's concert, at which John McCormack sang with the orchestra. He also sang a group of solos, accompanied by Harty – the kind of accompaniment singers must dream of, but rarely get.[15]

It was perhaps evident by this time that Esposito was ailing, a concern for which may well have instigated a further visit by Harty in July,[16] but, by dint of the enthusiasm of the RDS (and, very likely, some financial support from Cochrane), he was able to see him again when the Hallé went to Dublin on 31 October. On this occasion Harty conducted his 'Irish' Symphony, twenty-three years after he had gained his first experience with the work in front of an orchestra.[17] This was very likely the last time Harty would see his mentor, for in February 1928, after a rehearsal of a revivified DOS, Esposito suffered a heart attack during the night and was not expected to live. After unexpectedly rallying, he was persuaded by the RIAM to retire, and moved to Florence in 1928 to be with his family. How strange Dublin must have seemed when Harty went again with the Hallé in October 1928, and found that its most important luminary had departed.

At around this time it also appears that Harty and Nicholls ceased to work together as they had done in the past. After the war Nicholls joined Beecham's Opera Company; after that organisation ceased in 1920 she gave much time to the support of the BNOC (as a director), with which her husband was closely connected until his resignation in 1926.[18] After that it appears that their paths gradually diverged. There is also some evidence, albeit scant, that she suffered some form of chronic illness which curtailed her singing career in or around 1928. I was at this time that she sang her last role for the BNOC in Verdi's *Falstaff* with Barbirolli.[19] Of particular significance was the revival of the *Ode*

---

[15] Hirsch, 'Memories of Sir Hamilton', 71.

[16] *IT*, 20 July 1927.

[17] *MT* 68 (1927), 1131.

[18] See Nicholls, 'A Vignette', 26.

[19] See letter from Agnes Nicholls to Carice Blake (née Elgar), 24 Feb. 1934, *GB-HWRO*; see also Chapter 7.

to a Nightingale which had, at one time, been Nicholls's prerogative, but this role now passed to Isobel Baillie who became one of Harty's 'missions'. Baillie sang the *Ode* on numerous occasions in Bradford and Bournemouth, but on one occasion she experienced a lapse of memory during the performance, an error that weighed heavily with her. Harty wrote to reassure her:

> Your singing last night was beautiful, and don't worry over the little slip – that might occur to anyone. There is no doubt in my mind that if you keep your voice as it is at present, and go on improving in style, you will become the leading oratorio and concert English soprano.
>
> I am prepared to help you in any way and so when you need advice or a lesson in style and interpretation, ask me without constraint. I believe I can assist you in such ways. All this is private. I would not do it for anyone but someone, like you, of exceptional talent. You were a good girl last night – go on the same path![20]

Since Nicholls had largely given up singing professionally, there was no reason for her and Harty to perform together. Harty's musical attentions therefore passed on to Baillie, whom he ardently supported. Nor did Nicholls appear any longer, as was customary, at the traditional Wagner nights at the Hallé; her major roles of Isolde and Brünnhilde were supplanted by Florence Austral. Baillie also sang Wagner, but her more brittle voice was better suited to the 'lighter' music in *Lohengrin* and *Tannhäuser*. When tempted to try her hand at the heavier material, Harty, very much in a patriarchal capacity, chastised her:

> I see, by accident, that you have been singing such things as the closing scene from *The Ring* – I believe you know in your heart that this is not wise. Your voice is too lyrical and fresh for the kind of heavy-weight work.
>
> You will know that I am only writing in this way because I wish for your real success. I have really no business to interfere with what you consider right to do – but you know how straight-forward I am about music. I have been glad to do what little I could to help forward your charming talent but if you feel you must continue to sing music which cannot possibly suit your voice and personality then I must retire just wishing you whatever good luck remains for you in your musical life.
>
> I am really disappointed in you, Bella, I thought you had enough sense to see that in your own line you have most of the sopranos beaten – but in music of the type I refer to you are quite out of the picture and merely a source of gratification to your enemies. Don't be cross, I really believe what I am saying.[21]

Baillie took his advice and Harty, keen to see that his protégée was not hurt, took her to Bradford to sing in a Wagner programme.[22]

Though surrounded by friends and colleagues who venerated him, Harty nevertheless led an intensely private life away from the orchestra. Stephen Williams of the *Daily Express* remarked in 1931: 'He [Harty] lives a lonely life in

[20] Baillie, *Never Sing Louder than Lovely*, 94, quoting a letter from Harty to Baillie, 27 Jan. 1927.
[21] Baillie, *Never Sing Louder than Lovely*, 29.
[22] Baillie, *Never Sing Louder than Lovely*, 30.

a house in Eccles.[23] He shuns publicity, he affects the utmost fastidiousness in his way of life. He is an utterly charming man to meet, yet one can never be sure what subtle thoughts are lurking behind that bland expansive smile.'[24] Besides the retreat which was maintained for him by the Farrers at Lambrigg in the Lake District, Harty regularly made visits to Ulster to see his family. Holidays might last between four and six weeks and he would stay at Donaghadee, beloved of his childhood, on the Co. Down coast of the Ards Peninsula, where he would rent a house, 'Tir-na-Nog', close to the shore. He had many favourite haunts there and on the North Antrim cliff-tops. He enjoyed fishing in Scotland, but best of all were the Irish loughs of Corrib and Melvin. At Melvin, where he was well known to the local gillie, he kept a boat which he took regularly onto the loughs to fish. But in 1929, for reasons unknown, he suddenly gave up this pastime, perhaps with a view of spending his solitary hours elsewhere.[25]

During the summer of 1928 he enjoyed a rare bout of composition. In June he completed a Suite for cello and piano, a set of four movements which was published by Schott. Though it does not bear a dedication, it seems likely that it was intended for Squire, who often played it with Harty. 'An Irish Prelude' and 'A Wistful Song' allow the vocal character of the cello to shine through, these euphonious, slightly melancholy utterances contrasting with the more reflective 'Humoresque' and the *Urlicht*-style of the final 'Scherzo-Fantasy'. As Harty himself explained some years later to Beatrice Harrison, the work required gentle interpretation:

> I will tell you any ideas I have about them when we meet (and you can do the same to me). You will have seen for yourself that the Prelude is a sort of lazy Irish lilt and that the Humoresque and Scherzo-Fantasy are whimsical. It is necessary to keep the 'Wistful Song' from being too sentimental. It is really more a 'reverie'.[26]

Of the same date as the Cello Suite are *Three Irish Folksongs*. Attractive arrangements of three traditional tunes to words by P. W. Joyce ('The Lowlands of Holland', 'The Fairy King's Courtship', and 'The Game Played in Erin-go-Bragh'), the songs' simple verse schemes draw interest from Harty's skilful process of strophic variegation in the subtle piano accompaniment.

In August Harty participated in another of the congresses organised by the Incorporated Association of Organists (IAO). As before, he used the arena as a means of voicing his opinions on a variety of musical subjects, and on this occasion his attack on what he perceived as the nation's poor, indeed 'scandalously unpatriotic', attitude towards music amplified a view expressed in brief in the *Musical Times* article of 1920. In 'The Discouragement of English Music', Harty's vituperation had in part been fuelled by an exchange of letters with Cardus in the *Manchester Guardian* in July. Cardus, in reviewing a

---

[23] This was Harty's last place of abode in Manchester, at Ballinderry, Ellesmere Park, Eccles.

[24] Cited in Kennedy, *The Hallé, 1858–1983*, 17.

[25] See John Barry, 'Last Years', in *Hamilton Harty: His Life and Music*, ed. David Greer (Belfast: Blackstaff Press, 1978), 51–66, at 53.

[26] Letter from Harty to Beatrice Harrison, 23 Mar. 1939, *GB-Lcm*.

recording of the Philadelphia Orchestra and its salaried players, had somewhat clumsily described English orchestral players as 'well-intentioned amateurs',[27] a phrase which also provoked an angry rejoinder from Alfred Barker.[28] One of Cardus's main mitigating arguments was that the Hallé had always managed to exist on one rehearsal before each Thursday concert, and with difficult repertoire (such as Strauss's *Sinfonia domestica*), such a scheme was bound to be less satisfactory than the richer diet of rehearsals enjoyed by well-funded American orchestras. Harty joined the fray, equally insulted by Cardus's article,[29] and was keen to assert that many of the Hallé's performances expressed an élan where the over-rehearsed orchestras of Philadelphia, Boston, Berlin and Vienna he had witnessed at first hand to be 'dull and lifeless'.[30] Nevertheless, given the arduous negotiations he had experienced with the Manchester Corporation to establish the municipal concerts, and his irritation at the government's imposition of an entertainment tax, Harty's envy of state subvention on the European continent and private munificence in America was a source of deep frustration to him, and he was in no mood to compromise with the 'cynical indifference [and] ignorance' of politicians whose commercial attitudes distorted the value of great art.[31] But at the heart of his thesis, Harty lamented that British musicians did not enjoy the same approbation abroad as foreign musicians did here; this he blamed on an entrenched native belief that the foreign commodity was always superior, which meant that native music lacked both confidence and national character. 'I am trying to prove that two things mutually react upon one another', he claimed: 'the lack of national encouragement extended to native music and the absence of national character in much of the work we produce.' His message to the IAO was therefore one of collective power, and of the need to mobilise public opinion, the press, and the government to improve the conditions and financial aid to British music so as to obviate the endemic sense of national 'discouragement' which existing national policy sustained.

It was not an auspicious time to be asking for financial subvention from government. By 1928 the signs of economic depression were already evident, and the last thing available to music at this time was money. However, when the Hallé showed a small profit after its 1927–8 season, and new guarantors had come forward, there was a general feeling of satisfaction about the orchestra's future; moreover, they welcomed the suggestion from the *Manchester Guardian* for a rehearsal fund to support preparation for more challenging works.

The call for more substantial contemporary works was getting increasingly loud. In fact, some letters to the *Manchester Guardian* complained that, in order to hear Vaughan Williams, Schoenberg, Stravinsky and Honegger, it was necessary to go to neighbouring Liverpool.[32] In consequence, it appears that

---

[27] *MG*, 23 June 1928.

[28] *MG*, 29 June 1928.

[29] *MG*, 6 July 1928.

[30] *MG*, 9 July 1928.

[31] The full text of Harty's lecture is in *GB-Belqb*, MS 14/29/ix.

[32] *MG*, 12 July 1928.

Harty, perhaps a little reluctantly, was prepared to take note of the growing disquiet about the Hallé's repertoire. New items included Strauss's *Festal Prelude* (18 October 1928), Medtner's Second Piano Concerto (22 November 1928), played by the composer, and Dohnányi's *Ruralia hungaricus* (17 January 1929), which the composer conducted. There was the first hearing in Manchester of Kodály's *Háry János* (6 December 1928), two movements from Prokofiev's suite from his opera *The Love of the Three Oranges* (21 February 1929), the *Sinfonia sevillana* by Turina (for whose music Harty had a special predilection), and, with Harty ill, Ernest Ansermet was invited to conduct a programme mainly of modern works, among which were Honegger's *Chant de joie*, Stravinsky's *Petrouchka*, Lord Berners's *Fugue*, and Bliss's arrangements of Purcell, *Suite d'airs et du danses* (15 November 1928). In the event only the Bliss survived, but to give Harty his due, the works did reappear later in a concert which also welcomed his old friend Szigeti in Beethoven's Violin Concerto (6 December 1928).

Though some had called for less Berlioz in the programme, Harty was still determined to direct a full concert performance of *The Trojans* (1 November 1928), which attracted a good deal of friendly press attention, though to Cardus it fell flat.[33] At the end of the season, as continued proof of his belief in concert performances of opera, he conducted *The Flying Dutchman* for the first time in its entirety (13 March 1929). Of British repertoire, there were revivals of Elgar's *Falstaff* and the first hearing in Manchester of *The Music Makers*, which formed part of an ambitious choral evening with *Sea Drift* (with Roy Henderson) and Bax's new and extremely demanding motet *Mater ora filium* (7 February 1929) which must have put the Hallé chorus through their paces. But other new works by Eric Fogg, Victor Hely-Hutchinson and the prize-winning Swedish composer Kurt Atterburg, who won the prize of £2,000 guineas in a competition sponsored by Columbia for a symphony inspired by Schubert (whose centenary it was), prompted only disappointment from Cardus who was still hoping for a broader sweep to the Hallé's programmes.

The passing of Brodsky in January 1929, and of the Hallé's timpanist Willem Gezink, yielded warm tributes from Harty and Cardus.[34] With Carl Fuchs and the Speelman brothers, they were part of that fraternity of German musicians who had given loyal service to the city of Manchester since the days of Richter. What is more, Brodsky's sterling leadership at the RMCM had provided half of the Hallé's string players and several of its finest wind players. More devastating for Harty, however, was the news of Esposito's death on 19 February 1929. Harty heard from Esposito's daughter Vera:

> Your Miche is no more, as you will have guessed at once by the envelope. You have lost your best friend, I who know his heart so well can tell you. And I hope you love him as well as he loved you or even half as much as he thinks you did, it will still be a great deal. He measured others by himself, I suppose we all do.
>
> As I write he is lying so peacefully and all of us around him.

---

[33] *MG*, 2 Nov. 1928.

[34] See Neville Cardus, *Second Innings* (London: Collins, 1950), 114–8.

He is to be buried very quietly tomorrow morning at Trespiano out on the hills. I wanted San Miniato, but there is no more space there.

There will be a Requiem Mass sung for him by the Choir of Franciscan Monks at a monastery in Piazza Savonarolo, and another special Mass on Friday morning.

Dear Hay, I can't write any more now. Our friends and neighbours are coming to see him in numbers, and all admire him, many weep, and kiss his cold forehead, making the sign of the Cross.

Love him always as much as you can and remember him, he loved you greatly.[35]

A telegram of condolence was sent and a letter followed with the offer to arrange for a suitable inscription on Esposito's tomb. The quotation, signed 'H. H.', is two-and-a-half bars of music on a single stave.[36] After obituaries in the *Irish Times* and *The Times*, Harty furnished *The Irish Statesman* with an account of how indebted were many Irish musicians, including himself, to Esposito's redoubtable contribution to Irish musical life:

[It] was when he was playing in private for a few friends that he was at his finest both poetically and technically. I can never forget the impression I received on these occasions, not only of the depth and beauty of the music of composers like Beethoven and Chopin, but at the nobility of thought and the passion and romance of sentiment which dwelt in the soul of Esposito himself. He gave the best part of his life to teaching us in Ireland that poetic imagination and superficial facility are not enough in matters of art. It is our national failing in music to think that our Irish ease in conjuring up the vision of something emotional and poetic absolves us from the necessity of learning how to support it on a solid basis of learning and craftsmanship. It was in this way that Esposito served us so faithfully, and of all of his friends and pupils no one owes him more in this way than I do myself, or acknowledges it with more eagerness and gratitude. I shall always think of him as the most perfect musician I have ever met – and a still greater thing as the most beautiful and lovable nature with which I have ever been brought into contact.[37]

In a further letter from Vera, Harty was urged 'to keep Father's name alive a little',[38] but this was by no means an easy task. The musical environment of the late 1920s permitted little room for Esposito's unfashionable Romanticism. Harty made an effort to have the overture *Otello* published, but it was abruptly declined.[39] It was disappointing, but, to reassure Esposito's son Mario that his father's work would one day be appreciated for its value, he wrote in bullish mood:

Don't take the unintelligent criticism of this music as being insufficiently *modern* too seriously. Instead you should thank God for this fact. Your father was a Romantic composer, and as soon as people come around again to valuing sincerity

[35] Letter from Vera Esposito to Harty, 19 Nov. 1929, *GB-Belqb*.

[36] G. L. Aiello (ed.), *Al Musicista Michele Esposito nel primo centenario della nascita* (Castellammare di Stabia: M. Mosca, 1956), 63.

[37] Harty, 'Michele Esposito', 277.

[38] Letter from Vera Esposito to Harty, 27 Nov. 1929, *GB-Belqb*.

[39] Aiello (ed.), *Al Musicista Michele Esposito*, 56–7.

and simplicity in art, the work of your father will certainly have the recognition it deserves.[40]

As a further gesture, Harty, who was appointed a vice-president of the RIAM in 1930, campaigned for 'Esposito' prizes to be awarded for excellence on the pianoforte.

In spite of the hard economic climate, the Hallé orchestra boasted another profit of £140, and its indisputable reputation as Britain's most professional orchestra was confirmed by another visit to London to perform Berlioz's *Faust* for the BBC on 1 March 1929. The Hallé's high standing could also be measured by the impressive number of broadcasts and the high level of recordings which Harty oversaw. In 1928 alone he recorded Schubert's Ninth Symphony and most of the incidental music for *Rosamunde*, Brahms's Violin Concerto with Szigeti (a recording which Cardus maintained rivalled that of Heifetz)[41] and Mussorgsky's Prelude to *Khovanshchina*. There was also time within this busy schedule for him to record with Squire the Scherzo from his Suite for Cello and Piano, composed during June 1928,[42] which he and Beatrice Harrison premiered in London in November. The following year, recordings featured Solomon and the Hallé in Tchaikovsky's First Piano Concerto, Harty's arrangement of *The Londonderry Air*, the Scherzo of his 'Irish' Symphony, an orchestral arrangement of Schubert's 'Arpeggione' Sonata with Cassadó (its arranger), a popular rendition of Rimsky's *The Flight of the Bumble Bee* and the same composer's *Capriccio espagnole*. One recording that reached a huge number of gramophones was that of the children of Manchester Schools. On the back of the municipal concerts, and the specially reserved places for schoolchildren, Harty collaborated with the Manchester Education Committee for 250 of the city's working-class children (trained by a local teacher, Gertrude Riall) to participate with the Hallé in a municipal concert (4 March 1929) of Purcell's 'Nymphs and Shepherds', Handel's 'Let the Bright Seraphim', some of Brahms's *Gypsy Songs*, and an extract from Humperdinck's *Hansel and Gretel* (using orchestral arrangements by Harty and Fogg). Not only was this greatly appreciated throughout the city, but it reached a wider audience when Columbia recorded the Purcell and Humperdinck in June 1929. The record's impact was enormous – it sold more than a million copies and has since become iconic; in 1975 it gave rise to a reunion of the participants, and it even became the inspiration for Victoria Wood's 2011 play *That Day We Sang*. Delighted with the result, Harty repeated the experiment in March 1930 'with unmistakable affection and approval', Cardus remarked; 'he beamed upon them from time to time like an unusually benevolent uncle.'[43]

---

[40] Letter from Harty to Mario Esposito, in Aiello (ed.), *Al Musicista Michele Esposito*, 57 (from an Italian translation).

[41] *MG*, 7 May 1929.

[42] In accordance with his lionisation of Berlioz, Harty also arranged 'The Repose of the Holy Family' from *L'Enfance du Christ* in 1928, probably for Squire. It was a work of which he was immensely fond and, according to Baguley, he frequently included it in his concerts of chamber music.

[43] *MG*, 18 Mar. 1930.

On several occasions it had been noted that Harty's unwillingness to programme more contemporary works had not just been down to his own dislike of the music, for much of its new complexity and unfamiliarity demanded extra rehearsal time which was additional expense to an orchestra with finite resources. Some sympathised with him, others were doubtful; but it was clearly a question that bothered him repeatedly. His antipathy to musical modernism reared its head again at the Hull congress of the IAO in September 1929, when he delivered a paper on 'Some Problems of Modern Music'. It was, to a large extent, a regurgitation of his former address to the Manchester branch of the Union in 1924, and his language was no more temperate than before. He talked of the 'filthy desecration of the ultra modern', of a 'mental disease [that was] afflicting the present musical generation with special virulence' and of the 'fear of being left behind'. Composers of today, he claimed, could be divided into two groups: the serious pioneers seeking fresh methods of expression, and the charlatans who sought 'to go one better' in the production of ugliness and discord. The consequence of this kind of music to Harty was simply a recipe for 'restlessness, hardness, brilliance, grotesqueness and sardonic humour', which were, he believed, insufficient 'to give music enduring life'. Once again jazz – a symptom of 'feverish unrest' – was blamed for debasing serious music, comments which drew applause from Mackenzie, now a figure of a bygone age:

> I must congratulate you on the frankly spoken remarks regarding the present devilish concoctions which are offered us under the guise of music. Something to this same effect I wrote in my 'Musicians Narrative' (page 257 'L'Envoi') but it has been carefully ignored. I would gladly join you; but at my time of life cannot very well appear in the arena on crutches. Besides, I resent it so strongly that nothing will induce me to listen to any more of it. So, I am not even up to date thank God! I hope, however, that your speech will provoke a controversy ... which will come not an hour too soon.[44]

Mackenzie's letter symbolised the essence of Harty's 'lament' for a passing generation of composers and a pre-war Romantic era with which he closely identified.[45] 'Most of us', he contended, 'were born towards the close of a wonderfully lively time in music – a period which might be expressed by the formula Bach–Mozart–Beethoven–Brahms–Wagner. Strauss and Elgar are still with us and as far as one can see are at the end of that particular line.'[46] The assertion that music had seen the last of its great composers was familiar, but his refutation of modern developments and belief that music 'had wandered aside into barren and unfruitful wastes' ultimately articulated an aesthetic discourse at the very heart of musical creativity in the 1920s and 1930s. For England at least, it fairly represented the sense of post-war angst about the course of music, its function, and the kinds of polarised and eccentric criticisms it spawned in the work of Philip Heseltine and Lambert's *Music Ho!* (1934), and rather less

---

[44] Letter from A. C. Mackenzie to Harty, 4 Sept. 1929, *GB-Belqb*.

[45] As quoted in *MT* 70 (1929), 921.

[46] Quoted in P. Hammond, 'The Hallé Years and After', in *Hamilton Harty: His Life and Music*, ed. David Greer (Belfast: Blackstaff Press, 1978), 35–50, at 40.

eloquently in Van Dieren's *Down Among the Dead Men* (1935) and Cecil Gray's overlaboured *Survey of Contemporary Music* (1928).

Yet for all his publically expressed antagonisms, it is clear that Harty acknowledged his detractors, since the programme for the 1929–30 season was transformed in its openness to a wide range of new European and British works. In an interview for the *Daily Express* he made the following announcement:

> I know I have been accused in the past of neglecting modern works which Manchester people have a right to hear, and preserving a too conservative outlook. Well, I am going to alter all that.
>
> Next season we shall experiment to our heart's content. Previously I have been afraid, partly because I did not think the modern works as good as that music which for convenience we call classical, and partly because I did not feel that the Hallé Society could afford to risk experiments. However, we are going to take our chance.[47]

The audience expressed its most clamorous appreciation for Sibelius's Fifth Symphony; 'more – more of this Sibelius' was how Cardus, somewhat taken aback, expressed the response, even suggesting that Harty might repeat the work later during the season.[48] A week later Catterall appeared as a sympathetic soloist in Sibelius's Violin Concerto, which led Cardus to question how the Hallé had let him go.[49] For Cardus, however, the most impressive of Harty's interpretations of Sibelius was the Fourth Symphony (5 December 1929), which played to a less-than-full Free Trade Hall. Nevertheless, Harty was praised for his reading of the Finn's challenging, not to say enigmatic score; 'perhaps the subtlest symphony ever written' was Cardus's verdict, and he prophesied that Harty might well generate a renown for his performances of Sibelius equal to that he had for Berlioz.[50] In fact, Sibelius came to learn of Harty's authoritative readings of his symphonic works and expressed his appreciation in a letter a few years later:

> Let me express my profound gratitude to you for the interest and understanding you have always shown my music. During years [*sic*] I have followed your work and it was always with great satisfaction I knew my music to be in your masterful hands. Feeling happy about the opportunity to say to you this I beg [you] to accept my best regards.[51]

Of the late Austro-German Romantic repertoire, Harty's adventurousness extended to late Mahler as well as Strauss. On 27 February 1930, after three rehearsals, he conducted the first performance in England of Mahler's Ninth Symphony. The work made a deep impression on the audience, and Cardus noted:

---

[47] *Daily Express*, 25 May 1929.

[48] *MG*, 25 Oct. 1929.

[49] *MG*, 1 Nov. 1929.

[50] *MG*, 6 Dec. 1929.

[51] Letter from Sibelius to Harty, 11 Oct. 1934, *GB-Belqb*.

seldom indeed have the Hallé players so clinchingly proved their technical resource and their quick responsiveness to a strange musical aesthetic as on this occasion. Admirable, too, was Sir Hamilton Harty's control of the work, a control which combined sensibility to the inflected phrase … with a large-minded grasp of the structure's main lines.[52]

Harty's devotion to the nineteenth-century symphonic repertoire was reflected in an entire programme of symphonies by Beethoven, Brahms, and a 'new edition' of Schumann's First Symphony, in which Harty offered his own orchestration.[53] His performance of Elgar's Second Symphony, juxtaposed with three Strauss tone poems, was regarded by Cardus as 'the finest reading in Manchester so far'.[54] After the performance Harty wrote to Elgar full of warmth and admiration for the work:

> We were very sorry you could not be with us last night, as we were looking forward to trying to please you with our rendering of a work we love. I know that you do not care to discuss your music, but perhaps you will allow me to tell you of the deep impression your E flat symphony made this week at Manchester and London. My orchestra respect and love the work and take every care in its presentation. I know they feel as I do its nobility and power. Allow me to add that I feel it a great privilege to devote whatever talents I possess to your music and its adequate performance. (Excuse the stiffness of my words – my feeling is very sincere.)[55]

The London performance also elicited a euphoric letter to Harty from George Bernard Shaw:

> The symphony went wonderfully: I heard everything in it with the last inch of effect. The great rampage in the rondo came off with indescribable completeness. And you know how very seldom that can be said of an orchestral performance, especially in London, where the players are so clever that they can read everything and consequently never know anything. I have always said that we should get no really satisfactory performances of such works as those of Elgar and Berlioz until they were played without notes, not read. You produced that effect last night: the band seemed to be really in possession of the music. How you knocked it into them, and got it out of them, Heaven knows. I can only guess six months rehearsal. Anyhow it was so magnificent that I have written a line to Elgar about it.
> My wife was enchanted, and reviled me for not having made her come to all the other concerts. She declares, by the way, that all the Manchester players have precisely similar noses, and she wants to know whether you select them by that feature, as she thought that their ears were the important organs.
> As we met Lady Hamilton Harty at Madeira, and she seemed to like us, perhaps we shall have the pleasure of making your personal acquaintance some day when you are not too busy – if that ever happens.[56]

[52] *MG*, 28 Feb. 1930.

[53] *MG*, 14 Mar. 1930. Harty also later conducted his new 'edition' of the Fourth Symphony on 3 April 1933 with the LSO at Queen's Hall.

[54] *MG*, 24 Jan. 1930.

[55] Letter from Harty to Elgar, 25 Jan. 1930, *GB-HWRO*.

[56] Letter from George Bernard Shaw to Harty, 25 Jan. 1930, *GB-Belqb*.

Shaw's letter to Elgar was equally ecstatic:

> Harty and his Manchester men pulled off a stupendous performance of the E flat Symphony last night. They seemed really to know it bit by bit instead of merely reading it; it was not a matter of the notes producing the effect (which they often don't if the players don't mean anything except to earn their salaries) but an intended and exhaustive real performance. Harty was a dripping rag at the end, but he had mastered [it] and was feeling every phrase; he was kinder to some of it than you would have been yourself.
>
> As to that fortissimo in the Rondo, which is like nothing else on earth (Beethoven nowhere!), you should have heard it. *I* never heard it before!
>
> I write this as, if there were a question of a new recording of the symphony, and you were not yourself disposed to do it, it might be useful to know that you could trust Harty and the Hallé Band. Also, it is pleasant to blow off steam after an exciting evening.[57]

Backhaus appeared in Strauss's *Burleske* for piano and orchestra, Cassadó played Elgar's Cello Concerto, Suggia the Cello Concerto of D'Albert, and Schnabel gave an epic performance of Brahms's First Piano Concerto, one so powerful that it occupied most of Cardus's review the following day. Among the French novelties were Chabrier's *Marche joyeuse* and D'Indy's *Symphonie montagnarde* played by Cortot, while Harty's partiality for Respighi continued to manifest itself in two of the *Three Botticelli Pictures*. Russia was represented by Stravinsky's *Petrouchka* – Harty was still not ready for *The Rite of Spring* or any later works by that composer – Rachmaninov's *The Bells*, and Prokofiev's *Scythian Suite*, an example of futurist work which Cardus found unpalatable: 'By all means let us have modern music at the Hallé concerts. But let it be good.'[58]

It was, however, in the much greater concentration of modern works that the programme stood out. It was a brave move given the financial austerity of the depression. A flavour of Hungarian contemporary music was heard in Bartók's *Rumanian Folk Dances* and Kodály's *Psalmus hungaricus*. After several cancellations, Vaughan William's *A Pastoral Symphony* finally came to Manchester on 7 November 1929. This was accompanied by Warlock's *A Capriol Suite* in its full orchestral version, recently performed at the Promenade Concerts in London. There was also Holst's *St Paul's Suite*, Walton's *Façade* (conducted by the composer) and Ireland's *Mai-Dun*. Krenek's 'neo-romantic' *Potpourri* was performed for the first time in Manchester on 30 January 1930, 'but he runs a poor second to Constant Lambert', Cardus claimed, 'as an artist in idioms derived from jazz'.[59] What Cardus was referring to, of course, was the first public performance of Lambert's *The Rio Grande* in Manchester on 12 December 1929, conducted by the composer with Harty at the piano. Cardus called it a work of genius and was thrilled by the composer's assimilation and transformation of jazz: 'The work is a complete synthesis of jazz elements; we

---

[57] Letter from Shaw to Elgar, 25 Jan. 1930 (in possession of Simon Walker; henceforth SW).

[58] *MG*, 1 Nov. 1929.

[59] *MG*, 31 Jan. 1930.

have heard them before, rude and vulgar. Mr Lambert has by the alchemy of the imagination turned the clattering metal into something which often has a golden enough ring.'[60] Despite his outspoken antipathies to jazz, Harty had fallen in love with the piece and was duly praised for his control and touch.[61] The following evening, in a concert attended by Princess Mary, it was given its first London performance at Queen's Hall with the same performers (though with an understrength contingent of the Hallé choir) to similarly rapturous acclaim. After a second performance, by popular request, on 10 January 1930 (which entailed the swift and gallant co-operation of the St Michael Singers, trained by Harold Darke),[62] it was recorded the same month by Columbia.

There is no doubt that by the end of 1929 Harty and the Hallé occupied what seemed like an unassailable position in the league of British orchestras. Full of confidence, they decided to inaugurate a series of six concerts at Queen's Hall – three before Christmas and three after – which were advertised as the 'Hamilton Harty Symphony Concerts' during the seasons of 1929–30 and 1930–31 (held on Friday nights to avoid conflict with the regular Thursday fixture in Manchester); the programmes were, in many cases, repeats of those in Manchester. A heightened interest in the more regular presence of the Hallé spawned a new attitude to professionalism among the London orchestras. Those sponsored by Mrs Samuel Courtauld (under Sargent and guest conductors Klemperer and Walter) promised more rehearsal time, and, not to be outdone, the LSO and Royal Philharmonic Society raised their game in a similar manner.

Yet, even with this atmosphere of new-found competition, the winds of change were blowing. For some time critics such as Ernest Newman had been complaining that orchestral-playing in the capital was habitually poor and that a first-rate orchestra was needed. The visits of the Hallé to London in 1928 served to expose rudely to audiences that regular rehearsals under one conductor could produce results, a fact brought home again by the visit of the Berlin Philharmonic under Furtwängler in December of that year. Talk began to circulate that a body such as the BBC might be the ideal organisation to embrace a permanent orchestra. An alliance between the Royal Philharmonic Society and the BBC was suggested by Walford Davies in 1927, while Beecham, notwithstanding his opposition to broadcasting, was himself interested in forming a new orchestra after his experiences in New York, Boston and Philadelphia. Unfortunately, Beecham's negotiations with the BBC eventually foundered, but not after the press had already reported details of possible salaries and the putative name of the orchestra which should have remained private.[63] As the matter became more public, the LSO began to consider safeguarding its own position and decided to issue contracts for seventy-five of its players along with guaranteed recording work with HMV. As Beecham bowed out, a new scheme was hatched by Kenneth

[60] *MG*, 13 Dec. 1929.

[61] *MG*, 13 Dec. 1929; see also Shead, R., *Constant Lambert* (London: Thames Publishing, 1973; rev. edn, 1988), 61.

[62] *MT* 71 (1930), 351.

[63] Michael Kennedy, *Adrian Boult* (London: Macmillan, 1987), 138–9; See also N. Kenyon, *The BBC Symphony Orchestra, 1930–1980* (London: BBC, 1981), 15ff.

Wright, Julian Herbage and Edward Clark for the BBC to employ directly its own players.

At this point, it seems that Harty, who had been observing events from the sidelines, had become concerned about the new orchestra's personnel. For some years he had been extremely supportive of the BBC's aims to bring music to more people, and, according to Baillie, he had been asked at one stage to consider a 'high-powered position' at the Corporation, but was deterred by the bureaucratic responsibilities.[64] The BBC had been a valuable source of income to the Hallé Society and the Northern Wireless Orchestra, which Harty often directed, and a useful source of income to many Hallé players. However, the spectre emerged of how the BBC would fill the ranks of its new orchestra and, more precisely, *whom* it would recruit. In March 1929 a report in the *Manchester Guardian* seemed to calm fears that there would be a mass exodus of Hallé players to London,[65] and Harty felt that the magnetism of the Society (and loyalty to him) would be enough to keep them in Manchester. In a further column he added:

> I am, of course, aware that from time to time players have received lucrative offers from America and elsewhere, but they have refused them consistently, and I do not think that many, if any, of the members of the Hallé Orchestra would think for a moment of forsaking a position of which they are proud in the finest orchestra in England.[66]

But Harty was whistling in the wind, for the financial arrangements and security offered by the new BBC orchestra were too good to turn down. Catterall, his one-time colleague, had been snapped up as leader, as were Alec Whittaker (principal oboe) and Harry Barlow (tuba). Camden was also approached but, after some considerable heart-searching, refused the offer out of loyalty to Harty:

> The Hallé was my spiritual home but I realised that it was Sir Hamilton who made the orchestra what it now was, and I was loath to exchange my happiness in the musical life there for an unknown setting. ... Harty's 13 years with the Hallé was [*sic*], in my opinion (and in the judgment of many of those who also remember), an era there since unmatched.[67]

Camden's choice to stay undoubtedly touched Harty deeply, but he was furious at the way the BBC, in his view, had 'cherry-picked' through the British orchestras without proper consultation.[68] Fortunately these difficulties did not impair his friendship with Boult, with whom Harty always remained on good terms. This is confirmed by a sympathetic letter Harty wrote during a holiday to Cornwall after Boult had undergone an operation:

> I hope that by this you are in comfort again? The first day or two are the worst, I believe, and then one recovers strength quickly and without pain.

[64] Baillie, *Never Sing Louder than Lovely*, 31.
[65] *MG*, 14 Mar. 1929.
[66] *MG*, 14 Mar. 1929.
[67] Camden, *Blow by Blow*, 113.
[68] *MG*, 1 Oct. 1930.

I shall be returning to London on Saturday – and will certainly come to see you when I am allowed by your medical advisers. In the meantime do tell me if I can assist you in any little way as far as your work is concerned.

Any little friendly action I could do for you wd give me pleasure.[69]

At Torquay on 30 August 1930, as retiring president of the IAO, Harty used his speech (which by now had become something of an event) to berate the BBC for its high-handed, autocratic, centralising policy, its 'sincere if misguided idealism', and for entering into direct competition with the musical interests of private orchestras when its proper place was the studio rather than the concert hall. 'It was never meant that the BBC should have the trusteeship of large sums of public money in order to use this money to crush and imperil enterprise', he complained. 'With sublime self-confidence and an almost infantile disregard of the problems and difficulties involved, the BBC has now developed into a huge concert-giving concern. I contend that it has absolutely no right to do so.' Harty went on to criticise the BBC's arrogant and amateurish musical policy, the resentment that grass-roots orchestral players felt towards it, and how the considerable funds at its disposal – reported as being in the region of £100,000 a year – gave it the means to undermine struggling private orchestras. 'If certain players seemed to them to be desirable acquisitions, the fact that they were members of other orchestras were not allowed to stand in the way; make the financial inducements high enough and they were bound to come.' Pulling no punches, Harty referred to those working to create the BBC orchestra as 'the amiable bandits of Savoy Hill', a description unlikely to make him any friends at the Corporation.[70]

The BBC, on its part, was unrepentant and, in response to Harty's assault, reminded those in Manchester and the north generally that the BBC was in negotiation to provide specific sums of money to employ (and therefore support) orchestras such as the Hallé, the Liverpool Philharmonic and Leeds Symphony Orchestra. Cardus also penned a largely unsympathetic column for the *Manchester Guardian* urging the prophets of doom to face the facts of the modern age. Harty himself, during his speech to the Hallé's AGM, warned that the orchestra might easily lose its place as the country's premiere orchestra and become a second-rate band, but his pessimism was not shared widely. However, he rightly argued that the BBC did not provide any form of 'subsidy' to the Hallé in broadcasting its concerts; the Corporation had received good value for money. In the event, the Hallé only lost two players, but the Northern Wireless Orchestra was abolished and replaced with a 'Nonet' of full-time performers (dubbed the BBC Studio Orchestra), a move which provoked the charge that the BBC governors were starving the north to benefit London. It was a matter that ultimately required the Lord Mayor as an intermediary, so fraught had negotiations become.[71] Because of restrictions in their contracts, seven players

[69] Letter from Harty to Boult, Friday [n.d.], *GB-Lbl*, MS 72639 fol. 70.

[70] *MG*, 31 Aug. 1930; see also Kenyon, *The BBC Symphony Orchestra*, 46–7.

[71] *MG*, 1 May 1931. The Mayor's participation was also necessary because Harty was away for some of the time in Ireland.

in the 'Nonet' were unable to perform at certain times with the Hallé outside
Manchester, which ultimately compelled them to resign their positions. In this
way, Clyde Twelvetrees, a longstanding friend and colleague of Harty's, left the
orchestra.[72] It was a bitter pill, and though Harty naturally understood the
reasons (not least the much more substantial financial remuneration offered by
the BBC), he took it extremely personally.

There were other financial problems. Harty demanded a proper individual
broadcasting fee, a condition the BBC refused to consider on the grounds that
they were only in the business of paying fees to societies and organisations.
The Hallé, in order to retain its players, was forced to offer higher fees which
placed greater strain on the orchestra's already limited budget. To address this
problem the Society asked for higher broadcasting fees, but there was deadlock
as the BBC was compelled to make economies of its own.[73] Another of the BBC
projects left the Hallé bemused. Between 26 May and 21 June 1930 a series of
broadcast Promenade Concerts was arranged to be given by Harty and the
Hallé in Manchester, Liverpool and Leeds. 'The central idea', Harty announced
to the press, 'is to make music a friendly thing to the man in the street – or
the man who stands at the back of the hall on Hallé nights – at a price he can
pay for it.'[74] The BBC also voiced its enthusiasm for the project as the 'biggest
attempt at promenade concerts ever made outside London'.[75] The concerts were
well attended and pronounced a major success, yet, at the series's conclusion
the BBC maintained that it had suffered major losses and could not repeat the
experiment. Grommé was puzzled, particularly since Harty had accepted a third
of his normal fee, and contributed sums of money to ensure the success of the
enterprise (as had his friends).[76] Harty's personal generosity to the orchestra
can also be measured by the loss incurred by the Society for the two series of
'Hamilton Harty Symphony Concerts' in London. One suspects that, because the
concerts bore his name, he felt a personal responsibility for the venture. Losses
mounted to more than £3,000, a colossal sum, which Harty bore himself. What
is more, having entertained the orchestra to dinner in Manchester entirely at
his own expense, he did the same in London at the end of both concert series,
taking them to Pagani's – a restaurant much favoured among musicians for its
proximity to Queen's Hall.

The fractious relationship spawned by the controversy of the new BBC
orchestra and the abandonment of the Promenade Concert project in 1930 can,
in many ways, be seen as a significant watershed in Harty's relationship with the
Hallé. He may have been somewhat jaded by controversy, by Cardus's sniping,
and by the constant public gaze of the press. Rees gave a fascinating account of
one unproductive encounter:

[72] This problem was eventually alleviated by the formation of the larger Northern
Studio Orchestra in 1933, and the BBC Northern Orchestra in 1934, both of which
implemented more liberal contracts with the Hallé players.

[73] Rees, *100 Years of the Hallé*, 63–5.

[74] *MG*, 2 Apr. 1930.

[75] *MG*, 16 May 1930.

[76] *MG*, 1 Oct. 1930.

He was a most engaging conversationalist, and I remember a train journey with him and his great friend, J. A. Forsyth, who was then music critic of the London *Star*, when the talk ranged far and wide and one was content, for the most part, happily to listen. As a representative of the Manchester *Daily Dispatch* I had to beard him in the conductor's room at Queen's Hall, to ask his views on a musical matter then agitating some of the newspapers. He greeted me with that disarming smile which orchestras – and audiences – knew so well. I ask my question – and immediately saw that equally familiar glint in his eye. Seated in his chair, he shook his head. I repeated the question in another form. He quietly stood up, came towards me, put his hands on my shoulders, gently turned me around, and equally gently marched me to the door, opened it and deposited me in the corridor with a smiling 'good night'. The 'interview' was the most unproductive of 'copy' I ever had![77]

In March 1930 the house where he lived in Eccles was ransacked and burgled, an experience which must have left him with a sense of violation. It was made worse by the thieves' having made off with an appreciable amount of jewellery, a gold dress-watch, pearl vest buttons and a small jewel box. But what was most upsetting for Harty was the theft of several presentation items from the Hallé and a ring that had belonged to his father. There is no indication that the culprits were brought to justice.[78]

The 1930–31 season, which worked in tandem with the six London 'Hamilton Harty' concerts, continued the spirit of unfamiliar works as well as some significant revivals, the most notable being the *Grand Messe des morts* at an all-Berlioz concert on 13 November 1930. This was repeated at Queen's Hall on 14 November. Harty was particularly keen that this work should receive as much publicity as possible, and urged his agent Ibbs and Tillett to do all they could to raise the profile of this noteworthy concert.[79] 'And so he [Harty] raises once more the great Berlioz question', wrote *The Times*; 'no-one is better qualified to do so than he; the performance he gave was admirable in almost every detail of execution.'[80] Yet, for all the work's drama and effect, it was met with critical scepticism. *The Times* talked of its lack of melodic stamina and rhythmic weakness. Cardus, in the *Manchester Guardian*, disliked Berlioz's instrumentation: 'it is bad art whenever our minds are distracted from a contemplation of the aesthetic ends and instead are directed to a very conscious interest in the technical means.'[81] He attempted to sum up his frustration to the tenor Parry Jones, who sang in the performances:

I am afraid you may have felt a little hurt at some very unjust criticisms of your singing at my Berlioz concert in London, and I want to tell you not to take any

[77] Rees, *100 Years of the Hallé*, 67.

[78] MG, 11 Mar. 1930.

[79] Letter from Harty to Ibbs and Tillett, 8 Nov. 1930, in Christopher Fifield, *Ibbs and Tillett: The Rise and Fall of a Musical Empire* (Aldershot: Ashgate, 2005), 154.

[80] *The Times*, 15 Nov. 1930.

[81] MG, 14 Nov. 1930.

notice of them. For my part I was most pleased and delighted with what you did and was very angry and disgusted at what I read.

It is part of our lives as musicians to have these unjust criticisms sometimes, but I thought you might like to know that as far as Berlioz is concerned (and I trust my own judgment there before anyone's) I thought you sang his music most beautifully, and in just the right spirit. My own personal friends were also of that opinion.[82]

Support came from Sacheverell Sitwell:

This letter is just an entreaty to you to make a gramophone-record of the 'Chasse-royale' pour 'Les Troyens'. It is surely one of the most beautiful and haunting pieces of music in the world. Since having it at your concert I have thought of nothing else. I am sure there are many people like myself, who are not musicians, who find it one of the most inspiring things in the world, and have no opportunity to study it. This would be possible for us if only you would record it, and I really feel it is your duty to do so, however much you may dislike gramophones yourself.

The 'Marche Troyenne' is the most intoxicating piece of militarism. Your performance of it was superb.

Please forgive my writing to you but I enjoyed every minute of the concert and am a fanatical admirer of Berlioz. I have not enjoyed a concert so much for years.[83]

Bernard van Dieren, who had also attended the London concert, acknowledged Harty's courage in the face of a 'hesitant world':

Let me thank you most heartily for the superb performance you gave us of the Messe des Morts yesterday. It requires so much courage to present the work, as talent and power to conduct it. You have shown all these qualities and so overwhelmingly that a rabid Berliozian like myself feels that he may pay the tribute of words of gratitude in the Master's name to you.

I have studied Berlioz's works so devotedly and have so deep a personal affection for his personality and genius that I feel directly indebted to you for all you are doing to bring his work before the public in this country.

Your interpretation of the two songs was perfectly admirable, and I was profoundly moved to see at last a conductor who had grasped every detail of their unostentatious but overtly telling orchestration.

Berlioz may have found champions here before now, but only by performances such as yours may we hope to embrace a hesitant 'world of music' at last.[84]

The greatest honour, however, was a letter from the French Ambassador, Aide Florian:

You have not to thank me, I have to thank you and I am ashamed to have let you write to me before I had written to you. I have to thank you for a delightful evening and to congratulate you upon the wonderful direction you gave to the orchestra and to the excellent choir. Berlioz should have been pleased to attend your concert. But he who was the subject of passionate discussions during his life remains the

---

[82] Letter from Harty to Parry Jones, 26 Nov. 1930, *GB-Lbl*, MS Mus.1117.

[83] Letter from Sacheverell Sitwell to Harty, 18 Nov. 1930, *GB-Belqb*.

[84] Letter from Bernard van Dieren to Harty, [n.d.; 15 Nov.?] 1930, *GB-Belqb*.

object of the same discussions in our time and I suppose always shall remain. Such is the destiny of geniuses. And it requires some courage to present his works to the public which is generally following the line of least resistance and the fashion of the day. Allow me to express my admiration for your courage, skill and my hope for your enduring success.[85]

Sammons played Elgar's Violin Concerto (23 October 1930), Orloff appeared in Prokofiev's Third Piano Concerto (6 November 1930), and Schnabel returned to perform Brahms's Second Piano Concerto (15 January 1931), an event which Hirsch recalled. Schnabel had suffered a lapse of memory in the last movement and inadvertently missed out two bars. Harty immediately noticed this and indicated it to the orchestra. After the concert Schnabel, delighted with the performance, exclaimed:

> 'Do you know … the Hallé Orchestra is almost as good as the Berlin Philharmonic.'
> 'Do you really think so?', replied Harty, 'I think they are even two bars better!'
> Years later, I [Hirsch] asked Schnabel if he remembered the time when he played the Brahms in Manchester, with Sir Hamilton conducting. He replied, 'Shall I ever forget it – and the two bars I owed Sir Hamilton. Never, but never, in my whole life have I ever experienced such a magnificent accompaniment'.[86]

Mahler's *Das Lied von der Erde* was heard for the first time in Manchester on 11 December 1930 with the contralto Olga Haley and the tenor Frank Titterton. The audience was disappointingly small, but the reception for the work, tentatively performed according to Cardus, was enthusiastic. Harty's revelation of Sibelius resumed with the Third Symphony (16 October 1930), a repeat of the Fifth (22 January 1931) and *Night Ride and Dawn* (20 November 1930), though Cardus was unimpressed and felt that the music 'never came up to its promise'.[87] Harty maintained his fascination for twentieth-century Italian music in Respighi's Passacaglia in C minor, Sinigaglia's *Le baruffe chiozzote* and Pizzetti's *Concerto dell'Estate* (23 October 1930), while Ravel's *Bolero* (30 October 1930), new to Manchester, was repeated by popular demand. The most significant British work was Bax's imposing First Symphony (4 December 1930), which Cardus spent much of his time comparing with the more fluent and clearly expressed Third Symphony. However, Delius's *Dance Rhapsody* No. 2 and Bruckner's Fourth Symphony were casualties of the schedule, which was again a source of disappointment to subscribers.

In addition to the normal run of orchestral concerts in places such as Bolton, Burton, Bradford, Liverpool and Nottingham, Harty was also doing more in the south coast festivals which were beginning to evince a high standard of orchestral playing and varied programming. At Brighton in February 1931 he shared the podium with Vaughan Williams, Henry Wood, Lambert and Ronald, and at Hastings later that same month he conducted his own *Comedy Overture* and Elgar's Cello Concerto with Cassadó, then yielded the baton to Julius

[85] Letter from Aide Florian to Harty, 22 Nov. 1930, *GB-Belqb*.
[86] Hirsch, 'Memories of Sir Hamilton', 69.
[87] *MG*, 21 Nov. 1930.

Harrison while he played the solo piano part of *The Rio Grande* (a role which had revitalised his national reputation as a pianist).

While the difficult negotiations with the BBC over the contracts of the 'Nonet' ensemble were still under way, Harty made his first visit as a conductor to the United States. *En route* to California, where he was to fulfil most of his engagements, he stopped off in Boston long enough to conduct a single Sunday concert with the Boston Symphony Orchestra. Harty received an ovation and was brought back to the platform again and again. Such was the applause that critics unanimously declared it unprecedented since the time of Carl Muck.[88] A letter from a Manchester resident to the *Manchester Guardian* relayed the news of Harty's success:

> I have attended a large number of concerts here during the last year, and it was most gratifying to see the music-sated Boston public awakened from its apathy and applauding our own Harty. It must be heartbreaking for the majority of artists to appear in this city, for I have heard such artists as Roland Hayes and Walter Gieseking receive the most perfunctory applause. But tonight the ovation was nothing short of overwhelming, both orchestra and audience standing up and shouting themselves hoarse. The greatest demonstration followed the conductor's own 'With the Wild Geese'.[89]

In California Harty directed a series of three concerts with the San Francisco Symphony Orchestra at the Woodland Theatre under the aegis of the San Mateo Philharmonic Society between 6 and 11 July 1931. These concerts were managed by the Society's director, Leonora Wood Armsby, who, almost single-handedly, had persuaded the middle classes of her community to support an orchestra after the millionaires had withdrawn their financial aid owing to the Great Depression.[90] Harty directed a further eight concerts at the Hollywood Bowl with players who were mainly from the Los Angeles Philharmonic Orchestra. His programmes characteristically reflected his deep-seated affinity for the late Romantic era: the symphonies of Brahms, Dvořák, Schumann and Tchaikovsky, orchestral works of Berlioz and Wagner, Stanford's First *Irish Rhapsody*, Delius's *Brigg Fair* and *A Walk to the Paradise Garden*, his transcriptions of Handel, his arrangement of *The Londonderry Air*, and some of his own original orchestral works.[91] August was, for the most part, a period of vacation during which he was a guest of the San Francisco Bohemian Club along with John McCormack, Charlie Chaplin

---

[88] *San Mateo Times*, 2 July 1931.

[89] Letter from John Lougher to the Editor, *MG*, 2 July 1931.

[90] Leonora Armsby detailed this process of the San Francisco Symphony Orchestra's revival in her book *We Shall Have Music* (San Francisco: Pisani, 1960). Harty, widely quoted in American newspapers, greatly admired this example of American enterprise.

[91] This also involved the revival of two of his oboe pieces, 'Orientale' and 'Á la campagne', which were played by Henri de Busscher, one of the works' first exponents in London before the war. (De Busscher had settled in Los Angeles in 1920 and founded the De Busscher Chamber Music Society). The pieces were subsequently revived by the Hallé during the 1931–2 season with Fred Tilsley.

and Harpo Marx, but he was invited to conduct one further concert for the San Mateo Philharmonic (whose other guest conductors had been Damrosch, Walter and Monteux) before returning to England in September.

There were things Harty obviously liked about America, and in an interview with the *Manchester Guardian* he gave a full account of his impressions. One of the most obvious was America's material resources which enabled its orchestras to achieve a level of technical perfection by dint of additional rehearsal time and the ability to employ players from anywhere in the world. Endowments were generous and the enthusiasm of the supporters infectious. Yet passion and spirit could not be bought, and here the Hallé scored, but Harty felt ashamed that so much was expected from the orchestra when financial support was so meagre. At the beginning of the interview, and at the end, Harty gave more than a brief hint of his frame of mind. He was restive:

> I have received many flattering invitations from America and far-reaching ones, but I have not yet decided what to do. In any case, I am engaged to conduct in various places in America in the spring and summer of next year as a guest conductor. I have an invitation to conduct in Australia and return by California, and to conduct three symphony concerts in Honolulu. I have been invited to conduct in Moscow.[92]

For those who knew him well, Harty also seemed to exude a sense of exasperation and impatience. Writing home from Manchester, Hubert Foss, the musical editor of Oxford University Press, expressed misgivings to his wife about Harty's uneasy demeanour: 'Harty was kind but for some mysterious reason would not stop and chat. Barker … could not imagine why but says he's been quite funny and like this all season. He looks so old now. I feel quite sad about it.'[93]

The Society AGM announced a loss of £310, but favourable proceeds from previous years obviated a call on the guarantors. Income from BBC broadcasts and recordings with Columbia had all helped, but the resignation of seven players for the BBC's 'Nonet' had necessitated the audition and employment of new faces. This had proved a difficult process, especially acquiring a replacement horn.[94] Harty nevertheless reassured the Society in a letter from America that all personnel would be in place by the start of the new season.[95]

Harty's first tour of America seemed to fill him with added zeal to explore new works and, in spite of the Society's loss during the previous season, neither he nor the Hallé were deterred from announcing a similarly ambitious programme for 1931–2. Among the symphonic works – Sibelius's Fifth and Seventh and Bax's Third – was the First Symphony of Dmitri Shostakovich (21 January 1932). Cardus likened its programme to that of 'a very solemn student wrestling with

---

[92] *MG*, 3 Sept. 1931.

[93] Letter from Hubert Foss to Dora Foss, 11 Dec. 1931, in private possession.

[94] As a gesture of support to the Manchester College of Music, Harty endowed a three-year horn scholarship to encourage the development of this branch of orchestral playing.

[95] *MG*, 9 July 1931.

beasts in a composition class in any Leningrad conservatorium',[96] and his invective for Gershwin's *American in Paris*, which Harty greatly admired for its national character and energy, seemed extraordinarily reactionary:

> The new work of the night was not even amusing ... Mr Gershwin, when he wants to make a noise like a taxi-horn (in Paris) is actually witty and imaginative enough to introduce into the orchestra four real taxi-horns. The music is a decided addition to American humour. If the suggestion may be made in these columns, I suggest a 150 per cent tariff against this sort of American dry-goods. Mr Gershwin's symphonic poem (a technical term) contains one fairly good tune, which he ought to save up for his next musical comedy. But 'An American in Paris' is yet another argument against America – which as Oscar Wilde put it, was not discovered but detected.[97]

It was not one of Cardus's most creditable reviews and one feels at times that his purple prose, for all its craft and humour, occasionally hid a certain dilettantism. For all their cleverness, those reviews that ventured too close to the technical exposed an area of his critical capacity that, unlike Langford's perspicacious ear, was far from secure. His diatribe against Gershwin's score also revealed that, in many ways, he harboured prejudices against certain types of music in much the same way as Harty.

Among the new British works were Elgar's recently composed *Nursery Suite* (21 January 1932), Bax's *Overture to a Picaresque Comedy*, which the composer dedicated to Harty (19 November 1931), Lambert's hard-edged *Music for Orchestra*, a fine piece of Neo-classical contrapuntalism (29 October 1931), and Walton's Viola Concerto, played by Lionel Tertis (14 January 1932). Harty had great belief in Walton's music and was hugely impressed by the Concerto and the young English composer's progress. After the performance Harty asked Walton if he would write a new symphony for the orchestra, a commission to which the composer happily acceded. For Walton it was a 'rather portentous undertaking', but, as he wrote to Siegfried Sassoon, 'the Hallé is such a good orchestra & Harty such a magnificent conductor besides being very encouraging, that I may be able to knock Bax of[f] the map!'[98] But what Tertis most fondly remembered, in his Manchester debut, was his performance of Berlioz's *Harold in Italy*. 'Harty's interpretation excelled that of all the conductors I have known', he recounted.[99] 'We feel music in the same way', Harty explained to Tertis;[100] 'I have never forgotten our 'Harold' in Manchester, and the players there often speak of it and of your beautiful playing of the solo.'[101] Harty's admiration for Delius reached a climax in his first performance of *A Mass of Life* (18 February

[96] *MG*, 22 Jan. 1932.

[97] *MG*, 16 Oct. 1931.

[98] Quoted in Stephen Lloyd, *William Walton: Muse of Fire* (Woodbridge: Boydell Press, 2001), 112.

[99] Lionel Tertis, *My Viola and I* (London: Paul Elek, 1974), 70.

[100] Quoted in John White, *Lionel Tertis: The First Great Virtuoso of the Viola* (Woodbridge: Boydell Press, 2006), 122.

[101] Quoted in White, *Lionel Tertis*, 121.

1932) with Roy Henderson in the principal part for baritone. Cardus believed he had heard none better: 'Other performances have had a softer bloom at parts, and a more obviously ravishing texture. But none has gone deeper than last night's.'[102] Delius heard the performance by radio in Grez-sur-Loing and sent a telegram thanking Harty for a 'splendid performance and perfect understanding of work'.[103] Harty also conducted *Life's Dance* on 25 February, which elicited a second letter from Delius:

> Your kind and sympathetic letter gave me the greatest pleasure. Only one who felt and understood my music entirely could have given such a performance as you did.
>
> And last night, I listened in again to Northern Regional, and you gave again the best performance of 'Life's Dance' that I have yet heard. (And I have heard it often in Germany.) …
>
> I like Constant Lambert's 'Rio Grande'. I think he is the most gifted of the young lot. He has got something to say.[104]

As Delius's letter indicated, Harty also gave a further performance of *The Rio Grande* as pianist with Barker as conductor, though this work and Delius's symphonic poem were substitutes for *The Rite of Spring* which was cancelled. Jelka Delius, utterly devoted to the promotion of her husband's music, also wrote to thank Harty:

> To-day I am sending you a dictated letter from my husband and a photograph, taken just before his birthday, and which, I hope, you will receive safely.
>
> Delius looked just like that so rapt and happy during the memorable performance of the Mass of Life, from time to time remarking on some special beauty of the rendering. We both enjoyed it immensely, as well as the beautiful performance of 'Life's Dance' last night. Those are the glorious moments that lift us over many rather drab times.
>
> I am so glad that the Northern Regional comes through to us so well. Yesterday there was no fading and your Violin Concerto sounded splendid.
>
> It is my lot to manage the wireless set and I am always terribly anxious that any catastrophe might happen; as Delius is *so* keen to listen and enjoy it more than anything else when he can listen to such exquisite performances.[105]

This contact with Delius touched Harty deeply and he wrote again to Grez-sur-Loing asking about the availability of other works. He was also considering a concert performance of Delius's fourth opera, *A Village Romeo and Juliet*. Jelka replied:

> We were very glad to hear that you liked the photograph. When your letter came, I had already written to Roy Henderson. We were, of course, delighted with his

---

[102] *MG*, 19 Feb 1932.

[103] Telegram from Delius to Harty, 19 Feb. 1932, *GB-Belqb*. It is said that Delius considered Harty's reading of *The Mass of Life* superior to Beecham's, but never dared say so for fear of offending his greatest champion.

[104] Letter from Delius to Harty, 26 Feb. 1932, *GB-Belqb*.

[105] Letter from Jelka Delius to Harty, 26 Feb. 1932, *GB-Belqb*.

singing and on the telegrams to you he had put to thank the soli, chorus and orchestra, but I fear the post-lady here left out the soli.

The question of a uniform edition of my husband's works is a very difficult one and I hardly see how it can be done. So far, it has not even been possible to get the publishers to join hands in making a general catalogue of his works.

I enclose you today a list which we have made. The orchestral suite of 'Hassan' which is mentioned in Universal Edition, is not quite ready yet. It is the last thing my husband did with Fenby. I also mention the Negro Opera 'Koanga' which is not published.

I think it is a very good idea to give 'A Village Romeo and Juliet' as a concert performance, and my husband is very glad you intend doing it.

You have heard, of course, that Beecham is to conduct a Studio performance at the B.B.C. in May.

Delius is delighted that you are taking the 'Walk to the Paradise Garden' to Madrid.

The 'Songs of Farewell' are to be given on March 21st and 22nd at the Cortauld Concert. I wish you could hear it. It is by far the most important of the latest works, and Delius would like you very much to do it at the Hallé Concerts next season.

Eric Fenby has been very ill and is luckily better now.[106]

In addition to the works by Delius, Hindemith (who had premiered Walton's Concerto in London in 1929) was represented by his overture *News of the Day* in a programme which also included another American novelty – Charles Griffes's impressionistic *The Pleasure Dome of Kubla-Khan* – a work which complemented two other new French items, Debussy's Rhapsody for Alto Saxophone and Pierné's *Impression of a Music-Hall*.

In October 1931 Harty began his series of James W. Alsop Lectures at Liverpool University, a series which boasted a number of illustrious predecessors including Gustav Holst and W. G. Whittaker. Harty's choice, perhaps typically, was a subject he knew best by experience, 'The Modern Orchestra'. There were five lectures in all, on the evolution of the orchestra, the technical capacity of the woodwind and horns, the strings, brass, and, finally, a most interesting area where Harty talked publically for the first time about 'Conductors and Conducting'. In this he gave some clues as to his own approach, in particular the essence of a successful conductor:

When it comes to the poetical value of his readings, however ... he must depend for this upon things which are intrinsically musical and quite personal. If his *musical* imagining is of high enough quality and if he possesses as well those purely human sympathies which impress and influence all bodies of men under the control of a leader, then he will be a successful Conductor and his interpretations will possess a definite musical value.

The reason that there are so few great Conductors is that the several qualities required, some of them rather contradictory, do not often exist together in the same person. It is said that to be a great Conductor requires something of the Philosopher, something of the actor, of the Jesuit, of the politician, and a great

---

[106] Letter from Jelka Delius to Harty, 7 Mar. 1932, *GB-Belqb*.

deal of the artist to balance the mixture. The combination is rare, and so are really great Conductors. I have met with very few in my life.[107]

He fairly summarised the difficulties of a conductor when 'his own artistic conventions and ideals must go to the wall if he is to appreciate and to give first-class performances of works which outrage his artistic conscience.' How true this must have been of recent concerts with the Hallé. Harty quickly covered the question of 'stick technique' in order to move on to the more complex issues of analysis and interpretation. 'Sometimes he [the conductor] makes little pencil notes on the pages of the score to remind him of his intentions regarding these points' – a technique clearly visible in Harty's own scores.[108] He also held that modern conductors were divided into two categories:

> There are those whose only aim is to follow out what they conceive to be the composer's meaning by the most faithful attention to every detail, and who try to keep from any display of their own emotional reactions to the music, and those others whose interpretations are a true reflection of the personal impressions they receive. Each school has its own followers. Personally, I lean rather towards the latter class, for the reason that I prefer something that is living even if it may sometimes be wrong, to something that is perfectly correct and lifeless.[109]

It was for this reason that Harty so admired Nikisch. As for conducting in England, Harty credited Hallé and Manns for their encouragement of English composers and English orchestral playing, but for the art of conducting Harty paid tribute to Henry Wood as the guiding light. At this concluding point of his lectures the tone changed markedly as he both rejoiced at the list of outstanding native conductors (Beecham, Goossens, Coates, Ronald, Sargent, Harrison and Cameron) and lamented that they were given little reciprocal Continental recognition. Opportunities were also restricted by the present state of the few professional orchestras Britain possessed, the lack of funds and rehearsal time, and a distorted passion for foreign conductors. Added to Harty's gloomy equation were the lack of wealthy benefactors and, making clear reference to his war with the BBC, 'the semi-state interference in musical affairs' which was likely to do more harm than good by a 'disastrous lack of knowledge on the part of those charged with its administration.'

In the early part of 1932 Harty made appearances in Liverpool, Brighton and Hastings and, after an absence of many years, he was re-engaged by the LSO. Owing to the debacle with the BBC and its perceived monopoly, Harty was seen by the LSO as something of an ally in its own anxious dealings with the Corporation. Meetings with the BBC, presided over by Harty, took place on 9 November 1931 and 3 January 1932, resulting in a deputation to meet the Corporation's governors. Despite demands to confine the new BBC orchestra to the studio and to give broadcasts to existing orchestras, the meeting was

---

[107] H. Hamilton Harty, 'Conductors and Conducting' (typescript), *GB-Belqb*.

[108] Many of Harty's own printed scores have survived in the archive at *GB-Belqb*.

[109] H. Hamilton Harty, 'Conductors and Conducting'.

inconclusive.[110] More pressing, however, for the LSO, was its own survival after the death of its concert agent, Lionel Powell. Among those who came to the aid of the orchestra was Harty, who waived his fee for his appearance on 19 February 1932 at Queen's Hall and was willing to do so for a second concert on 20 March.[111]

After recording Elgar's *Enigma Variations* and *Dream Children* with Columbia in March 1932 (the last recordings he would in fact make with the Hallé), Harty travelled to Spain in April where he conducted the Madrid Philharmonic Orchestra in a concert of Beethoven, Delius, *With the Wild Geese* and his orchestration of Handel's *Polonaise, Arietta and Passacaglia*; Cassadó appeared as soloist in Elgar's Cello Concerto. He was widely complimented by the Spanish press, not least by Turina in *El Debate*.[112] On returning to England Harty entered into correspondence with the LSO, expressing a willingness to 'co-operate with the orchestra for next season's concerts'.[113]

Harty's interest in the affairs of the LSO was undoubtedly motivated by the more volatile situation in Manchester. 'The society's dignity is outraged when an important work like Stravinsky's "Rite of Spring" has to be withdrawn from a programme – because of considerations which have nothing to do with music', Cardus had complained, pleading for a greater democratisation of the Society as well as a larger number of guarantors.[114] The reason put forward was lack of funds for rehearsal, and it was true that the Society's finances had returned to a precarious state. A deficit of £1,583, diminishing reserves, and dwindling guarantors understandably posed a major artistic challenge to the committee and its conductor, but the decision was to carry on in the hope that, even in straitened times, things would improve. One initiative was the formation of a Light Orchestra to provide Promenade Concerts, which was to be directed by Barker. Another scheme, suggested by Harty, was to reduce the number of concerts per season to fifteen, and to combine with the Scottish Orchestra for a limited season to open the way to a larger number of concert engagements. This, he also argued, might increase the Hallé's leverage with the BBC. The committee, however, had no truck with this idea and wished to remain aloof from Harty's private war with the Corporation.[115]

To alleviate the financial pressure, Harty and the players agreed to accept a ten percent reduction in their fees. Harty's agreement, he told Grommé in a letter from Ireland in April, was also to be understood as an indication of his commitment to the orchestra. However, by this time, he was also asking the committee for greater flexibility:

---

[110] Foss and Goodwin, *London Symphony*, 129.

[111] LSO Minutes, 28 Mar. 1932, 109.

[112] Harty's ambassadorial role for British music in Madrid was repeated in November 1932, when he accepted an invitation from the National Institute of Radio Diffusion in Belgium to take part in a series of concerts directed by international conductors. This included Weingartner, Arbós and Monteux: see *MG*, 1 Nov. 1932.

[113] *MG*, 11 Apr. 1932, 167; see also Foss and Goodwin, *London Symphony*, 135.

[114] *MG*, 11 Mar. 1932.

[115] Kennedy, *The Hallé Tradition*, 239.

There are certain considerations which I should like to be understood. In the first place I should like to be assured of a certain amount of freedom in case of important engagements abroad. It is not a financial question but a question of my personal musical career and considering that anything that increases the musical prestige of your conductor reacts favourably on the Society, I do not anticipate that your Committee will offer any objection. I need not say that I would not think of abusing this liberty in any way and in case I wanted leave of absence from any concert would give the Committee as long notice as possible, and also assist them in every way to secure an attractive substitute. I have no immediate reason to suppose that I should have to exercise this freedom very often, if at all, but the possibility would be there and naturally it would be necessary that the principle should be admitted.[116]

Harty did his best to keep his powder dry, though he was, nevertheless, fully aware that the LSO was in a serious state of flux. Beecham, having foundered in his own negotiations with the BBC, was looking to form his own orchestra and there was a possibility that the LSO might be subsumed into this new organisation along with the New Symphony Orchestra and the Royal Philharmonic Society.[117] Sargent was also involved, but after what was considered a substantial breach of faith, where the allegation was made that the LSO had lost the confidence of the public and might soon cease to exist, the members of the democratic organisation rediscovered their courage to continue the orchestra's independent existence.[118] Beecham, meanwhile, went on to form the London Philharmonic Orchestra (LPO).

While all this manœuvring was going on, Harty made his second visit to America. After arriving in New York on 17 June 1932 he travelled across the country to California where, as a guest of the concert master Michel Piastro, he was due to conduct the San Francisco Symphony Orchestra in their seventh season of open-air concerts at the Woodland Theatre. In the audience were Harold Bauer, the well-known patron Mrs Sprague Coolidge, the composer Roy Harris, and Mischa Elman. Harty then moved on to conduct at the Hollywood Bowl, where he undertook a series of nine concerts. On 7 July excerpts from the first two movements of Mozart's Symphony No. 40 were recorded during a live broadcast which was part of a larger programme of leisure and cultural events devised to be available to holiday-makers and tourists who had come to attend the 1932 Summer Olympic Games in Los Angeles. The following day Harty directed a notable performance of *Hiawatha's Weddings Feast* with Mario Chamlee (the celebrated tenor of the Metropolitan Opera), and on 12 July the concert included the extraordinary fourteen-year-old violin prodigy Ruggiero Ricci (named that year as 'one of the world's most famous children') in Vieuxtemps's Fifth Violin Concerto in A minor.[119] Other concerts included his

[116] Letter from Harty to Grommé, 28 Apr. 1932, Hallé Society Minute Books.

[117] Foss and Goodwin, *London Symphony*, 136.

[118] Foss and Goodwin, *London Symphony*, 136–7.

[119] Harty also accompanied Ricci on the piano in Sarasate's *Zapateado*. During rehearsals the violinist Phillip Kaghan made some silent 'home movies' of Harty conducting the Hollywood Bowl Symphony Orchestra. These films are now in

arrangement of *The Londonderry Air*, Handel's *Water Music*, the Scherzo from his 'Irish' Symphony, *With the Wild Geese* and *The Mystic Trumpeter* (with the American operatic baritone Richard Bonelli).

While Harty was in America the atmosphere at the Hallé was beginning to turn sour. Grommé and the committee had agreed to reform themselves by taking on extra members to enhance the democratic will of the Society. At the AGM on 6 July 1932 dissent was also voiced about the Hallé's programming, and the committee was criticised for what was perceived as an over-deferential attitude towards its conductor:

> We want to put some salt in your tea. ... You put too much sugar in it and you give us the stuff you want whether we like it or not. If you don't give us someone to represent us we shall never get our views represented.
>
> We don't want your American jazz. We want someone on the committee who is not afraid of Sir Hamilton Harty and who will tell him what we think. You bow down to this gentleman too much. A lot of the stuff he puts on is rot. We want a man on the committee who will tell him so, even at the chance of displeasing him.[120]

But, in the light of Harty's previous letter, and the need to have some greater flexibility, Grommé and the committee were undoubtedly unsettled about Harty's commitment to the orchestra and quite evidently wanted to make new arrangements. On his return from America, Harty, who must have been aware of the Hallé's anxiety and resolve, contacted the LSO to '[express] his willingness to become conductor-in-chief of the [LSO] Symphony Concerts should the suggestion meet with the approval of the Board'.[121] The offer was made, Harty accepted, and without informing the Hallé – a somewhat discourteous gesture – it was announced to the press at the beginning of September. Although Harty had given assurances that this new appointment would not affect his work for the Hallé, it was bound to unnerve Grommé and the committee, who held that the permanent contract in Manchester was full-time (even if such flexibility had, in the past, been extended to Richter). In consequence they resolved not to renew Harty's contract at the end of the 1932–3 season. At Christmas Harty made it clear to the chairman of the Society that his agreement with them was effective until the end of the 1932–3 season and that he had no intention of making any plans until then.[122] Harty did not endear himself to the committee by announcing that he would also be absent from Manchester in January and February of 1933 for further engagements in America. This provoked Grommé to inform him, while there, that the committee was seeking to find a replacement; hence, when Harty returned to England in February, he immediately announced his resignation, an act he resented because he believed there was still room for renegotiation of his

archives at the University of California, Los Angeles (UCLA): see C. Niss, 'Sir Hamilton Harty at the Hollywood Bowl', *Le Grand Baton* 23(2), issue no. 61 (1990), 10.

[120] *MG*, 7 July 1932.

[121] LSO Minutes, 21 August 1932.

[122] Kennedy, *The Hallé Tradition*, 240.

contract. At one stage he threatened to make all correspondence available to the press, but, wisely, he thought better of this and steered clear of any unseemly wrangles or reproaches.

Harty's last season with the Hallé perhaps lacked the verve and colourful imagination of the previous two, but the audiences were reassuringly buoyant and, with a more healthy relationship with the BBC, many of the concerts were broadcast to the nation. There were some interesting new works: Pick-Mangiagalli's *Sortilegi* (2 December 1932); Sibelius's First Symphony (3 November 1932) and *Tapiola* (24 November 1932), which shared the same programme as Reznicek's *Donna Diana*; Walton's *Belshazzar's Feast* (17 November 1932); Respighi's transcription of Bach's Passacaglia and Fugue in C minor (10 November 1932); the Serenade for Violin and Small Orchestra (9 March 1933) by Frederick Kelly, the gifted Australian who had been killed during the war; Mosolov's *Music of Machines* (24 February 1933); and Strauss's *Schlagobers* (16 December 1932), which provoked Cardus to denigrate the composer's creative invention (somewhat prematurely in light of Strauss's 'Indian summer' of the 1940s). There was also an all-Brahms programme to mark the centenary of Brahms's birth (16 March 1933), a fine performance of *Messiah* (the 'most sensitive for years', Cardus proposed);[123] a second performance of *A Mass of Life* (2 March 1933); Ravel's *Tombeau de Couperin* (24 February 1933); and Saint-Saëns's Third Symphony (17 November 1932), which Harty had rarely directed. As for the promised symphony by Walton, it was not finished. The work was put down for the concert on 9 March 1933,[124] but Walton, knowing well that he was far behind with its completion, wrote to Harty to cancel it.[125]

The standard of soloists remained high. Hess gave Brahms's First Piano Concerto, Schnabel surprised the audience in his nimble performance of Weber's *Konzertstück* which acted as a foil to the profundity of Beethoven's Fourth Concerto, Solomon appeared in Tchaikovsky's First Concerto, Cassadó in Elgar's Cello Concerto, and Elman in Tchaikovsky's Violin Concerto. During Harty's absence in America Barbirolli, Monteux, Beecham and Elgar appeared as guest conductors (the last already a sick man, who conducted *The Dream of Gerontius* from a chair). Beecham, never one to miss the opportunity for a wry comment, hinted that it would not be long before he would conduct the orchestra again.[126]

Within a few weeks of the announcement that he was to become Conductor-in-Chief of the LSO, Harty began to spend more time in London with the orchestra's directors. The gaps left by those who had left the LSO for Beecham's new LPO made it necessary to recruit new players and, from Harty's point of view, it was imperative that the orchestra should retain and better its position in London. He also suggested that, if positions in the orchestra could not be filled

[123] *MG*, 23 Dec. 1932.

[124] *MG*, 10 Mar. 1933.

[125] Lloyd, *William Walton*, 113.

[126] *MG*, 3 Feb. 1933.

adequately by London players, members of the Hallé should be employed.[127] This proposal brought several of his old friends, including Alfred Barker, to fill the orchestra's vacant ranks temporarily. In terms of programming Harty evidently wished to exert as much of his own influence as possible, though the LSO's particularly democratic manner of operating meant that he could not easily impose his will. In the months before Christmas he conducted four concerts at Queen's Hall. The second, on 7 November 1932, included Ruggiero Ricci's London debut in Mendelssohn's Violin Concerto as well as in pieces by Ries, Bach, and Sarasate which Harty accompanied at the piano. The third concert, on 28 November, featured D'Arányi and Beatrice Harrison in Brahms's Double Concerto, as well as Harty's first performance of Prokofiev's 'Classical' Symphony. The remaining two concerts in March and April of 1933 were also worthy of note. In continuing his fascination with Gershwin's music, he conducted the American's Second Rhapsody for Piano and Orchestra with Solomon (20 March 1933), a performance which thrilled the soldier and author A. Corbett-Smith:

> Your 'Symphonie' last night was superb. For the first time in I don't know how many years I applauded with the greatest enthusiasm. I have been at the game too long to be easily moved. But from the opening half dozen bars I sensed that you were going to give us something really big. And you did! How the devil you maintain your energy through over two hours I cannot imagine. You must keep 'in the pink' of training. As always, too, your accompanying (e.g. in the Concerto) was exquisite. I vividly recall your old days 'at the Pianoforte'. And your playing and control of the 'Gershwin' was a magnificent piece of craftsmanship. Speaking to Norman Allin afterwards I remarked upon the stroke of genius evinced by the L.S.O. in securing you. And you have certainly put the fear of God into the orchestra. The whole performance was thrilling in the extreme.[128]

At this point Harty bade farewell to Manchester in the Hallé Pension Concert on 23 March 1933 with the music of Brahms, Wagner and his own 'Irish' Symphony. It was an emotional severance and an opportunity to reflect on thirteen years of music-making. Not for the first time did Harty get his facts wrong. On arrival in Manchester he believed that the orchestra consisted of only forty-five players; there were in fact seventy-two. But Harty's main point was that, because of the disruption of war and a procession of guest conductors, the Hallé had been left in a listless and enervated state. 'You honoured me greatly by handing over your orchestra to me', he declared, 'and as I hand it back to you I think I am not being immodest when I say I hand it back to you perhaps better than it was when I took it over.' After long and tumultuous applause for the 'Irish' Symphony, and a standing ovation, his final gesture to the audience before leaving the platform was to acknowledge his colleagues: 'Do something that will please me enormously. Applaud the orchestra for once.'[129] This was not in fact Harty's final appearance with the orchestra; that was reserved for

---

[127] LSO Minutes, 27 Sept. 1932; see also Foss and Goodwin, *London Symphony*, 138.

[128] Letter from A. Corbett-Smith to Harty, 21 Mar. 1933, *GB-Belqb*.

[129] *MG*, 24 Mar. 1933.

a concert in the Memorial Hall at Stratford-upon-Avon on 23 April. After that an uneasiness existed. The committee were unwilling to engage him and Harty, somewhat embittered by his last experiences, would not come. Some still hoped that reconciliation might be possible, among them Alfred Lomas – a Manchester businessman who had founded the Beecham Operatic Chorus and organised Rochdale Chamber Concerts, and who greatly lamented Harty's resignation. He wrote, in a private capacity, to Harty in 1936:

> The other day I had a talk with Neville Cardus, who asked me why the Hallé Society did not invite you to be a guest conductor.
>
> I told him that, personally, nothing would please me better, but the Committee understood that you would under no circumstances come to Manchester again.
>
> As N. C. doubted the truth of this, I decided I would write to find out, if you cared to tell me, whether the statement was true: or if it was true at one time, whether you had altered your opinion since. I have always felt you would like to conduct your old orchestra again, and I am sure they would like it. Also as a man of peace I don't like old disagreements and quarrels perpetuated. I am speaking merely for myself and in a private capacity and with no authority whatever from the Hallé Committee so there is no obligation even to reply, unless you care to do so. Tho' I hoped that you had not altogether forgotten the old days of the Hallé and the delightful chamber music that I was able to arrange with your help in Rochdale.[130]

Harty's reply was courteous but curt:

> I remember your Chamber Music Concerts at Rochdale and your kind hospitality in connection with them, for which I thank you again. You write to me courteously and I wish to reply to you in the same spirit.
>
> As you do not represent your committee in the enquiry you make, I cannot give you any definite indication of my probable attitude towards any official approach that might be made to me in connection with the Hallé concerts. I have not considered the question. Should contingency arise that would make it necessary I will do so.[131]

But it is evident from a letter to his old friend Hirsch, who was toying with the idea of leaving the Hallé in 1934, that his attitude to music in Manchester had been soured:

> It is not that I have a personal dislike to Manchester, but the fact that there is really no future for you or your boys there that makes me feel you would be much happier in London. You will know when it will be possible for you to make the change, and I wish I could help you more than I can at present. Certainly, when I get back I will do anything I possibly can and I hope you will never hesitate to call on me when I might be useful to you.[132]

It was an unfortunate and regrettable end to a highly productive and largely positive period of the Hallé's history at a time when the economic climate had

[130] Letter from Lomas to Harty, 6 Mar. 1936, *GB-Belqb*.

[131] Letter from Harty to Lomas, [n.d.], *GB-Belqb*.

[132] Letter from Harty to Hirsch, 30 Mar. 1934, *GB-Belqb*.

militated against any possible form of artistic prosperity. Yet Harty had achieved this with his inimitable energy and verve. Many lamented his resignation and departure, among them Camden who, in mentioning the clashes with members of the Hallé committee, pointed the finger at R. J. Forbes (the Principal of the RMCM): 'He had never liked him and took exception to Harty's part-time link with the LSO.'[133] With Harty gone, Camden immediately left for the BBC Symphony Orchestra and Hirsch moved to London in 1936. For these men, and for many in the orchestra, chorus and audience, Harty's departure marked the passing of a golden era.

[133] Camden, *Blow by Blow*, 124–5.

America and Australia:
An Unforeseen Romance

IN January and February of 1933 Harty fulfilled engagements as guest conductor of the Rochester Philharmonic Orchestra and the Cleveland Orchestra. Travelling over on the *Mauretania* he had to hurry to be with the Cleveland Orchestra for their first pair of symphony concerts on 5 and 7 January in Severance Hall.[1] In the Cleveland press, Adelle Prentiss Hughes, the manager of the orchestra, was heard to comment: '"You were fortunate to arrive as early as you did. … Fortune must have been with you and the ship." "I'll say fortune was with them," he [Harty] laughed. "The Mauretania brought over one of the big payments on the war debt from Great Britain to the United States".'[2] After the first concert the press took most interest in Harty's arrangement of Handel's *Polonaise, Arietta and Passacaglia* and Delius's *A Walk to the Paradise Garden*, both of which were new to the Cleveland concerts; at his second pair of concerts, on 12 and 14 January, most attention was devoted to Berlioz's 'Royal Hunt and Storm' (from *Les Troyens*) and Harty's own *With the Wild Geese*. After two pleasant weeks in Ohio, where he was constantly entertained to dinner by the orchestra's patrons and management, he went on to New York where he also conducted. There, on 18 January, the press was intrigued to cover the meeting of four great Irishmen – Harty, Oliver St John Gogarty the Free State Senator, John McCormack and W. B. Yeats – who were guests at a banquet thrown at the Waldorf Hotel by wealthy Irish-Americans. Harty also enjoyed the opportunity of hearing the sixteen-year-old Yehudi Menuhin at the Carnegie Hall in the company of Elman and McCormack.

With the season over in England, Harty moved back to London and bought a house at 1 Norfolk Street, in St John's Wood. Olive Baguley, who had worked closely with him at the Hallé, resigned her position at the Hallé, became his private secretary and moved to London to assist his new existence as a freelance professional conductor.[3] Her role was put in to effect early on for, in dealing with

---

[1] On 6 January 1933 the *New York Union-Star* reported that Harty was one of a series of 'try-outs' to replace the Cleveland Orchestra's regular conductor Nikolai Sokoloff, who was in his last season with the orchestra. Indeed, many thought that he would be Sokoloff's successor (see *Cleveland News*, 4 Jan. 1933). However, the announcement that he had been contracted by the LSO seemed to put him out of the running.

[2] *Cleveland News*, 5 Jan. 1933.

[3] In *The Hallé Tradition*, Kennedy referred to Baguley as Harty's 'intimate friend' and made the allegation that, 'in close concert' with Baguley, Harty 'more and more [took] affairs into his own hands' (p. 230). This caused an outrage with Baguley and other former friends of Harty, Camden and Maurice Johnstone (see letters in *GB-Belqb*). Later, in *The Hallé, 1858–1983*, Kennedy more bluntly claimed

the Directors of the LSO, there were difficulties over Harty's fees. The Directors understood that Harty had originally waived his fee in order to establish himself with the orchestra, yet there was now a demand for £250. The matter was deferred until the end of the season, when it was agreed that he should accept 25 guineas for each concert, though on the grounds that next season would see an increase. This clearly irritated the LSO Directors who felt that his 'great desire to be of the utmost help to the orchestra was rather contradicted by his evident desire to obtain a higher fee for his services.'[4] For the following season Harty received 50 guineas for each concert and an additional 20 guineas for each concert broadcast. Driving this hard bargain was not only symptomatic of his freelance status but also of Harty's desire to be free to accept engagements as he saw fit. For the LSO this was already a source of some friction, for in April 1933 Harty recorded Sammons and Tertis with the LPO in Mozart's Sinfonia Concertante (for Columbia), and this was seen as damaging to the LSO's own chances of securing recordings with the same company.[5] But Harty demanded his right to independence and the LSO were forced to accede, not least because Harty had further contracts that year to conduct the LPO in works by Balakirev, Berlioz, Smetana and Sibelius.

In July and August 1933 Harty was again in America to do six concerts 'under the stars' at the Hollywood Bowl. The Russian conductor Nicholas Slonimsky opened his concert on 15 July with a fanfare which Harty specially donated to the orchestra.[6] His own series of concerts began during the third week of festivities at which, on 27 July, Isobel Baillie made her American debut. Harty had worked a lot with Baillie in Manchester; indeed, there was a not a season in Manchester when she did not appear in a concert. Moreover, her place in the annual *Messiah* at Christmas was a fixture. However, this appearance in the Hollywood Bowl was the first time any British singer had been heard there: 'It was a magnificent setting,' she recalled; 'an absolutely natural amphitheatre with a seating capacity of twenty-five thousand – if there were some empty seats that night it was still the largest 'live' audience I ever faced in my entire career.'[7] Harty, too, was a brilliant success, and it was around this time that he earned the soubriquet the

---

that Baguley was Harty's 'mistress' (p. 17), an accusation based on assumption rather than hard evidence.

[4] LSO Minutes, 20 Apr. 1933, 246.

[5] LSO Minutes, 11 May 1933, 248.

[6] *San Mateo Times*, 15 July 1933. Harty presented his fanfare to the orchestra and it was used for several years afterwards as an indication to the Bowl audiences that the intermission was about to end: Niss, 'Sir Hamilton Harty at the Hollywood Bowl', 10. Harty also composed a fanfare for four trumpets and side drum for *Fanfare* – a short-lived periodical edited by Henry Leigh between October 1921 and January 1922. Besides articles by Poulenc, Wellesz and Cocteau, each issue contained a fanfare by a contemporary composer (such as Vaughan Williams, Bliss, Roussel, Poulenc, Holbrooke, Satie, Prokofiev, Bax, Auric, Milhaud, Wellesz, Malipiero and Havergal Brian). Harty's appeared in *Fanfare* 3 (1921), 51.

[7] Baillie, *Never Sing Louder than Lovely*, 47.

'Irish Toscanini', a flattering comparison with the venerated conductor of the New York Philharmonic Orchestra.

Before travelling to America Harty was delighted to receive a letter from Lord Londonderry, Chancellor of Queen's University, Belfast:

> As Chancellor of Queen's University of Belfast I am writing to inform you that the University desires to have the pleasure of conferring on you the Honorary degree of Doctor of Laws.
>
>   I shall be glad if you will be so good as to let me know at your early convenience whether you wish to accept the degree and whether you can attend in Belfast on Friday morning, 7th July, when the degrees will be conferred at the Graduation Ceremony.[8]

Of all the honours he had received, this degree, from his home town, was perhaps the sweetest. Even more significantly, the conferring of this doctorate cemented an important relationship between him and Queen's University, one that would be of great benefit to the institution in the future.

At the end of September 1933 Harty appeared as guest conductor at the Folkestone Festival (now in its fourth year) in a programme which included his 'Irish' Symphony and Lambert's *Rio Grande*, in which he habitually featured as the solo pianist. Soon after, the new season with the LSO began in which he was contracted to conduct eight of the concerts. Relations with the LSO Directors showed no signs of improvement. Harty wanted full control over his choice of programmes; the LSO, accustomed to retaining its own right to choose, resisted. Harty wanted to include *A Mass of Life* but the Directors considered this too expensive and opted for Verdi's *Requiem*. This disagreement raged throughout June and July but in the end the Verdi was selected. A further difficulty presented itself in finding a way to ask W. H. Reed, the LSO's longstanding leader, to relinquish his position (on the grounds that the orchestra needed younger blood to give it a more competitive edge). The decision came as shock to Reed, but he nevertheless agreed to stand down for the symphony concerts.[9] Reed subsequently became chairman of the orchestra, and, as a tribute to him, his Suite for Strings was performed at Queen's Hall on 6 November 1933.

For the concerts before Christmas Harty essentially conducted a repertoire of works with which he was entirely familiar: Delius's *A Walk to the Paradise Garden*, Kodály's *Hary Janos*, Mozart's Divertimento No. 17, Schubert's Ninth Symphony, Tchaikovsky's Sixth and Sibelius's Seventh, as well as *With the Wild Geese* and the Handel Concerto for Orchestra with Organ. Hess played Brahms's Second Piano Concerto, and Sammons Mozart's Violin Concerto, K216. At the conclusion of the mainly Berlioz programme on 4 December 1933 Harty conducted Elgar's First Symphony. Harty had always been on friendly terms with Elgar and had even expressed a great interest in the news that Elgar was planning a new symphony:

[8] Letter from Lord Londonderry to Harty, 24 Apr. 1933, *GB-Belqb*.

[9] LSO Minutes, 15 Sept. 1933, 12.

I have seen in some paper that you have a new symphony ready – or almost ready to produce. I hope there is some truth in this report. If so, how pleased and gratified I should feel if you would allow me to be responsible for the first performances in Manchester and London! We should take the utmost care in its preparation and it would be so interesting to do after many years what Richter did with the First Symphony.[10]

As is well known, Elgar never finished the work. This must have been a great disappointment to Harty, who by now had become one of the composer's most eminent interpreters. After the First Symphony had received an enthusiastic response from the press, Harty wrote a sympathetic letter to Elgar, who was by now in a Worcester nursing home:

I meant to write to you before this to tell you what a great pleasure it was to prepare and perform your A flat symphony at a recent LSO concert. The orchestra played the work with the greatest love and care, and the audience was, I know, deeply touched by the beauty and power of the music – as I was myself. I think, for a time, that I used to consider the 2nd Symphony much finer, but I am wavering in that opinion and don't really know which I like better, or if I have any choice. But do let me tell you of the deep admiration and love I have for your music and that I always feel it a great responsibility and privilege to conduct it.[11]

Elgar's reply expressed warm gratitude; it was his last letter to Harty:

Your very welcome letter reached me still in the nursing home. It is very cheering to receive such a warm tribute from so great a man as yourself. Nothing could give me greater pleasure than to hear that you take such a real interest in my music.

I heard that your performance of the A flat Symphony was fine and I am very grateful to you for all your kind care of it.[12]

In January and the first half of February 1934 Harty made his fourth visit to the America, where he made a return visit to the Rochester Philharmonic Orchestra and was guest conductor to the Chicago Symphony Orchestra. On his return he directed four concerts with the LSO. The first, on 19 February, featured Artur Rubinstein in Rachmaninov's Second Piano Concerto and a rare performance of Josef Holbrooke's symphonic poem *The Raven*. *The Times* gave it a lukewarm reception even though it was well received by the audience.[13] On 3 March Cassadó appeared in the world premiere of Bax's Cello Concerto, which the composer had specially written for him though the work was later championed by Beatrice Harrison. The novelty of Bax's concerto was followed on 14 March by a recital of contemporary works at the Wigmore Hall, with Murray Lambert and members of the LSO. This featured the first performance in England of *Prinz Csongor und die Kobolde* by the Hungarian Leo Weiner, Delius's Violin Concerto, Vaughan Williams's Neo-classical *Concerto accademico* and the first English hearing of Sibelius's *Three Pieces* for Violin and Orchestra. For

[10] Letter from Harty to Elgar, 30 Nov. 1930, *GB-HWRO*.
[11] Letter from Harty to Elgar, 16 Dec. 1933, *GB-HWRO*.
[12] Letter from Elgar to Harty, 19 Dec. 1933, *GB-Belqb*.
[13] *The Times*, 20 Feb. 1934.

Harty's last LSO concert of the season, on 19 March, he was to have conducted the premiere of Walton's First Symphony, but the work was still not ready. In its place he conducted two works in memory of Elgar, who had died on 23 February: his *Enigma Variations* and the *Introduction and Allegro*. A week earlier Harty had written to Elgar's daughter, Carice, offering his commiseration and words of admiration:

> I did not write to you before this (and this letter does not need any reply) for I know you have been overwhelmed by many unavoidable duties at the time of your father's death. But perhaps you will allow me to send you my very best sympathy with you in your bereavement. You must have had a terribly trying time during all these last months, and like many other people, I have often thought of what you must have been going through.
>
> I have always loved and revered your father's music, and just as much his dignified and quiet and serene life, and I know that he will always be remembered as a great Englishman as well as a great composer.[14]

Agnes Nicholls (signing herself 'Agnes Harty'), who now lived at 37 St John's Wood Road, also wrote recalling her vivid memories of *The Kingdom*:

> I am so sorry your father has passed on – sorry for you and for all of us, who will miss him very greatly, but not sorry for him if he was to suffer … I am always glad to think that almost the last thing I did before my illness was "The Kingdom" with him – such a happy day.[15]

After the two Elgar works, the audience stood during the playing of Berlioz's funeral march from *Hamlet* and, for the second half, enjoyed a fine performance of Brahms's First Symphony. 'It was a performance,' claimed the critic of *The Times*, 'which showed how foolish were the people who used to say that Brahms could not score and how unnecessary were the apologies which used to be made for his individual treatment of the orchestra.'[16]

Having already recorded his arrangement of the *Water Music* with the LPO in May 1933, on 12 March 1934 Harty recorded his arrangement of the Handel Concerto for Orchestra with Organ with Dawber and the LSO (again for Columbia); this was followed soon afterwards by his first performance of *Messiah* in London, on 30 March with the Royal Choral Society. One further obligation was undertaken – to join Arthur Bliss and Frank Bridge as one of three judges for the *Daily Telegraph* Overture Prize (won by Cyril Scott and his *Festival* Overture) – before making preparations to sail for Australia at the special invitation of the Australian Broadcasting Commission (ABC). By now the business of packing and travelling had become a tedious chore, as he explained to Harriet Cohen: 'One good thing about being dead is that in the

---

[14] Letter from Harty to Carice Blake, 11 Mar. 1934, *GB-HWRO*.

[15] Letter from Agnes Nicholls to Carice Blake, 24 Feb. 1934, *GB-HWRO*. The date of this performance of *The Kingdom* is unclear, but it may have referred to the one given at the Worcester Three Choirs Festival in September 1923.

[16] *The Times*, 20 Mar. 1934.

scanty clothing required in the next world, there is a promise of relief from packing. Oh. how I hate it!'[17]

The ABC were keen to provide a fillip to orchestral playing across Australia's vast continent and had arranged for Harty to be there for the months of May and June. Travelling on the Orient Line's *Ormonde*, Harty faced a long voyage to Perth, and while passing the hours on board he became acquainted with a thirty-two-year-old married woman, Lorie Irving Bolland (née Staughton). The wife of an officer seconded from the York and Lancashire Regiment to the Gold Coast (now Ghana) Regiment in West Africa, she was on her way to Australia to spend time with her family in Terang, Victoria (her husband was on active service in Ghana during much of 1934 and 1935). Lorie Bolland was not particularly musical, but she was a lively, educated, well-read and intelligent woman, highly engaging in conversation. Harty found her irresistibly attractive. She, in turn, must have been flattered by the close attention she received from one of the world's most eminent conductors. Confined to their nautical surroundings, they evidently saw a lot of each other and their friendship developed into a 'shipboard romance', at least from what can be deduced from the one passionate and very personal side of correspondence that has survived – from Harty.[18] Such was Harty's ardour during the course of the voyage that he was moved to write a piano piece for her birthday, *Spring Fancy* (dated 23 April 1934), a gentle romantic effusion in A major featuring a singing melody in the outer sections (rather in the style of Rachmaninov's D major Prelude, Op. 23 No. 4) and a more solemn hymn-like idea for the middle section in F sharp minor. The piece was an expression of unbridled adoration; a love that only came once in a lifetime. Yet, there was, of course, a substantial difference in their ages: she was thirty-two; he was fifty-four. He, for one, was fully cognisant of this age gap, but there was also a second complication: they were both married, Lorie for the second time.

The *Ormonde* docked in Fremantle, Western Australia, at the end of April and the pair made their way to Perth. At this stage Lorie and Harty were obliged to part. It was a painful moment and from that point, although he had to give his full attention to a busy schedule, his mind was also firmly fixed on the woman with whom he had fallen completely in love. In Perth he was given a royal welcome. At a lunch organised by the University of Western Australia and the West Australian Music Teachers' Association he delivered an address in which he outlined the repertoire he intended to bring before the people of Australia.

I have brought collections of the best compositions, because I consider it would be an insult to offer anything but the finest music to the Australian people. Every taste will be catered for, the wide range including Bach, Beethoven, Brahms, Wagner, Berlioz, Mozart, Handel, Dvorak, Schubert, Mendelssohn, Smetana,

---

[17] Letter from Harty to Harriet Cohen, 30 Mar. 1934, *GB-Lbl* MS Mus.1640.

[18] It seems more than likely that Harty would have retained Lorie's letters, but they were probably destroyed in 1940 when Harty's house was bombed.

Rimsky-Korsakov, Weinberger, Liadoff, Tchaikovsky, Debussy, Strauss, Cesar Franck, Delius, Percy Grainger, Elgar and Stanford.[19]

Besides the injection of a new and vital standard of orchestral playing, another item on Harty's agenda, which had been clearly endorsed by the ABC, was the popularisation of classical music in Australia. Rather like Walford Davies's broadcasts for the BBC, Harty's concerts and addresses were tailored to appeal to a wide range of the public and to draw them in on the grounds that 'high brow' was not the preserve of the educated, adult middle and upper classes. Wishing to appeal to children, he even went so far as to recall an experience with a niece in Dublin:

> In Dublin, Sir Hamilton told us, he has a small niece, Rosemary, who loves nothing more than riding her ponies. But when the Hallé orchestra was going to give a performance there not long ago, Sir Hamilton suggested that she be brought and be formally introduced to music. Consequently he put the Royal Box at Rosemary's disposal so that he could watch her reactions. First she seemed very interested. Then, as a Tchaikovsky concerto rose to its heights while he conducted it with suitable energy, he noticed Rosemary almost falling out of the box in her excitement. 'In fact, her mother seemed to be holding her by the legs', he added. Afterwards, he asked what she was saying. It was: 'Oh, Mummy. Is uncle winning?'[20]

In an interview with the *Perth News* Harty also gave a fuller account of his views about music, with a particular emphasis on Walton, whose talents he considered to be at the forefront of music in Britain at that time. Curiously, the same article billed Constant Lambert as an Australian composer, perhaps as a means of attracting Australian audiences, on the basis that his father George Washington Lambert was an Australian war artist (Lambert's music was represented by *The Rio Grande*, in which Harty would of course take an active practical role):[21]

> Discussing music generally, Sir Hamilton said that like the rest of the world England had passed through a period of what might be termed 'intellectual music', in which it was thought that the brain of the composer was more important than the heart.
>
> 'Now the time has turned in the direction of emotional significance', he said. 'Music has to appeal to people's hearts for it to live. If music was merely an intellectual pursuit I would have found something better to do, but it is the amount of pleasure and emotionalism that I derive from music that makes me love it and continue'.
>
> Sir Hamilton said that during the past few years in the returning mood of emotionalism, several successful works had been written by the Australian

---

[19] *Perth News*, 1 May 1934. This address also formed part of an earlier interview Harty had given with the Sydney *Morning Herald* (21 April 1934) before his arrival.

[20] *Melbourne Herald*, 9 May 1934.

[21] Lambert was born in England in 1905. His father had come to England in 1900, and after a short period in Paris, settled in London in 1902. He returned to Australia, without his family, in 1920.

composer [sic], Constant Lambert, who had made his name with 'Rio Grande'. In his opinion, this work was the only composition based on jazz rhythm which was significant enough to live.

'It is most artistic, and as I think it belongs to Australia I decided to include it in the forthcoming programme', he said.

Describing jazz as primitive and sensual and a hysterical, nervous reflex of the intellectual vogue, Sir Hamilton said that this form of music was the best example of a curious period in musical history, which had been but a passing stage. There was now a definite movement back to Viennese rhythm.

Sir Hamilton said that a composer who has rhythm to the forefront in London was William Walton, a very young man whose compositions had attracted much attention because of their mature nature. Walton's works were the strongest they had had in England for many years and the youthful composer's artistic tendencies were extraordinarily well developed for one so young.[22]

Harty then gave a broadcast to the entire nation and an interview for the magazine *The Home* before continuing his journey on the *Ormonde* to Adelaide. There he was entertained to a reception by the mayor:

The manager for the Australian Broadcasting Commission in Adelaide (Mr Hosking) said that Sir Hamilton Harty's visit should prove a tonic to music generally in Australia similar to that provided by Verbruggen [sic] and Marshall Hall in the past. …

Sir Hamilton Harty said that one got accustomed on visits to America and Europe to good orchestral playing, which had been the order for many years. Australia had made history in song [here he was referring particularly to his associations with Melba and Austral] and instrumental prowess but its orchestral music had been sporadic and had evidently not made continuous progress.

'The time has come when Australia should possess one of the principal orchestras of the world', he said. 'I am sure the material I will have to deal with will be good. It takes a long time for an orchestra to attain cohesion which is the chief beauty of orchestral playing.'

'Wireless', he said, 'could not avoid having far-reaching effects on the public taste. Through the BBC's generosity, orchestras have been able to remain alive in England over a critical period. The turn of the tide had now come, and people were gradually going back to the concert hall. The policy of the BBC to make as many people as possible acquainted with the best music had made people want to hear it first hand.' He advised listeners not to be afraid of the word classical, and not to have the wireless turned on always, but to get into the habit of selecting their items from the programmes and learning to appreciate the value of different music.[23]

On arriving in Melbourne Harty encountered the same enthusiastic welcome that he had met in Perth and Adelaide. On 8 May there was a reception at the Lyceum Club, and, a day later, by the Association of Music Teachers of Victoria at Melbourne Town Hall. On 11 May he was the guest of Melbourne University Conservatorium Past Students' Association and delivered an address which was

[22] *Melbourne Herald*, 9 May 1934.
[23] *Adelaide Advertiser*, 7 May 1934.

published in the *Melbourne Star* in which he touched on the political state of music and finance in England, its composition (again singling out Walton), and his vision for Australia's broadcasting commission:

Perhaps in no other country is the level of accomplishment in music as high as it is in England today. ... But while she had scores of first-rate musicians, England could lay claim to little individuality in music, so after all she was not very much better off, musically, than other countries. The one exception was composition. There England could lead the way, for her school of composition was the most promising in the world, and outstanding amongst the many brilliant young composers was twenty-seven-year-old William Walton, who had produced some of the significant works of the generation. Referring to orchestral music, Sir Hamilton Harty said that England was faced here with the same problem as Australia; that of finding the necessary money. There was no public or State support for orchestras, largely because the average man was chary of spending money on music since he would have nothing to show for it. The only hope lay with the BBC and he was confident that eventually the broadcasting commission, wisely guided, would take the place of a 'ministry of arts' in the encouragement and development of music. 'And I venture to prophesy that in time the same thing will happen here in Australia', he concluded.[24]

Harty undertook many interviews with the Australian press during his time in Melbourne and Sydney, and, perhaps feeling himself immune from the press at home, felt less inhibited in expressing his prejudices. On one occasion his deep-seated distaste for jazz gave rise to an outburst:

'Jazz, jazz, jazz!' yelled England's temperamental Irish conductor when 'Smith's Weekly' took pencil and paper to the Australian Broadcasting Commission's honoured guest.

'Don't talk to me of jazz, my lad! Jazz is a disease which has smitten music, and a disease, thank goodness that will soon be cured and, like all other complaints and diseases will only be spoken of in the same manner that old ladies refer to their asthma and appendix.

Jazz is finished, definitely', insisted Sir Hamilton Harty.[25]

But all the time Harty was preparing for his first concert in Melbourne, his first thoughts were for Lorie and whether they could meet together somewhere in the city. From Cliveden Mansions, in the eastern part of Melbourne, he wrote to her impatiently:

It may prove to be hopeless and vain – shall we make one more big effort? Some secret instinct tells me so loudly that if I ever want all of Lorie, I must be strong and patient and enduring and good. Excuse me if I am stupid (Hay No. 2 is biting and kicking with rage). I just don't know anything except that I am quite madly in love with you and following a blind instinct in writing like this. Give me a kiss and tell me if I am right or wrong. I hardly know.[26]

[24] *Melbourne Star*, 11 May 1934.
[25] *Smith's Weekly*, 19 May 1934.
[26] Letter from Harty to Lorie Bolland, 16 May 1934 (CB).

The first concert in Melbourne took place on the evening of 19 May. The ten days of rehearsals with the ABC Orchestra had been highly successful and the players had taken to Harty's methods and personality. The programmes at the Melbourne Town Hall on 19, 23, 26 and 30 May, all of them broadcast, were familiar and characteristically popular ones that he had given on many occasions in Manchester and America. The repertoire featured the Prelude to *Die Meistersinger*, Brahms's First Symphony, Mozart's Serenade *Eine kleine Nachtmusik*, Delius's *A Walk to the Paradise Garden*, Tchaikovsky's 'Air and Variations' from his Suite No. 3., excerpts from Berlioz's *Damnation of Faust*, Beethoven's Fifth Symphony, the Polka and Fugue from Weinberger's *Schwanda the Bagpiper*, his own arrangement of Handel's *Water Music*, and *With the Wild Geese*. The last of his Melbourne concerts, on 30 May, was an all-Wagner programme (in connection with which he gave a second broadcast talk for the radio). In general the Melbourne press were elated with the new energy that the orchestra exuded. The *Melbourne Age* described the first concert as a 'unique occasion in our musical history', while the *Melbourne Sun-News Pictorial* saw the event as the beginning of a new era:

> When the Broadcasting Commission's Symphony Orchestra rose at the end of its night to give its own three mighty cheers in concord with the long bruit of acclamations already ringing in the Melbourne Town Hall, it was an acknowledgement that its very being had been shaken by something epochal, something every man and woman present was bound to remember right through life, no matter who may be a guest conductor in time to come.[27]

Lorie managed to come up from her parents' home at Keayang (near Terang) in order to hear the second of the concerts. She stayed at the Alexandra Club, and this allowed her to see Harty for a brief time. The following day she left for Keayang, which provoked another passionate letter from Harty:

> You have only gone this afternoon Lorie and it seems a long time I have been here without you. Tomorrow I am obliged to rehearse both morning and afternoon and talk 'over the air' in the evening as well as dine with our friend Father Murphy and a selected band of his own colleagues. That is why I am writing to you at midnight for I doubt if I would have time tomorrow. Tonight boxing.[28] Much blood and thunder, not much science. And I pretended you were with me, and the whole time I was talking to you and telling you not to be upset.
>
> Lorie, I love you so much, so magically, so completely, that I can hardly talk about it. But I do know that it is all marching towards some end, some meaning which at present is not clear to me. I have the strongest feeling that we are on trial and that our invisible friends and protectors are not hostile any more but non-committed. It is as if they will judge us according to how we behave on this strange journey we have elected to travel hand-in-hand.

[27] *Melbourne Sun-News Pictorial*, 21 May 1934.
[28] As a life member and patron of the Victorian Amateur Boxing and Wrestling Union, Harty felt obliged to attend an evening of boxing during his stay in Melbourne.

Ah. I have no wisdom with which to sustain us both – only the dumb instinctive knowledge that we mustn't hurt other poor people who have never tried to hurt us. How, why, whence? I don't know any answer, but the journey is ordained by fate. That I am sure of.[29]

Another revealing element of the letter was Harty's belief in fate and the spirit world, a fact confirmed in his interview with Leonora Wood Armsby. There it had been divulged that Harty believed in the presence of the 'unseen world', a form of mysticism Armsby linked with the composer's Dublin-born cousin Willam John Warner, otherwise known as Count Hamon or Cheiro, a palmist, clairvoyant, astrologer and occult figure.[30] But what is perhaps most affecting about Harty's outpouring to Lorie is that he had fallen genuinely in love for the first time in his life, and sought a spiritual, even preordained answer to the mystery:

I must go to bed. It is not the actual work with the orchestra that is tiring, but the constant pouring of my own spirit and fancy into vessels clear and receptive, but so far tragically empty. But it is a glorious thing to be allowed to do this – a kind of justification for one's own self. Lorie (I love your name) when you go about your familiar house and garden, take me always with you and talk silently to me. Everything I do now is dedicated to my darling like some lonely and shy country poet might secretly dedicate his best and purest thoughts to some star as he walks in the silence of the summer night.[31]

Before the final concert on 30 May, Harty heard from Lorie to say that she would come up for the occasion. He responded with alacrity:

Of course, I am dying to see you. I shall be here after lunch. Do come, perhaps we could have a little walk?
    I am so glad you have come down. Have you got your seats? I directed them to be left at Scotts Hotel for you. Ring me up and say what time you will come.
    Tomorrow morning? Of course, you have to help me pack! Tonight after the concert, let's have a drink and sandwich here, your mother, you and Laelia. I have to attend a brief party with the orchestra, but will get away soon.[32]

Directly after the last concert, Harty travelled up to Sydney where he was contracted to conduct five more broadcast concerts on 9, 13, 16, 20 and 22 June, at the Town Hall. Lorie was forever on his mind and a letter followed her to Terang:

I could not let you be in Terang tomorrow without a word of love. Darling I am entirely given over to you – and my life is all full of sweetness because I think of you. There may be harried times in front of us, but I won't take such a gift with foreboding – 'let come what come may' – but Oh Lorie – may God grant that we are not too far or too often apart in the future.

[29] Letter from Harty to Lorie Bolland, 24 May 1934 (CB).
[30] Armsby, 'The Irish Composer-Conductor', 148.
[31] Letter from Harty to Lorie Bolland, 24 May 1934 (CB).
[32] Letter from Harty to Lorie Bolland, n.d. (CB).

Hampton Court is my address in Sydney. I will write from there. God bless you, my star.[33]

In Sydney Harty was given ample accommodation in Hampton Court, King's Cross. But he was tired and exhausted by the public attention that bombarded him the moment he alighted from the train. This he imparted to Lorie in the knowledge that, in several weeks, he would be leaving Australia:

Here I am in a *large* flat, feeling *very* lonely and rather upset and tired and a few things like that. I've been very extravagant and have a man unpacking for me at the moment. God, Lorie, *how* I hate this publicity. No sooner was I off the rattling prehistoric train when I was besieged by reporters, photographers and the like. Then a huge reception at the Town Hall at which most of the Cabinet were present. …

I had a bad time last night. I couldn't sleep and it suddenly came over me – the realisation of our parting in a few weeks. How are we going to stand it Lorie? And it is going to hurt you awfully too, if it were only me I would pretend to you not to feel it so much. I don't know what to do. … God, there are cruel things in this world. But there, that's not very brave or helpful is it. Let us be quiet and strong and hopeful in fate, that it is not always unkind to two lovers.[34]

He was entertained to a lavish civic reception on 2 June with Mayor, Charles Lloyd Jones (the chairman of the ABC), and representatives of the federal government, and there were numerous other events including a meeting and photographs with Arundel Orchard (former Director of the Sydney Conservatorium) and Edgar Bainton (the new Director) at the New South Wales Musical Association's 'at home'.[35] In addition to the official ceremony and the fact that Harty had now been in Australia for a month, the national press became more interrogative in tone. *The Sun*, for example, commented that Harty had, as yet, relatively little time to create a new standard of orchestral playing in the four weeks of his residence, and that the ABC should make him a more prolonged offer (for several years) to give orchestral music a new sense of national prestige.[36] The Australian Musicians' Union agitated for an entirely professional 'National Orchestra', a policy which its secretary, Cecil Trevelyan, avowed to bring before parliament and which acted as a prelude to a debate which raged for the rest of Harty's time in the Australian capital.[37] On his arrival in Sydney Harty was immediately interviewed about his opinion of orchestral music in Australia, and this contributed to the debate. He was bluntly honest about his experience:

I cannot speak of Sydney yet, but the lack of good orchestral music in Melbourne made me feel distinctly sad. The individual members of the Broadcasting Commission's band were all very intelligent and ready to learn. But there is no-one to teach them. Sometimes they surprised me by their inability to surmount even

[33] Letter from Harty to Lorie Bolland, 30 May 1934.
[34] Letter from Harty to Lorie Bolland, 1 June 1934 (CB).
[35] *Labor Daily*, 6 June 1934.
[36] *The Sun*, 2 June 1934.
[37] *Melbourne Herald*, 6 June 1934.

the most moderate technical difficulties. Then when I showed them the way, they would go home and spend hours practising passages to order to make themselves perfect. As a result, when the night of the first concert arrived, the orchestra was like an old motor car which had been accelerated to 80 miles an hour. Our career was spectacular and exciting; but perilous in the extreme.[38]

Harty then freely offered his advice, suggesting that there should be a role for the state, but, at the same time, a place for the conductor without interference. It was an autocratic agenda that reflected his own experiences, aspirations and responses:

Here in Australia you should have fine orchestras, equal to the best in the world. Melbourne and Sydney should each be a little Paris, a little Munich – a real cultural centre. These cities would then be famous for their orchestras, just as Boston and Philadelphia are famous now. People in London would say: 'Sydney? Oh, yes; they have an orchestra there.'

Why will Australians be content for their principal cities to remain mere backwaters, where there is no invigorating, progressive stream of cultural activity?

It would be worth-while for the Government of this country to say: 'We must have the very best that can be obtained.' There are only about five great conductors in the world now. You could afford to engage one of these. Were he sure of having a free hand, a brilliant conductor would be inspired at the thought of developing this fruitful and almost virgin field. But he must have a free hand. There lies the danger always. If a government is having a bridge built, or a railway line laid down, it does not dream of interfering with the experts who are in charge of the work. But, in the case of a musical expert, all sorts of officious people think themselves justified in interfering with his plans. The great musicians of the world will not put up with interference. If persons in authority tell them what to do, they simply drop their activities of the moment and go somewhere else.[39]

The rehearsal schedule in Sydney was arduous and Harty found the acoustics of the Town Hall unsympathetic, as he noted in a long letter to Lorie:

I am hard put to it here, as far as work is concerned, but it is owing to the poor acoustics of the Town Hall, which makes rehearsing torture. They tell me it is much better when full of people – I sincerely hope so, for I am exhausted with rehearsing in such disgusting circumstances. You've no idea how trying it is when you are trying to make something beautiful to hear nothing but a jumble of noise and echoes. Damn it! If I'd known I'd never have accepted to conduct here. But no matter, it's all in the day's work, and I must do my best with it.[40]

The first concert took place on 9 June. The main works of the programme were Brahms's First Symphony, *A Walk to the Paradise Garden* and *With the Wild Geese*, mixed with smaller works by Smetana, Lyadov, Rimsky-Korsakov and Weinberger. The following day the death of Delius was announced. This came

[38] *Morning Herald*, 2 June 1934.

[39] *Morning Herald*, 2 June 1934.

[40] Letter from Harty to Lorie Bolland, 8 June 1934.

as a shock to Harty, for he saw Delius not only as a musical colleague but as a personal friend. *Sydney 'Country Life'* printed his tribute:

> The death of a great composer like Frederick Delius represents an irreparable loss, not only to England, but to the whole world of music. It is too much to hope that many of like genius will in our lifetime so enrich the art of music and give such exquisite pleasure to music lovers. Like all musicians, I deplore his death – perhaps even more than most, for he counted for much in my musical and my private life.[41]

In Melbourne his performance of *On Hearing the First Cuckoo in Spring* had been relayed by the ABC to France so that it could be heard by the composer on short wave radio. As a further tribute, Harty swiftly arranged for *A Walk to the Paradise Garden* to be repeated at the second concert on 13 June along with Strauss's *Death and Transfiguration*. The rest of the programme included the Scherzo from Harty's 'Irish' Symphony, Beethoven's Seventh Symphony, the Prelude to *Die Meistersinger* and solo arias by the Irish soprano Laelia Finneberg.

While the concerts in Sydney were generating enormous excitement, Harty himself was in considerable emotional turmoil. His love for Lorie had completely consumed him, and there had been only a brief opportunity during the orchestral preparations for the concerts to spend time with her at Keayang. Back in Sydney he wrote to her from his lonely flat in Hampton Court, and poured out his heart:

> It's *too* absurd, *too* annoying, *too* silly, that this flat has two perfectly fine bedrooms each with 2 beds all very charming, and yet, poor darling, you can't come straight here and look after a rather disgruntled boy – and let him love you and be kind, and stay here and make tea in the kitchen – and *all* those things that I have such a *hellish* thirst for since I came to love you and you me. *Why* are you not at least my cousin? Is there *any* way – Lorie? God keep you. I am surrounded, covered, overwhelmed with love of you, as if I were half-dead already.[42]

But with each day Harty fretted that his proximity to Lorie would soon be destroyed by the obligation to sail for America. In addition, their predicament as married people, and the need to preserve the privacy of their relationship, naturally restricted their behaviour in public. In sending Lorie a copy of his *Antrim and Donegal* songs, he added a musical quotation in the most Tristanesque of keys, B major, with the words 'My Lagan Love'; in 1935 he sent her a copy of his song *The Wake Feast*, drawing attention to the music of bars 40–2 and to Alice Milligan's text 'She was my secret love'. The sense of 'forbidden love' Harty closely associated with the spirit of the doomed lovers of Wagner's *Tristan and Isolde*, the opening of which he quoted in his correspondence to her.[43] In his heart he probably knew that his passionate attachment to Lorie was a hopeless cause, yet he pondered and agonised constantly on the idea that, somehow, their affair might continue and that he could give up his career in

[41] *Sydney 'Country Life'*, 22 June 1934.
[42] Letter from Harty to Lorie Bolland, 1 June 1934 (CB).
[43] See letter from Harty to Lorie Bolland, 14 May 1934 (CB).

pursuit of a new, blissful happiness. His letters to her became longer and more tortured:

> I tell you I am not God – I don't know what strength I have, but anyway, I am determined to try and fight for this ideal of love, with which you have inspired me.
>
> For sure, darling Lorie, I know now that this one thing – this maddening physical union – is *terribly* important when you are truly in love, and, if we managed to part at all it would be with horribly sore and torn hearts.
>
> And then too, it would, with so few days to be together, make us terribly sad, maybe, for before my eyes would be the thought of parting from you, and leaving you sad and alone.
>
> O darling, do you understand finally that I am all in love with you and if it comes to the final show-down, I'd rather love the smaller game than not play for the great one. All my best instincts – all those mysterious Guardians – in whom I believe – everything tells me this is the true and right way – and one I *must* follow, or try to. So darling (there *is* that damn naughty honest lusty boy Hay too!) give me *everything*, all your caresses, your surest body to hold, your darling presence, all Lorie, mind, body, soul, spirit, thoughts, fragrance, and let us just face that one fact, that this our mystic experience is forbidden for the time being.
>
> And now, Lorie, there is Hay's heart and brain, wretched weak heart and brain, and there is the best I can do. But there is one thing I believe we might look forward to as possible. Even if we had to ask for it from those who have certain rights. I mean every year a couple of months freedom from all ties, all duties, all conventions. How wonderful to think all the year that we were going to be alone somewhere in the quiet places of the world, answerable to no-one but ourselves, unobserved, happy beyond words, divinely happy. O I think this might be given to us if we try to be strong and good. And you know, I could ask even your mother – and that others – without shame for this if I could come with a clear honest face and heart. Don't you think Lorie, this *might* be? I am privately tired of life, work, success, difficulties, occasional defeats, more successes, it seems so aimless. But, O God, if I had that joy to look forward to every year.[44]

The third of the four orchestral concerts in Sydney, though it concluded with Schubert's Ninth Symphony, was very much a showcase for British music on Harty's terms. It consisted of Stanford's *Irish Rhapsody* No. 1, a work he had conducted countless times, along with Elgar's *Enigma* Variations, *The Rio Grande* (directed by Lindley Evans with Harty, as usual, as soloist), the *Water Music*, and the third movement of Harty's 'Irish' Symphony. The next event, a performance of Mendelssohn's *Elijah* on 20 June, was undermined by the fact that the Town Hall organ, tuned to the old higher pitch, could not be used to support the chorus; this necessitated the use of a smaller instrument that required amplification by microphone.[45] Harty's final appearance, on 22 June, was essentially an all-Wagner affair save for a repeat of Smetana's *Bartered Bride* Overture and Franck's D minor Symphony. It was perhaps with some irony, given his antagonism to the formation of the BBC Symphony Orchestra, that Harty joined the call after the concerts had concluded for the founding of

[44] Letter from Harty to Lorie Bolland, 8 June 1934 (CB).
[45] *Daily Sun*, 20 June 1934.

a central, National Symphony Orchestra. Such an organisation would help to focus musical excellence and serve the nation's appetite for orchestral music. It would also be a sign of cultural prestige, but, at the same time, it would be necessary to strip each of the ABC orchestras of its best players.[46]

On 21 June Harty was guest of honour at a dinner organised by the orchestral players in Sydney. As a tribute, he was presented with a set of silver drinking cups. Brisbane had entertained some hope that he could travel north to Queensland to conduct there, but he was tired after a long, gruelling schedule, and took some time off. This included a visit to Sydney University as a guest of the Vice-Chancellor Dr R. S. Wallace, where he heard an impromptu recital on the War Memorial Carillon and agreed to compose a work for the instrument.[47]

On the eve of his departure he wrote another anguished letter to his beloved Lorie, haunted by a troubling uncertainty for the future:

> I have been very sad for days. Your darling letter to the boat was sent to me today. I sail tomorrow, and I have the conviction so plainly from it that you love me, perhaps as deeply as I do you, that I am comforted. Courage and optimism and humour are three things necessary to me before I can really live and I have taken a fresh hold and just made up my mind to wait for you, for I know we are meant for one another, and if I don't think you will be able to help loving me, nor I you. In a lovely letter from your mother, so delicate yet so understanding, she said that in our way she was sorry I had a soft Irish voice, for you would hear it all your life now in the sighing of the wind and the falling of the rain. Escape me never! You never can, for I have loved you and love you too deeply and truly. Do not leave me without letters. If you ever want to reach me in America, letters addressed to my agent Richard Copley ... will be forwarded wherever I am. I shall be in Hollywood, Chicago and New York until about August 28th. Then in London. O God, I do hope you may be coming there soon. If you ever speak of things to your mother, tell her that some things, like our love, are so big that one doesn't consider right or wrong, but only the necessity to be good and sweet and not hurt others.
>
> I leave part of myself here behind me, to be near you, and all my heart. Be happy and peaceful in your sweet Keayang, and think of me always with secret love and longing. O Lorie, don't worry about our human frailties. They are no more than the lines which love and suffering make upon our faces. Let us try and make this big thing that has happened to us ennoble us and, for the rest, give us strength in waiting.
>
> God bless you, my darling, Love me, *some day* we shall be together.[48]

He left Sydney on the *Monterey*, bound for California. On board, bereft of his love, he composed a short 'Portrait' with the dedication 'For Lorie' on 9 July, written on *Oceanic Line* notepaper with staves he had to rule himself. It was a miniature valedictory love song in the guise of a nocturne, thirty-three bars long, written in D flat, and marked 'dolce espressivo'; he sent it to her when he reached America.

[46] *Sydney Herald*, 30 June 1934.

[47] *Sydney Telegraph*, 2 July 1934.

[48] Letter fom Harty to Lorie Bolland, 26 June 1934 (CB).

In California Harty made yet another series of star appearances at the Hollywood Bowl, conducting Wagner, Berlioz, Beethoven and Delius, though this time Henry Wood was also there to direct some concerts of his own. Harty's concerts began on 10 July and his appearances, highly acclaimed by audience and press, ran for two weeks. With Wood he made a visit to the Metro-Goldwyn-Mayer studio and was a regular guest of the American 'breakfast clubs'.[49] Moving on to Chicago, he found the summer weather unpleasantly stifling. From his suffocating room in the Congress Hotel, he relayed to Lorie the news of his success in California:

> Hollywood was an enormous success. One thing I am and that is, a more powerful musician than before. I ought to pay you a large fee! Here I arrived today. In great simplicity, let me just say that it is like Hell – with the temperature at 109 in the shade (but there isn't any shade!). Finding myself amongst a nation of frank and copious perspirers has removed my self-consciousness in that direction – and I don't mind so much. Besides, I am become thin and *very* beautiful of figure! I stay here a fortnight or so, then, thank God England and coolness and sanity.[50]

As a guest of the Chicago Symphony Orchestra's longstanding conductor Frederick Stock, and its associate conductor Eric DeLamarter, Harty featured as one of the guest conductors in the orchestra's twice daily appearances at the Swift Bandshell during the city's World Fair celebrations. Though music occupied him during the day, the lonely evenings caused him to dwell on the parting from Lorie – a painful experience that had left its mark. The separation and loneliness gave rise to his longest letter, one that was consumed with a passion and yearning for the true love of his life, yet stoical for its trust in fate and 'spiritual guardians':

> You would be surprised to know the number of times I have written letters to you – and cables too – and torn them up because they did not exactly explain my thoughts.
>   But now, indefinite as my ideas still remain in part – I am writing to you exactly as I feel. O my darling – without the slightest wish to reproach you – you have made me suffer more than I could ever tell you. I am sure that was not your fault at all – just that two natures like ours happened to meet, and love – for I'm certain you love me too. You know – Lorie – you are, in my life at any rate – *a fatal woman*. There have been such in other past lives, and all life-experience – self-command – ideals – everything that one possesses – that *is* one, melts into one devastating love. I suppose the reason my ghostly helpers are so dismayed is that they fear I might give up the only thing that is really of any importance or meaning in my spiritual life – my poor little gift of music – for your sake. ... Perhaps I should be happier if I could do so, but that would be like murder – and thank God I can still say I cannot be completely broken by anyone. Well, how serious my darling girl! But I had to tell you my whole mind. The end of it is this – I am madly in love with you – and I expect shall always be – but I have made up my mind to leave everything in the hands of fate and to make no move to gain you

[49] *The Times*, 31 Aug. 1934.
[50] Letter from Harty to Lorie Bolland, 8 Aug. 1934 (CB).

on my own account. It is only this way that I can find any peace from the constant urging, the constant anxiety, the constant disapproval of those who love me and protect me though they are not visible. Something tells me I shall gradually get strength and knowledge and power to deal with the most stirring and wonderful thing that has ever come to me. For the present I admit with low bows to the mocking gods that I am their servant. But let them destroy me or cripple me, even they cannot stop my being Hay. I mean – if that is their object, the obliteration of my own pride and endurance is possible only with entire annulment.[51]

Not knowing when he might see Lorie again, he looked forward to 1935 with the possibility of another tour to America and Australia. Though lucrative in the fees he earned, and the adulation he received, the journeys were nevertheless exhausting and this physical element was now an important factor in his longer-term decisions:

Both America and Australia make approaches to me for next summer, but I don't know what I shall do. To tell the truth I'm damned tired of rushing about the world and want time to think and perhaps compose. We'll see. (By the way, *how* I hate American pens!) Just turn round for a moment. Do you mind my kissing your soft lips like mad for a minute? That's better – let's go on – America is so beautiful. In California anyway, but so shallow compared to your country, which, on the other hand, is sad underneath. I wonder why? I think it is living at the end of the world, and being descendants of those who had so many loves and ties so far away in England.[52]

Indeed, Harty's mind turned to his hide-away in Kendal with the Farrers as an ideal haven of privacy, away from the public gaze:

… and now in my little green study there that looks over the lawns up the hillside to a beautiful wood, there will hang the two pictures of you. I didn't explain too much – it wasn't necessary. So think of me there. You see, someway, I couldn't bear artists and singers and such like to come to my home in London and say – 'who is that lovely girl?' – it would be like a kind of desecration.

Do you like this idea of dwelling alone with me away up in the wild North? And do you like the way I want to keep you terribly private from everyone? Now I must stop. You cannot help seeing how I love you. It is not a case of conscious loving, it is just being completely in love.[53]

In September 1934 Harty arrived back in England tired and weary from his long tour. He had promised to conduct Berlioz's *Corsair* Overture at the last concert given by Dan Godfrey in Bournemouth on 30 September 1934 as a sign of his esteem for the great advocate of British music, but he was advised by his doctor to withdraw owing to eye strain.[54] Meanwhile, relations with the LSO were not proceeding well. Having spent many years in a position of 'benign dictator' with the Hallé, Harty was unaccustomed to opposition. Even before

[51] Letter from Harty to Lorie Bolland, 8 Aug. 1934 (CB).
[52] Letter from Harty to Lorie Bolland, 8 Aug. 1934 (CB).
[53] Letter from Harty to Lorie Bolland, 8 Aug. 1934 (CB).
[54] Lloyd, *Sir Dan Godfrey*, 203.

he embarked on his tour to Australia and America, the Directors were getting impatient with Harty's domineering attitude. Indeed, as far back as October 1933 it was minuted that 'the policy of the Board in engaging Sir Hamilton Harty for the majority of the Orchestral Concerts was not calculated to improve the prospects of the orchestra', and that engaging individual foreign conductors would have been a more satisfactory policy.[55] This matter was raised again in April 1934 and the decision was reached that Harty would not be engaged to conduct all the concerts in the 1934–5 season. He was furious and accused the LSO Board of a breach of faith,[56] in that he had turned down offers from abroad in order to make himself available for the orchestra's entire season. This confrontation, and the fact that Harty continued to record with the LPO for Columbia, only served to damage relations further. The inevitable outcome was the termination of his contract which, though not sought, left him freer to pursue his foreign engagements; the LSO reverted to its former policy, agreed among its members, of employing individual conductors.

During October and November of 1934 Harty worked closely with both the LPO and the LSO. After recording four movements of Mozart's Divertimento No. 17 with the LPO for Columbia, Harty began his last season under contract with the LSO on 22 October with an importation from America, Frederick Stock's orchestration of Bach's Prelude and Fugue in E flat. There were also Leo Weiner's *Hungarian Folk Dances*, Op. 18, which were heard for the first time in England, Mozart's *Eine kleine Nachtmusik*, and a spirited performance of Elgar's Second Symphony. For all the awkward politics behinds the scenes, there was no doubt that the amelioration of the orchestra was due to Harty's influence. The critic of *The Times* pointed out: '[The] London Symphony Orchestra has now no cause to suffer from an inferiority complex, and that its patrons have every cause to expect the best from its members throughout this season.'[57] Because of Beecham's illness, Harty stepped in to conduct the Royal Philharmonic Society on 1 November in a classical programme of Ravel's *Tombeau de Couperin* and works by Haydn and Mozart, which included Jan Smeterlin in Mozart's Concerto in F, K459. On 5 November, as a tribute to Holbrooke whose music he much admired, he repeated *The Raven* with the LSO; Backhaus appeared as soloist in Grieg's Piano Concerto, a work he had not conducted for some time, and the programme also contained Harty's arrangement for organ and orchestra of Handel's Concerto in D (with Harold Darke at the organ) and Rachmaninov's Second Symphony. Four days later he was back with the LPO to record two Berlioz overtures, *Beatrice and Benedict* and *The Corsair*, for Columbia before travelling to Liverpool to conduct the Liverpool Philharmonic in a northern regional broadcast. Such was Harty's new freelance existence. However, his health was not good and he had now formed a more realistic perspective of his Australian love-affair. He was, nevertheless, receiving letters from Lorie in Terang to which he continued to respond:

[55] LSO Minutes, 10 Oct. 1933, 28.
[56] See LSO Minutes, 16 Aug. 1934, 72.
[57] *The Times*, 23 Oct. 1934.

I didn't feel I could write to you lately, though your last letter made me wish to do so, very much. You see, I couldn't write as I felt, and I didn't want to write coldly and formally. Are you clever and understanding at present? Let me be straight and fearless. I've always known in my heart that there was disaster ahead of us if we gave in to our love. And I had to struggle on until I had grown an amount of philosophy about the whole thing. A bitter struggle – but no more about that. It has taught me breadth and I hope more kindness for others. So now I can write to you in calm and affection too.

Since I returned to England my health has been poor – too much hard work in recent years and somewhat mysterious affection of the heart (but not mysterious to *us*) has been making my life and work rather difficult and wearisome. Much sending for doctors about the need for a long holiday. But all at once I begin to grow better again and though I am bound by solemn oaths to have a real let-up next spring, I believe I can carry on quite decently till then. That's enough about me. I am being rather a special good musician at present thank God. The instruments which the Almighty sometimes [uses] to teach one breadth and delicacy are sometimes hurtful, but his operations are intended to purify and refine ... and God knows how they are sometimes needed![58]

He was also pondering how to respond to invitations from both America and Australia for tours in 1935. He had by now written the *Little Fantasy and Fugue* for carillon that he promised for Sydney University, and this received its first public performance on Christmas Day 1934. For Harty, however, the piece had a much more touching, personal significance:

Australia cables me continually about going out there next spring – about May – I don't know – and am temporising. For one thing there is the promise I gave to M M: the gentleman of the medical profession – and yet again – and furthermore – and in the first place – and principally ... well ... I hesitate to revisit what seemed a magic land just to see what gold I can extract from its mines. ... So I say nothing for the present. ... You know, the University of Sydney has a very nice Carillon – a peal of bells. They were very nice to me there – and so as a little return I have written a composition for these bells and sent it to them. Why should I hide from you that my secret idea was that someday you might be in Sydney and would hear floating down over the city something that vaguely reminded you of me. Something that would say to you – 'there are bells ringing in a red dawn with wild freshness and spring gaiety – and yet with something sad underneath, and why does that remind me of Hay?' And the reason is that Hay is just telling you of a certain dawn with a red fiery sky when the thought of you seemed to colour the whole world. ... I loved your last letter.[59]

On 22 November he was honoured by the Royal Philharmonic Society with the Society's Gold Medal which, at Harty's request, was presented to him by Lord Londonderry, Secretary of State for Air. A few weeks before, Londonderry had responded with delight to Harty's invitation:

[58] Letter from Harty to Lorie Bolland, 15 Nov. 1934 (CB).
[59] Letter from Harty to Lorie Bolland, 15 Nov. 1934 (CB).

I am indeed flattered by your request that the honour of presenting you with the gold medal of the Royal Philharmonic Society should fall on myself. If to be a lover of music and an Ulsterman are sufficient qualifications then I can indeed lay claim to both, and am delighted to do what you ask.[60]

The presentation formed part of a concert which Harty directed, consisting of *Beatrice and Benedict*, Brahms's Fourth Symphony, three movements from Mozart's Divertimento, к334, and Harty's own Violin Concerto, played by Paul Beard (at that time leader of the LPO). Writing for the *Manchester Guardian*, Walter Legge made the following comment on Harty's speech at the end of the first half of the concert:

> In a short speech of thanks the conductor made witty and pointed reference to the fact that much of his conducting is done abroad and said that since the medal is a tribute from musicians – men of his own profession – it will go with him as a mascot and a reminder of the faith that his fellow musicians in Britain have in him. As if to pay its tribute to the conductor, the orchestra played better than it has ever done for any man but Beecham.[61]

In commemoration of the honour, Lambert, author of the recently published *Music Ho!*, added the following warm words of esteem:

> It is impossible to think of anyone more deserving this great honour than Sir Hamilton Harty. Fame has come to him later than to some men, but his name stands all the more solidly because he has never sought the cheap and evanescent rewards of fashion. Unlike many famous conductors Sir Hamilton is a musician first and foremost. We never feel that he is using a piece of music as a vehicle for his own virtuosity; on the contrary, he draws attention not to himself but to the composer, and that surely is the highest degree of the conductor's art.[62]

As a critic, Lambert could be withering in his demolition of music and musical individuals, but he clearly admired Harty's conducting art and musicianship greatly.

However, the climax of 1934 for Harty was the much anticipated premiere of Walton's First Symphony on 3 December. Harty had requested the work in January 1932, when still in Manchester, but its progress had been frustratingly slow. According to Sacheverall Sitwell, Harty and Walton had met up at the Sitwell's family seat – Weston Hall, Towcester – to discuss the symphony.[63] But in the knowledge that the work would not be ready, Walton had written to Harty early in 1933 (when it was scheduled for performance by the Hallé in March), cancelling it, yet trying to keep him optimistic about its eventual production. Writing from Ascona, a Swiss town on the shore of Lake Maggiore, where he was living with the widow Baroness Doernberg, he explained:

---

[60] Letter from Londonderry to Harty, 16 Oct. 1934, *GB- GB-Belqb*.

[61] *MG*, 23 Nov. 1934; see also Sanders (ed.), *Walter Legge*, 19.

[62] *Sunday Referee*, 25 Nov. 1934.

[63] Letter from Sacheverall Sitwell to Olive Baguley, 25 May 1967, *GB-Belqb*.

I'm sorry that I've been so slow in producing my symphony, but actually I don't think it is any the worse for it, in fact, I hope & think, that it promises to be better than any work I've written hitherto, but that may be only an optimistic reaction to the months of despair I've been through, when I thought I should never be able to write another note. However the 1st movement is finished & the 2nd ought to be in another 10 days or so. But having disappointed you once, I feel chary about fixing any date to its ultimate completion, but it ought to be ready sometime next season.

I must say, I think it almost hopeless for anyone to produce anything in any of the arts these days. It is practically impossible to get away from the general feeling of hopelessness & chaos which exists everywhere, however one may try – so you mustn't think I'm an exception, & one capable of encompassing all difficulties – producing a masterpiece. But I'm trying my best.

I am very grateful to you for taking so much interest in the work, & I really hope to produce something worthy of your genius as a conductor.[64]

Trusting in his judgment of Walton's ability and artistry, Harty was prepared to wait, though, as is evident in a letter to Foss, he did experience temporary moments of exasperation. 'Why don't you go over to Switzerland,' he wrote impatiently, 'and wrest poor WW's baroness away from him so that he can stop making overtures to her and do a symphony for me instead! (Rather a good joke!)'[65] With the various cancellations of the symphony, the anticipation of its performance grew ever more intense; besides the LSO's claim on the work, the BBC were also planning to perform it alongside Elgar's new commissioned symphony. Harty programmed it for 19 March 1934, but it was still not ready, yet such was his faith in Walton's gift that he was ready to risk a further cancellation by programming it for the following December. 'I must look forward to the first performance of this work whenever it is finished', he wrote reassuringly to Walton, 'and I take it for granted that you will reserve this for me.'[66] So the wait continued, and the BBC also had to face disappointment in that the symphony would not be ready for the Corporation's May music festival. By March 1934 Harty explained to Foss, 'Tell Walton that next season's dates are being arranged and I hope the symphony will be one of our chief exhibits – good luck to him.'[67] In another letter to Foss of 13 September, Harty, who was off to Ireland for a week, reiterated his resolve to be patient until the finished object was ready and the composer contented:

'Ecco! Il Duomo!', as the little Fiesole tailor said to me after the 12th fitting of the suit he was trying to make for me. (I had at last, in despair, professed myself satisfied, and he was as sardonic as he dared.) Poor little man. It was a frightful suit.

[64] Letter from Walton to Harty, n.d. (January or February? 1933), *GB-Belqb*.

[65] Letter from Harty to Foss, 22 Feb. 1933, in private possession.

[66] Quoted in a letter from Walton to Kenneth Wright (of the BBC), Jan. 1934, in Lloyd, *William Walton*, 114.

[67] Letter from Harty to Foss, 30 Mar. 1934, in private possession.

I shall not be sardonic but very thankful when I can say these words to Willie W. – but the poor boy is right to wait until he is quite satisfied. I do hope (and think) it is going to be all right this time. But what a difficult accouchement! No matter – pass the chloroform, nurse, these are the authentic pains![68]

Nevertheless, Walton eventually acceded, against his wishes, to the symphony being performed incomplete, without its last movement, largely because he knew that a further cancellation would be final. This he explained to his friend Patrick Hadley: 'Harty, who has behaved like a lamb, was more or less willing to wait till March [1935], but the LSO said that another postponement would be fatal, & that if I agreed, they would do it without the finale.'[69]

On 3 December 1934, in a programme of Berlioz, Bach, and the first London performance of Glazunow's *The Kremlin* (which Harty had first produced at Manchester), the three movements of the symphony came directly before the interval. Even though it was recognised as being unfinished, it created an enormous impression and the very fact that it lacked its Finale only added to the continued sense of expectancy in the press's critical appraisal. As Walter Legge remarked:

That this still unfinished work should be thus presented is unfortunate for the composer, particularly as we learn that the opening bars and the last three minutes of the missing movement are already completed. It is not fair either to the composer or to the audience to expect a final opinion based on three movements, any more than it would be to estimate the worth of Sibelius's Fifth Symphony without having heard its superb finale.[70]

After the symphony's birth pangs, and with a sense of relief, Harty wrote to Foss, perhaps detecting that the work revealed something deeply personal and nervous:

I was satisfied that what powers I possess were all given to the Symphony the other night. Whether these are powerful or mediocre is not a thing I have any means of judging. One just hopes.

Someday I should like to talk to you about the young man. Enormously gifted, something further has to happen to his soul. Did you ever notice that nothing great in art has lived that does not contain a certain goodness of soul and a larger compassionate kindness? Perhaps he has not noticed it either![71]

One cannot help but observe that the work's emotional turbulence also articulated, by strange coincidence, something of Harty's own inner turmoil. To find some peace, he spent a short time in the days before Christmas with John McCormack (who had become immensely wealthy) at the latter's mansion home at Moore Abbey, Co. Kildare, but his stay was curtailed by news of his mother's serious illness. From the Devonshire Club in London, in a troubled and

[68] Letter from Harty to Foss, 13 Sept. 1934, in private possession.
[69] Quoted in Lloyd, *William Walton*, 118.
[70] *MG*, 4 Dec. 1934; see also Sanders (ed.), *Walter Legge*, 19–20.
[71] Letter from Harty to Foss, n.d. (Dec. 1934), in private possession.

tired frame of mind, he wrote a Christmas message to Lorie, who was still in Australia:

Do you like Christmas greetings to arrive about a month late, my dear Australian Beauty? I think you are so lawless and unconventional that you won't care when they arrive. It seems to me as I grow older that only sincerity matters at all, and that if one can only tell the truth, no harm can come of it to anyone. That is why I don't tell you that I'm not in love with you – for that would be a lie, and why I don't tell you that I am, because I know that's dangerous and forbidden. So what's left? Only your own imagination and insight, and *how well* you know the whole truth about us two, and our feelings for one another!

I wish … wish … wish … well, let me wish something that's not forbidden (by some mysterious counsellor and judge who stands beside me, invisible but certain). It is that you, my strange companion, may be so happy, so radiant, so untroubled, so peaceful and constant all this coming year. 'So prays your humble and respectful servant.' This one day out of the year I am quite idle. I don't want to work, or even think much, and all I have done is go to Fortnum and Mason's and leave sums of money with them for various friends to go in and buy themselves luxuries for Christmas. Now, after writing this, I will go across to Jermyn Street and subside in a Turkish Bath, in pursuit of a more perfect figure. That is being lazy with a purpose! I am sailing to America on the 29th and shall be there until the end of February. …

… Dear Lorie, please guess what I mustn't say. If you can only guess truly how happy you ought to be! Your beloved Major Conder sent me a whole lamb for Christmas. I've given it to the sailor's home in Liverpool. The poor devils will have a good meal anyway.

I don't know if I am a good musician or not, or whether I am nice or not. I'm just dead at the moment. Ever feel like that? I'll have to go one thing or the other, I know, be austere and simple and frugal and good, or get drunk. I can't stand this present middle road. Understand? I send a special very polite and, if I dared, affectionate message to your lady mother, who knew how to be sweet and stern at the same moment. As for you, guess![72]

At the end of December Harty left for America, where he was again guest conductor of the Rochester Philharmonic Orchestra, the New York Philharmonic Orchestra and the Chicago Symphony Orchestra, who also engaged him as an adjudicator of the national composition competition (along with Frederick Stock, John Alden Carpenter and Howard Hanson).[73] In Rochester he heard from Eugene Goossens, one of the orchestra's former conductors; in his reply he offered his own negative comments about the growing prevalence for conducting from memory, a practice adopted by Toscanini:

It was delightful to hear from you after all this time. I see Leon and Marie and Sidonie fairly often in London, and we speak of you on those occasions. I am here for about 3 weeks more. Everyone is very kind and the orchestra most willing and courteous. As for this conducting from memory stunt – I quite agree with you – and wonder what would happen if one of its exponents were asked to write you

[72] Letter from Harty to Lorie Bolland, 19 Dec. 1934 (CB).

[73] *San Antonio Express*, 3 Mar. 1935.

the scores of a single concert from memory! If they could not do this accurately in every detail then they are not fit to be compared to the ordinary conductor who at least has the composers detail definitely in front of him if he desires it. Perhaps it would be a good idea to offer 10,000 dollars to anyone who could write out a single orchestral programme in detail, without a single mistake – from memory. There would be few entrants!

Delighted to hear of the excellence of your orchestra [the Cincinatti SO] – that must be a great joy to you.[74]

Unfortunately, Harty was indisposed in New York and his engagement had to be taken by Hans Lange.[75] On his return at the end of February, and affected much by the cold weather in Chicago, he made his first appearance with the BBC Symphony Orchestra, a band for whom he had, in the past, expressed mixed affections.[76] The interpretations of music by Berlioz equalled expectations, but Sibelius's Fifth Symphony was, according to *The Times*, ragged, and Schumann's Piano Concerto with Backhaus, slovenly.[77] Harty was, in fact, suffering from neuritis and was unable to conduct the LSO on 18 March (this was undertaken by Ronald). Aiming to spend a few days in Scotland, he wrote of his plans to Lorie, who had now returned to England:

Lorie dear, welcome to England. For a fortnight or so I shall be away from London. An attack of neuritis in my shoulder prevents my conducting for the moment and I am following out 'doctor's orders'. By the way, in the course of my wanderings I shall be in Scotland and shall be seeing our old friend Sir Robert Greig.

Any messages for him? I shall be back here before very long and quite recovered I hope. It was the dastardly cold in America this winter that gave me this annoying neuritis. Do send me word where I can find you on my return. A line to the Devonshire Club will get me most quickly.[78]

He was sufficiently recovered to conduct his Violin Concerto with Paul Beard and the LPO at one of the Beecham Sunday Concerts on 31 March. On this occasion Beecham directed the rest of the programme, which allowed Harty to recapture his vigour incrementally, for, a week later, he needed to be at full strength to conduct his last LSO concert of the season in his own 'Irish' Symphony, Walton's Viola Concerto and Berlioz's *Harold in Italy*, both of which featured Lionel Tertis. Though played to a modest audience, it was a fine concert after which Tertis and Harty corresponded. Tertis was clearly thinking about arranging the Violin Concerto for viola, as Harty wrote 'If so be you find anything in my Violin Concerto worth your attention, I should be honoured

---

[74] Letter from Harty to Eugene Goossens, 27 Jan. 1935, *GB-Lbl*, MS Mus.1173, fol.52.

[75] *Winnipeg Free Press*, 26 Jan. 1935.

[76] Harty was one of several guest conductors, including Beecham, Weingartner, Coates, Stravinsky and Wood.

[77] *The Times*, 7 Mar. 1935.

[78] Letter from Harty to Lorie Bolland, 14 Mar. 1935 (CB).

and delighted. But be quite frank and simple about it, if either the music itself – or its adaptability, seems unsuitable.'[79]

Being free from the trammels of an orchestral contract, Harty was extremely busy in the recording studio during 1935. For Columbia in April he and the LPO recorded the 'Funeral March for the Last Scene of *Hamlet*' from Berlioz's *Tristia*, Bax's *Overture to a Picaresque Comedy*, and his own transcription of Handel's *Music for the Royal Fireworks*. The latter, along with the 1933 recording of the *Water Music*, was sent to Buckingham Palace as a gift to Her Majesty Queen Mary.[80] Later in the year he made further recordings, this time with the LSO and the Decca label, of Berlioz's Overture *King Lear* and the *Marche troyenne*, Haydn's Symphony No. 95, and his suite of five pieces by Handel. This suite not only included his much-performed *Polonaise, Arietta and Passacaglia* but also two items recently published by Universal: the *Introduction and Rigaudon* (the first taken from the Concerto Grosso, Op. 6 No. 10, scored for string quartet and string orchestra; the second from the opera *Ariodante*, orchestrated for a classical orchestra without clarinets).

Harty had no plans during the spring and summer for another American tour and there were only a small number of regional broadcasts to undertake for the BBC. Added to which, he was still suffering from the recurring neuritis which was of concern to his doctors. He took a cruise for several weeks to Jamaica, which provided some much-needed relaxation. Also, for the first time in many years, he began to devote time to composition, and more specifically to a new set of Irish songs. He was in contact with poetess Helen Lanyon, who was delighted that Harty was interested in her verse. She replied: 'I think the omission of the last verse of 'At Easter' makes a better effect as a song, more impersonal, and therefore of more general appeal. I wonder how you liked Jamaica.'[81] He also entertained hopes of seeing Lorie again, but it was now more and more evident that Lorie wanted some form of release, while he fretted, too, that his love for her was unrequited. In April he received a letter from her and gave the forlorn reply:

> Ah, don't make that mistake, darling, 'you loved me'. ... I love you now, madly, more than can be imagined. Oh, don't you see, I am trying to live for an ideal, perhaps a foolish ideal, and I have only just sense enough to see that this ideal would be ruined and destroyed by admitting freely the other most lovely thing into my spirit – you, my beautiful darling. Ah, Lorie, you will never know what battles I have been through, or how exhausted and indifferent to life I have been left.
>
> I am even too tired to care about my sacred calling, some blind force keeps me facing forwards in that, but I feel dead and uncaring as an artist. My darling Lorie, keep love for me silently in your heart. I shall have it all my life for you.
>
> Listen, if it were for the last time, I worship, love and adore you my sweet, for ever and ever, and nothing can ever change that.

[79] Quoted in White, *Lionel Tertis*, 122.

[80] See letter from Harry Verney, Private Secretary to HM the Queen, 7 June 1935, *GB-Belqb*.

[81] Letter from Helen Lanyon to Harty, 13 Aug. 1935, *GB-Belqb*.

Your mother, with her sad wise eyes on me, in Melbourne, must have known what would happen to us. ... Could we write to each other sometimes? Surely that?

My beauty, and I *have* to do this. Yes, perhaps, my sister may still be jealous. But she has told me lately that you are sweet and good, not the Lorie I once thought I saw on a hot night in the Red Sea, you remember?

Once more, darling Lorie, do you love me? Forgive my weaknesses.[82]

In July, with great effort, they were able to meet. For Harty it was a moment of catharsis after more than a year of pent-up unhappiness:

Seeing you again was wonderful. I don't know what is the strange and magical tie between us, and I won't even tell you the effect produced on my being near you again. There are things which I know are not allowed to us, that is one of them, I mean that I must not say things like that ... but you know them all.

Oh, anyway, it would not hurt you to tell me if you truly love me. ... I think you must be, even if you were a dead woman, oblivious to all else besides the warm vital messages I continually send out to you, without really intending to do so. If you love me, I mean in that mad desperate unthinking way I do you. I see very well why we cannot meet very often, and why we must keep such a strong hold upon ourselves, for it would be so easy to destroy the barriers, and then conflagration fierce and raging and then disaster and nothingness.

And perhaps that price would, after all, be a small one for realisation and an hour of blazing joy.

People talk of priests and of hermits and devotion to great ideals. Perhaps I am one of them, only my religion is not stuffy ethics, but music. ... Did you know that it was this that has kept me from hastening us both into glorious madness?

Keep our secret always unguessed by anyone – it is sweeter so.[83]

In August he underwent a minor operation to remove his tonsils, after which he made for his habitual Westmorland hideaway. 'As you see I am in my old retreat', he wrote to Lorie, explaining:

I left the Nursing Home there four days ago and was still a little "wonky" on my legs, so I thought I'd come here to this peaceful and quiet spot where I begin to feel much better again. ... Naturally, I think of you most of the time here, for this place is dedicated to the thought of you and the only people here are my host and hostess – you and myself! I feel as if I had been through a serious illness, in many ways, and am now convalescent and fresh, and I feel that nothing can hurt me very much in the future.[84]

There was good news: Walton had completed the Finale of his symphony, an event which was recorded in *The Times* after Harty had played it through on the piano with the composer 'in a quiet square in the city of London' during the first week of September.[85] In fact Walton's symphony in its three-movement form had received two further performances by Sargent at his Courtauld series

[82] Letter from Harty to Lorie Bolland, n.d. (envelope dated 12 Apr. 1935) (CB).
[83] Letter from Harty to Lorie Bolland, 14 July 1935 (CB).
[84] Letter from Harty to Lorie Bolland, 22 Aug. 1935 (CB).
[85] *The Times*, 5 Sept. 1935.

of concerts on 1 and 2 April 1934, where one or two commentators, including Vaughan Williams, had observed that its present state was convincing enough. Harty was buoyed up by the prospect of the symphony, which was due for its premiere on 6 November with the BBCSO. In the meantime, his annual visit to the Torquay Festival was greatly enhanced by the prospect of seeing Lorie again, though he could also not help feeling dejected by the inevitability of their parting:

> On Sunday morning I'll telephone to you, for then we can see whether the day invites us to the country, which I hope, if it is very wet, we will find something else to do. But you always remind me of the country someway. You are so sweet and lovely, and I hope it will be possible to go there. After these rigours, we will come home and change and then meet to dine together, and for once to eat and drink everything we like, bad or good for us!
>
> I will not tell you much now, or perhaps anytime, but I am so hopelessly in love with you that I am afraid to permit myself to think. Fancy you really loving me. I can hardly believe it. I shall be here until Saturday morning and Lorie, my sweet girl, I can't help it. I love you and every inch and thought of you with all my heart.
>
> Hay
>
> One thing I especially want you to do when we part on Sunday. Do you mind making it quite casual and quick as if we were meeting next day? I'm not looking for extra wounds, are you?[86]

At Torquay Harty conducted the municipal band in performances of Berlioz's 'Royal Hunt and Storm', Dvořák's 'New World' Symphony, Tomansini's *The Good-humoured Ladies* (an orchestration of Scarlatti), and Henri Casadesus's transcription of a Handel Sonata for viola da gamba, arranged for viola and string orchestra and played by the up-and-coming virtuoso William Primrose.

Although Harty's contract with the LSO had come to an end, he continued to work with them on a freelance basis but on an equal footing with other orchestras. In this way he accepted far more engagements for regional live broadcasts of studio concerts and grew closer to the BBC. This was signalled by the premiere of the complete Walton Symphony on 6 November, when Harty conducted the BBCSO. The public anticipation, generated by Edwin Evans in the *Radio Times* and Stephen Williams in the *Evening Standard*, was colossal.[87] Indeed, such was the exhilaration of the occasion that Harty kept an entire scrapbook of the ecstatic newspaper reviews. After the performance the *News Chronicle* reported Harty as saying that 'it was the finest work he had ever produced for the first time.'[88] Lambert was lavish in his praise for Harty's sympathetic reading, and rather originally described the Finale as a movement that '[recalls] the eighteenth century in that it represents a facet of experience and not a final attitude'.[89] But perhaps most gratifying was Cardus's critique in the *Manchester*

---

[86] Letter from Harty to Lorie Bolland, 9 Oct. 1935 (CB).

[87] See E. Evans, 'Unique World Premiere for a New Symphony', *Radio Times*, 1 Nov. 1935; S. Williams, 'An English Composer', *Evening Standard*, 5 Nov. 1935.

[88] *News Chronicle*, 7 Nov. 1935.

[89] *Sunday Referee*, 10 Nov. 1935.

Guardian, which judged his interpretation as 'absolutely right, and a remarkable act of sensibility and technical control'.[90] From Walton, whose comments Harty must have valued deeply, came the following brief communication:

> I should just like to let you know how very grateful I am to you for the infinite trouble care and energy you put into the performance last night. There is no way of describing it except by that well worn word inspired but it is certainly true in this case.[91]

The symphony was recorded by Decca with the LSO on 10 and 11 December. Such an event was then considered out of the ordinary, not least because the recording company agreed to take on a lengthy modern work by a composer who was not yet a household name.[92] It also proved to be Harty's last recording. Later, he conducted the work for a regional broadcast on 1 March 1936, a performance which prompted John Ireland to express his own approbation of Walton's talent:

> I feel I must write to thank you for your splendid performance of the Walton Symphony on Sunday night. It was the kind of performance any composer would envy, and Walton is very lucky to have such an interpreter of his work which in your hands impresses me as the finest British work since Elgar.
>
> The performance was masterly and extremely moving, and I shall always remember it as a vital musical experience.[93]

Two weeks after the elation of the Walton premiere, Harty gave another important first performance, this time of Bax's new Sixth Symphony. This took place within an interesting international context. The British Council for Relations with Other Countries had extended invitations to European music critics during the week of 17 November in order to hear three modern symphonies by British composers played by three London orchestras. Ronald conducted the LSO in Elgar's Second Symphony, Boult directed the BBCSO in Vaughan Williams's recent Fourth Symphony, while Harty concluded the week with the new Bax work on 21 November. At a luncheon on 18 November, organised by the Critics' Circle, Harty took the opportunity to air his long-held frustrations about the funding of orchestras and the lack of Continental appreciation for British musicians abroad. 'London', he complained:

> is often referred to nowadays, with complacency, as 'one of the world's musical centres'. Perhaps it is – for others. ... Music is, or should be, an international language, but up to the present there has been too much 'one way' internationalism in this country and I cannot see why we should feel any shame in pointing it out.[94]

Over the years Harty had been a stalwart supporter of Bax's music, and Bax had considerable trust in Harty's ability to understand his scores.

[90] *MG*, 7 Nov. 1935.

[91] Letter from Walton to Harty, 7 Nov. [1935], *GB-Belqb*.

[92] See Foss's account of the recording sessions in *The Gramophone*, Feb. 1953, 228.

[93] Letter from John Ireland to Harty, 3 Mar. 1936, *GB-Belqb*.

[94] Hamilton H. Harty, 'Music in England': luncheon for the Critics' Circle, London, 18 Nov. 1935, *GB-Belqb*.

On this occasion the composer gave the following advice about the slow movement:

> I think that secret of the second movement of the symphony is to keep the mood, throughout, *cool* and far-away, with no 'points' or rubatos. (The heading 'molto espressivo' is wrong and misleading.) Perhaps if we can make it a remote West-Highland unhuman dream it may turn out rather charmingly. But you of all people, know what to do about this.[95]

Reception of the Bax was mixed, though McNaught called it a 'glowing and supremely effective performance'[96] and *The Times* an example of the composer's 'unfailing sense of beauty'.[97] Bax himself was delighted and wrote to Harty directly after the concert:

> I must send you a line at once, *late* and rather drunk … and I am to thank you for that wonderful performance. You realized everything I wanted, and indeed took some of it into a work of beauty I did not know the work compassed. I am only afraid that no-one (except maybe yourself), will ever re-create to-night's experience for me. I am sure it was the best first performance any work ever had.[98]

After the Bax premiere Harty had another important engagement, this one with the LSO. At a concert on 2 December which included rare performances by him of Mozart's Symphony No. 30 (with Harty's usual reduced forces) and Dvořák's Seventh Symphony, he introduced the British public to Bizet's unknown, youthful Symphony in C. This had been discovered among the composer's manuscripts in the Paris Conservatoire by Jean Chantavoine in 1933, and was the subject of an article for the French journal *Le Ménéstrel*.[99] Douglas Charles Parker, Bizet's first British biographer, then introduced the manuscript to Weingartner, who directed the first performance in Basel on 26 February 1935. At first there was a certain confusion when John W. Klein erroneously announced the work as Bizet's 'Roma' Symphony,[100] a more mature work in the same key, which provoked a flurry of correspondence in the months that followed.[101] After the concert, however, there was no doubting the prodigious nature of Bizet's gifts, and among the enthusiastic press who heard inchoate shades of *Carmen* and *The Fair Maid of Perth*, Lambert urged a repeat performance the following season.[102] For Harty, it was the subject of another scrapbook to add to those of Walton and Bax.

After the success of the Bizet symphony Harty took himself off to Harrogate for some spa treatment. Although he had been able to conduct, the physical

[95] Letter from Bax to Harty, n.d. (Nov. 1935?), *GB-Belqb*.

[96] *Evening News*, 22 Nov. 1935.

[97] *The Times*, 22 Nov. 1935.

[98] Letter from Bax to Harty, 21 Nov. 1935, *GB-Belqb*.

[99] J. Chantavoine, 'Quelques inédits de Georges Bizet', *Le ménestrel* (4 Aug.–22 Sept. 1933). See also Parker's letter to *MT* 76 (1936), 155.

[100] J. W. Klein, 'Bizet's "Roma" Symphony', *MT* 75 (1935), 1078–9.

[101] See letters by John Russell and C. D. Parker to *MT* 76 (1936), 155.

[102] *Sunday Referee*, 8 Dec. 1935.

strain had exacerbated the problem of his arm and shoulder. Giving his apologies to the entrepreneur Sir Harry Preston, he wrote:

I have been suffering recently from neuritis of the arm and shoulder, which has made my work of conducting very difficult and very painful. After Christmas I am obliged to go to America on an orchestral tour, and my Doctors absolutely refuse to let me consider fulfilling these engagements unless I take steps to get rid of the neuritis which has plagued me so long. In the circumstances I have felt obliged to listen to their advice and after my next London engagement on December 2nd I have undertaken to transfer myself to Harrogate and to follow a course of treatment there. I am sure you will appreciate that it is only the really important question of health which prevents my accepting your most kind invitation, and I am really deeply disappointed that I cannot be with you.[103]

On 4 December he wrote to Lorie with the news that he would be undertaking a further American tour in January and February of 1936:

You may wonder why you have not heard from me since you left England. The reason is simple. I developed bad neuritis in my arm and shoulder and couldn't face using a pen. I managed to carry on with my engagements strangely enough. While conducting I was more or less free from pain, but afterwards it always came back, only worse than before. However, it is showing signs of abating and I hope to finish it off by a course of treatment here. You see, I don't want to face America in January with anything like that wrong. I sail on Jan 9th the 'President Roosevelt'. I shall be back in England early in March to fulfil a number of engagements including a rather amusing series of lectures over the wireless about music and people. I say 'amusing' because they have recklessly given me *carte blanche* to say just what I please, and I rather expect to raise up some trouble with certain sections of the public. I mean the fashionable and semi-fashionable sheep who try to influence the equally ignorant more honest sheep typified by the 'general public'". Poor 'general public'. I like them so much better than the pretentious sheep that browse in Mayfair fields.[104]

He was by no means over his love affair with her, and his belief in the paranormal informed a disturbed dream he had during his summer holiday in Westmorland:

That night I couldn't sleep, and lay awake until dawn, just as it got dimly light, a woman walked through the door of my dressing-room, crossed the room, by the foot of my bed, walked over to the wall, turned, as if puzzled, and walked out again. She was brown-haired, and her hair was done up at the back of her neck in a way that is not, I think, much used now.

I thought it was you. But you didn't look at me – you appeared troubled and puzzled. I asked my hostess if there was anyone in the house like the description I gave her. She said no, but that at dawn the dogs had been disturbed and howled and cried very fearfully.

[103] Letter from Harty to Sir Harry Preston, 27 Nov. 1935, *GB-Belqb*.
[104] Letter from Harty to Lorie Bolland, 4 Dec. 1935 (CB).

Then her husband got cross and I thought it better to shut up. Some people are afraid of ghosts.[105]

On Christmas Eve and Christmas Day Harty appeared in broadcasts with the flautist Lambert Flack and the harpist Sidonie Goossens in his orchestration of *In Ireland* (which had been completed in August); the programme also included his Concerto for Orchestra with Organ and Bizet's early symphony. In the new year he travelled to Ireland with Jelly D'Arányi to give broadcast concerts in Belfast and Dublin of his Violin Concerto, before making what would prove to be his last journey to America. He appeared again as guest conductor for the Chicago Symphony Orchestra and gave the American premiere of Walton's symphony there on 23 January 1936. Its reception was far from enthusiastic. In the *Chicago Tribune* the following day Edward Barry commented:

> The imposing Walton Symphony was finished only last year and performed in London under Sir Hamilton in November. Last night marked its first hearing, I believe, outside of England. It was rather coldly received by Chicago and there is good reason to think that the applause that followed it was intended for the conductor rather than the symphony. The reason was the obvious restlessness of the audience during the performance.[106]

The Chicago subscription concerts followed a pattern of a Thursday evening programme followed by a Friday afternoon matinée at which some of the music from the Thursday programme usually appeared. A further Tuesday afternoon matinée then often featured a work from the previous Thursday and Friday concerts. Harty's intention was to repeat the Walton symphony in both the Friday and Tuesday 'matinées', but at the Friday performance most of the audience walked out and those that remained offered only token applause after the Walton was completed. Harty was visibly astonished by this response to a work he believed in so implicitly. Indeed, so stung was he by the audience's reaction that he withdrew the work for the following Tuesday where it was due to be performed alongside Sibelius's Seventh Symphony. On the morning of the Tuesday a special announcement was printed in the press:

> Sir Hamilton Harty surrenders to the musical stand-patters of Chicago and withdraws the Walton Symphony for the symphony matinee today, substituting the Dvořák 'New World'. Too many walked out on the Walton and the famous Irishman decided that Chicago does not want it. He may be right, but there was a time when German audiences walked out on Dvořák.[107]

The Tuesday matinée, which went without a hitch, was Harty's last appearance with the Chicago Symphony Orchestra. On a happier note, De Paul University conferred an honorary doctorate on him, which was of great satisfaction to his sponsor, the Dean of the Graduate School Alexander Schorsch:

---

[105] Letter from Harty to Lorie Bolland, 4 Dec. 1935 (CB).

[106] *Chicago Tribune*, 24 Jan. 1936.

[107] *Herald Examiner*, 28 Jan. 1936.

It has been a great happiness to me that I was instrumental in having you honored. I am also very much indebted to you because of the intense pleasure and joy which your music and your company have given me. Do not forget to let me know when you are ready for the Hungarian goulash at my mother's. I am waiting hopefully to hear Liszt's 'Hunnenschlacht', and I know I shall like it. I am sure you'd capture the Hungarians with this composition. When you are next in our city, please come to our University at 64 East Lake Street so that I may show you more of it than you have already seen.[108]

Harty then enjoyed a brief vacation to Jamaica on board the *Ariguani* before undertaking further conducting engagements for the Rochester Philharmonic.

Returning to England, there was but brief time to prepare for a major performance in London of Berlioz's *Grande Messe des morts* and the *Symphonie funèbre et triomphale* at Queen's Hall on 4 March. For this the BBC had agreed to a considerable financial outlay to afford the major forces of the BBCSO and Choral Society and the BBC Military Band. Queen's Hall was packed. The massive additional brass was positioned in the two organ galleries and both sides of the balcony. Earlier, on 2 March at 9.15 p.m., Harty also broadcast an introductory talk on Berlioz. Although this was designed to provide prefatory information about the large-scale concert and the infrequent performance of such costly works, Harty also focused on the perennial partisan question of Berlioz's standing as a composer. He had already touched upon this issue in an article called 'The Approach to Berlioz', printed in *The Music Teacher* a decade before (in September 1926). With such mixed critical views of the Frenchman, the 'Berlioz problem' came to a head in 1928 when Hubert Foss convened a discussion in a well-known Soho restaurant to create a forum of debate among his champions and detractors. Harty and Van Dieren were enthusiastically for Berlioz, Edwin Evans, in the chair, was equivocal, whilst Percy Scholes, Percy Buck, M. D. Calvocoressi, Harvey Grace and Foss himself all voiced their reservations. The proceedings of the meeting were later printed in *Berlioz: Being the Report of a Discussion Held on December 17, 1928*, published in 1929 by Oxford University Press. To Harty, Berlioz was no less than 'an isolated genius … an architect, who without expert advice taught himself not only to design his own buildings but also to make his own bricks and erect his own scaffolding.' In this he could feel direct personal sympathy. But the secret of Berlioz's music was always, he ardently believed, driven by poetical rather than musical stimuli. It was this essential point he communicated to the Soho gathering in 1928 along with the imperative that the music was only truly successful when, in performance, it was injected with commensurate insight:

Among familiar technical accusations brought against Berlioz are that his melody is commonplace, his harmony thin, his modulations awkward, and his material demands as regards numbers excessive. A casual glance at his scores seems to support some of these arguments, and indeed there are not many even amongst his warmest admirers who have not been baffled and puzzled at times by what looks like weakness and ineffectiveness. But so many of these obscurities have

---

[108] Letter from Alexander Schorsch to Harty, 4 Feb. 1936, *GB-Belqb*.

proved to be no longer obscure when interpreted with a particular emotion or colour, the clue to which is to be found in something which does not seem to lie in, or be suggested by, the music itself, that one soon becomes chary of condemning other puzzles still unsolved.[109]

Critical reception to his BBC performance of the *Grande Messe* and *Symphonie funèbre* was, in the main, positive, and no more so than from Lambert, an avowed Berlioz admirer. His plaudits for Harty were unrestrained:

Although Beecham, like Monteux, shows a superb appreciation of certain aspects of Berlioz's genius, Harty has always struck me as the born Berlioz conductor. One is never made conscious of the interpretative side of the proceedings – it is as though the composer himself were directing the orchestra.

Admirers of Berlioz can never repay their debt to Sir Hamilton Harty, whose career as a Berlioz conductor reached its climax on Wednesday.[110]

Colles's review in *The Times*, however, was more predictably equivocal, and Harty wrote a letter of protest at some of the pejorative terms that had been used. Colles's reply typically encapsulated the polarised the views of Berlioz that continued to prevail:

Thank you for your letter. I always like to get a letter from a musician about music however much we may differ. Most of *my* correspondence with musicians is about themselves which is boring for me.

Now about Berlioz:-

1. First I plead guilty, although the sentence which you quote did not appear in *The Times*. Whatever was there said was 'chords for high flutes and a bass trombone'. It should have been 'a trombone bass', the point being not a particular kind of trombone or the number of instruments employed. Of course I know the passage well, and Berlioz 's quotation and explanation of it in the *Treatise*. When a concert ends only a little before 11 pm one has no time to go into details of orchestration.

2. I cannot agree that my notice was 'unfavourable'. I spoke of the *Requiem* as a work which every musician should hear as often as he can, and fully acknowledged its 'genius'. At the late hour I could only afford a few summary words as to the quality of the performance.

3. Generally speaking these differences about Berlioz puzzle me a bit. I can understand that the conductors' and the listeners' views are naturally different. What goes for little or nothing to the latter must be commonly interesting to the conductor who has to get it done.

But between two listeners the differences are equally acute, and what seems a positive offence to the one seems a stroke of genius to the other. I admit the genius but find it hard to swallow the 'offences'. The flutes and 8 tenor trombones seem to me not to be genius at all but a trivial display of ingenuity.

[109] H. Hamilton Harty, 'The Approach to Berlioz', *The Music Teacher* (Sept. 1926).
[110] *Sunday Referee*, 8 Mar. 1936.

Again the Berlioz enthusiasts want me to bow down to every note he wrote, and why should I? Most of his big works seem to me to be padded out with very poor stuff, and the reason for this surely is that he started with enormous conceptions which he then tried to body forth. Most of the big people have started with little shapes, Bach with organ and clavier preludes and fugues, Haydn, Mozart etc with slight sonata patterns etc, and such seeds have germinated till they reached to the B minor Mass, the *Creation*, and the *Zauberflöte*.

It is not, as has been often said of Berlioz, a matter of imperfect 'education' in the technical sense. He could acquire all the technique he needed in his own way. It is a matter of mental outlook towards what is big and what is little in ideas. Berlioz jumbled them up.

You may tell me that I am quite wrong about this, but the conviction remains as unshaken as is yours in the opposite direction.

If I used my conviction to warn people off Berlioz it would be wrong, but I don't. I think you perfectly right to do his works and to use all your conviction to display them at their best to the public – I congratulate you on a very fine achievement.[111]

Other letters nevertheless confirmed that Harty's promotion of Berlioz's grandest choral work had brought not only pleasure but fascination, too. From Frits Brase, conductor of the Dublin Philharmonic Society and head of the Army School of Music, came the following adulation: 'You saw and we heard how your audience enjoyed it. What an instrumentation, the use of the pedal notes of the bass Trombone and the solo part for that instrument. Those chords for the wind and the low Trombones, a shiver ran down my spine. You are a master conductor.'[112] A telegram of congratulations came from McCormack, and a note from Sacheverall Sitwell condemning *The Times* column:

Your concert was superb and wonderful. I do not believe there is another musician alive, German, Italian, or Russian who could have done it.

How maddening the 'Times' has been: it is a somnambulist paper and fell asleep long before 1840, or whenever the 'Symphonie funèbre et triomphale' was written.

Next year I do hope you will give 'La Impériale': and the 'Menace of the Franks', which Wootton says in his book has a magnificent march. Don't bother to answer this note, as it is only to tell you how much everyone in the audience enjoyed the concert. I cannot think the 'Tuba Mirum' ever sounded more terrifying.[113]

From Manchester he received a heart-warming letter from a loyal friend, who, having heard the Berlioz broadcast, was nostalgic for the old days at the Hallé when Harty's performances of Berlioz had been the stuff of legend:

It will, no doubt, afford you a certain amount of surprise to hear from me again, after the passage of time which has lapsed since the happy Manchester days. The excuse is that my knowledge of you these days is not so much *when* you will be in a certain spot, but *where* you *were* at a given time. I have in this way, however, followed your movements, and must say how pleased I was to hear your voice a

[111] Letter from H. C. Colles to Harty, 8 Mar. 1936, *GB-Belqb*.
[112] Letter from Frits Brase to Harty, 5 Mar. 1936, *GB-Belqb*.
[113] Letter from Sacheverall Sitwell, 7 Mar. 1936, *GB-Belqb*.

fortnight ago, and ten days ago to hear the magnificent Berlioz performance you gave at the Queen's Hall. With the aid of the Hallé programmes of the occasions when each of the items were given in Manchester, I was able to appreciate the grandness of the effect. The 'Funeral' Symphony particularly left a feeling of regret that yourself and Berlioz have been lost to Manchester. The 'Harty touch' is sadly missed at the Hallé these days, and there is a genuine feeling amongst a large section of the audience and also the Orchestra that it would be worth anything almost to have you back. There is not a remote chance of this, is there? Since you left, nineteen Conductors of all shapes and sizes have 'experimented' with the fine body of players which you, in your time, moulded into what everyone recognised as the Hallé Orchestra.

Next Thursday Beecham is attempting the 'Fantastique' of Berlioz, which is the first time since you went that a Berlioz item has appeared in the programmes. We are literally starved of good music. There are however still recordings of the Hallé under your baton, with which we can console ourselves, but they are all insufficient. The Brahms Violin Concerto recorded by you, with Szigeti, is still one of my treasured possessions.

Talking of records, could you inform if there is still in existence the performance of Wormser's 'L'Enfant Prodigue' which you recorded some years ago? For your efforts on the piano are as greatly appreciated by me as your larger efforts on the 'rostrum'.

Is all the globe-trotting congenial to you, or have you any regrets? I read something recently about yourself and the 'Philadelphia'. The world's finest ensemble, in my estimation, and one which would do you great credit as a conductor, but it would deprive this country of the even rare chances it has now of hearing your wonderful performances.

Whatever your decision, and wherever you go, you have the assurance that there are old friends who still think of you and wish you well, and not the least of these, myself.

May you have a just appreciation of your sterling worth, shown, wherever you may decide to go.[114]

Harty's final concert of the 1935–6 season was with the LSO. Besides the customary Berlioz and the Handel–Casadesus concerto with Primrose, it featured two works he had not conducted before: Bruckner's Sixth Symphony and Holbrooke's symphonic poem *Queen Mab*. His diary was, however, busy until July with broadcasts for the BBC in both London and Northern Ireland, which included an all-Sibelius concert (30 May), and, in Belfast, a further hearing of the Bizet Symphony (6 June). On 23 March he conducted the wind and brass of the BBCSO in a programme of Mozart's Serenade, K361, and Stravinsky's *Symphonies of Winds* (which he must have found aesthetically challenging). He encouraged young players such as the seventeen-year-old Russian émigré pianist Nina Milkina; he worked with Orrea Pernel, the young English violinist, the contralto Muriel Brunskill, the pianist Kendall Taylor, and Isobel Baillie, with whom he appeared as pianist in a BBC programme of his own songs on 13 June. It was quite like old times, before his years with the Hallé, but now he enjoyed a

[114] Letter from George E. Draper to Harty, 16 Mar. 1936, *GB-Belqb*.

new artistic freedom and success at the top of his profession. Yet, in spite of the adulation he received, he was aware of a persistent, gnawing tiredness, apathy, even an indifference, which, aside from the neuritis, he could not shake off. It was, unbeknown to him, the first signs of the cancer that would prematurely kill him, but for the moment he hoped that a holiday to Ireland would provide the customary, reliable and much-needed panacea.

The Last Years:
The Children of Lir – A Creative Codicil

HARTY often holidayed in Ireland during the months of May and June and 1936 was no exception. Although he usually frequented Donaghadee, Rostrevor or Carlingford Lough close to the Mourne mountains, on this occasion he spent the summer at Portballintrae, a delightful seaside village east of Portrush and west of the 'Giant's Causeway, rich in views and a bracing seascape. In England, perhaps in his favourite spot at Lambrigg, he had planned a period of quietness to fulfil a request from Universal (who had done well from his Handel transcriptions) to orchestrate some of Chopin's piano music; there was also the need to recharge his batteries in preparation for a European tour in the autumn to Poland and Yugoslavia.[1] But his friends were clearly concerned for his health and urged him to use his time in Ireland to recuperate as fully as possible. In his Portballintrae hotel Harty hired a piano and befriended some of the locals, including James Moore, a young organist in the town of Bushmills close by, who was delighted to establish the acquaintance of such an eminent musician and fellow Ulsterman. Harty, Moore, and the conductor DeLamarter from Chicago, who came to Portballintrae for a week, travelled around the locality in Moore's decrepit car. An additional visit came from a childhood companion, Sir William Thomson, who was now Professor of Medicine at Queen's University. Thomson grew up close to Harty in neighbouring Annahilt in Co. Down where his father was a dispensing doctor. Harty's father taught the Thomson daughters music, which left the boys to play; they remained firm friends despite the divergence of their professions. Thomson followed his father into the medical profession and rose to distinguished heights and, by the 1930s, he had reached the zenith of his career.[2] When Thomson became aware of Harty's presence in Ulster, and having been told of his condition by mutual friends, he travelled out to see him. After a preliminary examination he realised that his old friend was ill, but, because symptoms were still only slightly discernible, it was difficult to make an accurate diagnosis.

The fresh and stimulating air of the Antrim coast did Harty good, but the weather was poor. Bad news also came from the violinist Sybil Eaton about the death of Plunket Greene on 19 August:

> Harry [Plunket Greene] was too ill for me to read him your last letter. He was constantly given morphine throughout the last week, and his mind wandered (though not unhappily) a great part of the time. But he had occasional clear periods and in one of the last of these I said you had spoken of doing the Requiem

---

[1] See *The Times*, 23 Dec. 1938.

[2] H. W. Gallagher, 'Sir William Thomson, Physician', *Ulster Medical Journal* 42(1) (1973), 16.

or the Stabat Mater at the C. V. S. concert. And he said 'Tell him to do the Stabat Mater – it's a more original work.' I am writing to give you this message from him.

I know you loved him – I always remember your once saying to me that there would be other Kreislers and Casals – but never another Harry Greene. It is some comfort for us to know that he suffered practically no pain, that he was able to do his work till the end, and that he never knew he was walking off a platform for the last time.[3]

More to the point, Harty's underlying physical condition had not improved by the end of August, when he had to return to England to fulfil engagements. For a BBC broadcast on 28 August he performed Strauss's *Enoch Arden* at the piano with the speaker Henry Ainley, and during September and October it was time for the usual south coast music festivals at Folkestone and Torquay. At Folkestone, with a small but attentive band, he directed Brahms's Fourth Symphony, Stanford's Fourth *Irish Rhapsody* and his *Ode to a Nightingale* with Isobel Baillie, while at Bournemouth he conducted Beethoven's Violin Concerto with Issay Schlaen. Percy Whitlock, borough organist at the Municipal Pavilion, recalled the occasion and sensed from Harty's behaviour that things were wrong. At the morning rehearsal he gave the orchestra an unusually long fifty-minute break while he went to the station. Later, at the concert:

'[he] rolled in 10 min[utes] late as casual as you please. Monty [Birch, the leader of the orchestra] was just going on to conduct the Overture – & just saved HH from going on in hat and coat! He looked vague and dazed. Craen says he was tight … The band were thoroughly unhappy & couldn't see the beat properly.[4]

It is possible that Harty may have had too much to drink, but it is just as likely that the symptoms of his illness were beginning to reveal themselves. On 22 September he wrote his last letter to Lorie, who was again in Australia. In it he continued to blame the chill he had caught in Chicago for the succession of illnesses he had suffered since. Impatient with each doctor he had consulted, he was recommended to Oscar Brunler, whom, he had been informed, performed cures with the use of light rays:

This is a proper English autumn day. After a disappointing summer, cold and wet, here we are in the old misty foggy autumn days – which can only give place to winter permanently, and even that will be preferable to the present discouraging weather. … Since last winter in Chicago where I acquired a fierce chill in a blizzard, I have not been well. Cold after cold finally settled down into what is known as chronic catarrh, and for a long time I have been the sport and plaything of doctors – each with a different regime. A month in my native Northern Ireland didn't help much as it was cold and wet there. Since I came back here I have been a kind of storing place for all kinds of medicine which I hope will eventually have a good effect. But I am getting very tired of 'all that'.

… A friend of mine who is kind enough to be worried about my ill-health sent me to a famous Swedish scientist, a Dr Oscar Brunler, who performs wonderful cures by means of light rays, and also by means of his strong will-power. I have

[3] Letter from Sybil Eaton to Harty, 23 Aug. 1936, *GB-Belqb*.
[4] M. Riley, *Percy Whitlock* (London: Thames Publishing, 1998), 110.

been to him 3 or 4 times and he has burnt off most of the skin of my body, done me good all the same.

He is a tall and handsome man with a strong and good face, deeply lined by various spiritual experiences, and his simple faith is that all illness starts in the spirit and must be attacked there if the bodily reflection is to be cured. Very sound and logical, I think. He has some strange theories and holds that we are surrounded by invisible forces – 'Powers and principalities' – which can help us if we lay ourselves open to them. Some are evil – but still can and will help us. Evil and good are names invented by man – so he says – and the only right way to regard them is as manifestations of power. I agree with him to a great extent, but am still rather scared of the evil side. He is most interesting to talk with and has written many fine books on his pet subjects.

Last time I saw him, about a week ago, he collected all his 'ray' machines and put up a terrific barrage of light and heat. Towards the end, when I was almost exhausted, he suddenly turned the combined power – a blaze like fierce sunshine on my face. I nearly died. It was just like staring into the sun at close quarters. I was blinded and think I became unconscious.[5]

The visits to Brunler were ineffective, even though Harty continued a course of treatment with him. He informed Lorie that he had received an invitation from the Carl Rosa Opera Company to become their principal conductor. He demurred, though another invitation to Australia, this time for twelve months, was an attractive prospect: 'I said there were reasons why I'd like to go, and thought to myself, that'll keep you guessing! But I don't think it did someway! Now when the affair is decided, there *are* reasons why I *love* Australia better that anywhere. Guess!'[6] Yet, there was nothing in his letter that seemed ominous. After this their correspondence ceased for reasons which we can only surmise. Lorie, it appears, had always wished for their liaison to remain deeply private. Unlike Harty, who was estranged from his wife, Lorie had no desire to undermine her second marriage.[7] Whether she genuinely loved Harty is also a matter of some conjecture, but that she harboured some genuine platonic affection for him is surely indicated by her retention of all his letters. As for Harty, the end of the relationship must have come as a real sadness to him. He had, after all, spent many years both mentally and physically alone, and Lorie's sudden appearance in his life had brought both excitement and emotional energy. Whether he ceased to write to her at her request is unknown, though with the onset of his illness he may have reached this decision himself.

In early October he was in Torquay, where he shared the week's concerts with Boult and Albert Coates. On 9 October he conducted a live broadcast with the BBCSO in his *Comedy Overture*, Mendelssohn's First Piano Concerto with the Manchester pianist Edward Isaacs, and works by Sibelius and Pierné. Then came what was to be his last major public concert with the LSO, at Queen's Hall on 16 October, one that featured Rachmaninov in his *Rhapsody on a Theme of Paganini*,

---

[5] Letter from Harty to Lorie Bolland, 22 Sept. 1936 (CB).

[6] Letter from Harty to Lorie Bolland, 22 Sept. 1936 (CB).

[7] The matter, it appears, remained entirely unknown to her family, and is conspicuously absent from the autobiography which she later prepared.

Beethoven's *Leonora* No. 3, and Schubert's Ninth Symphony. The reception for Harty was enthusiastic but it was undoubtedly a strain. Thomson was called to London to examine him, and though he found nothing as yet to suggest that Harty was seriously ill, he advised him to cancel his European tour and to give up all engagements in London and elsewhere until after the new year. The announcement in *The Times* was peculiarly vague. It stated that Harty had 'an infection of the nasal sinuses' and might have to undergo an operation. In fact, what Thomson finally discovered was that his friend had an advanced malignant growth in the right antrum of the brain. This had been the underlying cause of his symptoms for a year or more. Harty went to stay with the Thomsons at their home in University Square in Belfast, where a number of specialists came to examine him. When the reality of his condition was finally discovered – the prognosis was fatal – Thomson decided to withhold the full truth, perhaps because, before Harty succumbed to the terminal effects of his illness, he might be spared for a year or two more where music-making and composition were possible. Hope was placed in the Radium Institute, and a protracted course of treatment was ordered for 1937. It must have been a harrowing time, not least because, after the radium treatment commenced, Harty had to endure the removal of his right eye in a surgical operation to remove the tumour. Not long after this he was able to return to his home in St John's Wood, where he was visited by Isobel Baillie. Her recollection of their meeting was poignant:

> I will never forget 'Hay' at his London home in St John's Wood shortly after he had undergone a serious and what was to prove an unsuccessful operation. He asked me to sing to him and I obliged with his *Across the Door*, a song I regularly included in my recitals devoted exclusively to his own compositions as well as in more general programmes. After the concluding *pianissimo* phrase 'his kiss upon my mouth' there was silence. Then, softly, he asked that I sing it again. We were both deeply moved and when I left there were tears in his eyes.[8]

Little could Baillie know that the language and passion of the song opened deeply personal, emotional wounds which he never felt at liberty to divulge.

An ordeal the radiation treatment might have been, but Harty showed signs of rallying. He continued to spend time with the Thomsons in Belfast, and a period of convalescence in the Great Northern Hotel at Rostrevor. He also spent days at his London home working, writing and answering letters, besides making tentative plans for the future. He received a welcome letter from Walford Davies in his capacity as Master of the King's Music. Preparations were well in train for the Coronation of George VI in May. 'It looks to me, at first glance', Davies wrote, 'as if the Overture might be exactly right for some part of the incidental music at the Coronation, and I, for one, shall be delighted if it can be included. I am sending it on to Bullock.'[9] In the event, Harty's arrangement of

---

[8] Baillie, *Never Sing Louder than Lovely*, 36. Baillie states that she never saw Harty again after their meeting, but this was not true, for they met again at the first performance of *The Children of Lir* in March 1939, when Baillie performed the wordless soprano part.

[9] Letter from Walford Davies to Harty, 27 Jan. 1937 (SW).

Handel's Concerto for Orchestra with Organ began the introductory music in Westminster Abbey at 8.45 a.m. on Coronation Day. During his absence from the capital he had not been able to attend Tertis's last public performance (in celebration of his sixtieth birthday) to hear *Harold in Italy* and the Walton Viola Concerto with the BBCSO under Ernest Ansermet. Tertis's retirement from the platform had been brought about by acute fibrositis in his right arm. Public sympathy and interest from the press had been, for the viola virtuoso, quite unexpected. In answer to a sympathetic letter from Harty came the reply:

> It has taken me all this time to try and answer your most beautiful letter to me – firstly because I am quite overcome that you, our greatest interpreter, should think so much of my puny efforts in the cause of music, secondly that with all the physical suffering you are going through, you write and comfort me, thirdly because I am still under daily treatment, fourthly because we have let the house, and are in the throes of the miserable job of packing up, and fifthly because I am just beginning to pull myself together and take stock of the situation – having said all this I sincerely hope you will soon be well again for all our sakes. I have taken to heart all the advice and gracious things you have said to me and I hope eventually to still be of some little use in the cause of our musical effort.[10]

To his close friend the tenor Parry Jones, who had recently appeared in the demanding role of Mephistopheles in the first hearing (as a BBC concert performance) of Busoni's *Dr Faustus* in England on 17 March under Boult, he wrote an encouraging letter after the press's response was lukewarm:

> I thought that both Busoni's conception of Mephistopheles as a high tenor, and your splendid reading of the part, were equally admirable. I don't think the press treated you half well enough, but they never do, and probably you have learnt to ignore them, which is the only proper attitude. It was, I thought, so specially stupid to quarrel with Busoni's idea of making Mephistopheles a tenor. Certainly to me, listening in, those blazing high passages which you did so extraordinarily well gave me the right idea of the Evil One, as being of flaming magnificence as well as of sinister and grotesque make-up.[11]

It was a fortifying letter to which Parry Jones replied with gratitude:

> I hardly know how to start to thank you for your lovely letter, and the grand things you say about my singing in Dr Faustus.
>
> It was a trying work to sing but I got great enjoyment out of it, and it was extremely interesting to have the opportunity of interpreting the role of Mephistopheles.
>
> The less we think about the press, and the less we take notice of them, the better for our sanity. I've never read such appalling ignorance as the critics displayed in their notices of Busoni's work.
>
> However, I've ceased to take notice of them, and shall take your advice, and just carry on to the best of my ability.

---

[10] Letter from Tertis to Harty, 29 Mar. 1937, *GB-Belqb*.
[11] Letter from Harty to Parry Jones, 11 Apr. 1937, *GB-Lbl*, MS Mus.1117.

> I can never thank you sufficiently for your … friendship, and your constant and unshakeable belief in me, which I can honestly say is a source of inspiration.
>
> Again my thanks and alas my very sincere hope that we shall very soon see you back in harness full of the strength of life.[12]

After the radium treatment was over, Harty spent a few weeks in mid-summer in Rostrevor and in the following July and August he made a further visit to Jamaica, where he benefited much from the sunshine and warmth of the Caribbean climate. When he returned to London he felt refreshed and, though not ready as such to take on any conducting engagements, he was invigorated enough to resume composition, something that had only occupied him intermittently throughout the 1920s. He had already begun to sketch material for a set of Irish songs in 1935, but now he put himself to the task with renewed commitment.

One of the major regrets that his illness had necessitated was the cancellation of engagements in London in the last part of 1936 and early 1937. This entailed handing over responsibility for a performance of Mahler's *Das Lied von der Erde* and Berlioz's *Romeo and Juliet* for the Royal Philharmonic Society in October and December respectively, Delius's *A Mass of Life* in Liverpool, and the first London performance of Harty's own piano concerto with Boult and the BBCSO, in which the composer himself was to have been the soloist. But perhaps the greatest disappointment came later in 1937 when Moeran announced that he had finally completed his symphony in Ireland that January, a work which Harty had commissioned at the Hallé in the mid-1920s and which had been almost completed before the composer had withdrawn it. Moeran began work on it again in 1934 and Harty was kept informed of its progress. In March 1935 Harty wrote to him after a conversation with the poet Robert Nichols:

> He [Nichols] spoke of your Symphony as being partly completed. This was good news, and I am looking forward so greatly to seeing the work fully completed with orch. parts ready – and the score lying between us as we discuss various points of interpretation! Good luck to your pen and may this summer bring you the necessary inspiration and lucky moods for work so that the Symphony may be finished.[13]

Harty did, however, begin to grow impatient as the completion of the work was put back continually, but it was all the more galling that when the work was finally finished, he was in no position to give its first performance. Moeran was then forced into an invidious position between Harty, the BBC, the Royal Philharmonic Society, and his publisher, Novello. In September 1937, feeling much better, Harty wrote to Moeran enquiring about the symphony. Moeran's reply was long and awkward:

> I am very glad to have your letter this morning, and to know that you are so much better in health. It is splendid to think of the prospect of your return to the concert platform before long. Now, about the symphony. In the first place, I am

[12] Letter from Parry Jones to Harty, 18 Apr. 1937, *GB-Belqb*.

[13] Letter from Harty to Moeran, 29 Mar. 1935, quoted in G. Self, *The Music of E. J. Moeran* (Exeter: Toccata Press, 1986), 104.

not altogether a free agent, as Novello & Co. have taken on it's [sic] publication and are dealing with the business side of things. When I was last in England early in the summer, I had a talk with Julian Herbage at the B.B.C. He proposed that the B.B.C. should earmark a symphony concert date for you to produce it at provided you were able to do so. I was given to understand, at the same time, that in the event of your delayed recovery, the symphony must not again be put off, but that it would have to go forward presumably under Boult's direction, or that of some other conductor, unspecified. I rang Miss Baguley, as you were at that time too unfit and ill to discuss it with, and told her the position.

From that day to this, I have not heard another word from the B.B.C. As I have said, Novello took on the work, and their terms were so fair and advantageous to me that I very naturally fell in with them. After all, it is not always easy to get publishers interested in large works these days. The next thing that happened was that Novello wrote to me in Ireland that they had fixed up it's [sic] production at a Philharmonic concert under Heward. I got into [sic] touch with him, and he would love to do it, but that if you were likely to be fit again for this season, he would prefer not to do anything to stand in the way of the original arrangement between you and myself.

Meanwhile, Novello told me that in drawing up the season's programmes there is a liason between the B.B.C. and the Philharmonic in the person of Owen Mase, who is on both committees, and that so far as a B.B.C. production with you conducting was concerned, it was apparently off on account of the unlikelihood of your being back in business this season. Now I tell you in strict confidence I was not keen on a first performance under Boult, and as Novello were getting restive about holding it up indefinitely, I had no alternative but to acquiesce in their arrangement with the Philharmonic. At the same time I must be frank, and admit to you that I did not like to turn down a proposal from the august Royal Philharmonic Society of so important a nature as the production of one's first symphony, especially in view of the fact that there was no definite alternative to look to at the time.

A possible exception might have been a B.B.C. performance, possibly only in the studio, under conductorship which might not have been sympathetic; in your absence, I would prefer him to anyone else I know in this country. That is the position, and I sincerely hope you understand. However, I feel sure you do after what you have said. Had I known earlier that you were recovering so unexpectedly quickly, I would have tried to get Novello to put off things for a time longer. I am most awfully disappointed that you will not be doing the first performance in London, but I do hope you will still see your way to take it on subsequently when you are back at work again.[14]

Moeran, diplomatically, attempted to sweeten the bitter pill for Harty by offering him the dedication:

> I wrote a great part of it with your conducting in the background of my mind, much in the same way that I have composed songs and chamber music for certain singers and players and am now engaged on a concerto for May Harrison.

---

[14] Letter from Moeran to Harty, 8 Sept. 1937, *GB-Belqb*.

It would be a great honour and pleasure to me if you would accept the dedication of the symphony. I had from the very first intended to ask your permission to do this when the work would be finished, and I very much hope you will agree. May I write your name at the head of the score?

I expect most good Irish hotels are lacking in quiet at this time of year. I came away from Valencia a fortnight ago, and am making a short series of visits about England. The Lyndhurst address, where my parents are spending the summer, will find me until the end of September. (Letters are forwarded.) I propose going back to Kerry on Sep. 30th. Having started my concerto there I want to finish it in the same surroundings. I am glad to say, it is progressing well – far easier to write than a symphony, but then I am an ex-violinist, which helps a lot.

I shall be passing through London to and fro during this month. I will ring up, as I would love to see you again soon. I should so like you to see my completed score one of these days i.e. if you won't feel inclined to shoot me, but I really don't see how I could have acted otherwise.

All best wishes for your continued improvement in health. If, by chance, you stay longer in Ireland, Parknasilla is ideal in October or, in fact, any part of Kerry. But don't come down there without letting me know. Valencia Island is my address after Oct. 1st.[15]

The Symphony in G minor was first performed by the Royal Philharmonic Society under the direction of Leslie Heward at Queen's Hall on 13 January 1938, and Henry Wood repeated it at the Proms in August of the same year. Given that, according to Dora Foss, Harty 'went over it bar by bar with him',[16] the disappointment must have been unimaginable. He never conducted the work, and to make matters worse between him and Moeran, there was a regrettable misunderstanding about Moeran's production of his Violin Concerto which Harty, in error, believed he was being offered in place of the symphony. He was clearly displeased and refused Morean's offer of the dedication:

Thank you for your letter. I think you must have misunderstood mine; I had no intention of bothering you with the score of my violin concerto. In fact, the ultimate production of it is quite in the air, so far as I am concerned, for it is not yet finished, and it may be a year or more before I am sufficiently satisfied with it to think of the question of performance. If you still have my letter, please have another look at that part of it: but perhaps I expressed myself badly. But surely you must realize that I would not ask you to take up a piece of that nature, especially in view of this muddle over the symphony.

It is a terrible disappointment to me that you do not feel inclined to accept the dedication. I have no wish to dedicate it to anyone else, so it must stand as it is without one; moreover, I cannot see that there is any valid reason or precedent whereby a large work should be inscribed to the conductor who directs it's [sic] first performance.

After all, you yourself gave the first performance of Arnold's 6th Symphony, dedicated to Boult.

[15] Letter from Moeran to Harty, 8 Sept. 1937, GB-Belqb.
[16] Biographical memory of Harty by Dora Foss, in private possession.

The fact of my work being dedicated to you would not, as far as I am concerned, cause me to take umbrage if you were not to find yourself in a position to play it for the time being, for I fully realize that after your long illness, you will need to take things easily, and also to make up for other activities which so unfortunately had to be deferred. I sincerely hope you will reconsider this, but take your time. There is no question of the score being engraved until next year.

I was in London early this week, and from what I have been able to gather, I have been badly let down over the symphony and yourself by a certain individual.

At present, I feel absolutely fed up and disinclined to think of music at all, having had my eyes opened as to some of the intrigues which take place under the auspices under which it is run in this country. It will be good to get back to Kerry soon, where the inhabitants may be less intellectual, but at any rate possess directness and honesty.

I sincerely hope you are enjoying your time in Co. Down, and that you will continue to make progress in your restoration to complete health and vigour.[17]

Fortunately Moeran persisted and the dedication appeared in the published score.

By the beginning of 1938 Harty was feeling better, but he was not as yet in a position to return to the conductor's rostrum. In September 1937 the LSO advertised their forthcoming season with Harty as one of their guest conductors; he was to have appeared on 2 February 1938. But neither this, nor a concert with the BBCSO at the end of January, was possible. Instead he devoted himself to composition work and completed his *Five Irish Poems* which were published by Boosey. Among Harty's numerous songs, many of them settings of Irish poetry and cast in an Irish idiom of synthetic modality and ornamentation, these are the most elaborate and inventive. The rhapsodic accompaniment of 'A Mayo Love Song', replete with rich, spread arpeggios, could almost be for harp rather than piano. Milligan's text, which tells of the lover parted by distance from his beloved, was also deeply personal to Harty. It is not hard to construe his longing for Lorie in the pages of this miniature, the passion of which is given full rein in the modified second strophe. At the song's climax there is a palpable cry from the heart as the voice rises to a high A flat, stressing the word 'shall' ('And we *shall* be, / Oh, Colleen lonely, beloved by me'), surely the expression of a vain hope that he would see Lorie again (Example 17).[18] It is a moment intensified by the unexpected juxtaposition of the tonic, D minor, with an F minor triad – a harmony which functions as the supertonic of E flat in conjunction with the dominant that follows. Yet this dominant is not permitted resolution and the tragic tonality of D minor is abruptly restored. Lanyon's 'At Easter' (from *The Hill o'Dreams and Other Verses* of 1909) attempts to diffuse the solemnity of mass, the miracle of the resurrection and the spring's awakening, to which Harty responded with an appropriately organ-like contrapuntal prelude, though, as the self-developing vocal melody expands upwards in range (from a low C sharp to a high G sharp), the accompaniment is more orchestral in timbre and texture.

[17] Letter from Moeran to Harty, 17 Sept. 1937, *GB-Belqb*.

[18] This is further corroborated by the fact that Harty sent Lorie an autograph copy of the manuscript of this song (now in private possession of CB).

Example 17 *Five Irish Poems*, 'A Mayo Love Song', climax

Example 17 *continued*

Of all the songs in the collection, this is the most resourceful in its illustration of the text and, with its colourful use of harmony, recalls the vivid settings of Colum composed before the First World War. For 'A Sailor Man', Harty, like Stanford before him, opted for the 'patter' style, requiring nimble delivery from the singer; and though the brilliance of this charming scherzo lies with the pianist, it is in the unaccompanied voice that the last gesture of humour resides. The ornamental style of *sean nós*, already evident in the rapid embellishments of 'A Mayo Love Song', are tangible in 'Denny's Daughter'. Harty would have known Stanford's setting of Moira O'Neill's poem, where the mood of lament is captured with an air of deft simplicity. By contrast, Harty portrays the acute sense of loss through lyric intensity, which is thrown into relief by the harnessing of O'Neill's refrain-like conclusion to each verse. Here the melodic material, in its pentatonic apparel, is highly affecting, as is the dramatic statement of the final bars. The climactic top B flat for voice ('Has left me *lone* for life'), which articulates both anger and regret, seems once more to point to the composer's own loneliness and inner melancholy. With permission from Yeats, he set *The Fiddler of Dooney* as a boisterous finale. The technical demands for the pianist, already present in the first song, are no less challenging in this rapid, quirky jig. Once again, Harty's design is essentially strophic, but each verse eccentrically concludes on the subdominant, before the final verse, harmonically modified, finishes with an unequivocal perfect cadence, a buoyant *tierce de Picardie*, and a mad scamper to the end.

The *Five Irish Poems* was one of several works that he been gestating in Harty's mind in the late 1930s. Another, according to Catterall, was a Concert Piece for Violin and Orchestra which never materialised.[19] But above all he was immersed in the composition of a large-scale symphonic poem, *The Children of Lir*. The incentive to write the work was recounted by John Barry who, in detailing the last years of Harty's life, described a walk along the Antrim coast with James Moore during his holiday of 1936, on which Harty encountered Sophia Rosamund Praeger's sculpture 'Finola and Her Brothers', a *bas-relief* of the Children of Lir, in the entrance hall of the old school-house along the Giant's Causeway with the Sea of Moyle beyond.[20] Moore related not only Harty's fascination for the piece, but also that it had awoken an idea for an orchestral work that had been creatively dormant for many years.[21] Harty took the best part of two years to complete the score – the manuscript of the full score is dated 'Nov. 1938' – though it is also evident from a sketch of the entire work in short score, dated 'Aug. 20. 1938', that he went on to revise it thoroughly. From surviving sketches Greer has shown, in considerable detail, how the work evolved with great care.[22] What is more, it is also clear from this study of the sketches that certain ideas had been developing in the composer's imagination since before the First World War, a fact which chimed with Harty's own comments to Moore after seeing the Praeger sculpture.

The legend of 'The Children of Lir' occupies an important position in Irish mythology as one of the stories of the *Three Most Sorrowful Tales of Erin* (*Trí truagha na scéalaidheachta*) and formed an important part of the harvesting of Irish writings during the nineteenth century by Eugene O'Curry. Several

[19] See letter from Arthur Catterall to Olive Baguley, 10 Sept. 1941, *GB-Belqb*.
[20] Barry, 'Last Years'. Praeger is thought to have completed the work in or around 1915, before showing it at the 37th Annual Exhibition of The Belfast Art Society in 1918.
[21] See Greer, 'The Composition of *The Children of Lir*', 78ff. Greer's essay provides a fascinating transcript of a television interview with Moore during the centenary of Harty's birth in 1979.
[22] Greer, 'The Composition of *The Children of Lir*', 90.

English translations became available during the later Victorian and Edwardian eras, namely P. W. Joyce's *Old Celtic Romances Translated from the Gaelic* (1879) and T. W. Rolleston's *Myths and Legends of the Celtic Race* (1911); it was no doubt from these that Harty formed his own impression for the programme of his tone poem.

The four children born of Lir and his first wife Aoibh were a girl, Finola, and three boys – Aobh, and the twins Fiachra and Conn. Aoibh died, but Lir's second wife, Aoife, the sister of Aoibh, was jealous of the love shown by the father for his children and the children for each other. With her magic, Aiofe turned the children into swans and they were cursed for 900 years, during which time they had to spend 300 years at Lough Derravaragh, 300 years in the Sea of Moyle (between Ireland and Scotland), and 300 years on the waters of Irrus Domnann, Erris, near the island of Inishglora. To counter the spell, they had to receive a Christian blessing by a monk (St Patrick had converted Ireland to Christianity during the time the children were swans). During the course of their cursed existence, the swans had the power of speech and possessed the gift of making glorious music. On Lake Derravaragh an unusual tranquillity prevailed, but when on the Sea of Moyle, forbidden to land, they had to withstand the cold and storm; Finola, the eldest, brought succour to her brothers by enveloping them in her plumage. During their final 300 years, on the western shores of Mayo, they suffered further hardship. Finally, on the shores of Erris Bay, they heard the sound of the first Christian bell from the chapel of a hermit who gave them sanctuary. Seized by Deoch, the wife of the King of Leinster, who wanted the swans for herself, Finola and her brothers were released from their bonds only to be transformed into withered beings of incredible age. Taken to the church, they died at the moment they were baptised and received into the Christian faith.

In his programme note for the first performance of his symphonic poem, Harty modified the story (which was also printed in the published full score) in order to suit his own personal reaction and experience. The focus of his programme was the church at Ballintoy where he had walked with Moore. An extremely picturesque place, its small church and graveyard look out over the sea to Rathlin Island and across to Scotland. It was here, Harty intimated in his note, that, fired by the idea of the sculpture, his imagination located the burial of the children 'within hearing of the bell which had brought their tragic sufferings to an end'.[23] Moreover, instead of leaving for the west coast, the children in Harty's account remained on the Sea of Moyle, a geographical simplification which gave a more concentrated edge to the programmatic dimension. Sensibly, Harty chose not to follow the story in detail, but rather to illustrate 'certain scenes and moods to which the musical sections of the work correspond.'[24]

Scored for a large orchestra with triple woodwind, the conception of Harty's tone poem was positively Straussian in its vibrancy and scale; lasting well nigh half-an-hour, it was his longest single movement, and went on almost as long as the complete Violin Concerto. Furthermore, it is evident from the virtuoso nature of the opulent instrumentation that Harty's technique and conception

[23] Queen's Hall programme note by Harty, BBC SO concert, 1 Mar. 1939.
[24] Queen's Hall programme note by Harty, BBC SO concert, 1 Mar. 1939.

had moved on considerably from his last work in the genre, *With the Wild Geese*, written before the First World War. In fact, in terms of elaboration and technical demands on the orchestra, the principal catalyst between *The Children of Lir* and *With the Wild Geese* was the final version of the 'Irish' Symphony, which revealed a much more brilliantly detailed and sumptuous approach to orchestration than the 1915 revision. Moreover, Harty's assimilation of 'Irish' ornamentation was executed with an even greater generosity – and here it shared that detail of embellishment from *sean nós* that appears incipiently in 'My Lagan Love' and, more confidently in 'A Mayo Love Song' – particularly in the rapid, scales, turns, mordants and grace notes of the flamboyant wind-writing. However, this dimension of the score was no mere superficial, nationalistic filigree, for it was sympathetically integrated into a more fully developed stylistic equation of melody, rhythm and harmony, and although Harty's approach to organicism – the 'working out' of his ideas – still essentially resided within the self-developing nature of his long thematic paragraphs (and these were substantial), the processes were more sophisticated, expansive and tonally wide-ranging. Moreover, one cannot also fail to respond to the more dissonantly chromatic resource of his harmonic language, which served to heighten the impressively pictorial nature of the images.

The much enlarged conception of Harty's structure is evident from the very opening in A major. In his programme note the composer called his first section an 'introduction', and this is true insomuch as the music eventually yields to a sonata Allegro in the manner of so many Romantic symphonic scores; yet its scale and the auspicious weight of the thematic ideas seem to militate against such a conventional rhetorical mechanism. This is apparent immediately in the imposing nature of the opening solo timpani, the solemn chorale for brass and low wind (the origins of which date from a sketch of May 1912),[25] and the antecedent idea for the full orchestra (Example 18). What is so thrilling about the presentation of these interrelated constituent parts is not only the dramatic and appealingly vivid nature of the ideas themselves, but the way in which Harty, from the outset, brings striking tonal variation to each recurrence. He went so far as to describe these opening gestures as 'the thoughts of one who stands on the Antrim Cliffs on a day of storm and tempest, and recalls the sorrowful story of the enchanted Children of Lir while gazing down on the turbulent Sea of Moyle – a picture of heaving waters, clouds of spray, and screaming seagulls.' This was surely autobiographical, for, as Greer has asserted, this person *was* Harty himself. After the turbulence of the Allegro's opening theme in A minor, and a plaintive link from the solo clarinet (by now a familiar *topos* in Harty's orchestral music), a secondary theme in F sharp minor (Example 19), highly elastic in its rhythmic character, issues forth as an evocation of the swans 'in all their grace and dignity ... facing their tragic future with bravery and defiance'. These two ideas are then allowed to combine until they reach a peak of intensity at what Harty described as the swans' 'rallying call', a clamorous figure for unison horns. Prefiguring the material of the Allegro, it leads to the first significant cadence, articulated by a return of the strident timpani idea.

[25] See Greer, 'The Composition of *The Children of Lir*', 83.

Example 18 *The Children of Lir*, opening

Example 19 *The Children of Lir*, secondary theme of introduction

This picture of the dreaming onlooker is then replaced by an Allegro, a much modified sonata structure depicting scenes from the legend. Harty's exposition presents two sizeable contrasting paragraphs, the first an illustration of the 'free open sea' in A minor (an idea which Harty had sketched some time earlier for a different work)[26] with an adjunct figure made up of juxtaposed augmented triads; the second a spacious, plangent melody in C major (though far removed from the traditional classical experience of the relative major) which conveys the 'passionate and sorrowful feelings of the swan-children'. To this expansive second subject Harty appended a balletic 'scherzando' ('telling of calmer seas and blue skies') somewhat redolent of Tchaikovsky in its felicitous scoring (Example 20). This material subsequently combines with a return of the second subject in which the sense of defiance and passion of the introduction is reiterated. With this affirmation of C major, and the formal end of the exposition – of such length that one's traditional perception of the form is thoroughly transformed – the conventional event, of development and tonal dissolution, is replaced by a nocturnal 'intermezzo' in G flat major. Harty requested in the score that the orchestra 'should play in a hushed and subdued manner, as if the sounds were coming from a distance' to evoke a 'long lazy ocean swell'. Muted strings, with solo violin and viola, provide a luxuriant background (enhanced by Harty's request to the cellos and basses to use a gentle downward 'portamento' for some of the larger intervals) against which Finola's haunting wordless lament for solo

[26] Greer, 'The Composition of *The Children of Lir*', 83.

Example 20 *The Children of Lir*, Scherzando

soprano emerges (Example 21). It was this scene of her, protecting her brothers on the rocky islet of Carricknarone, that Praeger captured in her sculpture. Harty closely associated it with Thomas Moore's verse which, with some deliberation, he quoted in his score and programme note:[27]

> Silent, O Moyle, be the roar of thy water;
> Break not, ye breezes, your chain of repose;
> While murmuring mournfully, Lir's lonely daughter
> Tells to the night-star her tale of woes.

Finola's melody had in fact been dormant in Harty's mind for many years, for it first appears in an orchestral sketch in F major dated 'Sept. 8 1914' and later in another sketch for an orchestral piece dated 'Sept. 1919'. Both are marked

[27] Harty's copy of Moore's *A Selection of Irish Melodies* survives at *GB-Belqb*. In 1934 Plunket Greene, who occupied a position on the board at Stainer & Bell, wrote to Harty asking if he might consider making some unison song arrangements of Moore's melodies for the publisher: see letter from Plunket Greene to Harty, 7 Apr. 1934 (CB).

Example 21 *The Children of Lir,* 'Finola's Song'

'Lento', as is one further undated sketch which confirms that Harty had been preoccupied with this material for an extended period of time.[28] What is also significant about Finola's melody is that its contours were important in generating the principal second subject of the symphonic poem, representing the swan children, a subtle 'family' interrelationship which Harty sought to create when he was working on the score.

The structural concept of Finola's 'intermezzo' was to create a more benign interlude as a foil to the otherwise more turbulent atmosphere of the symphonic poem. But the sense of tranquillity is by no means undisturbed, for Finola's euphonious lament turns into a cry of anguish at its peak on a high B for the soprano, and we are reminded of the troubled backdrop of the Moyle as her music is permeated by a sequence of descending augmented triads. At the intermezzo's conclusion the mood returns to the foaming Moyle and to a reprise of the 'sea' material. The musical context is, however, developmental for Harty reserves his climax of this section for the return of A minor and the 'sea' theme in full

---

[28] See Greer, 'The Composition of *The Children of Lir*', 86.

orchestral garb. With this *bona fide* recapitulation, the material of the exposition is recalled in a truncated and modified form. This is particularly conspicuous in the poetic restatement of the second subject (the swan-children's melody) and the brief allusion to the scherzando. The effect of this thematic truncation, as Harty suggested in his programme note, was to create 'a new note of urgency and anxiety in the music' as the swan children sense some form of impending change. An indication of this is marked by the return of Finola's song (in the arresting tonal area of A flat), whose connection with the second subject is even more perceptible. In this context, of course, the sense of urgency (rather than the former languidness) lifts the soprano voice to a climactic high C, at which point the bell of the church sounds. Vividly we are carried back to the music of the introduction, and to further reworking of the chorale and storm material. This is a portrayal of the transformed children, who, in their human form, 'noble and beautiful as ever, but incredibly old', are taken ashore to the little church where they die as they are baptised. This scene, captured by a melancholy cor anglais, tremolando lower strings, and the dissonance of E minor and F minor triads, is chilling. Harty described his coda as a 'meditation on the "sorrowful story"'. At its heart is the heroine, Finola, whose melody takes pride of place, initially as a triumphal apotheosis; but latterly it returns to the languid, benign mood of the intermezzo, epitomised by the rhapsodic musings of the solo violin and viola. The final gesture, in which we come full circle to the opening timpani motive, is masterly in its manipulation of the mediant–tonic cadence. All then seems calm, though, in the very last bars, Harty reminds us of the protagonist of the legend, the raging Moyle, heaving and foaming at the foot of the cliffs below.

The Children of Lir is undoubtedly Harty's orchestral masterpiece. Not only do we see the composer at his most fluent in terms of musical ideas, but it is also possible to observe how, over many years, he had benefited from his wealth of experience as a conductor of the world's greatest orchestrators – Tchaikovsky, Ravel, Respighi, Strauss, Rimsky-Korsakov, Elgar and Walton. Harty's handling of the orchestra is virtuoso by any standards and his ability to invoke a wide range of picturesque and emotional images is second to none. The larger structural scheme is also highly adroit. Besides the dramatic frame, which is brilliantly integrated and executed, Harty also managed to create a single-movement work in which the character of the four movements of a symphony are present within the heavily modified sonata design, and while the work can unquestionably be heard as absolute music, the interaction of programme and structural events is nevertheless compelling. Furthermore, with the knowledge of its autobiographical context, and the meaning it clearly held for the composer, it is most affecting to imagine Harty's own role in the depiction of the legend, for as James Moore commented, 'it was a sort of preview of his own death'.[29]

Harty's profile as a conductor was also assisted by the publication in 1938 of *The Orchestra Speaks*, a book surveying the rich panoply of native and foreign conductors during the 1920s and 1930s by the principal violist of the BBCSO, Bernard Shore. Although Harty had been absent from the 'circuit' for some time, Shore remembered him with great affection:

[29] Greer, 'The Composition of *The Children of Lir*', 75.

Intimacy with his orchestra is one of his characteristics; and only those who in his Manchester days worked with him in the Hallé Orchestra are really fitted to tell of this vital aspect of his life as a conductor. Many conductors do not need intimate acquaintance with their players and can achieve their finest results while remaining aloof from all personal contact, but Harty is one of those who wish to know their men. Cases are remembered in which he seemed to exercise something like a Svengalian influence over a player, giving him a sense of artistry that he was not able or willing to put forth for any other conductor.[30]

Shore also recalled that Harty aimed always for an atmosphere of chamber music, however large the orchestration. There was never a desire to over-rehearse and, always, there was a sense of 'listening to one another' with the object of a shared musical objective. Yet he also granted his players more freedom of self-expression than other conductors. Fondly, he would call them by their first names:

> Archie, I want you to play this with complete freedom, yet it must not upset the rhythmic figures in the accompaniment too much. Just play it with me by yourself, and I will show you what I mean. – Yes, that's very good, but I think it would be still better if you stayed on your top F just a little longer, and then hurried the next passage slightly. – I can keep the accompaniment going better. – Now, once more. – Yes, that's first rate. Now, my dears, we'll do it all together from the bassoon tune at letter B. – Archie, just one more thing before we leave it. – Can you take breath after the C sharp instead of in the bar before? – Good. – I won't try it again now, it will be all right.[31]

Shore also perceptively observed Harty's natural ability to accompany. As a concert conductor he was unsurpassed and this he attributed to his innate capacity as an accompanist and a rare intuition 'which enables him to anticipate the soloist's very thoughts'.[32] It was a fitting tribute and summarised the Irishman's unique, quiet and understated manner, at odds with Germanic discipline, which engendered a special affection from the players who served him.

While Harty continued to convalesce and regain his strength, he was forced continually to turn down various invitations to conduct. The American pianist, composer and conductor Ernest Schelling had heard of a possible visit to New York in the new year: 'I see that you are coming over very soon. Will you kindly let me know – I should so like to have you come to us for dinner, and [allow] a few musicians to have the pleasure of meeting you.'[33] But such an idea was unrealistic. In late January 1938 Boult was asked to take over a projected BBC concert of Elgar's Second Symphony and a Mozart piano concerto with Hess; a few days later Harty was still not well enough to appear with the LSO, who had optimistically advertised a concert for him at Queen's Hall in September 1937

[30] B. Shore, *The Orchestra Speaks* (London: Longmans, Green & Co., 1938), 95.

[31] Shore, *The Orchestra Speaks*, 97.

[32] Shore, *The Orchestra Speaks*, 98.

[33] Letter from Ernest Schelling to Harty, 31 Dec. 1937, *GB-Belqb*.

(together with Prokofiev, Mengelberg, Sargent, Toscanini, Boult and Wood).[34] In June 1938 he received a letter from his ophthalmic surgeon Robert Lindsay Rea which expressed his delight at Harty's gradual recovery:

> Your kindness and gratitude has touched me greatly. It bothered my dreams all last night but you would insist upon sending me the cheque and I am grateful – but not so much as to see you stepping out into life so fit and well again. I hope during the years to come we will see a great deal of each other and perhaps hear of each other.[35]

At the end of July Harty took a short holiday on the *Ariguani* to Jamaica and his arrival was proudly announced by the Kingston newspaper *The Daily Gleaner.*[36] In August, while enjoying a break in Clevedon, Somerset, he received sad news that his old friend and colleague Landon Ronald was dying. Harty remembered him fondly as 'a talented man of worldly gifts, but an indifferent musician, all told'.[37]

Refreshed from his holiday, he divided his time between London and Brighton where he found the necessary energy to complete *The Children of Lir* and prepare for his return to the conductor's podium. At the same time his business affairs were safely in the hands of his friend and accountant Alfred Chenhalls, an active member of the London Music Club who was keen for him to finish the scoring of his symphonic poem:

> I am very honoured to receive a letter in a handwriting that has become so unfamiliar, and incidentally to see that such handwriting is unshaken by what you have been through, which must have been enough to have shaken a normal person out of existence. I cannot say how glad I am that the miracle occurred, or how much I admire you in having bent your will to see to it that you are well and amongst us again. (Talking about handwriting, I am having this letter typed only because mine, unlike yours, is unreadable.)
>
> In a letter I have written Miss Baguley today I have reported the business position, so that you may put all thoughts of figures and tax out of your mind for another couple of months. And even then if you are still completing the scoring, or otherwise disinclined to talk of figures, I can get an extension. I am glad to say the tax authorities are as sympathetic as 10 years ago they appeared to have been the opposite.
>
> There is nothing I would like more than to accept your invitation to foregather for a meal to make up for those we have missed in the last two years, but having waited so long I can wait longer: the scoring of such a work must come first. It will be good to hear one which is the result of forced contemplation for two years instead of so many which these days seem to have been jotted down over the week-end.[38]

---

[34] *The Times*, 14 Sept. 1937.

[35] Letter from Robert Lindsay Rea to Harty, 30 June 1938, *GB-Belqb*.

[36] *Daily Gleaner*, 30 July 1938.

[37] See letter from Molly Landon to Harty, 13 Aug. 1938 (SW).

[38] Letter from Alfred Chenhalls to Harty, 23 Sept. 1938, *GB-Belqb*.

By November the news had spread that Harty was ready to resume work. The response, as a letter from his old friend Sacheverall Sitwell demonstrates, was heartwarming:

> I was not able to use my wireless last night, but I was delighted to hear that you are in the world of the living once more. I have often thought of you during your illness, and it seems too good to be true that you are conducting again. I expect you will have to go gently, at first; but how wonderful to be at work again! I shall never forget your great Berlioz evening.[39]

Even more rejuvenating was a letter from Professor Aloys Fleischmann of University College, Cork, inviting Harty to be the director of a proposed festival of operas, symphony concerts and plays in Cork along the lines of the Salzburg Festival. In fact Fleischmann and Harty had been in contact in the winter of 1937 about the prospect of inviting the Carl Rosa Company to Cork for such an event, an idea which had led Harty to make enquiries to the opera company's director, H. B. Phillips.[40] By November 1938 Fleischmann had evidently made some progress with support from the Irish Tourist Association and local patronage, and wanted to secure Harty's collaboration:

> I write to ask whether you would undertake to direct the Festival. A few days ago I chanced to discuss the whole scheme with Mr E. J. Moeran, who was confident that you might be so kind as to agree because of your interest in music in Ireland.
>   We visualise a series of about four symphony concerts, four or five operas (each of the latter, of course, to be repeated several times) together with performances of Irish plays by the Abbey Theatre Company, so that the Festival would last for some 14–17 days. If we should be so fortunate as to gain your interest and consent, would it be possible for you to let me know whether an English orchestra and opera company could be engaged for the first three weeks of August, 1940 (i.e. for one week's rehearsal and two weeks' performance), and would it be possible for you to give me a rough estimate as to the entire cost of such a scheme? This latter is somewhat urgent, since we cannot set about securing our guarantee until we know, roughly, what we shall have to expend.[41]

Harty responded positively, but reserved committing himself until he and Fleischmann had the opportunity to meet. As chance would have it, Harty mentioned that he was due to be in Ulster for some days' holiday in December and could travel down to Dublin. Fleischmann replied:

> I am glad to hear of your interest in the proposed Cork Musical Festival, and I should warmly welcome an opportunity of discussing the scheme with you within the next few weeks.
>   If it would not be too inconvenient, might I accept your suggestion of a meeting in Dublin? I am conducting in Cork on Dec. 9th, but should be free on any date from Dec. 10th to Dec. 17th. The Chairman of the Committee which has

[39] Letter from Sacheverall Sitwell to Harty, 23 Nov. 1938, *GB-Belqb*.
[40] Letter from Harty to Aloys Fleischmann, 1 Jan. 1938 (in possession of Ruth Fleischmann; henceforth RF).
[41] Letter from Fleischmann to Harty, 19 Nov. 1938 (RF).

been formed to organise the Festival (Mr Barry Egan) is anxious to join in the discussions, and Mr E. J. Moeran, who will be returning from England between the above dates, would, I imagine, be very glad to be asked to participate too – that is, if you are kind enough to agree.[42]

A meeting was fixed for 12 December at the Gresham Hotel in Dublin between him, Fleischmann and Egan, though quite clearly Harty was still smarting from his altercation with Moeran over the Symphony and Violin Concerto: 'if you don't mind I think I would prefer not to include Mr Moeran at this preliminary meeting, though no doubt his collaboration would be very helpful at a later stage.'[43] As it transpired, Moeran was not returning to Ireland until after Christmas, which saved both sides from any embarrassment. Fleischmann was also keen that, for sensitive political reasons, their discussions remain a private matter for the moment: 'Might I ask you to keep the proposed festival a secret until things have definitely materialised? Dublin would not be prone to look with favour on Cork's advancement in this respect.'[44] After the meeting Harty put down his thoughts for the festival in some detail and was happy to take full artistic responsibility. Nevertheless, he still entertained the possibility of engagements in America, and therefore reminded Fleischmann that his fee (of £1,000 plus expenses) would need to reflect a certain compensation for refusing these. He advised the Cork committee to engage the Hallé Orchestra and the Carl Rosa Company, and requested the presence of both an assistant conductor, naming DeLamarter of Chicago, and a qualified impresario. As for the operatic repertoire, he listed those operas he knew well and had conducted in the past – *Tristan and Isolde*, *Carmen* and *Pagliacci* – with *Shamus O'Brien* as the one exception.[45]

During the course of this correspondence Harty was readying himself for his first orchestral engagement since October 1936 – a BBC studio concert, eagerly awaited by the press. On 23 December 1938 he conducted his revised version of Schumann's Fourth Symphony, *With the Wild Geese* and his arrangement of Handel's *Music for the Royal Fireworks*, with which he had, by now, become inextricably associated. After Christmas he wrote to Lady Arthur Hill at Hillsborough, with whom he had kept in touch throughout his career. She had heard his broadcast:

> I can't say how much touched I was, at your kind remembrance of my birthday – thank you sincerely for your wishes. I was on the point of writing to you to express my pleasure at your return to the Concert World, and listened in to your performance last week with great enjoyment. It was so pleasant to hear the 'Wild Geese' again! Mr Matchett (Rector – Hillsborough) had previously sent me a cutting from the 'Newsletter' with your portrait and a most interesting article about your doings – so I knew that your long spell of invalidism had come to an

---

[42] Letter from Fleischmann to Harty, 26 Nov. 1938 (RF).

[43] Letter from Harty to Fleischmann, 28 Nov. 1938 (RF).

[44] Letter from Fleischmann to Harty, 30 Nov. 1938 (RF).

[45] Letter from Harty to Fleischmann, 14 Dec. 1938 (RF).

end! What a terrible time you must have had! I hope we shall hear the new work soon. Wishing you the best of luck in 1939.[46]

On Boxing Day 1938 he dined with Alfred Chenhalls, and there had met the publisher and bookseller Herbert van Thal. This chance meeting led, as Chenhalls's letter intimated, to a new project:

> You remember the chap you met at my feast Boxing Day who nearly worshipped you? His name is Hebert van Thal and he has an interesting and ambitious job in persuading famous people that they can write a book, autobiography, etc. at a profit to themselves (not to mention publisher and him).
>
> Will you see him and hear him out? You probably have heard what Sir Henry Wood got for his – and you have a better story to tell, and tell it better.[47]

It is not known whether Harty and van Thal met to discuss the idea of an autobiography, but what is evident, from the surviving pages of hand-written script, is that Harty did begin such a document, perhaps with the intention of publishing it at a later date. In his contribution to the BBC broadcast in 1951 Squire recalled the following:

> His last letter to me, written in 1940, stated that he was about to commence his autobiography, which I had so often urged him to write; and he added that when the proofs were ready, he would forward them to me immediately. But, alas! those proofs never came to hand. And never again did we meet, for, owing to the exigencies of war, we moved to the west of England for a long period.[48]

Harty therefore appears to have begun his memoirs in 1940. Though full of factual errors, especially in relation to dates and his age at various important junctures of his early career, it nevertheless provides a useful account of the decisions he made, his views, impressions and recollections. But by the time he commenced writing, he was a sick man, unable to complete more than twenty-seven pages.[49]

On 2 February 1939 he broadcast a concert of the 'Irish' Symphony and his arrangement of Handel's *Polonaise, Arietta and Passacaglia* after which he received a touching letter from Helen Henschel, the singer (and daughter of George Henschel):

> Sitting listening to your symphony, and still completely melted by the recollection of that perfect Handel Air, I cannot refrain from doing what I have often wanted to do since hearing from James Forsyth of your restoration to health: to tell you how happy a thing it is to know you are on the active list once more. Ill could we spare your sensitiveness, your poetry, your glorious and inevitable rhythm!
>
> Welcome back, and may many years of music-making be before you.[50]

---

[46] Letter from Lady Arthur Hill to Harty, 1 Jan. 1939, *GB-Belqb.*

[47] Letter from Alfred Chenhalls to Harty, 31 Jan. 1939, *GB-Belqb.*

[48] BBC talk, 1951.

[49] The remnant of Harty's surviving autobiography was reproduced and edited by David Greer in *Hamilton Harty: Early Memories.*

[50] Letter from Helen Henschel to Harty, 2 Feb. 1939, *GB-Belqb.*

From Edith Bairstow, the wife of Edward (now organist of York Minster and Professor of Music at Durham University), came further touching words:

> I feel I must write and tell you how *tremendously* I enjoyed your Broadcast on Thursday evening. The Handel was lovely, but your own Symphony is a gem. There is something you get out of an orchestra that no other conductor gets and it thrills me every time like no one else does. I hope you don't think me impertinent in writing but I do know that artists often suffer from too little appreciation.[51]

These broadcasts, however, were but a trial run for his first public appearance, at Queen's Hall on 1 March, when he would conduct the first performance of *The Children of Lir* with the BBCSO and Isobel Baillie as the solo soprano. It was the one work Harty directed in the programme, conducted from his manuscript because the BBC had organised the premiere somewhat hastily and Universal had not been able to prepare the published score in time (when it did appear it was dedicated 'To O. E. B.' – Harty's faithful friend and secretary Olive Baguley). The remaining works in the concert – Mozart's overture to *Don Giovanni*, Beethoven's Third Piano Concerto (with Solomon) and Vaughan Williams's *A London Symphony* – were directed by Boult. According to Cardus, who had travelled down from Manchester, Harty 'was given a tumultuous and affectionate welcome from a crowded Queen's Hall'.[52] His sympathetic assessment of the new work sounded strangely like those maxims which Harty had proselytised for years:

> His poem for orchestra, *The Children of Lir*, is an act of courage in these days when music is afraid not to sound obviously modern and when system is regarded as of more consequence than sensibility. Sir Hamilton trusts to the traditional stuff of his art, and by sincerity and the Irishman's gracious tenderness he has given us a work which appeals to the heart and moves us with beauty of tone and beauty of conception.[53]

Cardus was, nevertheless, critical of Harty's musical structure, and his misgivings were echoed to a greater or lesser extent by other critics. Some found fault with the piece's anachronistic stylistic lineage and over-elaboration, most of all *The Times*, which took Harty to task for the subject matter's irrelevance 'to a generation which has its own share of present miseries'.[54] Richard Capell of the *Daily Telegraph* was equally derogatory, and Norman Hay (under the pseudonym 'Rathcol') in the *Belfast Telegraph* perceived a looseness in the design.

But while the press was lukewarm, Harty was deluged by congratulations from fellow composers, friends and colleagues. From James Moore, who had listened to the broadcast from his home in Bushmills, came the following letter:

---

[51] Letter from Edith Bairstow to Harty, 4 Feb. 1939, *GB-Belqb*.

[52] *MG*, 2 Mar. 1939.

[53] *MG*, 2 Mar. 1939.

[54] *The Times*, 2 Mar. 1939.

Just got my breath after 'The Children of Lir': I can only say like the old county fellow in church, whom one day after a service said to me; 'It's not often we have the like of that!!' You can take what you like out of this rather doubtful compliment, but you can assume that I was thrilled by the whole performance. Everything was so perfectly balanced and there was an unmistakable Irish flavour about it all; not the vulgar crudeness that most people associate with Ireland but a certain atmosphere which is only possible when it is part of the make-up of the creator. It was good to know that you survived the ordeal of 'coming back' to the public 'gaze': you certainly seem to have got a 'harty' reception. When one looks back on a former legend which you have used, one is forced to the conclusion that 'your geese are all swans'!! no offence meant.[55]

Henry Wood was no less adulatory:

I had a chorus rehearsal tonight for 'Gerontius' but I managed to get home by three minutes to nine and heard your deeply impressive new work.

Bravo! Bravissimo. It sounded magnificently – the themes, the treatment, the orchestration – superb and wonderful. You have *indeed* enriched our list of big orchestral pieces tonight, by the 'Children of Lir'. Britain indeed owes you a deep debt of gratitude. And the orchestra played it superbly. I only regret that my wife and I were not in Queen's Hall.

All possible good wishes and good luck to you and I hope you will direct it at my 'Proms'.[56]

Infuriated by Capell's critique in the *Daily Telegraph*, Rutland Boughton sent a letter of encouragement:

The imbecility in today's Telegraph has made me so angry that I must send you a note to say that I wanted to hear your Children of Lir last night, and, as I remarked to my wife, every night this week. It was lovely – that I *know* because of the impression it left behind it. The real musical spirit of this country is in its Celtic strains or nowhere.[57]

There were also generous letters from Sir Ernest Cochrane, Rosamund Praeger, Paul Beard, Clarence Raybould of the BBC, and Walter Alcock from Salisbury Cathedral, and a shower of telegrams from Norman Allin, the Fosses, Walton, Alfred Barker, C. B. Rees, Arthur Catterall, Julius Harrison, Beatrice Harrison, Roy Henderson, and his friendly hosts at the Folkestone Festival.

After the dust had settled, Harty wrote to Beatrice Harrison expressing a sense of good fortune that his illness was behind him: 'I'm really very lucky to have come through a time of illness in such good shape and feel much obliged to the fates who arrange such things.' He had been contemplating a new work for cello, but although this had not come to fruition he put forward the suggestion that they might perform his suite together:

[55] Letter from James Moore to Harty, 1 Mar. 1939, *GB-Belqb*.
[56] Letter from Henry Wood to Harty, 1 Mar. 1939, *GB-Belqb*.
[57] Letter from Rutland Boughton to Harty, 2 Mar. 1939, *GB-Belqb*.

I have several times recently tried to write something on a decent scale for 'cello, but so far have not been satisfied with my attempts. But I hope, eventually to do something not too bad, when I get just the right idea.

I wish I had something new to offer you; it would be such a pleasure to hear you play it.

There came into my mind this morning the memory of four pieces – a little suite – which I wrote some years ago and which have only been played once – at a semi-private affair in London. They are not very serious pieces, but I think there are some nice things in them and that they could sound effective if played by someone imaginative and with the right kind of technique, and that means you! ...

Do sometime have a look at them – there might be something amongst the pieces that you would find suitable and pleasant. I should be much pleased if that were so. But don't touch them if they don't appear to be suitable to your purpose, because I shall quite understand, and two old friends and real musicians like ourselves can afford to be perfectly frank with one another.[58]

During his correspondence with Harrison, he was called away for one concert at the Bournemouth Festival at the last minute to take the place of Rafael Kubelik, who was detained in Prague. He directed his *Comedy Overture*. After the physical exertion of *The Children of Lir* and this unexpected visit to the south coast, he was keen to bring before the world his *Five Irish Poems*. Since December 1938 he had been in correspondence with Parry Jones, in whose career he had always taken an active interest:

Some new 'Irish poems' I have set to music are just published (Boosey) and I should like very much if you would look at them and see if you like them and if they 'fit' you to sing. If you are passing Boosey's just ask them for copies. 'Five Irish Poems'. My idea was that if you feel like it we might give them a send-off together at a short recital at the B.B.C. I have already spoken to them about this, and I think they are agreeable. So all depends on you – and I hope you will like them. The words are lovely anyway![59]

Their evening broadcast recital took place on 8 April, after which Harty planned to repeat them in Dublin. On 1 May, 'May Day', he took part in a concert at Queen's Hall organised by the Society for Cultural Relations between Great Britain and the USSR. Rutland Boughton conducted some patriotic Russian and English songs sung by the London Labour Choral Union, but the chief interest of the concert was Harty's conducting of the Sinfonietta No. 2 by the Soviet composer Nikolai Myaskovsky, with the London String Orchestra. The concert concluded with some Russian songs and negro spirituals sung by Paul Robeson. A week later Harty was in Dublin where, after many years absence, he was again an adjudicator at the Feis Ceoil for both the practical competition and the new entries by composers.[60] During the Feis activities he spent much time in discussion with T. J. Kiernan, Director of Irish Radio. Indeed, Harty had taken

[58] Letter from Harty to Beatrice Harrison, 14 Mar. 1939, *GB-Lcm*.

[59] Letter from Harty to Parry Jones, 20 Dec. 1938, *GB-Lbl*, MS Mus.1117.

[60] *IT*, 24 June 1939. Harty also adjudicated for some of the competition prizes for the Oireachtas in September 1939: *Irish Times*, 14 Sept. 1939.

a keen interest in the future of music in the Irish Free State since the inception of 2RN/Radio Éireann. On at least one occasion he assisted Godfrey Brown (of BBC Northern Ireland) and Vincent O'Brien with interviewing shortlisted candidates for the small Radio Éireann (RÉ) orchestra of twenty-three players,[61] and during RÉ's 1938–9 season of celebrity concerts he directed one concert from the studio.[62] While the Feis Ceoil of 1939 was under way he socialised with Harold Darke (who gave a organ recital in St Patrick's Cathedral on 12 May), old friends from the RDS days, Walter Starkie and Charles Rowe, and Kiernan, at the home of George Hewson, the organist of St Patrick's.[63] The following day Harty directed a studio concert for RÉ lasting an hour-and-a-half (including a five-minute introduction) entirely of his own music which included his *Five Irish Poems* with Parry Jones, *In Ireland* with the harpist Tina Bonifacio, 'Orientale' and 'À la campagne' for oboe and orchestra, and the *Fantasy Scenes (from an Eastern Romance)*.

To begin the programme, however, was another new work which Harty had completed in February 1939. This was *A John Field Suite*, a set of arrangements of individual keyboard movements (or in the case of the fourth movement, a Piano Quintet) by the Irish pianist and composer John Field. At some stage during his convalescence his attention had shifted from Chopin to Field, perhaps because Field's simpler textures and ideas were better disposed to original orchestration; in this context Harty enjoyed a *tabula rasa* in choosing his instrumentation, whereas in his Handel suites there had always been, in the background, an orchestral concept as a guiding principle. Harty's four movements – a Polka (the Rondo from Field's Piano Sonata in E flat, Op. 1 No. 1), a Nocturne (the Nocturne No. 5 in B flat), a Slow Waltz in E ('Remembrance') and a Rondo Finale (Rondo in E for Piano Quintet, 'Le midi') –were scored for an unusually small orchestra of single wind, horn, trumpet, harp, percussion, timpani (whose task was also to play a bell) and strings. Indeed, so chamber-like was the orchestral ensemble (reflecting, perhaps, his predilection for reduced ensembles in Mozart) that Harty may well have conceived it with the RÉ orchestra in mind. The work, delicately scored, has an intimacy which is particularly poignant in the Nocturne, a movement which has a romantic subtlety worthy of Weber or Mendelssohn.

Harty repeated *A John Field Suite* in a live broadcast concert for the BBC on 3 June with the BBCSO, and there were further broadcasts in June and July of Elgar, Delius and Mozart. A performance of his 'Irish' Symphony in July elicited a touching letter from John McCormack:

> Lily and aunty and I sat around the Radio last night and heard your Irish Symphony.
>
>   It brought back so many happy memories and made us so homesick. I don't mind telling you we all dropped a couple of tears and there was a great chorus of

---

[61] Richard Pine, *Music and Broadcasting in Ireland* (Dublin: Four Courts Press, 2005), 74.

[62] Pine, *Music and Broadcasting in Ireland*, 77.

[63] *IT*, 12 May 1939.

'nose-blowing' especially at the end of the slow movement. We talked about you for a long time afterwards and with deep affection. We would love to see you again. Is there any chance of you coming here for a couple of days – of course bring your Ration card!!!!!! Do come and let us talk of old times before its Chaplinesque Sadistic Megalomaniac destroyed our peace of mind.[64]

He visited Beatrice Harrison at her rural Surrey home, to play through the Cello Suite; they planned a recital in October.[65] Then he took some time off, with a cruise to the Azores and another stay at Rostrevor.

By this time all talk was of European conflagration, and with the onset of war there was much foreboding of what the future held for the nation's music-making. In addition – a sad reality for Harty – travel between Britain and Ireland was severely restricted. International events had also forestalled any further planning of the Cork Festival and Harty agreed with Fleischmann that 'undue haste just now would not be wise until indeed the international sky is much clearer than it is at present.'[66] The Cork Festival was cancelled. In September Harty wrote to Beatrice Harrison; their hopes of a recital together had been dashed:

> This sinful war has upset us all and ruined our plans. There is nothing to do but to take it all as quietly and calmly as we can. Some day it will be over and we can resume our normal lives again. Of course, my dear, you can count on me whenever your concert does take place. I am always your affectionate friend in that as in everything else.[67]

There was a handful of engagements with the BBC, which included Sibelius's Second Symphony (8 November) and Mozart's Clarinet Concerto with Frederick Thurston (25 November), and some concerts with the Liverpool Philharmonic, but the amount of concert-giving at this time of extremity was severely curtailed.

Early in January 1940, during a particularly cold winter, Harty gave a memorable performance of Elgar's Second Symphony with the BBCSO. Beatrice Harrison, whose memories of playing the Cello Concerto under the composer's direction, wrote an appreciative letter:

> The Elgar Symphony is just over, and words cannot ever ever express our gratitude, as well as thousands of listeners, for the glorious performance. The transmission was perfect oh! how we revelled in your wonderful climaxes, and different moods of the great work, which so few, who conduct it, seem to reach. We have not heard it for so long ever since he conducted it at a concert, when I was playing his Concerto with him. I do hope you are not feeling this cold too much. Everything here is frozen.[68]

[64] Letter from John McCormack to Harty, 3 July 1940, *GB-Belqb*.

[65] Letter from Harty to Beatrice Harrison, 23 June 1939, *GB-Lcm*.

[66] Letter from Harty to Fleischmann, 3 Aug. 1939 (RF).

[67] Letter from Harty to Beatrice Harrison, 28 Sept. 1939, *GB-Lcm*. Harrison continued to play Harty's music for cello throughout her life: see Harrison, *The Cello and the Nightingales*, 94.

[68] Letter from Beatrice Harrison to Harty, 3 Jan. 1940, *GB-Belqb*.

Harty's reply extolled the Elgar symphony:

> I am so glad you liked the Elgar. It is a work of nobility, I think, and few foreign
> works can compare with it. My love to you (and to the whole family) and I wish for
> you much happiness and success in 1940. Keep quiet and faithful and serene.

And in a brief postscript his hopes of performing the Suite had not dissipated.[69]

Between January and March 1940 Harty conducted the New Symphony
Orchestra at a number of concerts for the National Sunday League at the
Palladium in all-Beethoven programmes which included the pianists Louis
Kentner, Solomon and Hess. He appeared with the LPO at one of Beecham's
Sunday Concerts for the Royal Philharmonic Society on 1 February, when *A
John Field Suite* was given its first public performance. It was hastily published
by Boosey that spring, which, for the novelty of Field as 'a forgotten artist',
drew some interest from the musical press.[70] On 29 February he made what
would be his last appearance at Bournemouth, in the company of his old friend
Moiseiwitch. Such journeys as these, out of London, were strenuous for him, and
with the BBCSO moving to the Colston Hall in Bristol to avoid the bombing, it
meant yet more travelling to fulfil engagements with them. Yet he soldiered on
gallantly. On 14 February he and Tertis (who had come out retirement to help
the war effort) gave a performance of *Harold in Italy* as well as music by Bax and
Brahms, and there was more Berlioz at the end of March with the *Symphonie
fantastique.*

Harty longed for Ireland, and after he received good wishes from James
Moore for St Patrick's Day, he replied with a postcard. It was a painting by
Peter Scott of white-fronted geese in flight in the fading sunlight of evening.
On the back Harty wrote ruefully: 'I wish I was going over with them too.'[71]
His involvement with the Society for Cultural Relations renewed his contact
with Edward Clark, a keen Communist and, formerly of the BBC, a promoter
of new music. Clark wanted Harty to participate in the SCR's celebration of
the Tchaikovsky centenary, and, at first, Harty expressed interest in doing so.
But, with Germany's present non-aggression pact with the Soviet Union, it was
clear that associations with the SCR would be frowned upon, as he attempted to
explain to Clark:

> Being Irish is not always an advantage! I have made some discreet enquiries since
> we talked yesterday and have been warned, politely of course, that my collaboration
> in the proposed concert of Tchaikowski's music under S.C.R. direction would
> be looked at in certain important circles as unwise if not unpatriotic. With
> the rightness of this judgment I have no concern, though I do not agree
> with it.
>
>   Under the difficult circumstances, however, I feel that I must ask you to release
> me from undertaking. I am very sorry for many reasons – not least because I

---

[69] Letter from Harty to Beatrice Harrison, 5 Jan. 1940, *GB-Lcm*.

[70] *The Times*, 6 Apr. 1940.

[71] Postcard from Harty to James Moore, 23 Mar. 1940 (in the private possession of
David Greer).

should have liked to have been with you in this effort to honour the name of a great composer. The world is very mad at present![72]

After a broadcast of Elgar's First Symphony on 15 May the opportunity to mark Tchaikovsky's centenary came with the first of two broadcast concerts from the Colston Hall on 22 May, when he conducted the 'Pathétique' Symphony. On 25 August he made a visit to Manchester to conduct *A John Field Suite* with the BBC Northern Orchestra. The entire occasion had many sentimental associations, not least because, through the offices of Maurice Johnstone, Head of the BBC Northern Region, there was a chance to socialise with former players from the Hallé:

> The 'old guard' in the Northern Orchestra, that is to say players who were in the Hallé in your day, have expressed a keen desire to meet you apart from musical operations on August 25th. This wish is naturally shared by Mr Coatman, Gideon Fagan and myself and I have, therefore, been asked to write to you on behalf of the whole bunch of your loyal and humble servants, and to ask Olive and your good self to join us at lunch at the Grand Hotel between rehearsal and transmission. The party would thus consist of you two, some twenty or twenty-five Hallé boys, Mr Coatman, Gideon Fagan and myself. Olive will thus be the only lady present, but after her many years' association with the orchestra I am sure she will feel no embarrassment![73]

Harty made a guest appearance at a Promenade Concert (during Henry Wood's farewell season) on 3 September to conduct *the Children of Lir* with Isobel Baillie. All the time, however, it was evident that his illness had returned and that more radium treatment was needed. In May he had been fined at the Marylebone Police Court for displaying a light during the black-out, having been warned some days beforehand for a similar offence.[74] When the Blitz began in September 1940 his house at Norfolk Road, always vulnerable, was severely damaged by bombing. The house was left uninhabitable, and though he did his best to rescue what he could, much was totally destroyed. Needing to find somewhere to live, he retreated to Hove on the south coast where, after living in hotel accommodation for a few weeks, he found a flat at 35 Brunswick Square which allowed a view of the sea.

The radium treatment continued, which meant onerous visits to London sixty miles away. To the players, his frailty was now plainly visible. Gerald Jackson, who played first flute with the BBCSO, was haunted by his weakened constitution:

> His last years were tragic. When he came as a guest conductor after his final operation, his hands were trembling badly. It had therefore become necessary to drape the stand with green felt to muffle his uncontrollable and involuntary bangs.

---

[72] Letter from Harty to Edward Clark, 3 Apr. 1940, *GB-Lbl*, Add. MS 52256.

[73] Letter from Maurice Johnstone to Harty, 13 Aug. 1940, *GB-Belqb*.

[74] *The Times*, 13 May 1940.

This caused us considerable grief, for he had few equals among our niggardly reserve of true affection.[75]

Harty gave a broadcast with Solomon on 30 October, still with a view that he could accept engagements for 1941. But the concert he gave on 1 December at Tunbridge Wells was the last he could manage. The first trumpet of the BBC SO, Ernest Hall, remembered the experience with some sadness: 'I was very distressed when Sir Hamilton conducted the BBC Symphony Orchestra for the last time. He was a very sick man after his operation, and while he was conducting this concert, his hair fell over one eye, so devoid of vision, he did not attempt to move it. It was very pathetic.'[76] The Royal Philharmonic advertised a concert for him on 8 February 1941, but he was too ill, and it was instead taken by Leslie Heward.

In Hove he took short walks to the shingle beech and watched the sky lit up by distant guns and search-lights, and all this while he was nursed loyally by Baguley. In January he received a letter from his oldest friend and colleague, Squire, who had moved down to Exeter to escape the worst effects of the war:

> I couldn't resist a smile this morning when the wireless announced that all road-signs in Ireland were to be removed. Begorra! as if they ever were to be relied on. For my mind instantly reverted to that most remarkable 6-way sign-post outside Bundoran, when they all pointed the same way! And when I said to you: 'Why doesn't somebody put 'em right' – you (knowingly) answered: 'Ach! it's nobody's business!'
>
> How are you keeping, Laddie? We often speak of you. I hope to goodness those 'Reminiscences' haven't suffered thro the 'Blitz'. And were your windows blown in the same time as ours – on Dec. 21st? … That was sad news about the poor old Free Trade Hall [which had been bombed in December 1940]. Where will the Hallé orch. be housed now, I wonder?

But the 'Reminiscences', as we know, only existed as an incipient fragment. A week later he received a supportive letter from Henry Wood, who had also suffered from the bombing. There was also sad news of Frank Bridge's passing:

> We were terribly sorry to see that you did not conduct the Philharmonic Concert – and upon making some enquiry yesterday in London, we were told that you had been through rather a bad time lately – we were naturally very upset and we do hope you are now resting and making a complete recovery.
>
> We have not been lucky as our Suite of rooms at the Langham Hotel were boomed [sic] two days after we left the Bowdon. Then No. 4 Gran Avenue got it, although we hear our furniture has not been destroyed and someday, we hope to go back to our dear home. We are most comfortable here, only 30 miles from Kings X excellent train service and by a taxi to Bedford, I get up north easily. It seems I have had a lot of dates, since the Proms closed down, 5 Sundays starting with the opening concert of the Hallé in Manchester, followed by many dates in

---

[75] Gerald Jackson, *First Flute* (London: J. M. Dent, 1968), 92.

[76] From a note by Hall to Leonard Hirsch, *GB-Belqb*; quoted in Greer, 'The Composition of *The Children of Lir*', n. 23.

Blackpool, Morecambe, Workington, Carlisle, Hanley etc: dear Malcolm seems to enjoy being permanent Conductor, then not turning up, or at least, only when it suits his other engagements. *We* never did this when we had a permanent job. But *we* avoided Music Hall tours in the old days. It was rough on the Hallé to think he directed 2 shows a day the week before his first concert of the season. I pulled his leg at the Midland Hotel, by telling him I was *so sorry* he had *no* engagement, hard luck in war time. He took it very well.

I shall miss Frank Bridge very much. I am doing his Overture 'Rebus' at 2.H on Feb. 23rd and a memorial concert for the B.B.C. on March 12th. He was such a splendid straight fellow and his Suite 'The Sea' always had success.

Well my dear friend, take great care of yourself for such as you are very rare in these days. If we ever get back to Hove we shall look you up.[77]

It was a bitter-sweet letter from a fellow conductor. Wood did not realise, though, just how sick Harty was. As the cancer took hold, his immune system diminished and he contracted a chill on 17 February 1941 which quickly turned into septic pneumonia. Two days later, in the early evening, he died peacefully.

Harty's death joined a roll of other musicians: his countryman Herbert Hughes, Frank Bridge, Walford Davies, and (two years later) Leslie Heward, whose demise was considered premature. Indeed, among the numerous obituaries, which included a generously detailed one from John Russell,[78] was an article by Edwin Evans in which special tribute was paid to Bridge and Harty together – different sensibilities in many ways, but at their hearts deeply private individuals, each with a melancholy streak, who also shared, somewhat coincidentally, a prowess for composing, conducting, and playing both the pianoforte and the viola.[79] Boult conducted a memorial concert on 16 April at the BBC; a number of his works featured in the Hallé concerts which were now taking place at the Opera House in Manchester; and Isobel Baillie gave a programme of his songs in August. In Dublin the conductor Michael Bowles paid his own respects with a performance of *The Children of Lir* in December 1942 and on the second centenary of his death, in February 1943, it was broadcast by the BBC. But, save for a few isolated performances of *With the Wild Geese*, Harty's original works, which he had conducted with such conviction during his lifetime, fell quickly out of fashion after the war, leaving only his transcriptions of Handel and *A John Field Suite*, which remained extremely popular.

After the residue of his will was published in June 1941 (which left a sum of £6,865 – today about £300,000), there was the matter of what to do with his legacy of music and manuscripts. On 19 February 1943, exactly two years after his death, Norman Hay produced his own tribute, 'Hamilton Harty – Great Ulsterman', for the *Belfast Telegraph*. There he recalled the self-effacing reserve of his compatriot, quoting a letter Harty had written to him after Trinity College, Dublin had conferred on him the degree of MusD:

---

[77] Letter from Henry Wood to Harty, 15 Feb. 1941, *GB-Belqb*.

[78] Russell, 'Hamilton Harty'.

[79] E. Evans, 'In Memoriam: Frank Bridge and Sir Hamilton Harty', *Music Review* 2(2) (1941), 159–66.

'I really don't know what I've done to deserve this. I'm sure I couldn't pass the Mus.D. exam'. Such was the modesty, thoroughly genuine, of the man. But Harty had already graduated in another sphere; he was the child of that spirit-land of which Yeats sang, whence he came for a while to make music for our heart's delight.[80]

Hay wondered what memorial might be erected to Harty's memory, and thought that the founding of a first-rate Ulster Orchestra would be dearest to his heart.[81] This was not inconsistent with a conversation he had with Terry O'Connor (who led the RÉ Symphony Orchestra). Over a meal in Dublin, Harty intimated to him: 'Long I have had a dream of living the latter portion of my life over here – training and conducting a first-class orchestra, and helping forward Irish musical talent. Ah, well! That still may lie in the future. Who knows?'[82] Baguley, who had be importuned by various conductors and musical organisations (in both England and America) about acquiring Harty's music library, suggested it should come to Ireland. She had much appreciated Hay's article and wrote to him on the subject. Hay responded:

I am glad you liked my few words on our dear mutual friend, Harty. His was, as you say, an unique personality; and for that reason it is difficult to express one's feelings: but what I did write was written from a full heart; and I am so happy to think that it touched you who knew him and helped him so well and loyally.

James Moore and I often talk of him and he has told me how much Hamilton Harty owed to you in his last years.

Your idea of giving his music library to Ireland is a very pleasing one and I hope it will come to fruition. The only difficulty I can see is as to whether it should come to Ulster or to Eire in both of which parts of the country he and his work were equally loved. Anyhow, I shall be glad to hear from you when the time comes to put your idea into effect. Meanwhile I thank you for your letter, which I shall treasure.[83]

After the war it was decidedly, fittingly, to leave all of Harty's papers, manuscripts, books and music to Queen's University, Belfast, and the royalties to support the creation of the Hamilton Harty Chair of Music, established there in 1951. In addition, there would be an annual Hamilton Harty Memorial Concert, featuring at least one of his major works, and a travelling scholarship.

In 1947, after travel restrictions between Britain and Ireland had been lifted, Baguley took Harty's ashes to Hillsborough, where they were buried beneath a memorial bird-bath made of Limerick limestone and sculpted by Rosamond Praeger. It lies near the west door of the church. In 1964 Hillsborough paid its own tribute by the placing of a memorial plaque on Harty's childhood home in Ballynahinch Street; a similar tribute was paid by the Regency Society of Hove in 1976. Three years later a choir verge was fashioned in gold from the gifts Harty

[80] [Hay N.] Rathcol, 'Hamilton Harty – Great Ulsterman', *Belfast Telegraph*, 19 Feb. 1943.

[81] Rathcol, 'Hamilton Harty – Great Ulsterman'.

[82] BBC talk, 1951.

[83] Letter from Norman Hay to Olive Baguley, 22 Apr. 1943, *GB-Belqb*.

had received during the course of his life, on the head of which, symbolically, is a nightingale in full song. These memorials were of lasting importance, but perhaps the most powerful compliment to Harty were the recordings made by Bryden Thomson and the Ulster Orchestra between 1979 and 1983 on the Chandos label, where the full stature of Harty's powers as a composer were properly revealed.

There were also BBC broadcast talks in 1943 (by Eric Gillett), in 1946 for the Northern Ireland Home Service, and another shared by the North of Ireland and North of England Home Services in 1951 which featured contributions from Alfred Barker, Lady Harty, Norman Allin, Alice Harty, Terry O'Connor and Clyde Twelvetrees. Material from this interesting documentary was later included in *A Child of Lir* – a centenary broadcast by BBC Radio 3, written and presented by Bernard Keeffe in 1979. All of these accounts provided a glimpse of Harty's achievements, but they could not practically give an account of the phenomenally rich and active musical life he led, particularly after he arrived in London in 1901. It is perhaps forgotten today how pioneering was Harty's career as an accompanist before his time with the Hallé. Some still consider him the finest proponent of the art in Britain, and an exploration of those he accompanied, in the concert halls of London *and* during the 'chamber music interludes' with the major international orchestras, reads like an unbroken catalogue of the world's greatest soloists. For those who played with him, the effect of his tone at the keyboard, combined with his instinctive musical empathy, was spellbinding, and to the trained musician his abilities to score-read and transpose remain legend. To this end, he was the most consummate of musicians – which seems all the more extraordinary when one remembers he never received a formal lesson from a music college or university.

Much has been said of Harty's brilliance as a conductor, not least of his remarkable legacy to the Hallé Orchestra during a time of economic depression. He left an indelible mark on those who played for him – such was Archie Camden's regard that his favourite choice for his 'Desert Island Discs' was the Scherzo from the 'Irish' Symphony.[84] While he never tolerated slovenly playing, he encouraged a rare spontaneity, as Gerald Jackson recalled: 'Sargent was, and indeed always remained, on the attack. He could not let us *play* as did Beecham or Harty.'[85] As a conductor of concertos Harty was largely unsurpassed, a skill no doubt engendered by his prowess as an accompanist. As a British conductor among a rich crop, he maintained the contentious position that he and his colleagues suffered from a European chauvinism, and that British conductors did not enjoy the welcome among Continental orchestras that foreign conductors did in London, Manchester, Leeds, Glasgow and elsewhere. His two visits to Madrid and Brussels, somewhat understandably, did nothing to alter that view, though there was some compensation in his successful tours to America.

Harty's love of poetry and literature led him to Berlioz, with whose maverick unconventionality he naturally identified. What is more, obdurately defying

[84] BBC Radio 4, 11 Mar. 1968.
[85] Jackson, *First Flute*, 88.

all the Frenchman's critics, he remained a standard-bearer for Berlioz's genius through the regular programming of his works, to the point where they became a hallmark of his career and personality; his promotion of works such as the *Grande Messe des morts* and the *Symphonie funèbre et triomphale* remain pioneering landmarks in the composer's performance and reception history. He was also, by all accounts, a great interpreter of Mozart, Elgar, Delius, and Brahms (at a time when the latter was recovering from the invective as an old-fashioned, conservative composer), as well as much contemporary Italian music, notably Respighi. His readings of Beethoven and Schubert were at times eccentric, but he was a successful and enthusiastic proponent of Russian music, notably of Tchaikovsky, Balakirev, Mussorgsky and Borodin. His recording legacy, though extensive, communicates only a part of this interpretative aptitude. We have some Berlioz, but not, regrettably, the *Symphonie fantastique* in which he was considered supreme; we have no Delius, no symphonies of Brahms or Elgar, and no Respighi. As compensation, there is some Mozart, which is compelling in its detail and insight, and there is the wonderful recording of Szigeti in Brahms's Violin Concerto. His readings of his own works, *Scenes for an Eastern Romance*, *With the Wild Geese*, and the Scherzo from his 'Irish' Symphony, are also helpful clues to the interpretation of his own music.

In terms of musical outlook, which clearly had a major bearing on the works he chose to conduct, Harty's unwillingness to embrace the modernisms of Stravinsky (notably *The Rite of Spring*), the Second Viennese School, much of Bartók, Hindemith, and much of Vaughan Williams's and Holst's more challenging music stemmed from a deeply ingrained, anti-intellectual antagonism to developments which, he believed, had blighted much music of the twentieth century and threatened to sever that vital relationship between composers, performers, and music's most vital, indispensable patron, the audience. In this he was argumentative to the point of pugnacity. It is possible to attribute this, perhaps, to the lack of a university education where his aesthetic outlook might have been broadened, and the horizons of musical art questioned, but his views were also those espoused by Stanford, a fellow countryman he greatly admired, whose education and intellect were of the highest calibre. More likely, however, is the simple fact that he could not comprehend art as a purely mental activity, and that the emotional, even visceral response to music, as a means of human interaction, was paramount. This view was reflected in his work as a composer, as it was in the contemporary powers of those such as Lambert and Walton, who, he fervently believed, were carrying British music in the most productive direction. Supremely polished and professional, Harty's style was enduringly Romantic and persistently informed by the nationalist mindset (musically rather than politically inclined) in which he had grown up at the end of the nineteenth century, while his embracing of the Irish traditional repertoire had begun very much in the mould of Stanford and his mentor Esposito. This is evident in the 'Irish' Symphony, but in the composition of the *Comedy Overture* and *With the Wild Geese* his assimilation of the Irish idiom moved on from the simpler concept of arrangement to more inventive, innovative composition. This, as Harry White has asserted, made *With the Wild Geese* a 'seminal work in the history of Irish music'.[86] Indeed, by the time Harty had composed *The Children of Lir* in 1938 his distance from the Celtic revival, as White has stressed, enabled him to create a genuinely Irish work that was free from the constraints and limitations of folksong quotation. As for Harty's musical vocabulary, it was already suffering from accusations of anachronism after the First World War, and in the context of contemporary British music of the 1920s and 30s it seemed dated. However, in this post-modern age, that anxiety no longer carries the critical weight it once did, and we are able to perceive the subtleties, character and flair in Harty's music, especially in that for the orchestra, without the encumbrances of chronology, modernity or contemporaneity.

Finally, in assessing Harty the man, we still know relatively little about him. If he fostered political views, he assiduously kept them to himself. He loved Hillsborough, Ulster and Ireland, but ultimately identified himself as British. Of Irish affairs he remained aloof, yet his actions openly expressed a profound love for his country before and after partition. He cultivated a small circle of truly close friends, but his nature was gregarious enough to enjoy the larger social circle of an orchestra like the Hallé, which, over thirteen years, assumed a family atmosphere. Although in public he exercised autocratic tendencies – not uncommon among conductors – in private he appears to have been a rather shy, retiring, solitary figure, a fact confirmed by the refuge he cultivated near Kendal. His marriage to Agnes Nicholls was clearly unhappy, though on what basis it foundered is unknown. They may simply have been incompatible. Nicholls undoubtedly helped Harty's career in the first years of their life together, and their professional association lasted until the mid-1920s. Thereafter their paths parted and they lived separate lives. That they decided to abjure divorce may well have been to avoid scandal and the public gaze, and though their estrangement must have been obvious to his friends and colleagues, as well as to his secretary Baguley, it was never mentioned or discussed. Nicholls styled herself 'Lady Harty' until her death in September 1959, and this front of normality was retained when she appeared in the BBC documentary of 1951. Her final words were, perhaps, revealing:

> He was a man of great genius, and I have always felt that if he had not been the great musician he was, he might have been as great a poet or writer. His comparatively early death, and his previous months of illness, give me the feeling that his was, in some ways, an unfulfilled career.[87]

In terms of his musical aspirations, this may have been true. But it was not all that he craved. In the light of his strained domestic circumstances, a fleeting affair with Elsie Swinton before the First World War now seems more than conjectural, a fact surely corroborated by the surviving correspondence with the one woman he truly loved, Lorie Bolland. Here it is verified that, for much of his life, he was an intensely lonely man. Strangely driven by a sense of fate and a belief in the paranormal, he had probably accepted that, by the age of fifty-five, his loveless existence into old age was inevitable. His encounter with Lorie

---

[86] White, *The Keeper's Recital*, 117.

[87] BBC talk, 18 June 1951.

was therefore an extraordinary and unexpected happening which might have changed his life. With her he found love and his letters to her reveal a passionate, unreserved side not seen before in his personality. Yet, when this secret 'affair of the heart' ended, he must have been a broken man with a sense of loss that can only have grown more acute as his illness took hold and he faced the prospect of an uncertain future alone. It is therefore hard to escape this affecting impression of bereavement in the pages of some of the *Five Irish Poems* and *The Children of Lir*, pieces which embody a powerful inner loneliness belied by the optimism of his Handel transcriptions and the buoyancy of *A John Field Suite*. It was an emotional burden this remarkable, consummate musician and polymath carried to his grave with fortitude and courage at a time of great national crisis, unknown to his friends, colleagues and the wider world.

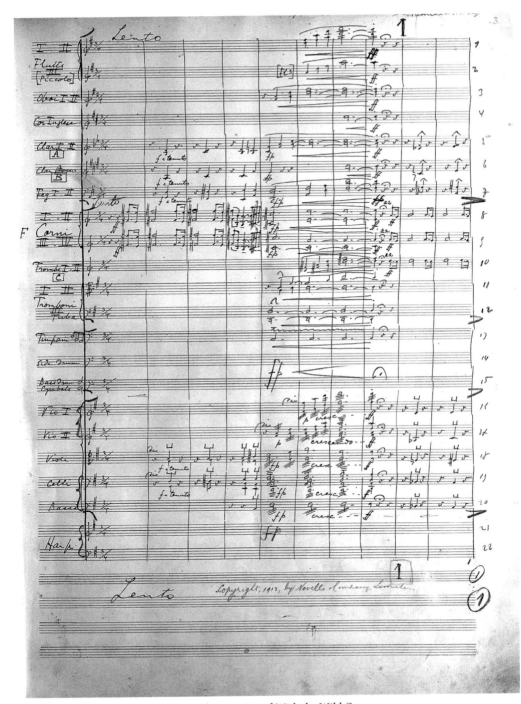

Fig. 3 The opening of *With the Wild Geese*

APPENDIX 1

List of Works

Abbreviations for sources:

GB-Belqb	Harty Archive, Queen's University, Belfast
GB-Lbl	British Library, London
GB-Lcm	Royal College of Music, London

A SOLO AND CHORAL WORKS WITH ORCHESTRA OR ORGAN

1 *I Heard a Voice from Heaven*, anthem SATB and organ (Revelation 14:13). Composed on the death of Queen Victoria, Jan. 1901. First perf. Bray, Christ Church, Jan. 1901; also sung at the funeral of Archdeacon Scott, Christ Church, Bray, Jan. 1912. MS *GB-Belqb*. Unpub.

2 *Ode to a Nightingale*, Op. 16, [Scena] for soprano or tenor and orchestra. Completed 1907. First perf. Cardiff Festival, Agnes Nicholls (sop), cond. Harty, 25 Sept. 1907. MS *GB-Belqb* (vocal score and full score). Pub. Brietkopf & Härtel (vocal score) 1907. Dedicated 'To my Wife'.

3 Triple chant, A major. In *The Irish Chant Book* (Dublin: Pub. Association for Promoting Christian Knowledge, 1907).

4 *Come Up from the Fields, Father* (from Walt Whitman, *Drum Taps*), chorus and orchestra. Completed 3 July 1912. MS *GB-Belqb* (vocal score only). Unpub.

5 *The Mystic Trumpeter* (from Walt Whitman, *Whispers of Heavenly Death*), baritone, chorus and orchestra. Completed April 1913. First perf. Leeds Triennial Festival, Thorpe bates (bar.), cond. Harty, 2 Oct. 1913. MS *GB-Belqb* (vocal score); *GB-Lcm* (full score). Pub. Novello (vocal score) 1913. Dedicated to Sir Stanley Cochrane.

B ORCHESTRAL WORKS

1 Overture: *The Exile*, Op. 2, C minor. Based on Thomas Campbell's poem 'The Exile of Erin'. Completed *c.* 1901. Unperf. during Harty's lifetime. First perf. Slough Parish Church, Windsor Sinfonia, cond. Robert Tucker, 29 Sept. 2001. MS *GB-Belqb*. Unpub.

2 An 'Irish' Symphony, Op. 7: (i) 'On the shores of Lough Neagh', D minor; (ii) 'The Fair Day', B flat major; (iii) 'In the Antrim Hills', F major; (iv) 'The Twelfth of July', D major. Completed 1904. First perf. Dublin, 18 May 1904, DOS, cond. Harty; rev. 1915, Leeds and Bournemouth, cond. Harty; rev. 1924, Manchester, Hallé Orchestra, cond. Harty, 13 Nov. 1924. MS 1904 version missing; MSS (1915 and 1924 versions) *GB-Belqb*. Pub. Boosey (1924 version) 1927. Dedicated to Louise Farrer.

3 *A Comedy Overture* [*Lustspiel Overture*], Op. 15, E flat major. Completed
Aug. 1906; rev. Dec. 1908. First perf. London, Queen's Hall (Promenade
Concert), Queen's Hall Orchestra, cond. Henry Wood, 24 Oct. 1907. MS
GB-Belqb. Pub. Schott 1909; Universal 1936.

4 *With the Wild Geese*, tone poem, E minor. Completed 1910. First perf.
Cardiff, 23 Sept. 1910, cond. Harty; Liverpool, LPS, cond. Cowen, 8 Nov.
1910; London, LSO, cond. Harty, 20 March 1911. MS *GB-Lcm*. Pub. Novello
1912. Dedicated to Nora O'Connor.

5 *Fantasy Scenes (from an Eastern Romance)*, suite in four movements (see
D2, *The Singer of Shiraz*, below): (i) 'The Laughing Juggler'; (ii) 'A Dancer's
Reverie'; (iii) 'Lonely in Moonlight'; (iv) 'In the Slave Market. Completed
1919. First perf. London, Queen's Hall, New Queen's Hall Orchestra, cond.
Harty, 23 March 1920. MS missing. Pub. C. E. Publishing *c.* 1920.

6 *The Children of Lir*, tone poem, A major. Based on the *bas-relief* by Sophia
Rosamund Praeger of 'Finol and Her Brothers'. Completed Nov. 1938.
First perf. London, Queen's Hall, BBC SO, cond. Harty, 1 March 1939. MS
(sketches and full score) *GB-Belqb*; two pages of piano score at Hillsborough
Church. Pub. Universal 1939. Dedicated to 'O. E. B.' [Olive Baguley].

7 Fanfare for four trumpets and side drum, in *Fanfare* No. 3 (1921), 51. MS
missing.

C CONCERTOS AND SOLO WORKS WITH ORCHESTRA

1 *Three Pieces* for oboe: (i) 'Orientale', G minor; (ii) 'Chansonette', D major;
(iii) 'À la campagne', A major. First perf. 'Orientale' and 'À la campagne',
London, Langham Hotel, Concert-Goers' Club, Henri de Busscher (ob) [?],
Harty (pf), 10 Nov. 1905; also Dublin, RDS, Henri de Busscher, Harty, Feb.
1911. First perf. all three pieces with orchestral accomp., London, Queen's
Hall, Promenade Concert, Queen's Hall Orchestra, de Busscher, cond.
Henry Wood, 7 Sept. 1911. MSS of orchestral versions of 'Orientale' and 'À la
campagne' (2 copies) *GB-Belqb*. Pub. Stainer & Bell 1911 (ob, pf); Stainer &
Bell 'Orientale' and 'À la campagne' (orch. version) *c.* 1931.

2 Violin Concerto: (i) Allegro deciso, D minor; (ii) Molto lento, C major;
(iii) Allegro con brio, D major. Completed 1908. First perf. Bournemouth,
Maria de Chastain (vn), cond. Harty, 18 March 1909; London, Queen's
Hall, Queen's Hall Orchestra, Szigeti (vn), cond. Harty, 24 March 1909. MS
missing. Pub. Schott (vn, pf) 1909; pub. (full score) C. E. Publishing 1920.
Dedicated 'To Joska Szigeti, in Friendship'.

3 *Variations on a Dublin Air* (also known as *Variations on an Irish Air* and
Variations for Violin and Orchestra), D minor. Completed 1 Sept. 1912. First
perf. London, Queen's Hall, LSO, Paul Kochański (vn), cond. Harty, 10
February 1913. MS (full score) *GB-Belqb*. Unpub.

4 *In Ireland*, fantasy for flute, harp and piano. Completed Feb. 1915; version
   for flute, harp and small orchestra completed Aug. 1935. First perf. Lambert
   Flack (fl.), Sidonie Goossens (harp), BBC SO, cond. Harty (BBC broadcast),
   24 Dec. 1935. MS (fl, pf) *GB-Belqb*; pub. Hawkes 1916. MS (orch. version)
   GB-Belqb; pub. Hawkes 1935. Dedicated to Miriam Timothy.

5 Piano Concerto: (i) Allegro risoluto, B minor; (ii) Tranquillo e calmo,
   E major; (iii) Con brio e vivace, B major. Completed Fiesole, Italy, summer
   1922. First perf. Leeds, Leeds Philharmonic, Harty (pf); also Bournemouth,
   Harty (pf), cond. Dan Godfrey, 28 Dec. 1922; also Manchester, Harty (pf),
   cond. Beecham, 15 March 1923. MS missing. Pub. two-piano version, C. E.
   Publishing *c.* 1923. Dedicated to Michele Esposito.

D THEATRE MUSIC

1 *Proud Maisie*, incidental music to play by E. G. Hemmerde: (i) Overture,
   A major; (ii) Entr'acte I; (iii) Entr'acte II; (iv) Act II Minuetto; (v) 'The
   White Cockade' (Alan's Song); (vi) Entr'acte III; (vi) End of Scene 1 Act IV;
   (vii) Interlude between Scenes 1 and 2 Act IV. Completed Feb. 1912. First
   perf. London, Aldwych Theatre, 12 March 1912. MS *GB-Belqb*. Unpub.

2 *The Singer of Shiraz* (A Persian Romance in Three Acts), incidental music
   to play by J. B. Fagan: (i) Prelude Act I Scene 1; (ii) Song Act I Scene I,
   'O Moon Arise from thy Couch in the East'; (iii) ['Intermezzo'] Act I Scene 2;
   Prelude Act I Scene 3; (iv) Song 'The Bee hath Stolen the Secret of the Rose',
   Act I Scene 3; (v) Prelude 'The Slave Market', Act I Scene 4 (also Act III
   Scene 2); (vi) Song 'O Sultan of the Shadowy Courts of Sleep' Act II Scene 1;
   (vii) Song 'O Wind of Dawn', Act II Scene 1; (viii) ['Dance'], Act II Scene 2;
   (ix) ['Dance'], Act II Scene 3; (x) Song 'Lo! All the Garden Sleepeth', Act II
   Scene 3; (xi) Prelude, Act III Scene 1; (x) Prelude, Act III Scene 3. Completed
   July and Aug. 1915. Unperformed? Libretto (typescript) and MS *GB-Belqb*.
   Unpub.

E ORCHESTRAL TRANSCRIPTIONS AND ARRANGEMENTS

1 *From the Water Music* [Handel], suite for orchestra: (i) Allegro; (ii) Air;
   (iii) Bourée; (iv) Hornpipe; (v) Andante espressivo; (vi) Allegro deciso.
   Completed 1920. First perf. (select movements), Manchester, Hallé
   Orchestra, cond. Harty, 18 Nov. 1920; also Birmingham, CBSO, cond. Harty,
   15 Dec. 1920; London, LPS, cond. Harty, 16 Dec. 1920. MS *GB-Belqb*. Pub.
   Murdoch 1922.

2 Concerto for Orchestra with Organ [Handel] (from Concerto 'B' in
   Chrysander's *Händel-Gesellschaft*): (i) Lento; Allegro ma non troppo;
   (ii) Grazioso; (iii) Tempo I (Lento); (iv) Con brio, ma non troppo allegro.
   Completed *c.* 1922. First perf. Manchester, Hallé Orchestra, Harold Dawber
   (org.), cond. Harty, 25 Jan. 1923. Pub. Universal 1934.

3 *From the Music for the Royal Fireworks* [Handel], suite for orchestra:
  (i) Overture; (ii) Siciliano; (iii) Bourée; (iv) Minuet. Completed 1923. First
  perf. Manchester, Hallé Orchestra, cond. Harty. MS *GB-Belqb* (MS missing).
  Pub. Murdoch 1924.

4 *The Londonderry Air* [Irish trad.]. Completed 1924? Recorded by Columbia,
  Hallé Orchestra, cond. Harty, March 1924. MS missing. Pub. Curwen 1924.

5 *Polonaise, Arietta and Passacaglia* [Handel]. (See F12 below.) Completed
  1926. First perf. Manchester, Hallé Orchestra, cond. Harty, 4 Nov. 1926. MS
  GB-Belqb. Pub. Boosey & Hawkes 1932.

6 *Introduction and Rigaudon* [Handel]. (See F12 below.) Completed 1935.
  Recorded with *Polonaise, Arietta and Passacaglia* for Decca, LSO, cond.
  Harty, 15 Oct. 1935. MS missing. Pub. Universal 1935.

7 *A John Field Suite*: (i) Polka (Rondo from Piano Sonata in E flat major,
  Op. 1 No. 1); (ii) Nocturne (Nocturne No. 5 in B flat major); (iii) Slow Waltz
  (Waltz in E major: 'Remembrance'); (iv) Rondo 'Midi' (Rondo in E major
  from Piano Quintet 'Le midi'). Completed Feb. 1939. First perf. Dublin (RÉ
  broadcast), RÉ SO, cond. Harty, 13 May 1939; London (BBC broadcast), BBC
  SO, cond. Harty, 3 June 1939; also London, Queen's Hall, LPO, cond. Harty,
  1 Feb. 1940. MS *GB-Belqb*. Pub. Universal 1939.

F CHAMBER MUSIC

1 String Quartet in A minor: (i) Andante, Piú mosso, A minor; (ii) Andante,
  A major; (iii) Allegro vivace, D minor; (iv) Serioso, Allegro, A minor.
  Completed 29 March 1898. Unperformed. MS *GB-Belqb*. Unpub.

2 Violin Sonata. Entered for the Feis Ceoil, Dublin, 1899. MS lost.

3 String Quartet No. 1 in F major, Op. 1: (i) Allegro con brio, F major;
  (ii) Vivace, D minor; (iii) Andante pastorale, B flat major; (iv) Allegro vivace,
  F major. Prize-winner, Feis Ceoil, Dublin, 1900. First perf. first movement
  only, Dublin, Feis Ceoil, Swan, Munster, L. Brett and M. Brett, [15] May
  1900. MS *GB-Belqb*. Unpub.

4 *Introduction and Allegro* for violin and piano. (See Greer 1979, 20n.) First
  perf. Hillsborough Castle [?], T. J. Lindsay (vn), Harty (pf), 12 Oct. 1900. MS
  missing. Unpub.

5 Two *Fantasiestücke* for piano trio (vn, vc, pf), Op. 3: (i) Andantino, A flat
  major; (ii) Allegro moderato, F major. Morrison Prize, Feis Ceoil Dublin,
  1901. First perf. Dublin, Feis Ceoil, A. Darley (vn)?, Carl Fuchs (vc), Harty
  (pf), May 1901. MS *GB-Belqb*. Unpub.

6 String Quartet in A minor, Op. 5: (i) Allegro ma non troppo, A minor;
   (ii) Vivace sempre leggiero, F major; (iii) Lento, A minor; (iv) Allegro con
   brio, Molto vivace, A major. Prize-winner, Feis Ceoil, Dublin, 1902. First
   perf. Dublin, A. Darley (vn), P. J. Griffith (vn), O. Grisard (va) and H. Bast
   (vc), 8 May 1902; also London, Copped Hall, Totteridge, A. Gibson (vn), J.
   Capron (vn), A. Hobday (va) and H. Trust (vc), 22 Dec. 1902. MS *GB-Belqb*.
   Unpub.

7 *Romance and Scherzo* for cello and piano, Op. 8. Prize-winner, Feis Ceoil,
   Dublin, 1903. First perf. Dublin, Feis Ceoil, C. Twelvetrees (vc), Harty (pf),
   18 May 1903. MS *GB-Lbl* Add. MS 54409, fols. 22–35. Unpub. Dedicated to
   W. H. Squire.

8 Piano Quintet in F major, Op. 12 (2 vn, va, vc, pf): (i) Allegro, F major;
   (ii) D major; (iii) Lento, A minor; (iv) Allegro con brio, F major. Winner
   of the Lewis-Hill prize for piano quintets 1904. First perf. first and second
   movements only, London, Concert Club, Bechstein Hall, E. F. Arbós
   (vn), T. F. Morris (vn), A. Hobday (va), P. Jones (vc) and Harty (pf), 29 Jan.
   1905; complete and rev., London, Langham Hotel, Concert-Goers' Club, 7
   Dec. 1906. MS *GB-Belqb*; also sketches of further rev. of opening of first
   movement *GB-Belqb*. Unpub.

9 *Three Pieces* for oboe and piano. (See C1 above.)

10 *Two Pieces* for cello and piano: (i) 'Waldstille' ('Wood Stillness'); (ii) 'Der
   Schmetterling' ('Butterflies'). Completed 1907? MS missing. Pub. Houghton
   1907; Forsyth 1924. Dedicated to W. H. Squire.

11 Scherzo for string quartet incorporating 'The Londonderry Air'. Completed
   1908, one of five movements commissioned by the Hambourg String
   Quartet (the others were by Frank Bridge J. D. Davis, Eric Coates and York
   Bowen). MS (parts only; vn 1, va and vc) in private possession. Unpub.

12 Suite for violin and piano: (i) Rigaudon; (ii) Arietta; (iii) Hornpipe;
   (iv) Passacaglia; (v) Polonaise; (vi) Siciliano; (viii) Allegro giocoso.
   Completed 1912? MS missing. Pub. (movements i–iv) Schott 1910; pub.
   (complete) Schott 1920.

13 *Irish Fantasy* for violin and piano. Completed 27 July 1912. First perf. Dublin,
   Antient Concert Rooms, A. J. Griffith (vn), Harty (pf), 8 Dec. 1912. MS
   GB-Belqb. Pub. Boosey 1912. Dedicated to P. J. Griffith.

14 *In Ireland* for flute, harp and piano. (See C4 above.)

15 *The Repose of the Holy Family* for cello and piano (arr. from Berlioz's
   L'Enfance du Christ). MS *GB-Belqb*. Unpub.

16 Suite for cello and piano: (i) 'An Irish Prelude', D major; (ii) 'A Wistful
   Song', F major; (iii) 'Humoresque', A major; (iv) 'Scherzo-Fantasy',
   D minor. Completed June 1928. First perf. London, B. Harrison (vc), Harty
   (pf), Dec. 1928. MS *GB-Belqb*. Pub. Schott 1928.

G WORKS FOR PIANO (AND HARP)

1 *Fantasia* for two pianos, Op. 6. Completed 1902. MS *GB-Belqb*. Unpub.

2 *Valse Caprice*. Completed *c.* 1904. MS *GB-Belqb*. Unpub.

3 *Idyll, Arlequin et Columbine*, Op. 10. Completed 1904. MS *GB-Belqb*. Unpub.

4 *Irish Fancies*: (i) 'At Sea; (ii) 'The Stream in the Glen; (iii) 'The Spanish Stranger'. Completed *c.* 1904. MS *GB-Belqb*. Unpub.

5 *Spring Fancies: Two Preludes* for harp: (i) A flat major; (ii) C flat major. Completed *c.* 1915. MS missing. Pub. Novello 1915.

6 Nocturne: *Spring Fancy*. Completed 23 April 1934. MS in private possession (CB). Unpub. For Lorie Bolland.

7 *Portrait*. Completed 'At sea, July 9 1934'. MS in private possession (CB). Unpub. 'For Lorie'.

H SOLO SONGS

1 *Sea Wrack* (Moira O'Neill). Completed 1901–2? MS *GB-Belqb*. Pub. Boosey 1905.

2 *The Song of Glen Dun* (Moira O'Neill). Completed 1902. MS missing. Pub. Boosey 1902.

3 *Bonfires* (W. L. Bultitaft). Completed Oct. 1903, orch. version for Nicholls. First perf. Norwich Festival, Agnes Nicholls (sop), cond. Harty, Oct. 1905. MS *GB-Belqb*; orch. version missing. Pub. Boosey 1905. Dedicated to 'H. B. S.'

4 *Rose Madness* (W. L. Bultitaft). Completed 1903? MS missing. Pub. Augener 1903?

5 *Now is the Month of Maying* (Anon., *c.* 1595). Completed March 1903. MS *GB-Belqb*. Pub. Boosey 1907.

6 *The Devon Maid* (John Keats). Completed July 1903. MS *GB-Belqb*. Pub. Augener 1903.

7 *Three Traditional Ulster Airs* (Seosamh MacCathmhaoil), folksong arrangements: (i) 'The Blue Hills of Antrim'; (ii) 'My Lagan Love'; (iii) 'Black Sheela of the Silver Eye'. Completed Jan 1905. MS *GB-Belqb*. Pub. Boosey 1905. Dedicated to Harry Plunket Greene.

8 *Collen's Wedding Song* (P. W. Joyce). Completed April 1905. MS *GB-Belqb*. Pub. Boosey 1905.

9 *The Ould Lad* (Moira O'Neill). Completed *c.* 1906. MS missing. Pub Boosey 1906.

10 *Three Flower Songs* (L. B. Hay Shaw), Op. 13: (i) 'Poppies', dedicated 'To Agnes [Nicholls]'; (ii) 'Mignonette', dedicated 'To Elsie [Swinton]'; (iii) 'Gorse', dedicated 'To Muriel [Foster]'. Completed *c.* 1906. MS missing. Pub. Boosey 1906.

11 *The Blue Hills* (John Arbuthnot). Completed Nov. 1906. MS *GB-Belqb*. Unpub. Dedicated to Frederic Austin.

12 *Lane o' the Thrushes* (Cahal O'Byrne & Cahir Healy). Completed May 1906. MS *GB-Belqb*. Pub. Boosey 1907.

13 *Come, O Come my Life's Delight* (Thomas Campion). Completed *c*. 1907. MS *GB-Belqb*. Pub. Boosey 1907.

14 *Song of the Three Mariners* (Anon. *c*. 1609). Completed June 1907. MS *GB-Belqb*. Pub. Boosey 1907. Dedicated to Lady Arthur Hill.

15 *An Irish Love Song* (Katherine Tynan). Completed 1908? MS missing. Pub. Chappell 1908. Dedicated to Benjamin Davies.

16 *Six Songs of Ireland*, Op. 18: (i) 'Lookin' Back' (Moira O'Neill), dedicated to 'F. O. M.'; (ii) 'Dreaming' (Cahir Healy), dedicated to Gordon Cleather; (iii) 'Lullaby' (Cathal O'Byrne), dedicted to Mis Rhoda von T. Lehin'; (iv) 'Grace for Light' (Moira O'Neill), dedicated to 'Miss Carmen Hill'; (v) Flame in the Skies' (Lizzie Twigg), dedicated to Louise Dale; (vi) 'At Sea' (Moira O'Neill), dedicated to A.[gnes] N.[icholls]. Completed April 1908. First perf. London, Bechstein Hall, Agnes Nicholls (sop), Harty (pf), 3 Nov. 1908. MS *GB-Belqb*. Pub. Boosey 1908.

17 *Your Hand in Mine* (Harold Simpson). Completed *c*. 1908. MS missing. Pub. Chappell 1908.

18 *By the Sea* (Moira O'Neill). Completed Jan. 1909. MS *GB-Belqb*. Unpub. 'Written for some private person. Whose name I have forgotten'.

19 *Three Sea Prayers from the Greek Anthology* (from the *Greek Anthology* trans. J. W. Mackail): (i) 'To the Gods of Harbour and Headland' (Antiphilus), completed 13 Oct. 1909; (ii) 'Saved by Faith' (Leonid of Tarentum), completed 14 Oct. 1909; (iii) 'To Apollo of Leucas' (Philippus), completed 15 Oct. 1909. First perf. London, Bechstein Hall, Agnes Nicholls (sop), Harty (pf), 16 Nov. 1909. MS *GB-Belqb*. Unpub.

20 *Song of the Constant Lover* (Sir John Suckling). Completed *c*. 1909. MS missing. Pub. Boosey 1909.

21 *Tell Me Not, Sweet, I am Unkind* (Richard Lovelace). Completed *c*. 1909. MS missing. Pub. Boosey 1909.

22 *When Summer Comes* (Harold Simpson). Completed *c*. 1909. MS missing. Pub. J. Church 1909.

23 *Scythe Song* (Riccardo Stephens). Completed Jan. 1910. MS *GB-Belqb*. Pub. Boosey 1910. Dedicated to Mrs Goetz (Miss Muriel Foster).

24 *An Exile's Mother* (Emily Lawless). Completed April 1911. MS *GB-Belqb*. Unpub.

25 *Homeward* (Harold Simpson). Complete *c*. 1911. MS missing. Pub. Novello 1911. Dedicated to Robert Radford.

26 *The Sea Gypsy* (Richard Hovey). Completed March 1911. MSS *GB-Belqb* (see D. Greer, 'Hamilton Harty Manuscripts', *Music Review* 47(4) (1986/7), 241, 245. Pub. Boosey 1912. Dedicated to Elsie Swinton.

27 *Five Irish Sketches for Voice and Piano*: (i) 'The Rachray Man' (Moira O'Neill) MS *GB-Belqb*; (ii) 'The Stranger's Grave' (Emily Lawless), MS *GB-Belqb*; (iii) 'Across the Door' (Padraic Colum), MS missing; (iv) 'Cradle Song' (Padraic Colum), MS missing; (v) 'A Drover' (Padraic Colum), MS missing. Completed *c.* 1911. Pub. as separate songs, Novello 1913.

28 *To the King* (Ricardo Stephens), piano with organ obbligato. MS missing. Pub. Chappell 1911.

29 *Heart of my Heart* (Emily Lawless). Completed *c.* 1910–12. MS *GB-Belqb*. Unpub.

30 *Nursie* (Lina Rathbone). Completed *c.* 1911–13. MS *GB-Belqb*. Unpub. Dedicated to Miss Mary Swinton [daughter of Elsie Swinton].

31 *Adieu, Sweet Amaryllis* (Anon., No. 12 from John Wilbye's *First Set of English Madrigals*, 1598). Completed *c.* 1911–13. MS *GB-Belqb*. Unpub. At the end of the MS there is a note 'From an old manuscript in the possession of John Broadley Esq of Bristol.'

32 *By the Bivouac's Fitful Flame* (Walt Whitman). Completed May 1912. MS *GB-Lcm*. Pub. Boosey 1912.

33 *A Rann of Wandering* (Padraic Colum). Completed *c.* 1914. MS missing. Pub. Novello 1914.

34 *The Wake Feast* (Alice Milligan). Completed *c.* 1914. MS missing. Pub. Novello 1914.

35 *My Thoughts of You* (author unknown). Completed Feb. 1920. MS *GB-Belqb*. Unpub.

36 *Carnlough Bay* (Irish melody). Completed 1921. MS *GB-Belqb*. Unpub.

37 *Antrim and Donegal*: (i) 'The Two Houses' (Moira O'Neill); (ii) 'The Little Son' (Moira O'Neill); (iii) 'Hush Song' (Elizabeth Shane); (iv) 'Herrin's in the Bay' (Elizabeth Shane). Completed 1926. MS *GB-Belqb*. Pub. Boosey 1926.

38 *Three Irish Folksongs*, folksong arrangements (P. W. Joyce): (i) 'The Lowlands of Holland'; (ii) 'The Fairy King's Courtship'; (iii) 'The Game Played in Erin-go-Bragh'. Completed *c.* 1929. MS *GB-Belqb*. Pub. Oxford University Press 1929.

39 *Five Irish Poems*: (i) 'A Mayo Love Song' (Alice Milligan); (ii) 'At Easter' (Helen Lanyon); (iii) 'The Sailor Man' (Moira O'Neill); (iv) 'Denny's Daughter' (Moira O'Neill); (v) 'The Fiddler of Dooney' (W. B. Yeats). Completed 1938. Pub. Boosey 1938.

I UNACCOMPANIED CHORAL MUSIC

1 *The Splendour Falls*, partsong SATB, n.d. MS missing. Pub. Vincent Music *c.* 1901.

2 *Owls*, partsong SATB (Tennyson), n.d. MS *GB-Belqb*. Unpub.

J DRAFTS AND SKETCHES

A large number of drafts of sketches survives of individual pieces. These are detailed in David Greer, 'Hamilton Harty Manuscripts', *Music Review* 47 (1986–7), 238–52.

K ARTICLES, BROADCASTS, LECTURES AND OTHER WRITINGS

The following survive complete. All *GB-Belqb* unless otherwise stated.

1 'Modern Composers and Modern Composition': lecture for the Manchester Organists' Association; published in *MT* 65 (April 1924), 328–32

2 'The Approach to Berlioz', *The Music Teacher* (Sept. 1926)

3 'Beethoven's Orchestra: A Conductor's Reflections', *Music & Letters* 8(2) (1927), 172–7

4 'The Discouragement of English Music', IAO Congress, 28 Aug. 1928

5 'Variations on a Theme by Haydn: Brahms': lecture given at the Royal College of Organists, 16 Feb. 1929

6 'Michele Esposito', *The Irish Statesman*, 7 Dec. 1929, 276–7

7 'The Art of Pianoforte Accompaniment', *c.* 1930

8 James W. Alsop Lectures, Liverpool University, 'The Modern Orchestra': (i) 'History and Growth of the Orchestra', 13 Oct. 1931; (ii) 'The Woodwind and Horns', 20 Oct. 1931; (iii) 'The Strings', 3 Nov. 1931; (iv) missing [10 Nov. 1931]; (v) 'Conductors and Conducting', 17 Nov. 1931

9 Broadcast talk for ABC, [May] 1934, in private possession (CB)

10 'Music in England': luncheon for the Critics' Circle, London, 18 Nov. 1935

11 'Berlioz': BBC broadcast talk, 2 Mar. 1936

12 'Autobiography' (*c.* 1940)

13 'The Problem of Berlioz', n.d.

14 'On Listening to Music', n.d.

List of Recordings

Listed below are as many of Harty's UK and USA recordings as I have been able to discover. As part of this work I should like to acknowledge the following:

Ehrlich, C., 'Appendix A: Discography', in *Hamilton Harty: His Life and Music*, ed. D. Greer (Belfast: Blackstaff Press, 1978), 133–40.

Niss, C., 'The Recordings of Sir Hamilton Harty', *Le Grand Baton*, issue no. 61, vol. 23(2) (1990), 16–37.

Hunt, J., *More Musical Knights: Harty, Mackerras, Rattle, Pritchard* (London: John Hunt, 1997; repr. edn. 2009), 7–70.

The discography is arranged in two sections: the first of Harty as conductor and the second as pianist (or organist). The recordings are listed by composer in alphabetical order, and for each composer in date order. The central column lists the works and artist(s) on the recording, and the third column the catalogue numbers(s). Undated recordings are listed at the end.

Abbreviations

CG	English Concert Gramophone
CHW	Recorded in the Central Hall, Westminster
C.	Columbia (Britain)
COL	Columbia (USA)
D.	Decca (Britain)
Decca	Decca (USA)
FTHM	Recorded in the Free Trade Hall, Manchester
GM	British Gramophone Monarch
Hallé	Hallé Orchestra
HMV	His Master's Voice
LPO	London Philharmonic Orchestra
LSO	London Symphony Orchestra
s/s	single-sided

1 AS CONDUCTOR

Anonymous

1922	Old English song: *Barbara Allen* Clara Butt, with orchestra	C. X263 s/s
1922	Old English carol: *The First Nowell* Clara Butt, with orchestra	C. X262 s/s

Bach, J. S.

1924 (20 Jan.)   Orchestral Suite No. 2 in B minor, BWV1067   C. L1557-8
R. Murchie – flute   COL 67069-70-D in M-13

1924 (20 Jan.)   'Air' from Orchestral Suite No. 3 in D major, BWV1068 C. L1615
COL 67068-D in M13

1924 (10 April)   Concerto in D minor for two violins   C. L1613-5
A. Catterall & J. S. Bridge – violins   COL 67066-8-D in M-13

Balakirev, Mily

1933 (12 Sept.)   *Russia* (Second Overture on Russian Themes)   C. DB1236-7
LPO   COL DB 1236-7 in M-234

Bax, Arnold

1935 (15 April)   *Overture to a Picaresque Comedy*   C. LX394
LPO   COL 68389-D

Beethoven, Ludwig van

1919   Romance No. 1 in G   C. L1340
D. Kennedy – violin

1922 (29 Aug.)   *Die Ehre Gottes aus der Natur*, Op. 48 No. 4   C. 7265
Clara Butt

1922 (30 Aug.)   *In questa tomba oscura*   C. 7267 s/s

1925 (6 April)   Piano Concerto No. 3 in C minor, Op. 37   C. L1686-9
William Murdoch – piano

1926 (26–7 Nov.) Symphony No. 4 in B flat major, Op. 60   C. L1875-9
Hallé (FTHM)   COL 67234-8 in M-47

Berlioz, Hector

1920 (13 Dec.)   *La Damnation de Faust*, 'Marche hongroise'   C. L1405
Hallé (FTHM)

1924 (29 Oct.)   Overture: *Le Carnaval romain*   C. L1650
Hallé (FTHM)   COL 67087-D

1927 (2 May)   *La Damnation de Faust*, 'Marche hongroise'   C. L2069
Hallé (FTHM)   COL 7188-M

1927 (2 May)   *La Damnation de Faust*, 'Danse des sylphes'   C. L2069
Hallé (FTHM)   COL 7188-M

1927 (2 May)   *Roméo et Juliette*, Scherzo 'Queen Mab'   C. L1989
Hallé (FTHM)   COL 67422D

1932 (18 Feb.)   Overture: *Le Carnaval romain*   C. LX291
Hallé (FTHM)   COL 68221-D

1931 (10 April)   *Les Troyens*, 'Royal Hunt and Storm'   C. DX291
Hallé (FTHM)   COL 68043-D

1933 (5–9 Sept.) *Roméo et Juliette*, 'Roméo seul et fête Capulets'   C. DB 1230-1
LPO; Leon Goossens   COL 1230-1 in M-234

1934 (9 Nov.)	Overture: *Le Corsair* LPO	C. DX644 COL 68287-D
1934 (9 Nov.)	Overture: *Béatrice et Bénédict* LPO	C. LX371 COL 68342-D
1935 (15 April)	Funeral March from *Tristia* LPO	C. LX421 COL 68429-D
1935 (16 Oct.)	Overture: *Le Roi Lear* LSO	D. K792-3 Decca 25539-40
1935 (16 Oct.)	*Les Troyens*, 'Marche troyenne' LSO	D. K793 Decca 25340

Bishop, Henry

| 1921 (23 March) | *Home, Sweet Home*
Elsa Stralia | C. 7262 |

Bizet, Georges

1920 (5 May)	*Carmen*, 'Je dis que rien ne m'épouvante' Elsa Stralia	C. 7247 s/s
1924 (24 Oct.)	*Carmen*, 'Parle-moi de ma mère' Miriam Licette & Frank Mullings	C. L1664
1924 (31 Dec.)	*Carmen*, 'La Fleur que tu m'avais jetée' Elsa Stralia	C. 7332
1926 (23 June)	*Carmen*, 'La Fleur que tu m'avais jetée' Aroldo Lindi	C. L1816

Brahms, Johannes

1920 (3–5 Dec.)	Violin Concerto in D major, Op. 77 Hallé (FTHM); Joseph Szigeti – violin	C. L2265-9 COL 67608-12-D in M-117
1924 (29 Oct.)	*Academic Festival Overture*, Op. 80 Hallé (FTHM)	C. L1637 COL 67085-D
1929	Hungarian Dance No. 5 in F sharp minor and No. 6 in D flat major Hallé (FTHM)	C. 5466 COL 2020-D

Bruch, Max

| 1925 (9 April) | Violin Concerto No. 1 in G minor, Op. 26
Hallé?; Albert Sammons – violin | C. L1680-2
COL 67152-4-D in M-30 |

Clarke, Jeremiah
(previously attributed to Purcell)

| 1927 (2 May) | Trumpet Voluntary [*Prince of Denmark's March*], arr. Henry Wood
Hallé; Alex Harris – trumpet; Harold Dawber – organ | C. L1786
COL 7136-M |

Davies, H. Walford

1927 (2 May)   *Solemn Melody*   C. L1986
                 Hallé (FTHM); Clyde Twelvetrees – cello; Harold Dawber –
                 organ   COL 7136-M

Debussy, Claude

1920 (13 Dec.)   *Prélude à L'Après-midi d'un faune* (abridged)   C. L1405
                 Hallé (FTHM)   COL 67053-D

Donizetti, Gaetano

1926 (24 June)   *L'elisir d'amore*, 'Una furtive lagrima'   C. L1832
                 Charles Hackett

Dvořák, Antonin

1923 (10 Apr. – 24 Oct.)   Symphony No. 9 [No. 5], 'From the New World'
                                                                          C. L1523-7
                 Hallé (FTHM)   COL 67000-4-D in M-3

1927 (2 May)   Overture: *Carnival*   C. L2036
                 Hallé (FTHM)   COL 67412-D

1927 (2 May)   Symphony No. 9 [No. 5], 'From the New World'   C. 9770-4
                 Hallé (FTHM)   COL 67355-9-D in M-77

Elgar, Edward

1920 (16 Sept.) *Sea Pictures*, Op. 37, 'Where Corals Lie'   C. 7246
                 Clara Butt

1927 (27 Jan.)   *The Apostles*, Op. 89, 'By the Wayside'   C. L1968
                 Hallé and Hallé Chorus (FTHM); Dora Labbette; Harold
                 Williams; Hubert Eisdell; Denis Noble; Robert Easton

1930 (30 Nov.)   Cello Concerto in E minor, Op. 85   C. DX117-20
                 Hallé (FTHM); W. H. Squire – cello

1932 (11 July)   *Dream Children*, Op. 43   C. DX325
                 Hallé (CHW)   COL 68002-D in M-165

1932 (11 July)   *Enigma* Variations, Op. 36   C. DX332-5
                 Hallé (CHW)   COL 67999-68002-D in M-165

Esposito, Michele

1922 (20 April) *Irish Suite*, Op. 55, movements 2, 3 and 5   C. L1434
                 Hallé (FTHM)

Giordano, Umberto

1927 (1 Sept.)   *Andrea Chenier*, 'Nemico della patria'   C. L2065
                 Cesare Formichi   COL 7146-M

Gounod, Charles

1919   *Faust*, 'Vous qui faites l'endormie'   C. 747
                 Norman Allin

1924	*La Reine de Saba*, 'She alone charmeth' Norman Allin	C. 756
1924 (31 Dec.)	*Faust*, 'Ah je ris!' Elsa Stralia	C. 7330
1925 (14 Jan.)	*Roméo et Juliette*, 'Je veux vivre dans cette rêve' Miriam Licette	C. L1665
1926 (17 Feb.)	*Faust*, 'Salut demeure' William Martin	C. L1789
1926 (25 June)	*Faust*, 'Salut demeure' Charles Hackett	C. L1832

Grieg, Edvard

| 1923 | Piano Concerto in A minor, Op. 16
Ignaz Friedman – piano | C. (unissued) |

Handel, George Frederic

1919 (5 May)	*Jephtha*, 'Deeper and deeper still' Frank Mullings	C. L1344
1919 (5 May)	*Semele*, 'Where'er you walk' Frank Mullings	C. L1344
1920 (13 Dec.)	*Water Music*, arr. Harty, Movements 1 and 3	C. L1404
1921–2 (10 Oct. – 20 April)	*Water Music*, arr. Harty Hallé (FTHM)	C. L1437-8 COL 50003-4-D
1924 (30 April)	*Pertenope*, 'Hark the tempest wildly raging!' Norman Allin	C. L1612
1933 (14 May)	*Water Music*, arr. Harty LPO	C. DX538-9 COL 68146-7-D in X-13
1934 (12 March)	Concerto in D major for Organ and Orchestra, arr. Harty LSO; Harold Dawber – organ	C. LX341 COL 68256-D
1935 (15 April)	*Music for the Royal Fireworks*, arr. Harty LPO	C. LX389-90
1935 (15 Oct.)	*Introduction, Rigaudon, Polonaise, Arietta and Passacaglia*, arr. Harty	D. K795-6 Decca 25610-11

Harty, Hamilton

1919	*Fantasy Scenes (from an Eastern Romance)*	C. 753-4
1924 (4 March)	*Londonderry Air*, arr. Harty	C. L1573
1926 (26 March)	*With the Wild Geese* Hallé (FTHM)	C. L1822-3
1929 (24 June)	*An Irish Symphony*, Scherzo Hallé (FTHM)	C. 9891 COL 7077M

1929 (24 June)   *Londonderry Air*, arr. Harty   C. 9891
                  Hallé (FTHM)

Haydn, Joseph
1927 (2 May)   Symphony No. 101 in D major, 'The Clock'   C. L2088-91
                  Hallé (FTHM)   COL 65351-4-D in M-76

1935 (14–15 Oct.) Symphony No. 95 in C minor   D. K798-9
                  LSO   Decca 25598-9

Humperdinck, Engelbert
1929 (24 June)   *Hansel and Gretel*, Dance Duet   C. 9909
                  Hallé (FTHM); Manchester School Children's Choir, Gertrude
                  Riall, choirmistress

Lalo, Edouard
1924 (18 July)   *Symphonie espagnole*, Op. 21   COL 67059-61 in M-14
                  Leo Strockoff – violin

Leoncavallo, Ruggero
1927 (1 Sept.)   *I Pagliacci*, 'Si può?'   C. D1487
                  Cesare Formichi   COL 2032M

Liszt, Franz
1931 (10 April)   *Hungarian Rhapsody* No. 12 in C sharp minor   C. LX132
                  Hallé (CHW)   COL 7243-M

Lyadov, Anatole
1924   *The Musical Snuffbox*   C. 980
                                                             COL 67096-D

Mascagni, Pietro
1920 (5 May)   *Cavalleria rusticana*, 'Tu qui Santuzza?'   C. 7242 s/s
                  Elsa Stralia, Frank Mullings

1925 (8 Jan.)   *Cavalleria rusticana*, 'Voi lo sapete'   C. 7330
                  Elsa Stralia

Massenet, Jules
1924   *Thaïs*, 'Helas enfant encore'   C. D1490
                  Cesare Formichi

1927 (1 Sept.)   *Le Jongleur de Notre Dame*, 'La Sauge est en effet précieuse'
                                                                    C. D1491
                  Cesare Formichi   COL 2030M

Mendelssohn, Felix
1931 (9 April)   Symphony No. 4 in A major, Op. 90, 'Italian'   C. DX342-4
                  Hallé (CHW)   COL 68007-9 in M-16

Meyerbeer, Giacomo

1925 (25 July)	*L'Africaine*, 'O paradis!' Charles Hackett	C. 7271
1926	*L'Africaine*, 'O paradis!' Heddle Nash	C. 9104
1926 (21 June)	*L'Africaine*, 'O paradis!' John O'Sullivan	C. L1828

Mozart, Wolfgang Amadeus

1920 (9 May)	*Die Zauberflöte*, 'In diesem heiligen Hallen; O Isis und Osiris' Norman Allin	C. L1384
1924 (10 April)	Violin Concerto No. 5 in A major, K219 Arthur Catterall – violin	C. L1592-5 COL 67055-8 in M-11
1924 (29 Oct.)	Overture: *Le Nozze di Figaro* Hallé (FTHM)	COL 67083-D
1926 (23 March)	Symphony No. 35, K385, 'Haffner' Hallé (FTHM)	C. L1783-5 COL 67209-11-D in M-42
1926 (30 March)	Bassoon Concerto, K191 Hallé; Archie Camden – bassoon	C. L1824-6 COL 67328-30-D in M-71
1933 (30 April)	Sinfonia concertante in E flat major, K364 LPO; Albert Sammons – violin; Lionel Tertis – viola	C. DX478-81 COL 68148-51-D in M-188
1934 (17 Oct.)	Divertimento in D major, K334, movements 1, 2, 3 and 6 LPO	C. LX 350-2 COL 68267-9-D in M-207

Mussorgsky, Modest

| 1924 (4 March) | *Khovanshchina*, Prelude | C. L1573
COL 67053-D |
| 1929 (24 June) | *Khovanshchina*, Prelude
Hallé (FTHM) | C. 9908
COL 67743-D |

Parry, C. Hubert H.

| 1927 | *Blest Pair of Sirens*
Leeds Orchestra; Leeds, Huddersfield and Sheffield Choirs;
Henry Coward | C. 9222 (unissued) |

Puccini, Giacomo

1919 (23 Sept.)	*La Bohème*, 'Che gelida manina' LSO; Tom Burke	C. 7205
1920 (23 May)	*Madame Butterfly*, 'Viene la sera' Elsa Stralia; Frank Mullings	C 7251 s/s
1920 (25 May)	*La Bohème*, 'Lovely maid in the moonlight' Elsa Stralia; Frank Mullings	C. 7253

1923 (20 July)	*La Bohème*, 'Che gelida manina' Charles Hackett	C. 7273
1924 (13 March)	*La Bohème*, 'Che gelida manina' Charles Hackett	C. 7366
1924 (24 June)	*Tosca*, 'Tre sbirri, una carozza' Cesare Formichi	C. L1579 COL 7102M
1924 (25 Sept.)	*Tosca*, 'Vissi d'arte' Miriam Licette	C. L1706
1924 (24 Oct.)	*Madame Butterfly*, 'Un bel dì' Miriam Licette	C. L1666
1924 (24 Oct.)	*Madame Butterfly*, 'Viene la sera' Miriam Licette; Frank Mullings	C. L1666
1925 (12 Jan.)	*La Bohème*, 'Si mi chiamano Mimi' Miriam Licette	C. L1665
1926 (15 Feb.)	*La Bohème*, 'Che gelida manina' William Martin	C. L1789
1926 (15 Feb.)	*La Bohème*, 'Ah Mimi tu più non torni' Marcel Rodrigo; William Martin	C. L1763
1927 (5 Sept.)	*Tosca*, 'Ella verrà per amor del suo Mario!' Cesare Formichi	C. L1949 COL 7156M

Purcell, Henry
| 1929 (24 June) | 'Nymphs and Shepherds' (from *The Libertine*)
Hallé (FTHM); Manchester School Children's Choir,
Gertrude Riall, choirmistress | C. 9909 |

Ravel, Maurice
| 1921 (20 Oct.) | *Ma mère l'oye* (Laideronette, impératrice des pagodes;
Jardin féerique)
Hallé (FTHM) | C. L1418 |

Rice, Edward Everett
| 1920 (20 Jan.) | *Dear Old Pal of Mine*
LSO; Tom Burke | C. 7233 |

Rimsky-Korsakov, Nikolai
1924	*Tsar Sultan*, 'The flight of the bumble bee'	C. 980 COL 67096-D
1923 (24 Oct.)	*Le Coq d'or*, Introduction and Wedding March Hallé (FTHM)	C. L1533
1929 (11 Feb.)	*Capriccio espagnol* Hallé (FTHM)	C. 9716-7
1929 (24 June)	*Tsar Sultan*, 'The flight of the bumble bee' Hallé (FTHM)	C. 9908

Rossini, Gioachino

1920 (20 April)	Overture: *Il barbiere di Siviglia* Hallé (FTHM)	C. L1428
1925 (8 Jan.)	*Semiramide*, 'Bel raggio lusinghier' Elsa Stralia	C. 7368

Saint-Saëns, Camille

1921	*Introduction* and *Rondo capriccioso* Daisy Kennedy – violin	C. L1335
1925 (9 Jan.)	*Le Carnaval des animaux*	C. L1617-9 COL 67104-6 in M-17
1925 (25 March)	Cello Concerto No. 1 in A minor, Op. 33 Hallé (FTHM); W. H. Squire – cello	C. L1800-2 COL 67216-8 in M-44
1927 (1 Sept.)	*Samson et Dalila*, 'Maudite à jamais!' Cesare Formichi	C. D1491 COL 2030M

Schubert, Franz

1923 (24 July)	*An Sylvia* Charles Hackett	C. 7274 (unissued)
1927 (2 May)	Overture: *Rosamunde* Hallé (FTHM)	C. L1998 COL 67309-D in M-343 COL 67388-D
1928	Overture: *Alfonso and Estrella* Hallé (FTHM)	C. L2122 COL 68322-D
1928 (14 Jan.)	Symphony No. 9 in C major 'The Great' Hallé (FTHM)	C. L2079-85 COL 67423-9 in M-88
1928 (27 April)	*Rosamunde*, Nos. 1, 2, 3a, 5, 6 & 9 Hallé (FTHM)	C. L2123-5 COL 69310-2-D in M-343
1929 (5 May)	*Arpeggione* Sonata in A minor, arr. Cassadó as Concerto with Orchestra Gaspar Cassadó – cello	C. LX1-3 COL 67781-3-D in M-139
1933 (17 Nov.)	Marche Militaire No. 1 in D major LPO	C. DX571 COL 7322M

Senaille, Jean-Baptiste

1926 (30 March)	Allegro spiritoso (*Premier livre de sonates*), arr. Camden Hallé; Archie Camden – bassoon	C. L1826 CO. 67330-D in M-71

Sibelius, Jean

1933 (17 Nov.)	*Valse triste* LPO	C. DX571 COL 7322M

Smetana, Bedřich

1933 (17 Nov.)   Overture: *The Bartered Bride*   C. DX562
                  LPO   COL 7314M

Stanford, Charles Villiers

1922 (20 April)   Overture: *Shamus O'Brien*   C. L1428
                   Hallé (FTHM)

Strauss, Richard

1923 (22 Oct.)   Suite: *Der Bürger als Edelmann* (*Le Bourgeois Gentilhomme*),
                  movements 1, 2, 4, 5, 8 & 9   C. L1552 and L1555-6
                  Hallé (FTHM)   COL 67107-9-D in M-16

Tchaikovsky, Piotr

1929–30 (30 Nov. – 8 Feb.)   Piano Concerto No. 1 in B flat minor, Op. 23
                  C. LX19-22
                  Hallé (CHW); Solomon – piano   COL 67789-92 in M-141

1932 (12 Feb.)   *Mazeppa*, Cossack Dance   C. LX240
                  Hallé (FTHM)

1923   Suite: *The Nutcracker*, Valse des fleurs   C. PLS1 s/s
        Hallé?

Thomas, John Rogers

1922   *Eileen Alanna*   C. X261 s/s
        Clara Butt

Tucker, Henry

1921 (23 March)   *Genevieve*   C. 7254
                   Clara Butt

Verdi, Giuseppe

1915   *Ernani*, 'Ernani involami'   C. 74005
        Elsa Stralia

1920 (3 May)   *Aida*, 'Pur ti reveggo'   C. 7248-9 s/s
                Elsa Stralia; Frank Mullings

1920 (24 June)   *Il trovatore*, 'Ah sì ben mio!'   C. L1816
                  Aroldo Lindi

1924   *La traviata*, 'Di Provenza il mar'   C. D1488
        Cesare Formichi

1924   *Rigoletto*, 'Signor? Va non ho niente'   C. D1488
        Cesare Formichi; Fernando Autori

1924   *Otello*, 'Credo'   C. L1579
        Cesare Formichi   COL 7102M

1924 (30 June)   *Rigoletto*, 'Cortigiani!'   C. L1578
                  Cesare Formichi   COL 7102M

1924 (14 Oct.)	*Aida*, 'Celeste Aida' Frank Mullings	C. L1349
1924 (15 Oct.)	*Otello*, 'Era la notte' Frank Mullings; Harold Williams	C. L1604
1925 (1 Jan.)	*Ernani*, 'Ernani involami' Elsa Stralia	C. 7329
1925 (8 Jan.)	*Il trovatore*, 'Tacea la notte' Elsa Stralia	C. 7329
1925 (12 Jan.)	*Otello*, 'Ave Maria' Miriam Licette	C. L1683
1926 (15 Feb.)	*La forza del destino*, 'Solenne in quest'ora' Marcel Rodrigo; William Martin	C. L1763
1926 (18 June)	*Otello*, 'Ora e per sempre addio' Aroldo Lindi	C. L1773
1926 (25 June)	*Aida*, 'Celeste Aida' John O'Sullivan	C. L1816
1926 (25–6 June)	*Otello*, 'Ora e per sempre addio' John O'Sullivan	C. L1806
1927 (2 Sept.)	*Otello*, 'Credo' Cesare Formichi	C. L1949
1927 (5 Sept.)	*Rigoletto*, 'Pari siamo' Cesare Formichi	C. L2065

Wagner, Richard

1920 (1 May)	*Tannhäuser*, 'O Fürstin!' Elsa Stralia; Frank Mullings	C. 7257
1920 (5 May)	*Tannhäuser*, Elizabeth's greetings Elsa Stralia	C. 7243
1920 (2 May)	*Die Walküre*, 'Leb wohl, du kühnes herrliches Kind!' Norman Allin	C. L1390
1920 (8 Aug.)	*Siegfried*, Hammer Song Frank Mullings	C. L1399
1920 (Nov.)	*Tannhäuser*, Pilgrimage to Rome Frank Mullings	C. L1383
1923 (24 Oct.)	*Götterdämmerung*, Siegfried's Funeral March Hallé (FTHM)	C. L1522
1924	Overture: *Die Meistersinger*	C. 976
1924 (29 Feb.)	*Parsifal*, Good Friday Music	C. L1550-1 COL 67015-6-D
1924 (2 Feb.)	*Tristan und Isolde*, Tristan's vision	C. L1551 COL 67016-D

1924 (11 April)	*Die Meistersinger*, 'Am stillen Herd' Frank Mullings	C. L1576
1924 (11 April)	*Die Meistersinger*, 'Was duftet doch der Flieder' Norman Allin	C. L1591
1924 (31 Dec.)	*Tannhäuser*, 'Dich teure Halle!' Elsa Stralia	C. 7368
1925 (14 Jan.)	*Parsifal*, 'Titurel der fromme Held' Norman Allin	C. L1628
1925 (14 Jan.)	*Tannhäuser*, 'Allmächtige Jungfrau' Miriam Licette	C. L1706
1925 (1 May)	*Tannhäuser*, 'O Fürstin!' Elsa Stralia; Frank Mullings	C. 7333 (second version)
1925 (2 Dec.)	*Lohengrin*, King's Prayer and Finale Kinsley Lark; Miriam Licette; Muriel Brunskill; Frank Mullings; Thorpe Bates	C. L1714

Walton, William

| 1935 (10–11 Dec.) | Symphony No. 1 in B flat minor
LSO | D. X108-113
Decca. 25600-5 |

Weber, Carl Maria von

1921 (23 March)	*Oberon*, 'Ozean du Ungeheuer!' Elsa Stralia	C. 7259
1925 (1 Jan.)	*Oberon*, 'Ozean du Ungeheuer!' Elsa Stralia	C. 7328
1927 (30 April)	Overture: *Abu Hassan* Hallé (FTHM)	C. L2091

Weinberger, Jaromír

| 1934 | *Schwanda the Bagpiper*, Polka and Fugue
LSO | C. LX193
COL 68311-D |

Weiss, Willoughby

| 1920 | *The Village Blacksmith* | C. 787 |

Wood, Haydn

| 1919 (18 Sept.) | *Wonderful World of Romance*
Elsa Stralia | C. 7240 |

Woodforde-Finden, Amy

| 1920 (16 Sept.) | *Kashmiri Love Song*
Clara Butt | C. 7245 |

2 AS PIANIST

Anonymous

1912	*Drink to me only with thine Eyes*	HMV 07869 s/s
	W. H. Squire – cello	
1915	*Drink to me only with thine Eyes*	C. L1017
	W. H. Squire – cello	COL A5832
1922 (April)	Folksong: *Come my Own One*, arr. G. Butterworth	
	Agnes Nicholls	C. (unissued)
1922 (April)	*Have you Seen but a Whyte Little Grow* (Jonson)	C. (unissued)

Bach, J. S.

1913	'Air' from Orchestral Suite No. 3 in D major, ʙᴡᴠ1068	
	W. H. Squire – cello	HMV 07877 s/s

Bath, Hubert

1916	*African Suite* 'Sunset on the Veldt'	C. L1042
	W. H. Squire – cello	

Biene, August van

1910	*The Broken Melody*	HMV 07884
	Cedric Sharpe – cello	C. D436
1915	*The Broken Melody*	C. L1017
	W. H. Squire – cello	COL 7067MÉÉ
1922 (29 Aug.)	*The Broken Melody*	C. 1017 (second version)
	W. H. Squire – cello	

Boccherini, Luigi

1916	Rondo from String Quartet in C major, Op. 37 No. 7, arr.	
	Squire	C. L1032
	W. H. Squire – cello	

Boellman, Leon

1916	*Variations symphoniques* (abridged)	HMV 07863
	Jacques Renard – cello	

Brahms, Johannes

1916	Hungarian Dance No. 2 in D minor, arr. Joachim	
	Isolde Menges – violin	HMV 2-07935 s/s
1916	Hungarian Dance No. 7 in A major, arr. Joachim	
	Isolde Manges – violin	HMV 3-7999 s/s
1919	Scherzo in C minor 'Sonatensatz'	C. L1337
	D. Kennedy – violin	
1919	Violin Sonata No. 3 in D minor, Op. 108 (Adagio and Scherzo)	
	D. Kennedy – violin	C. L1337

1924 (21 Oct.)   Clarinet Trio in A minor, Op. 114   C. L1609-11
                  Charles Draper – clarinet; W. H. Squire – cello
                                                    COL 67101-3-D in M19

Buck, Dudley
1911 (6 July)   *When the heart is young*
                  Agnes Nicholls   HMV (unissued) and HMV 03246 s/s

Cadman, Charles Wakefield
1926 (27 Feb.)   *At Dawning*   C. (unissued)
                  Isobel Baillie

Chopin, Frédéric
1913   Mazurka in C major, Op. 33 No. 3   HMV GC7890 s/s
                  W. H. Squire – cello

1915   Mazurka in C major, Op. 33 No. 3   C. D1334
                  W. H. Squire – cello

1915   Nocturne in E minor, Op. 72 No. 1   HMV 2-07933 and C. D355
                  Isolde Menges – violin

Clay, Frederic
1920 (25 Feb.)   *I'll Sing thee Songs of Araby*   C. L1369
                  Herbert Eisdell

Coningsby Clarke, Robert
1920   *Desert Love Songs*   C. D1421-2
                  Herbert Eisdell

Cowen, Frederic
1909   *At the Mid Hour of Night*   GM 03140 s/s
                  Agnes Nicholls

1909   *A Bride Song*   GM 13143 s/s
                  Agnes Nicholls

1921   *The Better Land*   C. 7260 s/s
                  Agnes Nicholls

Danks, Hart Pease
1914   *Silver Threads among the Gold*, arr. Squire   HMV 07879 s/s
                  W. H. Squire – cello

1915   *Silver Threads among the Gold*, arr. Squire   C. L1003
                  W. H. Squire – cello   COL A5832

1922 (30 Aug.)   *Silver Threads among the Gold*, arr. Squire
                  W. H. Squire – cello   C. L1003 (second version)

Debussy, Claude
1920   *Petite Suite*, 'Menuet'   C. D1434
                  W. H. Squire – cello

Delibes, Léo

1909	*Les Filles du Cadix*	M. 2-033003 s/s
	Alice Verlet	

Dunkler, Emile

1917	*Humoresque* (*Chanson a boire*), arr. Squire	C. L1201
	W. H. Squire – cello	
1918	*Reverie*, Op. 20	C. L1233
	W. H. Squire – cello	
1922 (30 Aug.)	*Reverie*, Op. 20	C. L1233 (second version)
	W. H. Squire – cello	

Dvořák, Antonín

1933	Slavonic Dance No. 1	C. DB1235
	Piano Duet with Myra Hess	COL DB1235 in M-234

Eccles, Henry

1915	Violin Sonata in G minor	HMV E343
	C. Warwick Evans – cello	
1916	Violin Sonata in G minor, arr. Squire and Harty	C. L1053
	W. H. Squire – cello	

Elgar, Edward

1916	*Rosemary*	C. L1117
	W. H. Squire – cello	

Fauré, Gabriel

1916	*Berceuse*, Op. 16	HMV 07887
	C. Warwick Evans – cello	
1917	*Romance sans paroles* in A flat, Op. 17 No. 3	C. D1377
	W. H. Squire – cello	

Foulds, John

1915	*Canadian Boat Song*	C. L1042
	W. H. Squire – cello	
1916	*A Keltic Suite*, Op. 29 No. 2, 'A Keltic Lament'	HMV 07889 s/s
	C. Warwick Evans – cello	

Gabriel-Marie, Jean

1911	*La Cinquantaine*	HMV GC7887
	W. H. Squire – cello	
1915	*La Cinquantaine*	C. D1325
	W. H. Squire – cello	

German, Edward

1924 (31 Dec.)	*Tom Jones*, 'Waltz Song'	C. 7323
	Elsa Stralia	

Glazunov, Alexander

1916	*Sérénade espagnole* W. H. Squire – cello	C. L1117

Gounod, Charles

1909	*Serenade*, 'Quand tu chantes' Alice Verlet	GM 2-33005 s/s
1913	*Ave Maria* W. H. Squire	HMV 07874 s/s
1911 (6 July)	*O Divine Redeemer* Agnes Nicholls	HMV (unissued)

Godard, Benjamin

1913	*Berceuse de Jocelyn*, 'Angels guard thee' W. H. Squire – cello	HMV 07871
1915	*Berceuse de Jocelyn*, 'Angels guard thee' W. H. Squire – cello	C. L1007
1915	*Staccato Valse*, Op. 128 No. 6 Isolde Menges – violin	HMV 2-07925 s/s

Grieg, Edvard

1919	Violin Sonata No. 2 in G major, Op. 13 Allegretto tranquillo and Allegro animato Daisy Kennedy – violin	C. L1336
1922 (23 June)	Violin Sonata in F major, Op. 8 Allegro con brio and Allegro molto Daisy Kennedy – violin	C. L1440

Hahn, Reynaldo

1913	*Si mes vers avaient des ailes* W. H. Squire – cello	HMV 07878 s/s
1915	*Si mes vers avaient des ailes* W. H. Squire – cello	C. D1334

Handel, George Frideric

1916	*Serse*, Largo in G major Cedric Sharpe – cello; Harty – organ	HMV 07890
1916	Violin Sonata No. 13 in D major, Larghetto, arr. Squire W. H. Squire – cello	C. D1354
1917	*Serse*, Largo in G major W. H. Squire – cello	C. L1201
1918	Menuet (not specified), arr. Burmeister W. H. Squire – cello	C. D1391
1918	Minuet in F (not specified), arr. Harty Isolde Menges – violin	HMV E206

Harty, Hamilton

1909 (10 May) *Lane o' the Thrushes* and *Come, O come my Life's Delight*
Agnes Nicholls   GM (unissued)

1909 (9 July) *Lane o' the Thrushes* and *Come, O come my Life's Delight*
(two takes)
Agnes Nicholls   GM (unissued)

Haydn, Joseph

1916 Andante in E flat (not specified)   C. L1032
W. H. Squire – cello

Jensen, Adolf

1916 *Murmelndes Lüftchen*   C. L1100
W. H. Squire – cello

Lambert, Constant

1930 (11 Jan.) *The Rio Grande*   C. L2373-4
~   Hallé, cond. Constant Lambert; St Michael's Singers
COL 70472-3-D in MX-52

Lemare, Edwin

1917 Andantino ('Chanson de l'ame')   C. L1233
W. H. Squire – cello

1922 (30 Aug.) Andantino ('Chanson de l'ame')   C. L1233 (second version)
W. H. Squire – cello

Leoni, Franco

1909 (9 July) 'Song of the Cruise'   GM (unissued)
Agnes Nicholls

1911 (18 Dec.) 'Song of the Cruise'   HMV (unissued)
Agnes Nicholls

Liddle, Samuel

1911 (6 July) *How Lovely are thy Dwellings*   HMV 03250
Agnes Nicholls

1911 (18 Dec.) *The Evening Sea*   HMV (unissued)
Agnes Nicholls

MacCunn, Hamish

1916 *Amourette*   C. D1347
W. H. Squire – cello

Méhul, Étienne

1916 *Le Jugement de Paris*, Gavotte   C. D1347
W. H. Squire – cello

Moore, Graham

1916	*The Blind Boy*	C. D1337
	W. H. Squire – cello	

Mozart, Wolfgang Amadeus

1912	*Ave verum*, к618	HMV 07870 s/s
	W. H. Squire – cello	
1923 (27 April)	Violin Sonata in A major, к526	C. L1494-6
	Arthur Catterall – violin	COL 67139-41-D in M-25

Nevin, Ethelbert

1920	*'Twas April*	C. D1419
	Hubert Eisdell	

Offenbach, Jacques

1911	*Tales of Hoffmann*, Barcarolle	HMV GC7885 s/s
	W. H. Squire – cello	
1915 (Oct.)	*Tales of Hoffmann*, Barcarolle	C. D1325
	W. H. Squire – cello	

Parker, Horatio

1909 (10 May)	*The Lark Now Leaves*	CG 3837
	Agnes Nicholls	
1909 (9 July)	*The Lark Now Leaves*	GM (unissued)
	Agnes Nicholls	

Pierné, Gabriel

1916	*Sérénade*, Op. 7	HMV 7898 s/s
	Cedric Sharpe – cello	
1916	*Sérénade*, Op. 7	C. L1100
	W. H. Squire – cello	

Pons, Charles

1909	*Laura*, 'Hymn d'amour'	GM 2-033004 s/s
	Alice Verlet; Charles Pons – organ	

Popper, David

1916	*Alsatian Melody*	C. L1028
	W. H. Squire – cello	
1916	Gavotte No. 2	C. L1028
	W. H. Squire – cello	
1920	*Papillon*, Op. 4 No. 3	C. D1415
	W. H. Squire – cello	

Rameau, Jean-Philippe

1916	*Platée*, Menuet	C. L1039
	W. H. Squire – cello	

Rossini, Gioachino

1909	*La Danza* Alice Verlet	GM 2-053004 s/s
1920	*La Danza*, arr. Squire W. H. Squire – cello	C. D1440

Rubinstein, Anton

1915	Melody in F major W. H. Squire – cello	C. L1003
1922 (29 Aug.)	Melody in F major W. H. Squire – cello	C. L1003 (second version)

Saint-Saëns, Camille

1913	*Le Carnaval des animaux*, 'Le Cygne' W. H. Squire – cello	HMV 07872 s/s
1915	*Le Carnaval des animaux*, 'Le Cygne' W. H. Squire – cello	C. L1007

Sammartini, Giuseppe

1922 (31 Aug.)	*Old Italian Love Song* W. H. Squire – cello	C. L1513 (unissued)
1923 (12 March)	*Old Italian Love Song* W. H. Squire – cello	C. L1513 (second version)
1924 (1 Feb.)	*Old Italian Love Song* W. H. Squire – cello	C. L1513 (third vrsion)

Schubert, Franz

1920	*Wiegenlied* W. H. Squire – cello	C. D1440
1923 (24 July)	*An Sylvia* Hubert Eisdell	C. D1419

Schumann, Robert

1919	Violin Sonata in A minor, Op. 105 Daisy Kennedy – violin	C. L1338-9
1920	*Kinderszenen*, Op. 15, 'Träumerei' W. H. Squire – cello	C. L1337

Seligmann, Hippolyte

1920	*Chanson grecque* W. H. Squire – cello	C. D1434

Squire, William Henry
(all W. H. Squire – cello)

1911	*Serenade*	HMV 07868 s/s
1915	*Serenade*	C. L1039
1916	*Harlequinade*	C. D1354
1920	*Danse magyare*	C. D1425
1920 (12 Feb.)	*Meditation*	C. L1513

Sullivan, Arthur

| 1909 (10 May) | *My Dearest Heart*
Agnes Nicholls | GM (unissued) |
| 1911 (18 Dec.) | *My Dearest Heart*
Agnes Nicholls | HMV (unissued) |

Tartini, Giuseppe

| 1910 | Violin Sonata in G major, Op. 2 No. 12, Adagio cantabile | |
| | C. Saunders – violin; Jacques Renard – cello | HMV 08028 s/s |

Thome, Francis

| 1911 | *Andante religioso* | ? |
| | C. Saunders – violin; Jacques Renard – cello | |

Tosti, Paolo

| 1911 (18 Dec.) | *Goodbye*
Agnes Nicholls | HMV 03266 |

Tucker, Henry

| 1921 | *Genevieve*
Clara Butt | C. 7254 s/s |

Wagner, Richard

| 1920 | *Tannhäuser*, 'O star of eve'
W. H. Squire – cello | C. D1415 |

Widor, Charles

| 1911 | *Serenade* | ? |
| | C. Saunders – violin; Jacques Renard – cello | |

White, Maude Valérie

| 1911 (6 July) | *The Spring has Come*
Agnes Nicholls | HMV (unissued) |
| 1911 (18 Dec.) | *So we'll Go no More*
Agnes Nicholls | HMV (unissued) |

Wieniawski, Henryk

| 1915 | Polonaise in D, Op. 4
Isolde Menges – violin | HMV 2-07923 s/s |

Wolstenhome, William
1918   *Peasant Dance*   C. D1391
              W. H. Squire – cello

Wormser, André
1916   *L'Enfant prodigue*, incidental music   C. 607-9

Zarzycki, Alexander
1919   Mazurka, Op. 26   C. L1339
              Daisy Kennedy – violin

NO DATE (OR OTHER DETAILS MISSING)

Anonymous
              Mary of Argyle   C. D1329
              W. H. Squire – cello

Biene, August van
              Valse apache
              W. H. Squire – cello

Cui, César
              Orientale   C. D1369
              W. H. Squire – cello

Gade, Niels
              Two Noveletten
              W. H. Squire – cello

Gillett, Ernest
              Passepied   C. D2065
              W. H. Squire – cello

Goossens, Eugene
              Old Chinese Folksong   C. D1377
              W. H. Squire – cello

Gossec, François-Joseph
              Tambourin   C. D1329
              W. H. Squire – cello

Rossini, Gioachino
              La Danza, arr. Squire   C. 7895
              W. H. Squire – cello

Silesu, Lao
              Mon cœur est pour toi   C. D1369
              W. H. Squire – cello

Squire, William Henry
(all W. H. Squire – cello)

Chansonette	C. D1401
Tarantella	C. D1401
When you Come Home	C. D1327
Danse rustique	C. D1372

Bibliography

❧ Books, articles and theses

Aiello, G. L. (ed.), *Al Musicista Michele Esposito nel primo centenario della nascita* (Castellamare di Stabia: M. Mosca, 1956)

Amis, J., *A Miscellany: My Life, My Music* (London: Faber & Faber, 1985)

Armsby, L. W., 'The Irish Composer-Conductor: Sir Hamilton Harty', in L. W. Armsby, *Musicians Talk: Impressions of Musicians, with Plates* (New York: Dial Press, 1935), 144–8

—— *We Shall Have Music: The Story of the San Francisco Symphony Orchestra* (San Francisco: Pisani, 1960)

Armstrong, William, 'Dr Theodor Lierhammer on the German Lied', *The Etude* 22(6) (June 1904)

Baillie, Isobel, *Never Sing Louder than Lovely* (London: Hutchinson, 1982)

Barlow, Michael, *Whom the Gods Love: The Life and Music of George Butterworth* (Exeter: Toccata Press, 1997)

Barnes, A., and M. Renshaw, *The Life and Work of John Snetzler* (Aldershot: Ashgate, 1994)

Barry, John, *Hillsborough: A Parish in the Ulster Plantation* (Belfast: William Mullan, 1962)

—— 'Hillsborough Years', in *Hamilton Harty: His Life and Music*, ed. David Greer (Belfast: Blackstaff Press, 1978), 1–22

—— 'Last Years', in *Hamilton Harty: His Life and Music*, ed. David Greer (Belfast: Blackstaff Press, 1978), 51–66

Beecham, Thomas, *A Mingled Chime* (London: Hutchinson & Co., 1944; repr. 1987)

Benjamin, A., 'A Student in Kensington', *Music & Letters* 31(3) (1950), 196–207

Bliss, Arthur, 'Aspects of the Present Musical Situation', *PRMA* 49 (1922–3), 59–77

Boult, Adrian, 'The Orchestral Problem of the Future', *PRMA* 49 (1922–3), 39–57

C. [= H. C. Colles], 'Hamilton Harty', *Musical Times* 61 (1920), 227–30

Camden, Archie, *Blow by Blow: The Memories of a Musical Rogue and Vagabond* (London: Thames Publishing, 1982)

Cardus, Neville, *Autobiography* (London: Collins, 1947)

—— *Second Innings* (London: Collins, 1950)

—— *Talking of Music* (London: Collins, 1957)

Compton-Hall, R., *Submarines at War, 1914–1918* (Penzance: Periscope Publishing, 2004)

Dibble, Jeremy C., *Charles Villiers Stanford: Man and Musician* (Oxford: Oxford University Press, 2002)

—— *Michele Esposito* (Dublin: Field Day Publications, 2010)

Evans, E., 'Arthur Bliss', *Musical Times* 64 (1923), 20–23, 95–9

—— 'In Memoriam: Frank Bridge and Sir Hamilton Harty', *Music Review* 2(2) (1941), 159–66

Fifield, Christopher, *Ibbs and Tillett: The Rise and Fall of a Musical Empire* (Aldershot: Ashgate, 2005)

Foss, Hubert, and Noel Goodwin, *London Symphony: Portrait of an Orchestra* (London: The Naldrett Press, 1954)

Gallagher, H. W., 'Sir William Thomson, Physician', *Ulster Medical Journal* 42(1) (1973), 15–27

Graves, Charles Larcom, *Hubert Parry,* 2 vols. (London: Macmillan, 1926)

Greer, David, 'Hamilton Harty Manuscripts', *Music Review 47(4)* (1986–7), 238–52

—— 'A Dowland Curiosity', *The Lute* 27 (1987), 42–4

—— 'The Composition of *The Children of Lir*', in *Musicology in Ireland*, ed. G. Gillen and H. White, Irish Musical Studies 1 (Dublin: Irish Academic Press, 1990), 74–98

—— 'Hamilton Harty's Swansong', a lecture delivered on 19 February 1991 to commemorate the fiftieth anniversary of the death of Sir Hamilton Harty

—— 'Irish Music Between the Wars: The Case of Hamilton Harty', in *Glasba med obema vojnama in Slavko Osterc*, ed. Primo Kuret (Ljubljana: Festival, 1995), 254–61

—— *A Numerous and Fashionable Audience: The Story of Elsie Swinton* (London: Thames Publishing, 1997)

—— (ed.), *Hamilton Harty: His Life and Music* (Belfast: Blackstaff Press, 1978)

—— (ed.), *Hamilton Harty: Early Memories* (Belfast: The Queen's University, 1979)

Grew, Sydney, 'National Music and the Folk-Song', *Musical Quarterly* 7(2), 172–85

Hammond, P., 'The Hallé Years and After', in *Hamilton Harty: His Life and Music, ed. David Greer* (Belfast: Blackstaff Press, 1978), 35–50

Harrison, Beatrice, *The Cello and the Nightingales: The Autobiography of Beatrice Harrison*, ed. Patricia Cleveland-Pech, with a foreword by Julian Lloyd-Webber (London: John Murray, 1985)

Harrison, May, 'Delius', in *A Delius Companion*, ed. C. Redwood (London: John Calder, 1976), 101–6

Hirsch, Leonard, 'Memories of Sir Hamilton', in *Hamilton Harty: His Life and Music, ed. David Greer* (Belfast: Blackstaff Press, 1978), 67–74

Howes, Frank, 'A Note on Harty's 'Irish' Symphony', *Musical Times* 66 (1925), 223–4

Hughes, Angela, *Chelsea Footprints: A Thirties Chronicle* (London: QuartetBooks, 2008)

Hunt, John, *More Musical Knights: Harty, Mackerras, Rattle, Pritchard* (London: John Hunt, 1997; repr. edn 2009)

Jackson, F., *Blessed City: The Life and Works of Edward C. Bairstow* (York: William Sessions, 1996)

Jackson, Gerald, *First Flute* (London: J. M. Dent, 1968)

Kennedy, Michael, *The Hallé Tradition: A Century of Music* (Manchester: Manchester University Press, 1960)

—— *The Hallé, 1858–1983: A History of the Orchestra* (Manchester: Manchester University Press, 1982)

—— *Adrian Boult* (London: Macmillan, 1987)

Kenyon, N., *The BBC Symphony Orchestra, 1930–1980* (London: BBC, 1981)

Klein, J. W., 'Bizet's "Roma" Symphony', *Musical Times* 75 (1935), 1078–9.

Langford, Samuel, *Musical Criticisms,* ed. Neville Cardus (London: Oxford University Press, 1929)

Ledbetter, Gordon T., *The Great Irish Tenor* (London: Duckworth, 1977)

Lloyd, Stephen, *Sir Dan Godfrey: Champion of British Composers* (London: Thames Publishing, 1995)

—— *William Walton: Muse of Fire* (Woodbridge: Boydell Press, 2001)

Lochner, L. P., *Fritz Kreisler* (New York: The Macmillan Co., 1950)

Lucas, J., *Thomas Beecham: An Obsession with Music* (Woodbridge: Boydell Press, 2008)

McCormack, John, *His Own Life Story* (New York: Small, Maynard & Co., 1918; repr. edn New York: Vienna House, 1973)

McCormack, Lily, *I Hear You Calling Me* (London: Allen, 1950)

McCormack, W. J., and P. Gillan, *The Blackwell Companion to Irish Culture* (Oxford: Blackwell, 1999)

Midgley, S., *My 70 Years' Musical Memories* (London: Novello, 1930)

Mitchell-Hedges, F. A., *Danger My Ally* (London: Elek Books, 1954)

Moore, Gerald, *The Unashamed Accompanist* (London: Ascherberg, Hopwood & Crew, 1943)

—— *Am I Too Loud?* (London: Hamish Hamilton, 1962)

Newton, Ivor, 'At the Piano', *Music & Letters* 24(2) (1943), 107–10

Nicholls, Agnes, 'A Vignette', *Opera* (July 1923)

Niss, C., 'Sir Hamilton Harty at the Hollywood Bowl', *Le Grand Baton* 23(2), *issue no.* 61 (1990)

Patterson, Annie, 'The Characteristic Traits of Irish Music', *PRMA*, 23rd sess. (1896–7), 91–111

—— 'Herbert Harty', *Weekly Irish Times*, 7 July 1900

Pine, Richard, *Music and Broadcasting in Ireland* (Dublin: Four Courts Press, 2005)

Plummer, D., 'Hamilton Harty: A Catalogue of his Manuscripts Held by the Library of Queen's University, Belfast' (MA dissertation, Queen's University, Belfast, 2006)

—— 'Hamilton Harty's Legacy with the Hallé Orchestra (1920–1930): A Reassessment', *Journal of the Society for Musicology in Ireland* 5 (2009–10), 55–72

Plunket Greene, Harry, *Interpretaton in Song* (London: Macmillan, 1912)

—— 'Leonard Borwick: Some Personal Recollections', *Music & Letters* 7(1) (1926), 17–24

—— *Charles Villiers Stanford* (London: Arnold, 1935)

Rees, C. B., *100 Years of the Hallé* (London: MacGibbon & Kee, 1957)

Riley, M., *Percy Whitlock* (London: Thames Publishing, 1998)

Ronald, Landon, *Myself and Others: Written Lest I Forget* (London: Sampson Low, Martson & Co., 1931)

Russell, John F., 'Hamilton Harty', *Music & Letters* 22 (1941), 216–24

Sanders, A. (ed.), *Walter Legge: Words and Music* (London: Duckworth, 1998)

Self, G., *The Music of E. J. Moeran* (Exeter: Toccata Press, 1986)

Shaw, George Bernard, *The Perfect Wagnerite* (London: Constable & Co., 1923)

Shead, R., *Constant Lambert* (London: Thames Publishing, 1973; rev. edn, 1988)

Shore, B., *The Orchestra Speaks* (London: Longmans, Green & Co., 1938)

Sitwell, Osbert, *Left Hand Right Hand!* (London: The Reprint Society, 1946)

Smyth, E., *What Happened Next* (London: Longmans Green, 1940)

Stanford, Charles Villiers, 'Some Recent Tendencies in Composition', *PRMA* 47 (1920–1), 39–53

Stoupe, R. I., *Hillsborough Parish Church: The Organs* (Belfast: McCaw, Stevenson & Orr, 1972)

Szigeti, Joseph, *With Strings Attached: Reminiscences and Reflections* (London: Cassell & Co., 1949)

Tertis, Lionel, *My Viola and I: A Complete Autobiography* (London: Paul Elek, 1974)

Warren, R., 'Orchestral Music', in *Hamilton Harty: His Life and Music*, ed. David Greer (Belfast: Blackstaff Press, 1978), 89–115

White, Harry, *The Keeper's Recital: Music and Cultural History in Ireland, 1770–1970* (Cork: Cork University Press, 1998)

White, John, *Lionel Tertis: The First Great Virtuoso of the Viola* (Woodbridge: Boydell Press, 2006)

Wood, Henry J., *My Life of Music* (London: Victor Gollancz, 1938)

Zuk, P., 'Music and Nationalism', *Journal of Music in Ireland* 2(2) (2002), 5–10; 2(3) (2002), 25–30

❧ *Radio broadcasts about Harty*

19 February 1943 (BBC): talk by Eric Gillett; typescript *GB-Mcm* Man.Mus.49

15 April 1946 (BBC Northern Ireland Home Service): tributes to Sir Hamilton Harty; *GB-Lbbc*

3 October 1951 (BBC North of Ireland and North of England Home Service): documentary talk with various contributors; *GB-Lbbc*

4 December 1979 (BBC Radio 3): *A Child of Lir*: centenary broadcast written and presented by Bernard Keeffe

1979 (RTÉ Radio 1): documentary by Philip Hammond; RTÉ Sound Archives, tape no. LAA1154

❧ *Concert programmes*

Australian Broadcasting Commission: Programmes, 1934 season

Cleveland Orchestra: Programmes

Hallé Concerts Society: Programmes, 1920–33

Hamilton Harty Symphony Concerts: Programmes, 1929–30 and 1930–31 seasons

London Symphony Orchestra: Programmes

Royal College of Music: Programmes

Index of Harty's Works

Numbers in bold type refer to musical examples or facsimiles.

General Index

Music in Britain, 1600–2000

Titles listed here were originally published
under the series title *Music in Britain, 1600–1900*,
ISSN 1752-1904

Lectures on Musical Life
William Sterndale Bennett,
edited by Nicholas Temperley, with Yunchung Yang

John Stainer: A Life in Music
Jeremy Dibble

*The Pursuit of High Culture: John Ella and
Chamber Music in Victorian London*
Christina Bashford

Thomas Tallis and his Music in Victorian England
Suzanne Cole

The Consort Music of William Lawes, 1602–1645
John Cunningham

*Life After Death: The Viola da Gamba
in Britain from Purcell to Dolmetsch*
Peter Holman

*The Musical Salvationist: The World of Richard Slater
(1854–1939) 'Father of Salvation Army Music'*
Gordon Cox

*British Music and Literary Context:
Artistic Connections in the Long Nineteenth Century*
Michael Allis